The Talent Management of Indie Authorship

The Talent Management of Indie Authorship

From American Independent Cinema and Short "Films" to Pay-TV and Streaming

Andrew Stubbs-Lacy

EDINBURGH
University Press

Edinburgh University Press is one of the leading university presses in the UK. We publish academic books and journals in our selected subject areas across the humanities and social sciences, combining cutting-edge scholarship with high editorial and production values to produce academic works of lasting importance. For more information visit our website: edinburghuniversitypress.com

© Andrew Stubbs-Lacy, 2024, 2026

Grateful acknowledgement is made to the sources listed in the List of Illustrations for permission to reproduce material previously published elsewhere. Every effort has been made to trace the copyright holders, but if any have been inadvertently overlooked, the publisher will be pleased to make the necessary arrangements at the first opportunity.

First published in hardback by Edinburgh University Press 2024

Edinburgh University Press Ltd
13 Infirmary Street
Edinburgh EH1 1LT

Typeset in Monotype Ehrhardt by
Cheshire Typesetting Ltd, Cuddington, Cheshire,
and printed and bound by CPI Group (UK) Ltd,
Croydon, CR0 4YY

A CIP record for this book is available from the British Library

ISBN 978 1 4744 8264 6 (hardback)
ISBN 978 1 4744 8265 3 (paperback)
ISBN 978 1 4744 8266 0 (webready PDF)
ISBN 978 1 4744 8267 7 (epub)

The right of Andrew Stubbs-Lacy to be identified as the author of this work has been asserted in accordance with the Copyright, Designs and Patents Act 1988, and the Copyright and Related Rights Regulations 2003 (SI No. 2498).

Contents

List of Figures   *vi*
Acknowledgements   *vii*

Introduction   1

1 Producing with Indie-Auteurs: The Coen Brothers and an Indie Periodisation   22
2 Managing Indie-Auteurs in an Era of Media Convergence: Steve Golin, Propaganda Films and Anonymous Content   57
3 Propaganda/Films: The Indie-Auteur and the Legitimation of Short-Form Production   88
4 Packaging Indie-Auteur Television: The Single-Director Model, Cinematization and the Pursuit of Legitimacy   118
5 Navigating Specialty Film's Decline and Disruption: Specialty Film, Studio Blockbusters and the Maverick Male Myth   148
6 Black Agents and Agency: Charles D. King, Macro and the Talent Management of Black Indie-Auteurs   176

Conclusion: The Migration of Indie-Auteurism and New Directions   213

References   219
Index   252

Figures

1.1	Hi steals Huggies in the trailer for the Coens' screwball comedy, *Raising Arizona*	30
1.2	A comedy beyond belief: *Raising Arizona*'s poster in a quirky indie style	32
1.3	A still from *The Hudsucker Proxy* trailer	39
1.4	'A fake masterpiece': *Gambit*'s poster crediting the Coens	44
1.5	The poster for *Intolerable Cruelty*	45
1.6	A still from the R-rated *No Country for Old Men* trailer	51
2.1	Anonymous Content's logo	59
2.2	Propaganda Films' logo	60
2.3	Anonymous Content's commercials directors by race and gender at five-year intervals from 2010 to 2020	78
3.1	A still from Spike Jonze's music video for 'Drop'	94
3.2	A still from Spike Jonze's grainy music video for 'Praise You' made in the style of an amateur production	95
3.3	A still from Spike Jonze's music video for 'Buddy Holly'	96
3.4	A still from Wong Kar-Wai's 'The Follow'	104
3.5	A still from Guy Ritchie's 'Star' showing the Diva cowering from paparazzi on the red carpet	106
3.6	A still from Dee Rees's *The Box* commercial	113
4.1	A season three poster for *Burn Notice*, part of USA's 'blue skies' programming	130
4.2	A *Mr. Robot* season one poster features a dark cityscape and displays the protagonist's introversion in what represents a break from USA's 'blue skies' programming	131
4.3	'It's personal': *The Girlfriend Experience*'s season one poster	142
5.1	A still from the trailer for *The Revenant*	159
5.2	A still from the trailer for *Beasts of No Nation*	170
6.1	A poster for Tyler Perry's *Diary of a Mad Black Woman* featuring Perry starring as Madea	190
6.2	*Judas and the Black Messiah* poster	204

Acknowledgements

First, I owe a substantial debt of gratitude to Hannah Andrews for her immeasurable and unwavering dedication in nurturing this project as it began as a PhD under her supervision. I also offer my thanks to everyone who gave important advice and support as the PhD crossed between two institutions, moving as it did from the University of York to Edge Hill University, including Ruxandra Trandafoiu, Claire Parkinson, Philip Drake, Owen Evans, Phil Jackson, Jenny Barrett, Mita Lad, Debbie Chadford, Julie Climpson, Duncan Petrie and Kristyn Gorton. A big thank you must also go to Paddy Hoey, Yannis Tzioumakis and Paul McDonald for reading early drafts and offering valuable constructive feedback, as well as to Matt Freeman for encouraging me to undertake the PhD in the first place.

Thank you to the editors at Edinburgh University Press, Gillian Leslie, Sam Johnson and Kelly O'Brien, as well as to the reviewers of my monograph proposal. My thanks also go to everyone who helped me to work through ideas and supported my research for this project, including Kristine Krueger at the Margaret Herrick Library, staff at the BFI Reuben Library, and Denis Seguin for spending time searching out an old article, as well as Darnell Hunt, Emily Caston, Leora Hadas, Kim Wilkins, Wyatt Moss-Wellington, Michael Knowles, Matt Steele, Mark McKenna, Sharon Coleclough, Robert Marsden, Stephen Griffiths, Tatiana Ursachi, Ryan Hewitt, Dan Jones, Jodie Williams, Stephen Tate, Ben Tirunawarkarisu, and Andrea and Jonathan Lacy.

This book would not be possible were it not for the love and support that I receive every day from my friends and family, including Sue Roberts, David Stubbs, and Dorothy and Arthur Stubbs, among many, many others. Finally, this book is dedicated to my wife, Hannah Stubbs-Lacy, for all the love and support that she has given me during this project, and to our newborn son, Ethan (who, Hannah wants me to point out, hasn't put in quite as much effort as her to date in supporting me on this journey).

Introduction

In 2013, NBCUniversal removed James Schamus, a former co-founder of the independent production and sales company Good Machine and co-producer of indie movies such as *Trust* (Hartley, 1990), *Safe* (Haynes, 1995), *Walking and Talking* (Holofcener, 1996) and *Happiness* (Solondz, 1998), as the CEO of Focus Features in what marked the beginning of a period of uncertainty for the specialty film division. Schamus had been the division's CEO since 2002 when Universal[1] acquired and absorbed Good Machine to create Focus until the studio decided to replace him with Peter Schlessel, who ran another of Universal's film divisions, FilmDistrict, which was absorbed into Focus in the process. Under Schamus's leadership, Focus had concentrated on releasing often critically acclaimed indie or specialty films such as *Brokeback Mountain* (Lee, 2005), *The Kids Are All Right* (Cholodenko, 2010) and *Moonrise Kingdom* (Anderson, 2012). Yet Schlessel was reportedly tasked with producing and distributing more commercial genre pictures like the horror movie *Insidious* (Wan, 2010), which was FilmDistrict's first release.[2] Pointing out that Universal was also relocating Focus's offices from New York to Los Angeles in a move that indicated that the division would be run with less autonomy than before, *Variety* reported that Focus's restructuring was 'a blow for independent directors and producers' who would now have one less buyer for their films.[3] With Universal's restructuring of Focus having been preceded since 2008 by Warner's closure of Warner Independent, Paramount's closure of Paramount Vantage, and Disney's sale of Miramax, *Variety* thus motioned to a general decline in indie or studio specialty filmmaking.

Less than eighteen months after Focus's restructuring, Amazon Studios appointed Schamus's former partner and co-founder of Good Machine, Ted Hope, as the head of Amazon Original Movies. Amazon Studios' vice president at the time, Roy Price, announced that Hope's appointment would benefit filmmakers 'who too often struggle to mount fresh and daring stories that deserve an audience'.[4] *Variety*, meanwhile, couched Hope's appointment in less altruistic terms when it reported that the move was proof that Amazon was 'poaching independent filmmakers' to make not only television, such as Jill Soloway's *Transparent* (Amazon, 2014–19) and Whit Stillman's *The Cosmopolitans*[5] (Stillman, 2014), but also now feature films.[6] Undoubtedly Amazon sought to use Hope as a means of attracting indie filmmakers into working with the company as the producer had cultivated a reputation for supporting them effectively during his time at Good Machine. During the downturn in indie filmmaking, Hope had repeatedly professed his support for members of the community who he perceived as sharing his values, and did so after Universal removed Schamus when he tweeted, 'To me this really means the end of indie film – as we once knew it ... Schamus = superstar'.[7] Hope had also long advocated for a return to a more 'authentic' indie cinema made away from the Hollywood studios and, in the early 2010s, had begun expressing a belief that the internet could facilitate this,[8] which was rhetoric that fit neatly with Amazon's tech brand if not its corporate status. While Universal's removal of Schamus from Focus was greeted as harming indie filmmakers, Hope's appointment created an impression of Amazon as their benefactor or saviour. Moreover, when Amazon and Netflix paid $10 million and $7 million for indie features *Manchester by the Sea* (Lonergan, 2016) and *The Fundamentals of Caring* (Burnett, 2016), respectively, at the 2016 Sundance Film Festival, the trade press interpreted it as an example of the streaming giants' 'dominance'.[9]

These narratives of Hope and Schamus's hiring and firing help to set the stage for what this book is about. The narratives characterise American independent and indie film as a form of 'quality' specialty production that is driven by innovative, daring and original filmmakers who are often ignored or suppressed by the Hollywood mainstream. This characterisation is consistent with how American independent cinema has tended to be described since the 1980s when institutions, including certain film festivals, art-house cinemas, film magazines and specialty distributors, began to promote it as a cultural category that was meant to be distinct from Hollywood and other less culturally legitimate forms of independent film production, such as exploitation fare.[10] Hence, the independent filmmaker became increasingly important to the legitimation of independent and indie film as it was conceptualised as an authentic autonomously produced alternative to the Hollywood mainstream.[11] As this version of indie film became increasingly lucrative, however, the Hollywood studios expanded into the arena and increasingly used the indie label (and the independent filmmaker) as a valuable marketing tool for targeting niche middle-class educated adult audiences just as Amazon and Netflix had begun to do in the 2010s.[12] While promotional, extratextual and critical discourse often describes the independent filmmaker in these terms as a form of transcendent originality, though, this book departs from these old-fashioned but nevertheless still prevalent conceptions of authorship to instead examine the independent filmmaker, or rather the indie-auteur, as a discursive construction and brand that is managed by talent intermediaries, including producers, talent agents and talent managers.[13] While a significant amount of scholarly work has considered the centrality of authorship to indie film, therefore, this is the first book-length work to explore the roles that talent intermediaries play in constructing, mobilising and managing indie-auteur brands and, in turn, shaping ideas of indie and specialty production.[14]

I explore especially some of the individuals and institutions responsible for constructing and managing indie-auteurism as a branded discourse, their reasons for doing so, and the various economic, industrial and cultural functions and repercussions of its usage. I investigate the roles that talent intermediaries play in constructing and managing indie-auteurism, the strategies and practices that they adopt, and their motivations. I also explore talent intermediaries' relationships, interactions and dealings with other individuals and institutions, including above-the-line personnel (those figures generally labelled 'the talent'), especially the directors and writer-directors themselves,[15] the financiers of media projects, and the distributors. As a result, I investigate some of the projects around which indie-auteurism is mobilised, why it is mobilised around those projects specifically, and what this reveals about indie culture and broader media industry strategies and systems. At the same time, I investigate what role indie-auteurism plays in shaping the reputations of talent intermediaries and their clients and collaborators and how it might be used to enhance their employability and opportunities. I also investigate whether there are correlations between the types of figures branded as indie-auteurs and the intermediaries working with them, explore the types of products that indie-auteurism is used to package and promote, and analyse what indie-auteurism's usage reveals about relationships between media industry employers and employees and about producer and distributors' conceptions of their projects' intended audience. I also explore the themes or properties that indie-auteurism commonly conveys and the functions and repercussions of generating such meanings. Of particular interest is whether indie-auteurism generates meanings that reflect or obscure industrial and economic realities, whether or not it sustains or breaks down cultural distinctions and hierarchies, and who benefits as a result.

In an era of media convergence

I analyse the management of indie-auteurism in an era of media convergence. This is a period since the 1980s that has witnessed a coming together of media due to the emergence of digital and online technologies and a consolidation of media ownership facilitated by neoliberal government policies favouring 'deregulation' and 'free markets'.[16] While the period since the 1980s saw the emergence of the so-called quality iteration of American independent cinema, I explore how indie-auteurism as a branded discourse is mobilised and dispersed widely to sell a range of specialty content as well as many goods and services that are often produced and distributed by Hollywood studios and other major companies. Although most scholarly work on indie-auteurs has concentrated on their work in film, this book explores how indie-auteurism is also mobilised around certain television series, commercial spots, music videos and, to a far lesser extent, non-profit campaigns, virtual-reality productions, and documentaries. Moreover, while most studies of convergence focus either on changes in the organisation of the industry and its impact on labour or on the emergence of digital platforms and its effects on the production, distribution and reception of content, this book centres on talent intermediaries who play an important role in facilitating industry recruitment processes, make themselves appear to be capable of 'discovering' talent, and package and market certain productions. As Timothy Corrigan has stated, 'from its inception, auteurism has been bound up with changes in industrial desires, technological opportunities, and marketing strategies'.[17] Instead of treating indie-auteurs as figures who work to overcome the constraints of the industry to express their individual visions, therefore, I connect them to talent intermediaries, talent networks and, in turn, wider media industry practices.

I analyse the construction and management of indie-auteurism by talent intermediaries operating at the higher echelons of Hollywood and American screen media production where stardom and auteur brands are most visible and widely dispersed. Agents and managers operating at this level tend to have direct lines of communication to studio executives and often represent high-profile clients on big-budget projects, unlike intermediaries at boutique or very small companies that interact mostly with casting professionals as they help to gain their out-of-favour clients work on modest productions or in smaller roles.[18] The era of convergence has also witnessed consolidation across Hollywood's top talent agencies and management companies following a series of mergers and acquisitions.[19] This consolidation has seen the largest talent agencies and management companies expand and diversify their businesses, part of which has seen talent agents and managers increasingly taking on greater roles in the development of non-studio productions by pairing talent with a script and arranging co-financing deals, including sometimes by pre-selling distribution rights internationally and on home video.[20] While Violaine Roussel has explored how the 1980s marked the emergence of this independent packaging practice where agents began representing not only people but projects,[21] I explore how the practice has come to increasingly form the basis of a promotional strategy that involves generating value around certain productions by creating positive associations with indie film, and especially the indie-auteur.

Scholars including Geoff King and Yannis Tzioumakis have debated whether indie film has lost its relevance or has experienced a 'new dawn' following the decline of studio specialty filmmaking and emergence of low-budget digital technologies respectively.[22] Yet examining the management of indie-auteurism in an era of convergence opens up new possibilities not only for understanding the future direction of indie production but also for understanding its history. As Tzioumakis himself acknowledged in 2011:

> In today's age of media convergence ... it becomes increasingly important to locate the study of one particular media form and institution – in this case American independent cinema – within a wider context in order to account for the wealth of influences, associations, trends and tendencies that characterise it. Given that this work has appeared only in very recent years, there is still great potential for a rigorous examination of independent filmmaking within several wider contexts.[23]

Likewise, in an article intended to contribute to understandings of the history of media convergence, Dan Leopard argued that to understand how 'autonomous art practice as a metaphor of agency ... transfer[s] from individuals to institutions', it is necessary to explore the dispersion and migration of ideas across 'discourse networks', including sources, channels and receivers.[24] While Leopard traced discourses of autonomy from avant-garde artists and filmmakers of the 1950s to its expansion to the mainstream institutions of the 1970s, he concluded by gesturing to the contemporary period as he explained that 'The notion of an autonomous form of art practice still plays as large at Sundance with its auteurs of independent cinema as it does on the Internet with its activist's vision of "information wants to be free"'.[25] Although some scholarly work has already begun to map indie production in relation to convergence, especially in regard to intersections between indie film and television, including in the form of two edited collections, *Indie Reframed* and *Indie TV* (the latter of which I have contributed to),[26] much more work needs to be done. Thus, this book explores the relationship between convergence and ideas of autonomous modes of production surrounding the different types of projects that indie-auteurism is used to market and sell as it contributes to more expansive and comprehensive histories of different categorisations of specialty media.

I see the migration of indie-auteurs between sectors as an ongoing movement that is performed by a type of freelance labour and managed by talent intermediaries in pursuit of the conditions deemed necessary for achieving critical and commercial success. As Denise Mann explains, in post-Classical Hollywood talent gained some leverage after studios released them from long-term contracts, but their independence was 'never more than comparative and highly circumscribed' because 'much of the control' over their careers shifted to talent agents, managers and publicists.[27] Moreover, Roussel points out that 'Agency leaders know that they must institutionalize the necessary circulation of their artists between complementary sectors, and toward what they believe to be the most promising new areas'.[28] Indie-auteurism's management across sectors thus fundamentally challenges conceptualisations of the figures around whom it coheres as both autonomous and as filmmakers. For this reason, I define indie-auteurism as a discursive construct attached to authorial figures associated loosely with American independent or indie film. Doing so, I leave open the potential for figures to be constructed as autonomous artists even when their connections with independent or indie film have not yet solidified or have diminished following their migration to other sectors. Tracing intermediaries' work across sectors and their roles in the migration of talent thus points to the problems of conceptualising media within neat genre categories.

Scholars including Philip Drake, Peter Krämer, Mark Gallagher and Jason Sperb have conceptualised independence in post-Classical Hollywood, where talent became freelance and studios adopted the package-unit mode of production, as a form of autonomy that filmmakers secure when they negotiate with employers from a position of strength.[29] For Drake, a filmmaker's leverage hinges on their 'reputational capital', composed of their recent performance in the business, the critical and commercial reception of their work, and their 'embeddedness within key industrial, institutional and social networks'.[30] More recently, Carol Vernallis, Holly Rogers and Lisa Perrott, and Jonathan Gray and Derek Johnson,[31] have explored the migration of certain directors between sectors, including film, television and advertising. Yet none of this work explores the roles played by talent agents and talent managers nor how directors' auteur brands gain value from their association with indie film as a differentiated cultural category.

Sherry Ortner, however, provides a useful conceptual framework for exploring indie-auteurism within an era of convergence by proffering that indie cinema can be understood as both a field of cultural production where participants gain recognition through their associations with it while competing with one another for reward and greater recognition at the same time.[32] Ortner points out that indie cinema's institutions, including film festivals and art-house cinemas, which she calls its 'cultural apparatus', perform 'a kind of double interpellation, defining filmmakers as both independently creative and part of a collaborative community'.[33] As a result, Ortner shows how the institutions that are involved in generating an indie culture participate not only in legitimating certain films as authentically indie,[34] but also in the process of building and maintaining brands and professional legitimacy. Ortner also argues that scenes must be understood 'historically, as emerging at a particular point in time, and eventually dying out'.[35] In this sense, Ortner says, scenes can be thought of as 'cultural movements' that appear to challenge the established culture before losing momentum and leaving behind a 'partially reconfigured field'.[36] While indie film as a cultural category appears to become increasingly difficult to sustain during an era of media convergence,[37] therefore, Ortner's conceptualisation of the scene prompts us to consider how indie filmmaking continues to have a cultural resonance and influence through the indie-auteur figures that are associated with it.

Amazon Studios' appointment of Hope and its efforts to position itself as a benefactor of struggling indie filmmakers captures how indie-auteurism has become a tool used to promote a range of products and services in this era of convergence. On the surface, Amazon's investment appears to have been intended to promote Amazon's Instant Video streaming service by making it seem to be a site that was offering more original and innovative film and television content than the Hollywood studios, the multiplex theatres, and broadcast and cable television channels. While Amazon's cultivation of associations with indie film and Price's assertion that indie filmmakers' stories 'deserve an audience' catered to middle-class educated audiences with cultural and economic capital who could afford to subscribe, the fact that Amazon Instant Video is offered with Amazon Prime means that it is ultimately meant, as Karen Petruska discusses, to increase the volume of orders placed through Amazon's online shopping business.[38] Although Amazon's investment in indie film differentiated its service from the Hollywood mainstream and made the company seem to be a benefactor of daring filmmaking, the fact that it is a major conglomerate that has sought to dominate markets by suppressing workers' wages and undercutting its retail rivals indicates that it is not on the side of independents at all. This is particularly problematic given that the era of convergence is one that has witnessed an intensification of precarious employment conditions as major companies have successfully lobbied governments to reduce workers' protections for their benefit.[39]

Examining the indie-auteur within an era of convergence thus places indie culture within a wider political context. While Ortner considers independent filmmaking to be a form of social critique and resistance to the neoliberal social order,[40] Claire Molloy argues that neoliberalism explains American independent film's depoliticisation as the studios increasingly used indie-auteurism as a tool to differentiate between their products while the more politically charged independent filmmaking was pushed to the margins.[41] In this context, Molloy argues that the indie-auteur came to represent a type of neoliberal mobile creative labour that is monetised and valued for its high level of autonomy and ability to move between sectors creating products that sell widely.[42] This all helps to provide a reminder about why examining indie-auteurism matters in the first place; that is, it addresses issues of diversity in cultural production that are at stake because of consolidation of ownership and neoliberal policy. By tracing indie-auteurism's role in selling a range of products, therefore, I scrutinise depictions of indie-auteurs in promotional and critical discourse as daring, maverick, independent filmmakers and consider whether indie-auteurs are critical of consolidation or whether indie-auteurism might really be a symptom of it.

Analysing anonymous figures and their 'rhetorical manoeuvring'

Talent intermediaries, especially talent agents and managers, can be conceptualised as some of the media industries' most anonymous figures. On one hand, talent intermediaries elude inspection because they work behind-the-scenes, perform broad and complex roles across many projects and sectors, and actively resist becoming very visible to the public as they protect trade secrets and limit the potential for their associations with deal-making to undermine their collaborators' and clients' stardom and artistic legitimacy.[43] On the other hand, talent intermediaries can be conceptualised as anonymous figures because, paradoxically, they seek to build their brands and reputations by actively cultivating associations with anonymity.[44] Talent intermediaries' mobilisation of a discourse of anonymity can be found in abundance in press reports surrounding independent and indie film producers. Schamus and Hope, for example, evidently achieved a degree of notoriety from their reputations for supporting indie filmmakers behind-the-scenes. This discourse of anonymity is captured particularly neatly, though, in a 2002 article tellingly titled 'The Misfits', published by *L.A. Weekly*, in which its author, Paul Cullum, explained:

> For every director or writer or actor who lends his or her talent to big films that wind up smart, or to little films that turn out edgier or more subversive or less programmatic than might be expected, there is inevitably an independent producer toiling in obscurity, who actually makes it happen.[45]

Some companies, such as the major Hollywood management firm Anonymous Content, which is owned by producer Steve Golin, who is a subject of Cullum's article and of this book, also make anonymity an explicit part of their brand. The company's logo is 'Anonymous Content' written in bold white font against a black background with a figure resembling an executive or talent manager carrying a briefcase hidden within the letter 'A'.

The discourse of anonymity surrounding talent intermediaries involved with indie or specialty productions is effective because it creates an impression of the director as an autonomous artist and creative visionary working apart from Hollywood and its profit-driven agendas and standardised modes of production. Yet, recognising that indie-auteurism is a valuable tool that is managed and mobilised to market products and services, including Hollywood's own, I take the discourse of anonymity to be a form of what I call 'rhetorical manoeuvring' that obfuscates talent intermediaries and their clients' and collaborators' actual roles, and preserves misleading impressions that indie production prioritises art over commerce. Rhetorical manoeuvring can, on one hand, be understood as a form of soft selling where industry figures appear to reject very aggressive and obvious promotional strategies entirely or replace them with subtler ones that appear more suited to the purported goals of indie production. On the other hand, it can be understood as a form of what John Caldwell calls 'industrial reflexivity', where the industries' workers self-represent, critique and reflect on their own labour.[46] Branding functions, in these terms, as Catherine Johnson explains, to imbue 'all elements of production – not just product development, launch and promotion, but also the labour of workers and the ways in which they talk about that labour'.[47] Accordingly, I see talent intermediaries as being akin to the 'cultural banker', as identified by Pierre Bourdieu, as figures who accumulate cultural capital from their perceived success in 'discovering' talent and mobilise this capital to position certain figures as indie-auteurs and market their works as being of exceptional quality.[48] Intermediaries and their rhetorical manoeuvring thus contribute to what Bourdieu calls the 'charismatic' ideology, which attributes creation to individual authorial figures and, in doing so, suppresses the question of what 'authorizes the author, what creates authority with which authors authorize'.[49]

To map indie-auteurism, uncover the anonymous figures behind it, and decipher their rhetorical manoeuvring, I take a cultural production approach that involves analysing the extratextual, promotional and critical discourse surrounding case studies in the form of different screen media productions. I analyse extratextual discourse in the form of practitioner interviews, Q&A sessions, and conference speeches, promotional discourse in the form of interviews, press releases and marketing materials such as posters and trailers, and critical discourse in the form of trade and popular press reports and reviews. Talent managers are technically different from agents because they tend to represent fewer clients and offer more long-term strategic career advice, usually collect a 15 per cent rather than 10 per cent commission from their clients' earnings, and are legally prohibited from procuring employment but are permitted to engage in production.[50] The book focuses more on talent managers than it does on talent agents because their direct contributions to production often bring them a greater visibility as they engage in promotional activities at public forums that make managers more accessible to study using extratextual, promotional and critical materials.

As Jonathan Gray explains, marketing materials, which, borrowing a term from Gérard Genette, he calls paratexts, are often audiences' first encounters with film and television productions and, as such, establish the frames and filters that create the interpretive perimeters surrounding them.[51] Journalists and critics are also 'privileged paratextual creators' in that they have negotiated relationships with the institutions and individuals that they report on, and they provide a range of promotional functions and act as gatekeepers between the industries and their consumers.[52] While I rely on press reports for important information, I reconstruct their official and often PR-infused narratives by paying attention to the institutions circulating them and scrutinise them using existing scholarly research, a wider range of trade press publications, and companies' financial disclosures in the form of quarterly and annual reports.

While scholars such as Norman Fairclough and Penny Powers have set out rules for conducting discourse analysis,[53] I borrow from Tzioumakis a less bounded model that has already proven productive for examining American independent and indie film.[54] Doing so is essential for tracing the contours of indie-auteurism as a discursive construct that I propose is often productively vague, associated with unquantifiable ideas of quality, highly malleable, widely disseminated and as complex as the systems of production from which it emerges.[55] I combine macro- and micro-industrial perspectives to explore how talent intermediaries and their collaborators operate in specific and changing industrial and cultural contexts. Doing so, I build on Tzioumakis's exploration of 'periods' and 'waves' of independent and indie film, which involves examining the different strategies used by 'individual production companies ... [and] distinct market sectors and "classes" of producers' at the micro-industrial level during broader periods of convergence.[56] I also build on Derek Johnson, Derek Kompare and Avi Santo's framework for examining media industry management in general to explore how the management of indie-auteurism is shaped by intermediaries through a form of tactical negotiation between the rules that institutions create and individuals' agency.[57] Doing so I view talent intermediaries as a kind of 'organisational linking pin' that join talent management and production operations, client and institution, labour and authorship, and production and consumption.[58] Accordingly, I explore the strategic responses of talent intermediaries to changing industrial, economic, technological and cultural circumstances, as well as the opportunities and obstacles that emerge for developing and promoting specialty content packaged with indie-auteurism at given moments in time.

Cultural and social hierarchies

This book also explores relationships between the management of indie-auteurism and cultural and social hierarchies and inequalities. While many critics and some scholars have analysed 'the cinematic' as a set of textual properties that can be found in other media such as high-end television drama,[59] this book sees ideas about 'cinematization' as part of legitimating strategies that elevate certain works by associating them with cinema.[60] As Michael Newman and Elana Levine explain, in the convergence era, cinematization has become television's most ubiquitous legitimating discourse as certain shows and modes of consumption are elevated over television's less respectable genres and traditional modes of engagement.[61] In turn, the cultural and social positions of the elite, middle-class, well-educated and disproportionately male audience associated with these legitimated modes are sustained, while more marginalised groups, such as the working classes, the unemployed, the disabled, the elderly and women, who are associated with traditional television, are usually denigrated.[62] While Newman and Levine and many other scholars have explored cinematization as a form of cultural legitimation, I simultaneously explore how certain figures and their intermediaries gain professional legitimacy and marketability through their association with these modes as cinematization makes indie-auteurism increasingly valuable.

In the era of convergence, White men have remained overrepresented in screen media production while women and people of colour have remained significantly underrepresented.[63] These inequalities are mirrored within Hollywood's top talent agencies and management companies, where most talent intermediary roles, especially at the most senior levels, have been populated by White males from middle-class backgrounds.[64] These inequalities are also particularly pertinent in indie culture where the maverick White male auteur has been a defining feature and holds significant value in the promotion of specialty content, including indie film and so-called quality television, as they often cater to the tastes of White male middle-class audiences.[65] As Taylor Nygaard and Jorie Lagerwey explain, 'The aesthetics of innovation, complexity, and "art" typically labelled "quality" television are in fact an aesthetics of Whiteness, a result of the racist historical understanding of desirably affluent audiences as White'.[66] This image of the indie-auteur as a maverick and innovator is also mirrored in promotional and critical discourse surrounding the intermediaries and company executives who collaborate with them as they are regularly constructed as 'great men' or 'great leaders'.[67] This dynamic is epitomised by Cullum when he described the independent film producers that he profiled for *L.A. Weekly* as 'mavericks, visionaries, savants', as well as more worryingly, 'bullies, cardsharps [and] egomaniacs', whose personalities he claimed are necessary to make the movies that nobody else will make.[68]

With UCLA's *Hollywood Diversity Report*s having hypothesised that talent intermediaries acting as gatekeepers may contribute to wider inequalities in production,[69] I explore how the management of indie-auteurism may play a role in maintaining the maverick auteur discourse and in sustaining the employability and privileged positions of certain White male directors and their more anonymous collaborators. To do so, I investigate a kind of value chain that sees talent intermediaries and distributors draw on perceptions about which productions sell and who the target audience is when making decisions about who to hire and what types of properties they need to display to market productions. More specifically, I explore cultural and professional legitimation as talent intermediaries, their auteur-director clients, and the core intended audience often end up reflecting one another socio-economically as they secure a collective value that potentially sustains their privileged positions in media production and consumption. As Roussel explains, talent intermediaries usually:

> work at anticipating and satisfying buyers' expectations without challenging the categories they use to express them: they feel like they have no other choice than

slipping their clients' profiles into such constraining moulds ... thus reinforcing this typecasting system by playing along with it.[70]

More broadly, Tom Kemper argues that professional personalities, reputations and brands are institutional and industrial because they are 'developed within systemic practices'; that is, they are shaped 'through the routine relationships ... established by means of and within the studio system'.[71] Thus, I explore how talent intermediaries guide specific figures to present and position themselves as indie-auteurs as they gain value in the wider industry and marketplace.

Although many of my case studies centre around the management of White male indie-auteurs by White male intermediaries who have arguably benefited disproportionately from their associations with indie culture, I also consider the potential implications for people of colour and women who too often encounter greater difficulties accessing finance and distribution and face an increased precarity in employment.[72] I consider why many women directors and directors of colour are often excluded from talent intermediaries' management of indie-auteurism as well as what this reveals about indie culture more broadly. Acting on Cynthia Baron's point that studies of studio specialty film have tended to create a misleading impression that indie production lacks diversity entirely,[73] however, I also explore some of the instances where indie-auteurism has been constructed and mobilised around women and people of colour. Doing so, I explore what contextual circumstances were involved, whether the management strategies and indie-auteur discourse were reshaped in the process, and what this reveals about the role of gender and race constructions and discourses in indie culture. As a result, I consider women and people of colour not only as victims of unfair conditions but also as important players in indie and specialty production. While Roussel posits that talent intermediaries can sometimes be engaged imperceptibly in the 'progressive and collective rearrangement' of industrial and cultural divisions and hierarchies,[74] then, I explore to what extent this occurs through talent intermediaries' management of indie-auteurism across screen media. What is partly at stake is whether media convergence displaces or solidifies the class of producers and talent who receive the opportunities to make and sell specialty content, whether it relaxes or inhibits the 'proper interpretations' talent, producers, distributors and marketeers seek to impose upon their products, and whether it reshapes and diversifies indie-auteurism or merely helps it to migrate and multiply.

A note on Harvey Weinstein and sexual abuses in Hollywood

I do not analyse the work of Harvey Weinstein in this book. Yet the crimes that he is now known to have committed, and the culture of sexual harassment, sexual abuse and intimidation in Hollywood that have been allowed to exist and which revelations about his crimes helped to expose, demand attention and raise important questions. In 2017, Weinstein, arguably the most famous and influential independent and indie film producer during the previous three decades, was revealed to have committed dozens of acts of sexual abuse, including rape, against models, actors, and personal assistants and employees at his now former companies, Miramax and The Weinstein Company.[75] Many of these sexual assaults took place in the US, UK, France and Italy in Weinstein's offices and hotel rooms where he was staying, often after he invited the women in under false pretences to audition for roles in his films or to watch some rushes, and for parties during film festivals.[76] Weinstein also reportedly employed a number of assistants who helped to facilitate the meetings, as well as attorneys, publicists and eventually former Israeli spies who helped to cover up his behaviour by getting victims to sign non-disclosure agreements or tracking journalists and planting fake news stories to discredit victims or frighten them away from reporting his crimes.[77]

The *New York Times* also reported that talent agents and managers eager to profit from Weinstein's 'star-making films' instructed actresses to 'meet him alone at hotels and advised them to stay quiet when things went wrong'.[78] The *New York Times* singled out the Creative Artists Agency (CAA), reporting that at least eight of its agents were told that Weinstein had abused female clients but casually dismissed the complaints or told the clients that charges were not worth pursuing because they were difficult to prove and might harm their careers.[79] Consequently, complaints against Weinstein were reportedly not passed to senior management and the agency continued to send actresses to private meetings with him.[80] These reports prompted CAA to issue a measly public apology 'to any person the agency let down for not meeting the high expectations we place on ourselves, as individuals and as a company'.[81] Moreover, actress Rose McGowan was reportedly raped at the 1997 Sundance Film Festival, then aged 23, after she was instructed to meet Weinstein by Jill Messick, her manager at the time at Addis-Wechsler & Associates, at the Stein Eriksen Lodge in Park City.[82] McGowan reported the assault to Messick, which led Addis-Wechsler & Associates' owners, Nick Wechsler and Keith Addis, to confront Weinstein in an encounter that Wechsler says prompted the producer to promise that he would pursue psychiatric treatment.⁸³ Despite McGowan's allegations about Weinstein, however, Wechsler says that he felt compelled to continue working with the producer because 'Sometimes he was the only game in town'.⁸⁴ Furthermore, Messick became the vice president of Miramax only a few months after the assault, much to the astonishment of McGowan and Messick's then assistant, Anne Woodward.⁸⁵

The revelations surrounding Weinstein led to the #MeToo Movement as other victims of sexual assault in Hollywood and society more broadly began to tell their own stories.⁸⁶ Amazon's Roy Price, for instance, was suspended and later resigned as the head of Amazon Studios in October 2017 after Isa Hackett, a producer on *Man in the High Castle* (Amazon, 2015–19), alleged that he had repeatedly propositioned her during production.⁸⁷ Hackett's complaints prompted McGowan to tweet Jeff Bezos, Amazon's chief executive and founder, saying that she had told Price repeatedly that Weinstein had raped her only for the head of Amazon Studios to respond dismissively that it 'hadn't been proven'.⁸⁸ At the time, Amazon Studios was partnering with the Weinstein Company to finance and distribute two television series, *The Romanoffs* (Amazon Studios, 2018) with Matthew Weiner and an untitled project created by indie-auteur David O. Russell. Days after McGowan's tweets, Amazon broke their ties with the Weinstein Company.⁸⁹

During the promotion of *The Romanoffs*, which Amazon went on to produce and distribute after taking the project on, Weiner was himself accused of sexually harassing a former *Mad Men* (AMC, 2007–15) staff writer, Kater Gordon, while working late one night by telling her that she owed it to him to let him see her naked.⁹⁰ Weiner denied the incident by saying that he could not recall saying that and that he never felt or acted 'that way' towards Gordon.⁹¹ In 2022, allegations that Russell had a history of bullying and abusing colleagues on set resurfaced along with reports that, in 2011, he had engaged in sexual misconduct with his nineteen-year-old niece.⁹² Regarding the latter incident, Russell, who did not face charges, reportedly told police at the time that his niece had been acting 'very provocative and seductive' and consented to him touching her.⁹³ Other figures that I discuss in this book have been accused of inappropriate or abusive behaviour too. Indie-auteur Cary Fukunaga has been accused of engaging in inappropriate workplace behaviour and harassing young women on and off set.⁹⁴ Keith Redmon, a talent manager and a producer of feature films including *The Revenant* (Iñárritu, 2015), was dismissed from Anonymous Content after he was accused of multiple incidents of sexual misconduct, including harassment and inappropriate workplace behaviour.⁹⁵ Producer

Scott Rudin, who was revealed to have used racial slurs in comments about Barack Obama's film tastes following a hacking of Sony's computers in 2014, has more recently been accused of engaging in a pattern of aggressive and bullying workplace behaviour that included smashing a computer monitor on an executive's hand, throwing a baked potato at the head of one assistant, and throwing a stapler at another.[96] Rudin was, alongside Weinstein, one of the indie film producers that Callum celebrated for being a maverick, visionary, egomaniac and bully.[97]

These events thus raise several important questions. First, they raise questions about the level of power that certain producers can attain and the different, sometimes very harmful, ways that they can wield it. Weinstein built much of his reputation from managing indie-auteurs to produce, distribute and market projects such as *Sex, Lies, and Videotape* (1989) with Steven Soderbergh, *Clerks* (1994) and *Chasing Amy* (1997) with Kevin Smith, and especially *Reservoir Dogs* (1992) and *Pulp Fiction* (1994) with Quentin Tarantino. Weinstein subsequently used his reputation for delivering sometimes critically and commercially successful films, and building stars, to allegedly influence and control female actors, as well as colleagues, assistants, talent agents and managers. This exemplifies how producers can use their power to not only enhance reputations, marketability, employability and careers, but also tarnish and destroy them or, worse, threaten to destroy them to coerce people into vulnerable situations and ensure their silence. Second, Weinstein's alleged behaviour raises questions about what exactly autonomy means and who it benefits. The *New York Times*, for example, speculated that the autonomy that Disney gave Miramax to maintain its creative culture after taking over the company in 1994, 'could have inadvertently created opportunities for misconduct that Mr. Weinstein exploited'.[98]

Third, Weinstein's actions raise questions about the consequences of the culture that exists within Hollywood and the media industries, especially as a result of gender inequalities and the fact that men occupy most of the employer, producer and talent agent and manager roles. Finally, Weinstein's crimes show the disparity between the prestige and glamour that comes from managing indie-auteurism and forms of stardom and the behind-the-scenes realities. Much of the behaviour and interactions between individuals working in Hollywood takes place, as Caldwell has argued, in private locations including elevators, bars, and hotel rooms and corridors.[99] These interactions undoubtedly shape screen media history, but they are also practically off-limits for scholars, with even police detectives conducting undercover operations finding Weinstein's alleged assaults difficult to prove.[100] I do not explore the behind-the-scenes interactions in this book, therefore, but work instead on mapping and scrutinising the management of indie-auteurism as a discursive construct that has increasing promotional value in the era of media convergence but also a wide number of consequences.

Chapter overview

This book is made up of six chapters. Each explores specific sets of case studies, which are mostly examined chronologically. As such, the chapters' time periods often intersect as each chapter deals with overarching themes as a means for exploring broader issues, changes and continuities, within the era of convergence. Chapter 1 explores several different producers' collaborations with eminent indie-auteurs, the Coen brothers, during three different periods of contemporary American independent film as set out by Tzioumakis. Doing so, the chapter maps a model of indie-auteurism that has been managed during these different periods to shed light on how the Coens' indie-auteur brands have been sustained, to explore different instances of intersection between the Coens' indie-auteur brands and the brands of their producers, and to unpack what this reveals about indie culture.

Chapter 2 is the first of four chapters that explore two integrated talent management and production companies founded by Steve Golin, namely Propaganda Films and Anonymous Content. Chapter 2 explores both companies in broad terms as it examines their changing operations in an era of convergence as both companies were acquired and ceased to be independent. Doing so, the chapter explores how Propaganda's and Anonymous's owners' decisions and the companies' changing operations in an era of convergence impacted the types of productions that the companies made and, in turn, the opportunities that they offered to indie-auteurs. The chapter considers Golin's collaborations with indie-auteurs such as Michel Gondry, David Fincher, Michael Moore, Jocelyn Moorhouse, Antoine Fuqua and others. Chapter 3 then examines Propaganda's and Anonymous's operations in short-form production in the shape of commercial spots, branded content and music videos, and investigates specifically how the companies differentiated and elevated their short-form productions by mobilising indie-auteurism and positioning them effectively as short films. The chapter focuses especially on Spike Jonze's music videos, *The Hire* (Anonymous Content, 2003) as a form of branded content executive produced by Fincher and directed by auteurs including Guy Ritchie, Wong Kar-Wai and Alejandro G. Iñárritu, and Dee Rees's work on a commercial named *The Box* (2018) for Walmart.

Chapter 4 examines Anonymous's expansion into high-end television drama in the 2010s as the company produced shows such as *The Knick* (Cinemax, 2014–15), *True Detective* (HBO, 2014–), *Mr. Robot* (USA Networks, 2015–19), *Maniac* (Netflix, 2018) and *The OA* (Netflix, 2016–19) with figures including Steven Soderbergh, Cary Fukunaga, Sam Esmail, and Brit Marling and Zal Batmanglij. The chapter examines especially how Anonymous's managers and producers packaged several of their productions with an indie-auteur attached as single-series directors as a means for promoting the shows as cinematic indie innovations to differentiate them within a crowded television marketplace. Chapter 5 examines Anonymous's operations in film during the mid-2010s as its executives and clients navigated the downturn in studio specialty production. The chapter makes the case that the studios' reduction of investment in specialty film was not only a challenge that needed to be overcome but also provided a context and narrative that bolstered impressions that indie-auteurs and their producers are artists-at-heart. Doing so, the chapter considers Anonymous's collaborations with clients including Patty Jenkins, Edgar Wright, Gavin Hood and Mark Webb, but homes in on two specialty features in the form of *The Revenant* and *Beasts of No Nation* (2015) shot by Iñárritu and Fukunaga respectively. Collectively, Propaganda and Anonymous provide an excellent opportunity for exploring the management of indie-auteurism across media sectors, for exploring the relationship between the branded discourse and broader industrial, cultural and social hierarchies, and for working towards a more connected screen media history.

While Chapters 2 to 5 explore how Propaganda and Anonymous built their brands mostly around managing White male maverick auteurs, Chapter 6 analyses Charles D. King, a former agent and the first Black partner at the William Morris agency, and his management and production company, Macro, as they have built their brands around amplifying the voices of people of colour in screen media production. The chapter explores how King and Macro, with which Anonymous has come to share ownership, adhere to broader Hollywood studio systems while simultaneously seeking to differentiate themselves from Hollywood's established talent intermediary practices and endeavouring to shift the cultural and commercial possibilities for Black talent and Black intermediary businesses. Analysing King and Macro's work with several different Black indie-auteurs, including Tyler Perry, Tim Story, Ryan Coogler and Shaka King, on projects such as *Diary of a Mad Black Woman* (Grant, 2005), *House of Payne* (Debmar-Mercury, 2006; TBS, 2007–12; BET, 2020–), *Barbershop* (Story, 2002) and *Judas and the Black Messiah* (King, 2021), the chapter explores how they manage and mobilise indie-auteurism and in what ways it intersects with broader notions about Blackness. Over the six chapters, therefore, the book aims to trace the management of indie-auteurism to expand on the history of American indie cinema and specialty production and to shed much needed light on the roles that talent intermediaries play in cultural production in an era of convergence.

Notes

1. At the time, Universal was itself owned by Vivendi.
2. McClintock and Siegel (2016).
3. Stewart (2013).
4. Spangler (2015).
5. *The Cosmopolitans* ended up being a 'TV Movie'.
6. Lang (2015).
7. Stewart (2013).
8. King (2013a) p. 19.
9. O'Falt (2016); Lang and Setoodeh (2016).
10. Tzioumakis (2017b); Perren (2012) pp. 16–20; Newman (2011) pp. 1–11.
11. Newman (2009); Newman (2011) p. 226.
12. Tzioumakis (2006) p. 247; King (2005) p. 56; Newman (2011) p. 45; Molloy (2017) pp. 368, 375.
13. For classical conceptions of authorship in film, see Truffaut (2008) pp. 9–18; Sarris (2008).
14. As James Lyons (2016, p. 58) says, 'there is an overdue assessment of the function of such power brokers in the recent history of the specialty film sector, offering additional nuance to the conceptualising of "independent" production'.
15. Some of the indie-auteurs that the book analyses also take on a producer, director of photgraphy, and editing roles.
16. Holt (2011) p. 3; Jenkins (2006) p. 3; Schatz (2017) p. 259.
17. Corrigan (1998) p. 40.
18. Roussel (2017) p. 29.
19. See, for example, McDonald (2008); Roussel (2016).
20. Roussel (2017) pp. 180–1.
21. Ibid., pp. 180–1.
22. King (2013a) p. 259; Tzioumakis (2012) p. 14, (2013) pp. 38–9.
23. Tzioumakis (2011) p. 332.
24. Leopard (2009) pp. 158–9.
25. Ibid. p. 159.
26. Badley, Perkins and Schreiber (2016a); Lyons and Tzioumakis (2023).
27. Mann (2008) pp. 23, 48.
28. Roussel (2017) p. 47.

29. Drake (2013); Gallagher (2013); Krämer (2013); Sperb (2013) pp. 116–22.
30. Drake (2013) p. 145.
31. Vernallis, Rogers and Perrott (2020); Gray and Johnson (2021).
32. Ortner (2017). See also Straw (2001); Bourdieu (1993).
33. Ortner (2017) pp. 47–8.
34. Newman (2011) p. 180; King (2005) p. 14.
35. Ortner (2017) p. 45.
36. Ibid. p. 45.
37. Tzioumakis (2012) p. 14; Sinwell (2020) p. 11.
38. Petruska (2023) p. 239.
39. Curtin and Sanson (2016).
40. Ortner (2013) p. 3.
41. Molloy (2017) pp. 368–9.
42. Ibid. p. 380.
43. On talent agents, see Mann (2008) p. 36; For a similar argument around managers and executives in the media industries see Lotz (2014) p. 27.
44. Mann (2008) p. 39.
45. Cullum (2002) p. 35.
46. Caldwell (2008) pp. 4–5.
47. C. Johnson (2012) p. 21.
48. Bourdieu (1993) pp. 76–7. See also Roussel (2017) p. 102; Ortner (2013) pp. 158–63.
49. Bourdieu (1993) p. 76.
50. See, for example, McDonald (2008).
51. Gray (2010) p. 36; Genette (1982).
52. Gray (2010) pp. 166–7. See also Gallagher (2013) p. 112.
53. Fairclough (1995); Powers (2007).
54. Tzioumakis (2006).
55. On the complexity of systems of cultural production, see, for example: Williamson (2016) p. 21; Hesmondhalgh (2013) pp. 4–33; Wasko (2005) p. 21.
56. Tzioumakis (2012) p. 18.
57. Johnson, Kompare and Santo (2014) p. 10.
58. On the concept of industry figures as 'linking pins', see Havens (2014) p. 39; Turow (1992); Likert (1967).
59. For critics, see for example: Seitz (2015); Hale (2015). For scholars, see Richards (2021); Sexton and Lees (2021).
60. Newman and Levine (2012) pp. 5–6; Jaramillo (2013); McCabe (2013); Andrews (2014) p. 10; Caldwell (1995) p. 12.
61. Newman and Levine (2012) pp. 5–6.
62. Ibid. pp. 5–6.
63. Hunt et al. (2018).
64. Roussel (2017) pp. 53–4.
65. On the maverick indie-auteur, see: Perkins (2016) p. 140; McHugh (2016) p. 142. On specialty screen production and its audience, see: Newman (2011) pp. 2–3; King (2005) pp. 16–17; Nygaard and Lagerwey (2020) p. 155.

66. Nygaard and Lagerwey (2020) p. 155.
67. Lotz (2014) p. 29.
68. Cullum (2002) p. 34.
69. Hunt et al. (2018) pp. 28–32.
70. Roussel (2017) p. 129.
71. Kemper (2010) p. x, original emphasis.
72. Warner (2016); Ndounou (2014) pp. 1–5; White (2016) p. 44.
73. Baron (2016) p. 204.
74. Roussel (2017) pp. 131, 177.
75. Anon (2018a); Holpuch and Lartey (2018); Moniuszko and Kelly (2018).
76. Moniuszko and Kelly (2018); O'Carroll (2017).
77. Carroll and Levin (2017); Farrow (2017).
78. Twohey et al. (2017).
79. Ibid.
80. Ibid.
81. Chmielewski (2018).
82. Dominus (2017).
83. Ibid.
84. Twohey et al (2017).
85. Dominus (2017).
86. Rife (2017).
87. Anon (2017a).
88. Ibid.
89. Bowden (2017).
90. Nordyke (2018).
91. Ibid.
92. Rao (2022).
93. Ibid.
94. Roundtree (2022).
95. Belloni (2021).
96. Siegel (2021a).
97. Cullum (2002) p. 34.
98. Twohey et al (2017).
99. Caldwell (2008) pp. 4–5.
100. Holpuch (2017).

CHAPTER 1

Producing with Indie-Auteurs

The Coen Brothers and an Indie Periodisation

Since the emergence of the so-called quality iteration of American independent film in the 1980s, few filmmakers have sustained reputations as indie-auteurs as successfully as the Coen brothers, Joel and Ethan. As an increasing convergence between Hollywood and the independent film sector began to occur and intensified, and studios focused increasingly on making indie films with more commercial properties,[1] the Coens, alongside a handful of other figures such as Steven Soderbergh, Richard Linklater and Spike Lee, managed to maintain careers as filmmakers who could appeal to wider audiences while sustaining reputations as indie-auteurs retaining control over their productions to make work that was meant to be different from the Hollywood mainstream. The brothers did so even as they often worked with the major studios and their subsidiary divisions.

The Coens have sustained reputations as indie-auteurs while continuing to find employment in Hollywood in part because of the textual properties of their work. In particular, the Coens' quirky sensibility, dark tone and play with genre has helped to differentiate their films from the Hollywood mainstream and to appeal to niche audiences while simultaneously not alienating them from mass mainstream audiences with more conventional tastes.[2] While the textual properties of the Coens' films have been relatively widely discussed, however, this chapter explores how the Coens' reputations as indie-auteurs have been constructed and maintained through their collaborations with various producers and does so within three different periods of contemporary American independent film identified by Yannis Tzioumakis, namely independent, indie and indiewood, that represent an increasing convergence between Hollywood and the independent film sector.[3]

More specifically, the first section looks at the Coens' work with Circle Films' Ben Barenholtz and Jim and Ted Pedas, who distributed the brothers' debut feature *Blood Simple* (1984) before producing their next three films, *Raising Arizona* (1987), *Miller's Crossing* (1990) and

Barton Fink (1991). The next section explores their collaboration with Joel Silver on *The Hudsucker Proxy* (1994). The third section analyses their work with Brian Grazer and Scott Rudin on *Intolerable Cruelty* (2003) and *No Country for Old Men* (2007), respectively. Doing so, the chapter scrutinises simplistic conceptions of the relationship between indie-auteurs and producers that see the producers if not ignored altogether then often framed in binary terms as either meddling Hollywood figures that threaten creative autonomy (Silver and Grazer), or as ideal independent producers that are motivated by creative rather than commercial imperatives and invest their energy in facilitating the creative visions of auteurs by protecting them from administrative and financial burdens (Circle and Rudin).[4] As a result, the chapter uses the Coens to map a model of indie-auteurism that has been managed during three periods of American indie film and, by linking the brothers and their works to specific audience constituencies, draws out some of the key cultural connotations and appeals that this model of indie authorship often has.

'Everything's been done with a handshake': Circle Films as ideal independent film producers

The Coen brothers made their debut feature, *Blood Simple*, outside Hollywood by raising finance from a 'weird mixture' of private investors that included wealthy family members and friends, including doctors, lawyers and entrepreneurs, based mostly in New York, Texas and their home city of Minneapolis.[5] After completing the film, the Coens reportedly approached the studios about securing distribution but were turned away because the studio executives considered *Blood Simple* too difficult to market.[6] The studios thought it was 'not easily pigeon-holed generically', Joel Coen explained as he positioned the film as more innovative than most mainstream fare.[7]

Forging ahead without a distributor, the Coens submitted *Blood Simple* to festivals including Dallas's USA Film Festival, the Cannes Film Festival, Toronto's Festival of Festivals,[8] and the New York Film Festival. Doing so brought *Blood Simple* acclaim from audiences, judging panels and wider critics. At Toronto, *Blood Simple* finished as a runner-up for the audience's 'most popular film' award and one critic described it as a 'deliriously arty horror film' and 'nasty stylish send-up of film noir'.[9] This demonstrates, as Geoff King and Claire Molloy have discussed, how narratives of the discovery of filmmakers are prevalent in the history of independent film and tend to emerge especially in the extratextual and critical discourse surrounding festivals.[10] More broadly, Thomas Elsaesser explains that festivals build their brands around discovering new filmmakers, which effectively puts them 'in the business of making new authors'.[11] Hence festivals contribute to filmmakers' reputations and add value to their films in the wider market by giving them awards and providing them with opportunities to secure positive press coverage.[12]

Prior to the New York Film Festival, Annette Insdorf described *Blood Simple* as a 'sophisticated' American independent film made by a debut filmmaker, Joel Coen (because he was credited as the director), that deserved to secure distribution.[13] Very shortly after, Circle Films, which Ben Barenholtz and Jim and Ted Pedas founded earlier that same year, acquired it. Of Circle's acquisition, Barenholtz later commented, 'I've seen a lot of first films, and there was something about this film that was so good and so natural'.[14] The only other debut feature that had impressed Barenholtz as much as *Blood Simple*, he claimed, was David Lynch's *Eraserhead* (1977), which was a film that Barenholtz had, not coincidentally, distributed through his previous company, Libra Films.[15] Barenholtz thus contributed to the narrative of *Blood Simple*'s discovery as he suggested that Circle had found a film that was very rare in quality. More specifically, Barenholtz's comparison of *Blood Simple* to *Eraserhead* and the Coens to Lynch positioned him as a producer with a track record for spotting genius, elevated the Coens to the level of auteurs, and made *Blood Simple* appear to be innovative.

The discovery narrative was also effectively repeated around *Blood Simple*'s theatrical release as Circle distributed the film to art-house cinemas in major cities around the US. While *Blood Simple* was screening at Cinema 1 in New York, for instance, Jennifer Dunning encouraged 'adventurous' audiences to make a 'discovery' and 'try something new'.[16] In the *San Diego Reader*, Duncan Shepherd lamented that cinemagoers in the city were having to 'make do' with *Missing in Action 2* (Hool, 1985) while the Coens' debut film was being made available to audiences in Los Angeles.[17] The fact that *Missing in Action 2* was distributed by Cannon, an independent company, shows how a quality iteration of independent film, one underpinned by indie-auteurism and notions of textual difference from the Hollywood mainstream, were emerging at that time, and taking on greater prominence than industrial dynamics in the discourse of independent film.[18] This narrative of *Blood Simple* and the Coens' discovery captures how the brothers' indie-auteur brands were being constructed as they were situated in critical and extratextual discourse within an American independent film culture that appears to struggle for exposure.

Yet not all critics celebrated *Blood Simple* as an authentic independent feature. In the *Village Voice*, J. Hoberman described *Blood Simple*'s opening at Cinema 1 as a sneaky attempt to pass the film off as 'a kind of middlebrow equivalent' to Hollywood exploitation.[19] Hoberman also implied that the film was a form of advertisement that the Coens had created to secure the attention of Hollywood, which are sentiments that have been echoed by scholars including Geoff King.[20] Hoberman used language drawn from retail as he stated that *Blood Simple* has 'the heart of a Bloomingdale's window and the soul of a résumé', and that 'the only thing it's really independent of is some anxious producer worrying whether the audience will get the joke'.[21] Hoberman's reference to the absence of an anxious producer is indicative of how producers, particularly those operating nearer the centre of the Hollywood mainstream, are often regarded as antithetical to the creative aspects of filmmaking.[22] Suggesting that a producer would have worried about the Coens' comedy somewhat undermines Hoberman's own argument, as it indicates that their comedy was in fact not very typical of the mainstream. While critics' opinions of *Blood Simple* sometimes differed, however, they each ultimately advanced the notion that exclusivity, sophistication and adventure were key characteristics of authentic independent film.

By positioning *Blood Simple* against the mainstream, critics reinforced cultural and social hierarchies positioning independent and indie film and their audiences above mainstream film and mass audiences. Although critics appeared to confirm Newman's finding that exclusivity is a 'marker of indieness',[23] they ignored the fact that limited screenings can represent smaller distributors' efforts to overcome practical limitations and compete in an increasingly consolidated marketplace saturated by studio films.[24] The fact that the Coens also made the decision to screen *Blood Simple* at festivals after struggling to secure studio distribution was symptomatic of the independent film period when an infrastructure dedicated to the development of quality American independent film had only just emerged.[25] Indeed, Joel Coen indicated that *Blood Simple*'s limited distribution was a consequence of Circle lacking the capital and resources needed to distribute and market the film more widely when he pondered if the film could be successful with a wider audience. Coen stated:

> I'm curious if it'll work with more of an exploitation audience ... What would be really gratifying to us is if it works with more of a Times Square audience. Joe Bob Briggs [a drive-in movie critic] said it was the one movie Joe Bob would consider going indoors to see. It wasn't intended as an art film or anything.[26]

Coen also rejected Hoberman's review describing *Blood Simple* as exploitation and entertainment rather than art. 'That's a distinction that I've never understood', he stated, before adding, 'If somebody goes out to make a movie that isn't designed primarily to entertain people, then I don't know what the fuck they're doing'.[27]

Although Joel Coen's comments appear to be about *Blood Simple*'s appeal and tap into cultural debates about art, they may be understood as rhetorical manoeuvring designed to position the brothers advantageously in the marketplace. Around the time that Coen made these comments, the brothers were looking for business partners to finance their next film or films. Hence, Coen was attempting to distance the brothers from traits, including a disinterest in entertaining audiences and securing mass appeal, that may have limited their commercial potential and made them undesirable business partners. Coen's eagerness to see *Blood Simple* succeed with a wider audience was thus about enhancing their brand and leverage in negotiations. While Coen's comment points to the overlaps that exist between quality indie and exploitation film, he was not seeking to abolish cultural categories and hierarchies but was instead working to sustain notions of cultural difference to create impressions about the breadth of their appeal and box-office potential. The Coens' appeal to niche and mainstream audiences simultaneously, which Newman identifies,[28] was therefore a part of the brothers' early branding strategy.

Coen emphasised that the brothers were seeking to secure a deal for their next film or films that would give them more money for production but also allow them to retain significant creative freedom.[29] Four months later, the Coens secured a multipicture production deal with Circle that appeared to fulfil the brothers' criteria. The deal involved Circle agreeing to produce and finance up to four films in the $5 million to $10 million budget range by securing distribution with Twentieth Century Fox. Such deals are typical of independent film economics, where completion bonds are used by producers to secure production funds from banks upfront, providing that they have an agreement in place to sell the completed film to a distributor. With Circle securing distribution through Twentieth Century Fox, though, the deal was also symptomatic of an increasing interdependency between independent production companies and major Hollywood studios.[30] While Tzioumakis has argued that such deals made aesthetics, rather than industrial realities, increasingly central to definitions of independent film,[31] Circle and the Coens presented their deal as though it was designed to maintain the brothers' independence. Doing so preserved and enhanced impressions of the brothers' autonomy despite their increasing proximity to Hollywood, and boosted Circle's and its executives' reputations by positioning them as ideal independent producers who disavowed Hollywood bureaucracy to empower their indie-auteur directors to create their art.

Announcing the deal, for example, Ted Pedas emphasised Circle's continuing relationship with the Coens following the company's distribution of *Blood Simple* by stating, 'We believed in them, and they believed in us – it's a sort of marriage we've put together. Everything's been done with a handshake all along, and they stuck right by us'.[32] Seemingly forgetting that wedding ceremonies are usually concluded with a kiss, Pedas made Circle's relationship with the Coens appear to have developed organically through mutual trust and goodwill. As Geoff King has explained, extratextual and critical discourse often implies that the truest form of indie filmmaking is one that develops organically unlike 'the more cynically confected product of an industrial conjecture' associated with Hollywood.[33] Circle's Head of production, Jim Jacks, thus also stated that, unlike the Hollywood studios which he said usually dictate the movies that filmmakers should make, Circle would enable the Coens to make the films of their choosing.[34] Ted Pedas again distanced Circle from Hollywood bureaucracy when he later recalled negotiations with Twentieth Century Fox over the distribution of *Raising Arizona* by explaining that he got exasperated by all the bureaucracy involved.[35] According to Pedas, he told a Fox executive, 'Have all your people in one room. No more faxing, no more meetings, we're going to settle this thing … that's the way we do business in Washington'.[36] Circle's deal with the Coens also reportedly gave the brothers final cut. Circle's executives emphasised the brothers' final cut rights to position the films that they created as authentically indie-auteur products. 'Circle has a contract with the Coen Brothers', Barenholtz stated, 'So if you come to me wanting something, I can only give you what I have. And I *don't* have artistic control. So you either take it or leave it'.[37] Furthermore, Joel Coen deflected scrutiny over their arrangement with Fox and the larger budgets of their films by asserting that the budgets merely serviced their creative process. 'The extra budget lets you do things that are not possible with $800,000', Joel Coen stated, 'But the production process is still the same'.[38]

Of course, the Coens' relationship with Circle's executives was not a romantic coupling and notions projected in the extratextual discourse about its organic development are contentious. In fact, Barenholtz had turned down the opportunity to invest in *Blood Simple* before its production and a Circle 'staffer' reportedly brought the film to the company's executives' attention after its screening at Cannes.[39] As Amanda Lotz points out, portraits of media industry executives fulfilling their masterplans often obscure the roles of employees in 'narrow[ing] the universe of perceived options available to the manager as decision-maker'.[40] Instead of immediately recognising the Coens' natural talent or genius,

Circle acquired *Blood Simple* after it became a property that was garnering acclaim and becoming marketable for theatrical distribution.

The Coens' lawyers also reportedly ignored Circle's first offer to acquire *Blood Simple*, which forced the company's executives to almost double the size of their bid.[41] Jacks also admitted that the Coens had leveraged their increasing marketability during the negotiations over their co-production arrangement by telling him, 'Since we've got all this heat, why don't we make the deal for four pictures?'[42] Jacks's comment about the Coens' 'heat' may be an example of overstatement that was intended to enhance Circle's brand and share value by creating an impression that the company had secured a major asset. At the time, Circle was invested in cultivating a reputation for offering filmmakers autonomy and innovative deals as the company reportedly sought to sign other indie-auteurs such as Spike Lee to similar multipicture production deals.[43] As well as highlighting the bureaucracy that was involved in striking the deals between the Coens and Circle, these comments reveal how the brothers pursued deals that were more favourable financially. Although Joel Coen described having more money and larger budgets as a means for giving them greater creative licence, larger budgets are directly tied to the filmmaker and their intermediaries' abilities to secure larger fees. While certain sections of the press regarded the Coens to be among a new wave of independent filmmakers who were shunning Hollywood in favour of 'greater artistic control and profit participation',[44] the Coens' deal with Circle and Fox, as well as their efforts to secure studio distribution for *Blood Simple*, indicates that the brothers were well aligned with the Hollywood mainstream, and its commercial imperatives, to begin with.[45]

The length of the Coens' agreement with Circle was significant because it offered the brothers security at a time when their reputations and marketability were growing but unestablished. The deal also gave Circle an asset that they could retain in the medium-term and incentivised the company to invest in the Coens' careers and develop their marketability further. The construction of the Coens' brands is particularly evident in the trailers for their film collaborations with Circle, which can be understood as part of the brothers' developing 'brandscape', which, as Finola Kerrigan explains, is a process where name talent gain brand associations across a series of marketing materials based on previous consumption experiences.[46]

Circle's R-rated trailer for *Blood Simple*, a noirish thriller that tells the story of a cuckolded husband, Marty (Dan Hedaya), and his botched plan to kill his wife (Frances McDormand) and her lover (John Getz), begins with a title insert featuring a quote from *Newsweek*'s film critic David Ansen that describes the film as 'The most inventive and original thriller in many-a-moon' and a 'A maliciously entertaining murder story'. Afterwards, the trailer cuts to a field at night and tracks from an empty parked car to a man digging what turns out to be a grave. As the camera tracks, a quote that is finally attributed to Alfred Hitchcock written in bold white text appears slowly and in four parts across the top of the screen. The quote reads, 'It is very difficult, ... very painful ... and it takes a very, very long time ... to kill someone'. The Hitchcock quote is the only indication of the macabre humour that features more prominently in the film. Diegetic sounds of the man digging and chirping insects, and two non-diegetic sounds of a loud percussion instrument, accentuate the eerie quiet. After the camera stops, the soundtrack builds and the remainder of the trailer cuts to a series of images edited to the tempo of the score. The images include Marty crawling along a road at nighttime as his wife's lover, Ray, stalks him with a shovel that he drags beside him; Marty sliding a stack of cash to his private detective, Visser (M. Emmet Walsh), along a coffee table with the heel of his boot; Ray attempting to fire a gun to save himself from being buried alive, close-ups on the gun failing to fire, and the gun being wiped of fingerprints; Marty's wife Abby appearing in the cross-hairs of a gun and jumping away before being shot; Abby and Ray having sex in a dark hotel room under a white sheet; Visser screaming in agony from the other side of a window which subsequently cracks under pressure; and Visser shooting at Abby from the other side of a room partition causing bright white light to shine in through the bullet holes before Visser begins to punch his way through. Though the trailer features screaming and panting, it includes no dialogue.

Circle's trailer clearly promotes *Blood Simple* as an inventive thriller, one that was implicitly made to appear superior to most thrillers being made in Hollywood at that time. The trailer features key thriller iconography, but the quotes and the shot and scene setups make the film appear innovative. In this regard, the trailer is designed to make the film appeal to multiple audience constituencies comprising members who are drawn to conventional storytelling norms and others who are drawn to genre innovation. The Hitchcock quote creates an impression of *Blood Simple* as being authored at a time when the Coens' marketability remained limited. Like Barenholtz's comparison of *Blood Simple* to *Eraserhead* and the Coens to Lynch, Hitchcock is invoked to create an impression of the Coens as auteurs capable of making canonical works akin to the films of the so-called Master of Suspense. Although the Coens' names do not appear, Circle's trailer clearly contributed to the construction of a brandscape where the Coens were implicitly presented as auteurs of dark violent thrillers that were critically acclaimed and somewhat different to the mainstream.

The Coens' next film, *Raising Arizona*, was a screwball comedy that recalled Classical Hollywood movies such as *Bringing Up Baby* (Hawks, 1938) as it told the story of Hi (Nicholas Cage), an incompetent thief and ex-convict, and his wife and a former police officer, Ed (Holly Hunter), as they kidnap a baby quintuplet, Nathan Junior, because they are unable to conceive. Fox's trailer exhibits a quirky style throughout with the use of fast-paced dialogue, deadpan comedy, quick camera movements, unusual framing and a high-tempo score. For instance, the trailer begins with Hi escaping after committing a robbery while wearing pantyhose over his head that squishes and barely disguises his face (see Figure 1.1). When Hi attempts to hijack a getaway vehicle, the vehicle's driver responds in a deadpan manner and Southern drawl, 'Son, you've got a panty on your head'. When Hi instructs the driver to 'Just drive fast', the driver accelerates immediately and forces Hi to run along beside the car as he holds on. Afterwards, the trailer includes: a low to the ground shot of Hi head-on hunching as he attempts to gather up and return to their cot the other quintuplets; a long tracking shot where the camera races up ladders, through a second-floor window, and down the throat of Florence Arizona (Lynne

Figure 1.1 Hi steals Huggies in the trailer for the Coens' screwball comedy, *Raising Arizona*. (Source: Photofest)

Dumin Kitei) who, after discovering that Nathan Junior has been taken, is wailing in front of a very colourful abstract painting that helps to create a psychedelic effect; low to the ground shots of Hi, whose hair is very messy and face is scrunched up, as he is wrestled to the ground in one scene and in another is pulled from beneath a car while he futilely grabs at the concrete; a fast-paced exchange between Hi and Ed as they attempt to unconvincingly answer a question about the child's name; Nathan Junior in his car seat pulling his hood over his face as Ed makes a sudden U-turn; and two of Hi's fellow convicts explaining with deadpan delivery that they broke out of the jail because 'the institution no longer had anything to offer them'.

Raising Arizona's trailer concludes with a voice-over narrator calling the film 'A comedy beyond belief'. This tagline, which is also used on the film's poster (Figure 1.2), anticipates buzzwords such as 'quirky' and 'offbeat' that would become prominent in the marketing of indie films during the 1990s and 2000s.[47] The Coens' quirky sensibility is reinforced when Hi appears to agree with the voice-over by responding, 'Well, it ain't Ozzie and Harriet'. Appearing as metatextual commentary, Hi's reference to ABC's sitcom, *The Adventures of Ozzie and Harriet* (1952–66), reinforced the impression that *Raising Arizona* was different from the mainstream. This quote gestures to a cultural hierarchy, one that I discuss in more detail in Chapter 4, that privileges indie cinema over traditional television and its more conventional genres such as the sitcom. Given that, in the film itself, Hi and Ed are also shown sitting on their sofa watching television, which is large in the foreground, before they decide to kidnap Nathan Junior, it is clear that *Raising Arizona* and its trailer use television to represent a mundanity that contrasts to *Raising Arizona*'s not-so-*Ozzie and Harriet* liberating indie adventure. The trailer ends with a title insert describing *Raising Arizona* as a Circle Films presentation and a 'Ted and Jim Pedas/Ben Barenholtz production'. This insert indicates how *Raising Arizona* was being used by Circle to promote the company and its executives as much as it was the Coens. Although the Coens' names do not appear on the trailer, the paratext creates an impression of the film's difference from the mainstream, exhibits a style that invokes a sense of the film's authorship, and lays the foundations for constructing the brothers' reputations for being quirky filmmakers that enjoy playing with genre.

The Coens' next film, *Miller's Crossing*, is a gangster picture that tells the story of Tom Reagan (Gabriel Byrne) as he seeks to play two rival gangs off against each other to protect himself and his boss and friend, Leo (Albert Finney). Fox's trailer depicted *Miller's Crossing* as a mostly conventional gangster and prestige picture. The trailer begins with a title insert with white text against a black background explaining that *Miller's*

Figure 1.2 A comedy beyond belief: *Raising Arizona*'s poster in a quirky indie style. (Source: Photofest)

Crossing was selected to open the 1990 New York Film Festival. The trailer then cuts to a worm's-eye-view of a bowler hat being blown through a woodland and a voice-over narrator informing us that *Miller's Crossing* is 'From the makers of *Blood Simple* and *Raising Arizona*' and depicts 'a world where nothing is as it seems to be'. The narrator says a variation of the latter, spoken as 'No one is what they seem to be', at the end of the trailer as the hat is blown further away. In between, the trailer introduces us to the film's main characters and credits the film's stars, which besides Gabriel Byrne and Albert Finney includes Marcia Gay Harden and

John Turturro. It also features clips with typical gangster genre iconography and scenes, including 1920s- and 1930s-era sets and costumes, shootouts with pistols and Thompson submachine guns, Ford Model A and Oakland Six cars, a crystal chandelier that spins as bullets hit it, and a period saloon that explodes.

Of the Coens' feature film collaborations with Circle, *Miller's Crossing* was the most expensive with a budget of approximately $15 million and this is exhibited in the trailer through its inclusion of expensive-looking sets, its cast and special effects. Fox's trailer for *Miller's Crossing* is, therefore, indicative of the Coens' upward career trajectory, the brothers' increasing integration into Hollywood, and the studio's greater focus on more commercial properties during their collaborations with indie-auteurs. Although the trailer once again did not use the Coens' names specifically, its reference to the brothers' previous two films bolstered their construction as auteurs by associating them with their own oeuvre. Moreover, while Fox promoted *Miller's Crossing* as a fairly conventional gangster picture, the trailer's tagline, 'a world where nothing is as it seems to be', and its reference to the film's festival selection, still create a sense of its difference from the mainstream and associate it and the Coens with quality.

Barton Fink, the Coens' next and final film in their partnership with Circle, is a dark comedy that becomes increasingly dystopian after its eponymous protagonist (John Turturro), a playwright, struggles with writer's block after he moves to Hollywood and begins to lose his grasp on reality. The trailer opens with a voice-over narrator informing us that *Barton Fink* was the unprecedented winner of the Cannes Film Festival's three major awards, which title inserts name explicitly as Best Picture, Best Actor and Best Director. Most of the first half of the trailer has a light-hearted tone and sometimes quirky style as Fink experiences the absurdity of Hollywood before the trailer becomes much darker in the second half as it portrays his mental health decline and the film's dystopia. As the trailer ends with the film's title appearing on the screen, the letters seeming to be being typed in a random order, the narrator informs us that *Barton Fink* is 'A new film by Joel and Ethan Coen'. With the Coens' names being used explicitly in a trailer for the first time, this demonstrated how the brothers were now firmly constructed as auteurs and that they were associated with quality and genre innovation, properties that were clearly used to differentiate their films as exceptional works and, increasingly, to promote them as unmissable movie events.

Accordingly, this section has shown how Circle played a crucial role in constructing the Coens as indie-auteurs and did so by providing both practical support and by performing a rhetorical function by positioning themselves as ideal independent producers granting the brothers the autonomy that they purportedly deserved. In doing so, however, Circle and the Coens played on cultural hierarchies elevating niche production over mass media and emphasised the brothers' autonomy as they obscured their increasing alignment with Hollywood and the brothers' pursuit of wider appeal from the start.

'The last man anyone would associate with "quality cinema"': the Coens and Joel Silver

After concluding their partnership with Circle, the Coens turned their attention to making *The Hudsucker Proxy*. Despite eventually becoming their fifth feature film, the Coens reportedly wrote *Hudsucker* in collaboration with their friend and fellow indie-auteur, Sam Raimi, while the three of them shared a house together in Los Angeles just prior to the release of *Blood Simple*.[48] Although the Coens intended to make *Hudsucker* their second film, the $40 million[49] that it required meant that making it was not possible within the parameters of Circle's financing model.[50] In these terms, *Hudsucker* could be understood as a manifestation of the transition from the independent to indie film periods. The Coens renewed their interest in *Hudsucker* following *Barton Fink*, but again reportedly struggled to secure investment until their then-agent, Jim Berkus at the United Talent Agency, reportedly introduced them to producer Joel Silver.[51] Silver subsequently secured finance from Warner Bros., which acquired North American rights, and several smaller companies including Working Title and its then parent PolyGram Filmed Entertainment, which acquired rights for some international territories.[52]

If Circle represented ideal producers dedicated to supporting quality alternative independent film, then critics suggested that Silver was the archetypal Hollywood mainstream producer whose commercial imperatives represented a barrier to creativity. With Silver having produced several Hollywood action movies such as *Lethal Weapon* (Donner, 1987) and *Die Hard* (McTiernan, 1988), critics perceived him to be the 'antithesis' of the Coens' 'offbeat independence' and 'the last man anyone would associate with "quality cinema"'.[53] Hal Lipper, for instance, wrote:

> Viewers who embraced the Coens' ferocious independence with every release since *Blood Simple* and *Raising Arizona* may consider their association with the very symbol of Hollywood greed disheartening. It's almost as if they sold their souls to make their Cannes-sweeping *Barton Fink*. And, now, with *The Hudsucker Proxy*, the Devil has come to collect.[54]

Similar attitudes appeared in reports of Silver's appearance at film festivals with Sheila Johnston, for example, writing that 'the king of the genre picture's' presence at Cannes, where he was attempting to secure distribution for *Hudsucker*, summed up Hollywood's view of the festival as a market.⁵⁵

As critics resorted to perpetuating simplistic distinctions between art and commerce, they obscured the realities of Silver's collaboration with the Coens. Contrary to critics' disparagement, Silver performed an important role in *Hudsucker*'s production and promotion. On one hand, Silver performed important practical roles that included raising the finance needed to make *Hudsucker* and securing distribution. On the other hand, Silver performed a symbolic function that was used to promote *Hudsucker* and, paradoxically, sustain the Coens' reputations as indie-auteurs. Rather than representing a barrier to the Coens' creativity, Silver's reputation as a commercial producer reinforced the brothers' indie-auteurs brands by making their autonomy seem to be a deserved and natural facet of their ability to create indie films. While the purportedly ideal independent producer effectively acts as a guarantor of the filmmaker's autonomy, therefore, notions about the meddling producer indicate that the creative aspects of filmmaking should reside with the auteur-director by default.

During the promotion of *Raising Arizona*, Ethan Coen stated: 'We haven't worked with enough money to corrupt our production instincts … If anybody out there will give us the money, we're willing to try'.⁵⁶ Coen's comment indicates how the brothers playfully balanced their need for investment with attempts to build and sustain their marketability as indie-auteurs by contrasting themselves to the Hollywood producer or investor. Joel Coen performed a similar rhetorical manoeuvre in relation to Berkus when, during the promotion of *Hudsucker*, he stated, 'Berkus wants us to have mortgages. He would like nothing better than for us to be heavily in debt. He's an agent. He wants the money to keep coming in'.⁵⁷ It is also pertinent that two of the Coens' earliest films, *Barton Fink* and *Hudsucker*, are about individuals becoming corrupted by industry and featured representations of meddling bureaucrats. While *Barton Fink* followed a pompous playwright ingratiating himself within Hollywood and depicts his fraught interactions with a Hollywood studio chief and agent, *Hudsucker* focused on the exploitation and corruption of Norville Barnes (Tim Robbins), a mailroom trainee, at the hands of the Hudsucker Industries and its greedy and scheming boardroom. As a result, the Coens' collaboration with Silver provided a parallel narrative that they mobilised to promote *Hudsucker* and reinforce their indie-auteur brands. Doing so, however, hinged on and sustained simplistic distinctions between the indie-auteur and the Hollywood intermediary, art and commerce.

A key virtue associated with indie film, Geoff King notes, is 'honesty'. This privileging of honesty, which sits beside notions about organic indie production, is reflected in critical and extratextual discourse rejecting marketing strategies seen as potentially misrepresenting products in favour of strategies seen as 'remaining true to the nature of the product'.[58] While straightforward binaries distinguishing between inauthentic commercial and honest authentic forms of marketing are widely circulated in critical discourse, however, Hollywood talent strategically align themselves with promotional strategies matching their branded reputations. For instance, the Coens have gained reputations for being evasive, cryptic and difficult interviewees,[59] which creates an impression that they are resistant to traditional and often compulsory mass mainstream marketing techniques. The Coens have also made a point of dismissing the test-screening of films for audiences as they portray themselves as valuing artistic integrity over Hollywood's purportedly standardised modes of production and mass appeal. Though they confess to sometimes screening their films for friends, the brothers claim that they are 'more concerned with getting it right from [their] own point of view than worrying about the audience'.[60] In contrast, Silver has described test-screenings as a necessary 'process' that functions like a 'referendum' as he associates himself with popularity, accessibility and mass appeal.[61]

While Silver claims to value the general audience's opinions, he seems to value critics' opinions less. When Silver was attempting to secure distribution for *Hudsucker* at Cannes, for instance, some critics condemned him for making them 'peripheral' by barring the press from viewing *Hudsucker*'s promo reel.[62] Such protestations about the activities of Hollywood producers at festivals were not unique to Silver. As Noah Cowan wrote of Sundance:

> In recent years, the Sundance audience has been drawn less from the filmmaking community and more from the so-called 'industry' studio guys and agents. Their sheer numbers have meant that attention is being diverted from small, worthy projects to flashy Hollywood calling cards. This is not why Sundance was formed and is not what it should be about.[63]

The appearance of Hollywood producers and studio executives at festivals was arguably symptomatic of the transition between the independent and indie film periods and the increasing convergence between Hollywood and independent film. If, as Newman asserts, indie is 'communally rather than critically defined',[64] then these critics saw indie's community as being redefined by Hollywood producers such as Silver. Critics' disparagement of figures such as Silver thus highlighted their anxiety about independent film and its institutions becoming delegitimised and redundant. Critics suggested that festivals such as Cannes and Sundance were showcases for alternative works that were being intruded upon by Hollywood executives and implied that their own roles in the discovery of independent films was being weakened. By expressing their anxieties, however, these critics encouraged cohesion within the core indie community. Yet their doing so was problematic as this cohesion was built around vague notions of artistry and authenticity and depended on a continued exclusion of the masses.

In order to survive, the indie community must occasionally accept new members, which it does in part by matching candidates against already accepted figures.[65] Yet *Hudsucker* shows that this matching process can be prompted by the very same Hollywood promotional strategies that the community often denigrates. At the 1994 Sundance festival, for instance, Warner Bros. and Silver screened *Hudsucker* to coincide with the tenth anniversary of *Blood Simple*'s release and its Sundance Jury prize award success. Although *Hudsucker* was not made independently of Hollywood, recalling *Blood Simple* was designed to legitimate it as a similarly authentic indie-auteur production. The strategy also reinforced the festival's own brand, based as it was on notions that the festival provides a cultural value by helping to discover new independent filmmakers.[66] In turn, *Variety* reported on the festival by explaining that many young filmmakers in attendance confessed to facing a dilemma between making work that they could sell versus work that they were personally proud of.[67] *Variety* quoted David O. Russell, whose debut feature, *Spanking the Monkey* (1994), was being screened:

> Some would like to jump into the studio system, some would like to stay marginal and radical.
> I would like to follow a tough balancing act like the Coen brothers or the early Jonathan Demme, which is where you make films that have a lot of integrity but also find a market and a loyal following.[68]

While Russell matched himself against figures already accepted in the indie community, he also helped to show how the Coens' careful manoeuvring and construction as indie-auteurs had helped to make pursuing commercial success and collaboration with the studios increasingly acceptable.[69] Hence, Russell's comment highlighted the contradictions inherent in the ideals of the indie community. That is, while Silver's presence at Cannes was denigrated as symptomatic of the festival's commercialisation, the Coens were celebrated for penetrating a wider market.

Silver also promoted *Hudsucker* on 'Time Online', an online forum for *Time* magazine hosted by AOL. Since Silver was promoting the Warner Bros. distributed film, his participation represented an early example of synergy for the media conglomerate AOL Time Warner, which was subsequently established following a merger between AOL and Time Warner in 2000, that was symptomatic of a period of increasing consolidation in Hollywood.[70] On one hand, Silver's use of Time Online as a form of synergy anticipated his role in cross-promoting *The Matrix Reloaded/Revolutions* sequels (both Wachowski, 2003) and *Enter the Matrix* videogame (Atari, 2003). On the other hand, Time Online anticipated more recent strategies used by festivals including South by Southwest to increase their exposure.[71] Yet in contrast to notions that festivals are valuable platforms for independent films, critics received Silver's contribution to Time Online negatively as though it was indicative of Hollywood's corporate core. Katherine Monk, for instance, described Time Online as 'the biggest load of hooey to hit the media's whirring fan' in recent memory and likened Silver to a car salesman, one operating on the 'information superhighway'.[72] While festival attendees are usually depicted as sophisticated and discerning audiences, Monk described the online audience in attendance derogatorily as action movie fanboys 'jam[ming] up the channels sucking silicon patootie' and drooling 'electronic slobber'.[73]

During the event, Silver also claimed that he had 'learnt a lot' from the Coens and that watching footage made him 'feel proud'.[74] Silver's comment thus indicated that an exchange of knowledge occurred in making *Hudsucker* that ran counter to notions about the Hollywood producer imposing procedures on indie-auteurs. Silver positioned himself as an enthusiastic fan of the Coens' work and gave them the credit for its production. 'I really didn't produce this movie. This is a Joel and Ethan Coen film', Silver stated.[75] Yet Silver added that *Hudsucker* was 'the most commercial movie the Coen brothers have made'.[76] Although at risk of damaging the Coens' reputations as indie-auteurs, Silver's comment represents rhetorical manoeuvring that was designed to cater to a niche and mainstream audience simultaneously by promoting the film as an authentic indie-auteur work that was unusually accessible. Silver's comment was also designed to enhance his own reputation by portraying himself as being capable of bringing commercial success to specialty films as well as action movies. Silver's posturing was ultimately undermined, though, as *Hudsucker* earned only $2.8 million at the North American box-office.[77] Nevertheless, Silver's contribution to Time Online reveals how a Hollywood producer operating in an online forum at the intersection of corporate Hollywood participated in disseminating indie-auteurism more widely and did so by playing up cultural notions about niche modes of production and the Hollywood mainstream.

As well as advocating for test-screenings, Silver has claimed responsibility for 'testing and tweaking' trailers.[78] *Hudsucker*'s trailer may thus be interpreted as a meeting point for Silver and the Coens' authorship. On one hand, *Hudsucker*'s trailer exhibits properties associated with the Coens' oeuvre, such as their unusual or quirky comedy and play with genre. In the trailer, for instance, Norville Barnes asks rhetorically, 'Would an imbecile come up with this?' before proudly revealing a circle drawn in pencil on an otherwise blank page that is meant to depict his invention of the hula-hoop. Norville's reveal is immediately followed by the trailer's narrator pronouncing *Hudsucker* a film 'From Joel and Ethan Coen', thereby implicitly connecting the quirky comedy to the brothers' sensibilities. Other examples of quirky comedy in the trailer include one Hudsucker board member failing to commit suicide by running across the board's table and through the headquarter office's top floor window after it has been reinforced with plexiglass (Figure 1.3); a close-up of Norville asking Amy (Jennifer Jason Leigh), an undercover reporter, out on a date to watch *The King and I* before Amy slaps him and Norville wrongly assumes that she did so because he suggested the wrong play; and Norville telling the press that nobody expected his invention to cause 'this much hoopla' with no pun intended. On a few occasions, the trailer also cuts to

Figure 1.3 A still from *The Hudsucker Proxy* trailer. (Source: Photofest)

characters in the film that appear to be responding to its other moments. The Hudsucker executives laugh hysterically immediately after another scene where Norville mistakenly informs the press that the board did not appoint him because they thought he was 'a schmo', and two high-society women attending a ballroom gala gasp after the narrator describes the film as a 'comedy of fame'. Recalling Hi's metatextual commentary, 'Well, it ain't Ozzie and Harriet', these reaction shots in *Hudsucker* depict a self-awareness about the audience responses that each moment should elicit that signals the Coens' confidence about their ability to entertain and once again gesture to their play with genre.[79]

On the other hand, the trailer promotes *Hudsucker* as a more light-hearted film than it really is. The trailer begins with a tracking shot towards the Hudsucker Industries' headquarters, which is footage that is not from the film. The shot is accompanied by the voice-over narrator stating, 'Once upon a time, the American dream was power, wealth and success, but ... the American dream is about to get a wake-up call'. This dialogue, with its fairy-tale allusions accompanied by the snowy New York setting and festive score depict a relatively light-hearted comedy with a happy resolution. In turn, the trailer hides the film's darker tone and content by omitting a substantial part of Norville's character arc where he succumbs to wealth, power and sex after he becomes the Hudsucker Industries' president. As well as adding a darker dimension to the film, Norville's transgressions complicate clear distinctions between right and wrong, good and bad. Rather than being morally pure, Norville is susceptible to the trappings of business and capitalism. By adopting a lighter tone and conveying an uncomplicated message, *Hudsucker*'s trailer appears to adhere to marketing approaches favoured by Hollywood to promote its mass mainstream films in general.[80] While the trailer's uncomplicated message may suggest that Silver did have a role in designing it, however, it is worth remembering that any suppression of the Coens' authorship by the trailer is not necessarily also an erosion of the film's independent political critique. In other words, although Norville's corruption could be interpreted as a comment on capitalism, it was more likely intended to signal the Coens' authorship by paralleling narratives in extratextual and critical discourse about the corruption of the indie-auteur by the Hollywood producer and their money.

Dynamics between the Coens and Silver were mobilised explicitly in another paratext in the form of *Hudsucker*'s published screenplay, which included a fictional interview written by the Coens between Silver and an imaginary Professor of Cinema Studies, Dennis Jacobson. In the interview, Silver claims that Ethan Coen had wanted to play *Hudsucker*'s leading role and was dejected after the producer insisted on casting Tim Robbins before he pathetically began mouthing Robbins's lines from a corner of a room during filming.[81] Claiming that the Coens oppose the use of movie stars, the fictional Silver also declared: 'God forbid someone should actually be enticed into the theatre to see one of their movies'.[82] Consequently, the fictional interview contrasts the indie-auteur as a sensitive artist uninterested in commercial success against the meddling Hollywood producer who appears to be driven by box-office receipts. These portrayals are meant to be ironic and are designed to appeal to niche educated and middle-class audiences who have the knowledge necessary for recognising it as such as well as the means for purchasing ancillary products. By targeting existing fans of the Coens and *Hudsucker* following its theatrical release, the published script is symptomatic of distributors' efforts to cultivate and exploit intense audience engagement through non-theatrical markets.[83] The fictional professor may also be interpreted as part of the Coens' mocking of the intellectualisation of film and as an attempt to preserve their reputations as indie-auteurs in part by dissuading audiences from thinking too seriously about the production and industrial realities of their films.[84]

Citing the film's intertextual references and irony, critics credited *Hudsucker* to the Coens. David Ansen, for example, called *Hudsucker* a 'postmodern pastiche' for 'movie-buffs', one bearing the Coens' 'unmistakably independent stamp'.[85] Some critics also suggested that the Coens' irony and intertextuality was antithetical to Silver's purportedly mainstream sensibility and made the film less accessible. Desson Howe, for example, stated that while 'populist Joel Silver' had helped make *Hudsucker* more accessible than the Coens' previous films, it remained 'pointlessly flashy', 'overloaded with references to films of the '30s', 'arcane' and 'exclusive'.[86] Similarly, Geoff Brown wrote:

> No one could accuse the devisers of *Miller's Crossing* and *Barton Fink* of going Hollywood. Even their new film's title, *The Hudsucker Proxy*, flies in the face of America's multiplex punters. Hudsucker? Proxy? Dictionary, please. Although the physical dimensions may be bigger and glossier, the brothers are still playing the pastiche game they have made their own since *Blood Simple* a decade ago.[87]

As a result, critics made *Hudsucker* appear to be an authentic indie-auteur work and portrayed Silver as a Hollywood producer whose role was confined to the film's financing and distribution.[88] Such comments amounted to a further simplification of Silver's role and ignored any possibility that Silver may have had an affinity for the film's narrative and intertextuality. In fact, Silver had written his thesis on the Classical Hollywood filmmaker Preston Sturges, which, Joel Coen argued, made him more knowledgeable than him and his brother 'about the antecedents' of the movie.[89] Consequently, critics repeated simplistic cultural notions about the differences between independent film and Hollywood, the indie-auteur and Hollywood producer, and their apparently appropriate niche and mainstream audiences.

'We are apart from it [Hollywood] ... because we write our own stuff': Brian Grazer, Scott Rudin, and packaging as creation

After *Hudsucker*, the Coens collaborated with London-based Working Title on four films, *Fargo* (1996), *The Big Lebowski* (1998), *O Brother, Where Art Thou?* (2000) and *The Man Who Wasn't There* (2001). These films have become some of the most critically acclaimed of the brothers' careers and helped to grow their reputations as indie-auteurs. Even though Working Title had been owned by conglomerates since 1991,[90] the company's co-chairs, Tim Bevan and Eric Fellner, positioned themselves as ideal independent film producers providing the Coens with creative freedom as they marketed the films as authentic indie-auteur productions.[91] While choosing to work with producers who appeared to give them autonomy, the Coens also managed to sustain their reputations as indie-auteurs because they chose to only make films that were based on their own original screenplays. Doing so allowed the Coens to insist that they had autonomy even as they worked with major Hollywood studios. 'We are apart from it [Hollywood] in terms of production because we write our own stuff', Ethan Coen stated, 'We don't have to go through the usual Hollywood development process, with all that entails'.[92] During the 2000s, however, the Coens began to direct features that were based on source material that they did not write. These features included *Intolerable Cruelty* (2003), *The Ladykillers* (2004) and *No Country for Old Men* (2007). In these cases, the brothers were hired by producers to rewrite or adapt source material before production began. Accordingly, this section analyses the Coens' collaboration with Brian Grazer, a producer associated with the Hollywood mainstream like Silver, and Scott Rudin, a purportedly ideal producer dedicated to supporting the visions of his auteur-directors, on *Intolerable* and *No Country*, respectively. In doing so, it explores how the producer as a kind of creator may complicate the attribution of indie-auteurism and what this may reveal about indie culture more broadly.

Intolerable is a romantic comedy that depicts Miles Massey (George Clooney), a divorce attorney, and Marilyn Rexroth (Catherine Zeta-Jones), a gold-digger, as they fall in love while simultaneously using marriage for commercial gain. The Coens initially became involved with making *Intolerable* in 1995 when Imagine Entertainment, a production company co-owned by Grazer and his partner, Ron Howard, hired them to rewrite the script, which already had first drafts written by Robert Ramsey and Matthew Stone. Yet after the Coens completed their script, *Intolerable* was put into turnaround by Universal, which had the rights to distribute Imagine Entertainment's productions.[93] The Coens' decision to rewrite *Intolerable*'s screenplay prompted some commentators to express alarm. Josh Levine, for example, stated that although the brothers had previously 'refused to work as hired guns on anyone else's picture' or 'rewrite adaptations or screenplays for anyone but themselves', they were now breaking 'from their usual working methods'.[94] Describing *Intolerable* as a pure 'moneymaker', Levine suggested that the brothers had taken the unusual step of pursuing commercial reward. With the brothers not yet having committed to direct *Intolerable*, however, Levine concluded his discussion by stating that 'thankfully' they did not plan to be involved in the making of it.[95]

Levine's assertion that the Coens' decision to rewrite *Intolerable*'s screenplay marked a break from their usual practice was wrong. In fact, the Coens' rewrite of *Intolerable* was a continuation of their practice because they had been writing and rewriting scripts for producers on a freelance basis even before *Blood Simple* was released in 1986. Speaking in 1999 about their freelance writing, Ethan explained: 'We've done writing assignments before, but mostly adapted scripts for studios, for other people on an unattributed basis'.[96] Joel Coen added, 'We generally don't like to put our names on things we don't control'.[97] By claiming to exert control over their names, Joel Coen suggested that their names signalled their authentic involvement with a project and was as a mark of quality. To do so, Coen made a distinction between their apparently superior feature-film directing work and their other for-hire work. Coen's rhetoric pays off when commentators such as Levine distinguish between their freelance screenwriting and their feature-film directing. As Mark Gallagher argues, however, rhetoric that compartmentalises filmmakers' experiences represents flimsy attempts to preserve notions of creative independence.[98]

Like Jacks's comments about the Coens having 'heat', Joel Coen's comment also suggested that their names carried value and were worth controlling. Yet Coen's comment ignored the fact that they were relatively unknown in their early careers, as evidenced by the fact that their names did not appear prominently in the trailers for their first three films. This reveals that the Coens were less marketable than Joel Coen suggested and indicates that their names might not have needed controlling at all. Since the 2010s, though, the Coens *have* been credited in promotional and

Figure 1.4 'A fake masterpiece': *Gambit*'s poster crediting the Coens. (Source: Photofest)

critical materials as the writers of *Gambit* (Hoffman, 2012; Figure 1.4), *Unbroken* (Jolie, 2014), *Bridge of Spies* (Spielberg, 2015) and *Suburbicon* (Clooney, 2017), not to mention as executive producers for the television adaptation, *Fargo* (FX, 2014–23). This crediting not only indicates the brothers' increased marketability but also shows that, at least later in their careers, they willingly put their names on work that they did not control.

The issue of control and marketability is important because Imagine Entertainment had not planned to market *Intolerable* as a Coen production when they hired them to rewrite its script. As paratextual materials surrounding the film show, Imagine Entertainment conceived of and promoted *Intolerable* as a mainstream genre picture and star vehicle. Universal's poster, for instance, clearly makes *Intolerable*'s lead stars, Clooney and Zeta-Jones, the basis for watching the film (Figure 1.5). Both actors are dressed glamorously and fittingly for major Hollywood stars, with Clooney in a suave grey suit matching his swept silvery hair and Zeta-Jones in a low-cut red silk and figure-hugging evening gown. Although looking longingly at one another, the poses that each actor adopts, Clooney with a slight smirk and raised eyebrow and Zeta-Zones hiding her wedding ring hand behind the other, gestures to how the characters are concealing their

Figure 1.5 The poster for *Intolerable Cruelty*. (Source: Photofest)

real intentions. These poses gesture to the character's efforts to outsmart, or rather out seduce, one another, which is also indicated through the taglines, 'Engage the enemy' and 'A romantic comedy with bite'. The names of each actor appear beneath them and above the film's title in prominent upper-case black font. Ironically for a film that the Coens wrote and directed, the brothers' names do not feature prominently on the poster and appear only in very small print at the bottom amongst the long list of credits that include the film's other, but typically more anonymous, senior cast and crew.

The trailer, too, promotes *Intolerable* as a romantic comedy and emphasises its Hollywood stars. Clooney and Zeta-Jones are shown in many clips usually appearing as glamorously dressed as they are in the poster. Interspersed between clips from the film are the credits, which appear on one half of the screen in large black font against a background resembling a wooden coffee table. Credits are given to Universal Pictures, Grazer, Clooney and Zeta-Jones, and the Coens. In the other half of the frame beside each of these credits is a Polaroid photo with different still images of Clooney and Zeta-Jones that gesture to their photogenic qualities and Classical Hollywood stardom. While these credits show how Imagine Entertainment and Universal deemed the Hollywood stars to be more important in selling *Intolerable* than the Coens, the inclusion of a credit for Universal and Grazer shows that the brothers were very much working within the Hollywood mainstream. Thus, the trailer also features a title scene that sees the camera tracking down a typical sunny and palm-tree adorned Hollywood boulevard and a voice-over that sets up the film's narrative by announcing, 'When a marriage hits the skids, and there's a fortune to protect, Miles Massey is the best there is. Now, a man who is used to winning, is about to lose his heart to a woman who bites back'. The tone and linear description of the narration as well as the accompanying music is cliché and contrasts with the trailers for the Coens' earlier films, which emphasised their unconventional narratives and the brothers' play with genre.

According to John Caldwell, Grazer belongs to a group of studio executives who regularly 'lapse into creative-speak' when discussing business and increasingly take film credits even if they may never appear on set.[99] Caldwell argues that these practices help executives such as Grazer to advance their careers and cultivate buzz surrounding their companies, which, he says, can prove detrimental to project development since it 'trumps the need to spend precious time and resources in actual market research or content creation'.[100] Grazer's contribution to *Intolerable* may be understood in these terms as being responsible for the Hollywood conventions and standardisation exhibited in the trailer. Yet it is important not to generalise about the producer's taking of credit or see it as always inherently detrimental to a project. Grazer persisted in developing *Intolerable* for six years despite reportedly working in difficult conditions and following setbacks in casting and financing as Universal's parent company, MCA, was acquired by Seagram.[101] The fact that *Raising Arizona*'s trailer included a credit for Circle's executives but none for the Coens also complicates straightforward distinctions about ideal independent and Hollywood producers and their taking of credit. Moreover, producers have historically received far less recognition for their films' successes than directors whose taking of credits is more readily accepted despite it playing a role in enhancing their own careers too.

Because of the role that Grazer played in developing *Intolerable*, many critics regarded him negatively as being responsible for making it overly commercial, formulaic and sentimental. James Christopher, for instance, attributed *Intolerable*'s 'box-office driven desire to please' to Grazer and asserted that, despite being 'natural subversives', the Coens look 'desperately weak when they're paid to fudge it'.[102] Liam Lacey commented that the adapted script was 'a little too safe' because 'producer Brian Grazer [had] told the Coens it was time to swing lower for an on-base hit after a series of rarefied, daring box-office misses'.[103] Elvis Mitchell stated that 'Between a lethargic trailer propped up by *Gimme Some Lovin'* and the mainstream-sentimentalist producer Brian Grazer's name on the credits, there's plenty of reason for an involuntary recoil'.[104] Whereas critics reviewing *Hudsucker* reduced their scrutiny of the Coens' collaboration with Silver because the brothers wrote the script with Raimi outside Hollywood, critics reviewing *Intolerable* denied the Coens' indie authorship and increased their scrutiny as they recalled that the brothers had been hired by Grazer.

Some critics also debated whether *Intolerable* represented a mainstream romantic comedy or an indie subversion. Philip Booth commented that Grazer's name on the credits, the stars 'at the top of the bill', and 'the chosen genre', proved that the Coens had gone mainstream. Christopher claimed that Grazer was a producer who had 'generated millions from untreated Hollywood slush', and had forced the Coens to dump the satire 'for a fairytale ending and a grandstanding Republican speech about the importance of marital values'.[105] Jessica Fellowes wrote that 'The brothers are better known for offbeat movies such as *The Big Lebowski* and *Fargo*, but *Intolerable Cruelty*, a romantic comedy, appears to kow-tow to the mainstream demands of Hollywood'.[106] Disagreeing, Geoff Pevere called *Intolerable* an 'anti-romantic comedy' where the Coens took aim at Beverly Hills' 'culture of wealth, vanity and Botox injection'.[107] Likewise, Geoff Andrew claimed that the Coens had provided a 'distinctively wacky series of variations on generic themes' and refused to include 'even a single second of heartfelt emotion'.[108] Michael O'Sullivan also asserted that audiences 'expecting the kind of light, romantic romp that one television commercial [had] been trying to pitch it as may be tempted to sue for false advertising'.[109] Despite disagreeing over the film, these critics each saw indie and the indie-auteur as antithetical to the Hollywood mainstream and the romantic comedy.

As Erin Pearson argues, critical discourse rarely clearly defines indie film and instead tends to position it against what it is not.[110] Critics' responses to *Intolerable* are particularly problematic because of the negative associations that generic has with mass audience tastes and the romantic comedy with women. At worst, these critics reject feminised culture entirely and, at best, suggest that feminised culture might be accepted or improved if it is subverted or changed. In this dichotomy, most women are framed as lacking the taste and sophistication necessary to create and appreciate innovative work. These problematic connotations become even more pronounced considering the promotional, extratextual and critical discourse surrounding *No Country*, a violent thriller that depicts Llewelyn Moss's efforts to evade a hitman after he takes a large amount of money that he finds in the desert near the site of a failed drug deal.

Scott Rudin acquired the rights to Cormac McCarthy's novel *No Country for Old Men* prior to its publication in 2005. To do so, Rudin used funds advanced to him by Paramount under a first-look arrangement that he had with the studio until 2004 before he signed a new deal with Disney.[111] At the time, Disney and Paramount's specialty divisions were in a state of transition. Disney had hired Daniel Battsek, a former executive in distribution, to replace Miramax's co-founders, Bob and Harvey Weinstein, while Paramount appointed John Lesher, a former talent agent, as the president of Paramount Classics, which he rebranded as Paramount Vantage. Along with Fox Searchlight, Focus Features and Warner Independent, Vantage and Miramax were symptomatic of an increasing convergence between Hollywood and independent film, and were responsible for the dominant expression of American indie film at the time, which Tzioumakis says constituted indiewood.[112] Unlike earlier specialty divisions, these indiewood-era divisions made more expensive acquisitions and developed projects in-house as they sought to release films with greater commercial potential.[113] In doing so, the divisions increasingly sought more marketable subject matter, stars and brand-name directors, before running costly marketing campaigns and distributing films widely.[114] This shift led the parent divisions to not only provide greater financial support but also increasingly scrutinise their divisions' operations and financial returns.[115] In this context, Rudin capitalised on Miramax's and Paramount Vantage's new executives' eagerness to prove themselves, on their demand for more marketable material, and on Battsek's lack of experience in production and limited connections to talent, by packaging and selling *No Country* with the Coens as well as *There Will be Blood* (2007) with indie-auteur Paul Thomas Anderson. As Rudin explained, 'I wanted to see if they'd do these two filmmaking teams and great pieces of material together and kickstart both Vantage and Miramax'.[116]

Miramax and Vantage shared distribution rights for *No Country*. Miramax had initially been scheduled to handle international distribution and Vantage the domestic distribution before this arrangement was reversed just months before the film's release after it became apparent that Vantage already had a full domestic slate. While the trade press had earlier claimed that the studios' indie divisions represented a 'strong, growing business' that gave producers such as Rudin more opportunities than ever, the reversal of rights revealed the confusion that existed between the two revamped studios and was symptomatic of the challenges that studio divisions generally faced in the indiewood period.[117] As Rudin himself attested, 'figuring out the relationship' between Vantage and Miramax made for 'a confusing time'.[118]

Miramax, Vantage and Rudin developed a marketing strategy that promoted *No Country* as an authentic indie-auteur production by positioning the Coens and McCarthy as creative equivalents. On hiring the Coens to write the screenplay before convincing them to direct, for instance, Rudin claimed that he would have only ever wanted to have made *No Country* with the Coens because, he said, they were 'the filmmaking-language equivalent' of McCarthy.[119] Noting that McCarthy and the Coens were 'a magic alchemy', *Variety* reported that all *No Country*'s marketing materials emphasised the film's 'literary and cinematic pedigree'.[120] Yet the Coens were reluctant to align themselves with McCarthy or attach importance to their script's fidelity to the novel. When asked if they felt any 'sense of responsibility' to McCarthy, Joel Coen responded:

> The responsibility you feel, if you put it in those terms, is kind of clarified when you take the job. We were asked to do this, so we said to Scott [Rudin], 'Here's how we see doing it; does that jibe with how you want it done?' – 'cos he's the employer. Once that was set, we felt we could do whatever we wanted, within the agreed terms. But we didn't feel any specific responsibility to the material or Cormac McCarthy. The thing for us was to preserve aspects of the book the studio or the producer might baulk at: so we said, 'If we make this, you do know it's going to be violent?' That's what the story's about. There was also the peculiar aspect of the book that a central character dies abruptly and, essentially, offscreen. That was also something we wanted to preserve. Not that we wanted to slavishly follow the novel or felt an obligation to change anything; indeed, there were things we were puzzled by and we had no problem throwing them out of the window. It was just that certain things made the story more interesting to us, so we kept them.[121]

Coen's decision to invoke Rudin as the employer appears surprising given the negative connotations surrounding their earlier collaboration with Grazer. While appearing to shed light on the brothers' screenwriting process, however, Coen's comment is an example of rhetorical manoeuvring because invoking Rudin acts to establish an industrial context that distinguishes their work from McCarthy's. While the Coens claimed that their original scriptwriting made them separate from Hollywood earlier in their careers, therefore, they were now invoking the Hollywood context and adaptation process to preserve a notion of their dogged individuality and independence, their authorship and the value of their brand.

Coen's comment invoked Rudin's reputation as an ideal producer to create an impression of the brothers as enforcing their creative vision despite working with the Hollywood studios. For instance, Miramax and Vantage reportedly pressured the Coens to cast a star as Llewelyn Moss in the lead role instead of Josh Brolin, who the brothers considered to be an 'ordinary guy' necessary for playing the part.[122] In the face of this pressure and the reportedly difficult conditions created by the collaboration between the two studios, Joel Coen described Rudin as an 'unbelievable ally'.[123] Meanwhile, Rudin stated, 'When you work with filmmakers like this you end up being led by their instincts: They're incorruptible. It's very easy. You go down the road behind them and make sure the brush is clear in front of them'.[124] Rhetoric about the Coens' incorruptibility recalls comments that the brothers made during the promotion of *Raising Arizona* and *Hudsucker*. While positioning the Coens as indie-auteurs and Rudin as an ideal producer, however, the idea that the brothers should need a producer to steer them in the right direction and help to enforce their creative vision is one that undermines notions of their incorruptibility and independence in the first place.

Miramax, Vantage and Rudin designed their marketing strategy to appeal to two core audience constituencies: the niche specialty audience and men. Of the latter, Lesher asserted that *No Country* was 'a really good, muscular movie that works well with older men; it's violent and visceral'.[125] As Hannah Andrews argues, however, these two audience constituencies are not necessarily mutually exclusive as promotional discourse around specialty content often seeks to appeal simultaneously to a 'masculine, exclusive and elitist set of sensibilities'.[126] These joint appeals are evidenced clearly in *No Country*'s R-rated red-band trailer. The trailer begins with Chigurh (Javier Bardem), a hitman and bounty hunter, assassinating an innocent older man with a bolt pistol (Figure 1.6). Afterwards, deep red blood bursts onto the screen and with it a credit attributing *No Country* to the Coens followed by another crediting McCarthy. As a result, the R-rated trailer reinforces an impression of the Coens as being responsible for reproducing the violence in the novel for the screen and seems to confirm that they succeeded in exerting their will over the studios just as Joel Coen suggested.

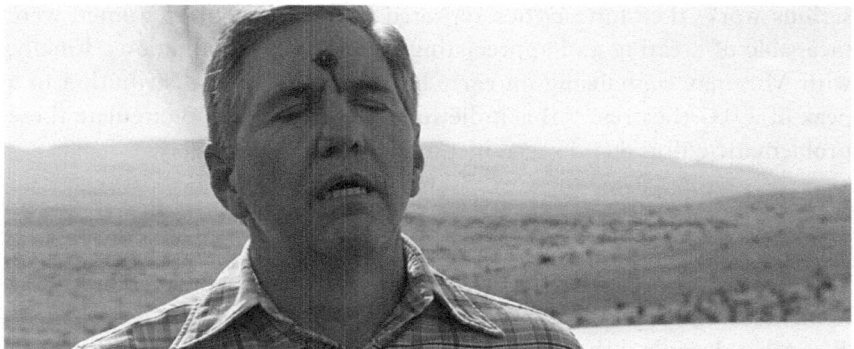

Figure 1.6 A still from the R-rated *No Country for Old Men* trailer. (Source: Author's own screengrab)

Attributing the film's violence to the Coens proved effective as critics described *No Country* as a quality feature akin to their earlier dark and violent thrillers such as *Blood Simple*, *Miller's Crossing* and *Fargo*. In turn, critics distinguished *No Country* from the Coens' previous two features, *Intolerable* and *The Ladykillers*. Anthony Lane, for example, called *No Country* a 'return to the dark, simmering days of their best work' that 'all but wiped out' the 'travesty' of *Intolerable* and *The Ladykillers*.[127] Ian Nathan described *No Country* as a 'neo-western' that shared DNA with *Blood Simple* and *Fargo*, and marked a 'return to form' after the brothers' 'below par' and 'crap' recent work.[128] Such reviews also suggested that *No Country* was a superior film to *Intolerable* and *The Ladykillers* because it was more intelligent and mature, and less sentimental and frivolous. Peter Howell stated that '*No Country for Old Men* is top-drawer Coen Bros., a return to form after the comic distractions of *The Ladykillers* and *Intolerable Cruelty*. It's a film that engages the mind and touches the soul'.[129] Jeff Vice described *No Country* as a 'serious work' that was the brothers' 'most assured movie in years'.[130] Unlike *Intolerable* and the romantic comedy, therefore, critics regarded *No Country* as sitting comfortably within the indie-auteurs' oeuvres. Thus, Rudin's strategy of pairing the Coens with McCarthy enabled the film to avoid the same accusations of commercialism, Hollywood standardisation and dumbing down that greeted *Intolerable* and *The Ladykillers*. Moreover, the positive reception of *No Country* that followed Rudin's targeting of male audiences, in contrast to *Intolerable*'s denigration as a romantic comedy, confirms that indie-auteurism is usually conceived of as masculine and not feminine. As Michelle Schreiber explains, indie film remains 'dominated by the male auteur model'.[131] By describing *No Country* as a more intelligent and serious work, therefore, critics repeated notions that most women were incapable of creating and appreciating proper indie productions. Finally, with Miramax capitalising on early buzz by expanding distribution to a peak of 2,037 theatres,[132] this indiewood picture helped to circulate these problematic cultural and social hierarchies even more widely.

Conclusion

The neoliberal notions circulated by the trade press during the development of indiewood features including *No Country* and *There Will Be Blood* that described the studio divisions as a robust and growing business providing indie-auteurs and their intermediaries with more opportunities than ever ultimately turned out to be wrong.[133] As Tzioumakis has explained, the indiewood model became unsustainable after the costs of producing and marketing the films approached the same level as those of the features being released by the majors.[134] Although indiewood arguably ceased to be the dominant expression of American indie cinema by the end of the 2000s, however, many figures branded as indie-auteurs have continued to work on specialty features released by the majors and their remaining subsidiaries, while some figures have found new opportunities working on feature films made for streaming services such as Netflix, Amazon Instant Video and Apple TV+, and in television.

Since *No Country*, the Coens have continued to sustain their reputations as indie-auteurs as they resumed their collaboration with Working Title on *Burn After Reading* (2008) and *Hail Caesar!* (2016), made *The Ballad of Buster Scruggs* (2018) for Netflix, and even as they have taken a hiatus from working together as Joel has made *The Tragedy of Macbeth* (2021) for Apple and Ethan has made *Drive-Away Dolls* (2024), billed as a 'lesbian roadtrip comedy', for Focus Features and Universal.[135] Indeed, many of the Coens' films have been canonised and their work and success has continued to inspire and influence other indie filmmakers. While scholarly and critical discourse has tended to frame the Coens' indie-auteur brands as a product of their sensibilities, however, this chapter has shown that their brands have been constructed, managed and maintained by producers providing practical and rhetorical functions. Far from being a cause for celebration, though, the chapter has shown that the Coens' ability to sustain their reputations and associations with indie film has often hinged on and reinforced certain problematic dynamics between the mass mainstream and niche specialty production, art and commerce, and even masculinity and femininity.

Having analysed the Coens' collaborations with several producers to explore a model of indie-auteurism that has been constructed and managed during the three periods of indie film set out by Tzioumakis, the remainder of this book goes on to explore how indie-auteurism has been managed more widely during an era of media convergence, often to promote media productions and products that mostly reside outside of Tzioumakis's film-centred periodisation. By tracing the migration of indie-auteurs across media, the book opens new avenues towards a broader understanding of American indie film and specialty media. In doing so, it remains alert to which figures manage to secure these privileged positions as indie-auteurs as well as to the industrial, cultural and social connotations that the migration of indie-auteurism carries.

Notes

1. Perren (2012) p. 27; Schatz (2017); Tzioumakis (2013) p. 37; King (2009) p. 271.
2. Newman (2011) p. 180; King (2005) p. 107.
3. Tzioumakis (2013).
4. On descriptions of Silver and Grazer as meddling Hollywood producers, see: King (2014) p. 103; Redmond (2015) p. 22; Palmer (2004) p. 52; on notions of the 'ideal' producer, see: Spicer, McKenna and Meir (2014) p. 3.
5. Klemesrud (1985).
6. Ibid.
7. Ibid.
8. Festival of Festivals later became the Toronto International Film Festival.
9. Scott (1984).
10. King (2005) p. 27; Molloy (2010) p. 34.
11. Elsaesser (2013) p. 87.
12. Ibid. p. 85.
13. Insdorf (1984).
14. Klemesrud (1985).
15. Ibid.
16. Dunning (1985).
17. Shepherd (1985).
18. Tzioumakis (2006) pp. 210, 266.
19. Hoberman (1985).
20. King (2005) p. 107.
21. Hoberman (1985).
22. Bernstein (2008) p. 180; Spicer, McKenna and Meir (2014) p. 3.
23. Newman (2011) p. 240.
24. Tzioumakis (2006) p. 209.
25. Tzioumakis (2013) p. 31.
26. Attanasio (1985a); see also Hall (1991).

27. Hinson (1985).
28. Newman (2011) p. 180.
29. Seidenberg (1985).
30. Tzioumakis (2006) p. 249.
31. Ibid. p. 266.
32. Attanasio (1985b).
33. King (2017) p. 60.
34. Attanasio (1985b).
35. Hall (1991).
36. Ibid.
37. Chanko (1990).
38. Leon (1987).
39. Van Gelder (1989); Hall (1991).
40. Lotz (2014) p. 29.
41. Hall (1991).
42. Attanasio (1985b).
43. Hall (1991).
44. Attanasio (1985b).
45. Claire Molloy (2017, p. 373) argues that indie-auteurs who move to Hollywood do not shed their alternative politics but are rather more aligned with the commercial mainstream to begin with.
46. Kerrigan (2017) p. 185.
47. In his work on the 'quirky' sensibility in the films and paratexts of Wes Anderson, James MacDowell (2013, pp. 54, 62) identifies the films of the Coens as 'important precursors'.
48. Pulleine (1985); Ansen (1985); Klemesrud (1985).
49. At the time of making *Blood Simple*, *Hudsucker*'s budget was expected to be around $25 million.
50. Attanasio (1985b).
51. Clark (1994).
52. Ibid.
53. Ryan (1994); Pendreigh (1994).
54. Lipper (1993).
55. Johnston (1993).
56. Leon (1987).
57. Clark (1994).
58. King (2017) p. 66.
59. Richardson (1990b); Ryan (1994); Billen (1994).
60. Johnston (1991).
61. Boston University (2010).
62. Johnston (1993).
63. Cowan (1993).
64. Newman (2011) p. 50.
65. Ibid. p. 51.

66. For a detailed discussion of festivals' own brand building, see Elsaesser (2013) p. 85.
67. Brodie (1994).
68. Ibid.
69. See also: Pierson (1996) p. 121.
70. On consolidation and synergy, see Murray (2005).
71. Tryon (2013) pp. 166–9.
72. Monk (1994).
73. Ibid.
74. Ibid.
75. Ibid.
76. Ibid.
77. BoxOfficeMojo (n.d.b).
78. Boston University (2010).
79. On the Coens' play with genre, see Newman (2011) pp 141–81.
80. King (2017) p. 67; Kerrigan (2017) p. 184.
81. Quoted from Bergan (2001) p. 150.
82. Ibid.
83. Klinger (2010).
84. The Coens engaged in a similar practice some years later when they wrote Mortimer Young (George Ives), a fictional film historian, for a bonus feature for the Blu-Ray release of *The Big Lebowski*. Young mistakenly called the film 'The Grand Lebowski' before stating that it 'slipped beneath the waves critically and commercially on its first release … during the catastrophic period of synergy' (Coen and Coen, 2011).
85. Ansen (1994).
86. Howe (1994).
87. Brown (1994).
88. Likewise, R. Barton Palmer wrote that *Hudsucker*'s box-office failure was down to Silver's failure to package the film properly, in a manner that was authentically aligned with the film's narrative. While calling into question Silver's abilities, however, Palmer perceived the film's commercial failure as reinforcing the Coens' indie reputations when he writes:

> More than anything else, perhaps, the Coens' experience with *The Hudsucker Proxy* demonstrated that, unlike other independent filmmakers such as Steven Soderbergh and David Cronenberg, they were not suited, and might never be, to conceiving big-budget films aimed at a mass audience. (Palmer (2004) pp. 11, 52)

89. Rea (1994).
90. In 1991, Working Title was acquired by PolyGram Filmed Entertainment, which itself was a division of Philips. Through a series of mergers since 1999, Working Title has become a division of Universal, which has itself been owned by Seagram and Comcast.
91. Hollywood Reporter (2014).
92. Gritten (1999).

93. Cling (1995).
94. Levine (2000) p. 161; see also Patterson (2007).
95. Levine (2000) p. 161.
96. Gritten (1999).
97. Ibid.
98. Gallagher (2013) p. 23.
99. Caldwell (2008) pp. 239, 242.
100. Ibid. p. 244.
101. Cling (1995).
102. Christopher (2003).
103. Lacey (2003).
104. Mitchell (2003).
105. Booth (2003).
106. Fellowes (2003).
107. Pevere (2003).
108. Andrew (2003).
109. O'Sullivan (2003).
110. Pearson (2017) p. 165.
111. Cieply (2007).
112. Tzioumakis (2012) p. 169.
113. Ibid. pp. 163–8.
114. Ibid. p. 169.
115. Ibid. p. 169; Tzioumakis (2006) p. 264.
116. Anon (2007).
117. Thompson (2007).
118. Anon (2007).
119. Ibid.
120. Thompson (2008).
121. Andrew (2008).
122. Anon (2007).
123. Ibid.
124. Ibid.
125. Thompson (2007).
126. Andrews (2014) p. 151.
127. Lane (2007).
128. Nathan (2008).
129. Howell (2007).
130. Vice (2007).
131. Schreiber (2013) p. 97.
132. BoxOfficeMojo (n.d.a).
133. Thompson (2006).
134. Tzioumakis (2012) pp. 163–9.
135. Kemp (2022).

CHAPTER 2

Managing Indie-Auteurs in an Era of Media Convergence

Steve Golin, Propaganda Films and Anonymous Content

In a 2004 *Los Angeles Times* article titled 'He's the real deal for artists', Michel Gondry, the auteur-director of the indie feature film *Eternal Sunshine of the Spotless Mind* (Gondry, 2004), attempted to articulate why the film's producer, Steve Golin, was a 'magnet for gifted filmmakers'.[1] To do so, Gondry did not focus on his relationship with Golin on set but instead chose to focus on an instance of male bonding by recalling how the producer had comforted him during the editing of *Eternal Sunshine* after his girlfriend ended their relationship. After explaining that Golin let him sleep in his house and in the same bed, and reassuring the shocked interviewer that nothing sexual happened, Gondry stated:

> When I needed someone, emotionally, he was there, not just for someone who was his director, but for me. You couldn't say that about many Hollywood producers. I can't imagine wanting to sleep in the same bed with Joel Silver![2]

After Gondry's story, the article featured quotes from other figures who worked with Golin, including his former assistant and a then-ICM agent, David Unger, and Charlie Kaufman, who wrote *Eternal Sunshine* and *Being John Malkovich* (Jonze, 1999), which Golin also produced. While Unger said that Golin had a unique ability to connect with filmmakers and 'loves the subversive quality that makes an artist unique', Kaufman stated that Golin was always trustworthy and 'creatively helpful'.[3] The article also featured several quotes from Golin who described his struggle in getting *Malkovich* made, called being a producer a lonely, depressing and terribly undervalued job, explained that he no longer tolerated temperamental behaviour from artists, and discussed the producers whom he admired. On the latter, Golin stated: 'I admire producers like Saul Zaentz and Scott Rudin, because I think we're alike – we have to make movies we care about ... But getting them made is tough'.[4]

Recalling my discussion of the Coen brothers' collaborations with Joel Silver and Scott Rudin in the previous chapter, this *Los Angeles Times* article demonstrates neatly how Golin cultivated a reputation as an ideal producer dedicated to supporting auteurs to fulfil their creative visions and create high-quality innovative work. Although the article focuses specifically on Golin, the narrative that it perpetuates is symptomatic of how he has actively worked to project the values that he embodies as an ideal producer back onto his two companies, Propaganda Films and Anonymous Content. Indeed, Golin's ability to do so has been of strategic importance for his companies as their brands were built around creating high-quality works with auteurs, including not only feature films but also music videos, commercials, branded content and television. Moreover, alongside their production activities, both companies operated talent management divisions that cultivated reputations especially for managing directors and, in turn, discovering and empowering auteurs. Although Golin is himself not a talent manager, his reputation for successfully facilitating the creative visions of gifted filmmakers, coupled with his roles as CEO of the companies and mentoring of producers and managers such as Michael Sugar, Keith Redmon and Doug Wald, figures whom critical discourse has labelled as his 'lieutenants', has helped to create an impression that Propaganda's and Anonymous's producer-managers must have the good taste necessary for spotting auteurs and facilitating their visions too.[5]

While scholarly accounts of authorship and specialty modes of production have tended to study media types separately,[6] therefore, Golin, Propaganda and Anonymous represent exceptional case studies for demonstrating how tracing talent intermediaries' work across sectors can shed light on how authorship discourses can be managed and mobilised between media, how authorial figures are embedded in wider talent networks, and how media histories are in fact often intertwined. Although I aim to offer an expansive perspective on the contemporary history of specialty production during an era of convergence, however, it is also important to recognise that it is methodologically impossible to give a full and detailed account of all aspects of Propaganda's and Anonymous's operations concurrently. To make the study of the two companies manageable, this chapter will provide a broad look into Propaganda's and Anonymous's changing business models, operations and ownership, particularly as they relate to the companies' management of auteurs and production of specialty projects, before the following three chapters home in on specific areas of production in the shape of their short-form, television and feature film work respectively. In this chapter, the first four sections focus particularly on how Propaganda's and later Anonymous's expansion and management of auteurism across media was facilitated or impeded by their executives' and investors' decision-making, market forces and industry consolidation, with the third section analysing Michael Moore's debut feature, *Canadian Bacon* (1995), to show specifically how Propaganda's operations were impacted. The last section analyses Propaganda's and Anonymous's talent management decisions in relation to race and gender, considering how the companies' management of indie-auteurism may have contributed to racial and gender inequalities in screen media production.

As I mentioned in this book's introduction, Anonymous's brand and logo, which appears at the beginning of several of its productions, including *Spotlight* (McCarthy, 2015), and has a figure carrying a briefcase hidden within the letter A, is one example of the discourse of anonymity surrounding the ideal indie film producer and talent intermediary (Figure 2.1). Though Propaganda's branding requires more decoding, it functions similarly (Figure 2.2). The 'R' in Propaganda's logo is reversed to draw attention to the PR or public relations work that its talent managers engage in to shape promotional and critical discourse and build its clients' brands. Understood in broad terms, propaganda films also resemble commercial spots if both media forms are interpreted as attempts to persuade audiences of a thing's value (whether that thing is an idea, activity, service or commodity). The company's logo also alludes to Soviet-era communism with the 'N' also reversed to gesture to Cyrillic script, bomber planes flying through spotlights above a city and a figure in the foreground resembling a military officer. Yet the logo may also depict a film set, with the spotlights representing set-lighting and the figure being a director. The allusion to communism arguably gestures provocatively to the company's efforts to

Figure 2.1 Anonymous Content's logo. (Source: Author's own screengrab)

Figure 2.2 Propaganda Films' logo. (Source: Author's own screengrab)

cultivate a reputation for offering directors creative freedom by appearing to be a space that is less hierarchical and driven by commerce than the Hollywood studios. Given Propaganda's profit imperatives, however, its brand deliberately mystifies the company's role in a way that displays its dexterity in managing rhetoric and reputation, particularly in terms of its ability to position commerce and commercial practice as art and creative practice. Accordingly, the case of Propaganda provides an example of how branding in general is a form of communication that, as Celia Lury points out, is 'not direct, symmetrical or reversible' as it performs and inhibits exchange between producers and consumers.[7]

While Propaganda and Anonymous have attempted to mystify their roles and hide in plain sight as they seek to sell their services to clients and distributors, the following chapters reverse this process as they analyse promotional, extratextual and critical discourse surrounding them. Considering that all texts contain 'the ghosts of authors not mentioned',[8] the chapters shed light on Propaganda's and Anonymous's talent management and production operations to explore their roles in constructing auteurism to promote productions as high-quality specialty works.

'Everybody thinks we have unlocked some secrets about the 18 to 24 market': Propaganda Films, MTV and music video

Propaganda Films was founded in 1986 by producers Steve Golin and Sigurjón (Joni) Sighvatsson, and directors David Fincher, Dominic Sena, Nigel Dick and Greg Gold. Propaganda began as an integrated talent management and media production company dedicated to managing directors, cinematographers and editors in the production of music videos before expanding into commercial spot, feature film and television production, and talent management. Although Propaganda's co-executives claimed that they wanted to remain independent in 1990,[9] in 1988 they had sold a 49 per cent stake to PolyGram, a major record label and entertainment company that was itself a subsidiary of Philips Electronics, and in 1991 sold them the remaining 51 per cent. In 1998, the company was broken up after Philips sold PolyGram to Seagram, which owned Universal.

Before establishing Propaganda, the company's co-founders had very limited success working in the media industries. For instance, Golin and Sighvatsson graduated from the American Film Institute before producing two minor independent films, *Hard Rock Zombies* (Shah, 1985) and *American Drive-In* (Shah, 1985). Meanwhile, Dominic Sena had worked as a cameraman and occasional music video director, and Fincher had worked in visual effects for George Lucas's Industrial Light and Magic and had directed a few music videos, including most notably for Rick Springfield for whom he also directed the concert film *Beat of the Live Drum* (1985). Because of its co-founders' relative obscurity and the popular and trade press's lack of interest in music video production, very few press reports exist on Propaganda's early years. In fact, reporters did not report substantially on Propaganda until 1989 and 1990 after it had already become the largest music video production company in the United States, was expanding into other screen media, and had secured investment from PolyGram.

Jack Banks's 1996 work on the emergence of MTV, however, helps to explain how Propaganda managed to become the leading music video production company. After launching on cable in 1981, Banks explains, MTV quickly became the dominant channel for music video in part because it had shared ownership with large cable multiple systems operators.[10] This co-ownership gave MTV guaranteed subscribers and enabled it to exercise control over music video distribution by, for instance, insisting that record companies grant early exclusive access to 30 per cent of their videos.[11] With MTV having created what Banks describes as a form of contractual vertical integration, record companies began increasingly commissioning work from a handful of established production companies.[12] Propaganda benefited especially from MTV's exclusivity contracts because the company and its directors already made videos for many of the major record labels' most popular and promising musicians including Madonna, Janet Jackson and Sting; the 30 per cent that effectively guaranteed them substantial exposure on MTV.

The exposure of Propaganda's videos on MTV had the circular effect of increasing the reputations of the company and its directors, which the company leveraged to secure more commissions and command greater fees.

In 1990, the *New York Times* reported that Propaganda's market 'share gave the company dominance of MTV and late-night music video shows',[13] while *Premiere* asserted that Golin and Sighvatsson 'seemed to have a special talent for ferreting out hot young directors' who 'quickly became the kings of MTV'.[14] Accordingly, Propaganda was able to command budgets with a 15 per cent markup on production costs and its top music video directors were able to secure fees of over $100,000.[15] Speaking in 1991, one record label executive explained that Propaganda was the most expensive music video production company but 'since [it] has consistently delivered results ... you don't hear many complaints'.[16] Speaking with anonymity, this record label executive may have been a PolyGram executive incentivised to increase the fees of its subsidiary company.

The success of Propaganda's music videos on MTV also created an impression that Propaganda and its directors had a special ability for appealing to young audiences.[17] 'Because we became the biggest in [music] videos', Sighvatsson stated, 'everybody thinks we have unlocked some secrets about the 18 to 24 market. We're perceived as image makers, and I think that has spilled over into commercials'.[18] While 'spilled over' depicted a fortuitous or organic process, one that was not necessarily driven by commercial imperatives, Propaganda leveraged the company and its directors' reputations to expand into commercials where its director clients began making spots for major brands, including Nike, Pepsi, Nintendo and Levi's, as they targeted youth audiences. By 1990, Golin and Sighvatsson were boasting of the efficacy of its business model as they declared that Fincher's and Sena's careers had gone 'through the roof' as the fees that they commanded for music videos increased from $5,000 to $140,000 before rising to $600,000 for commercials.[19] Such boasting not only helped to increase Propaganda's share price but also acted to recruit new aspiring clients for whom the company's talent management strategies served as a model.

While Banks provided important insight into MTV and its role in the consolidation of the music video industry, however, he perpetuates certain simplistic ideas about the relationship between music video directors and producers and the record labels, which also sustains broad distinctions between art and commerce. Specifically, Banks argued that the music video producer and director 'want to create an artistic work' unlike the record companies that are driven by commercial endeavours,[20] which are notions that have been expressed by critics and other scholars too.[21] Banks also stated that producers and directors have 'limited creative autonomy' because the record companies underwrite and own the clips.[22] Conceptions of music video directors and producers as artists striving to create work despite commercial pressures, however, represent a continuation of the same romantic notion of authorship that can be found around all types of purportedly legitimate forms of cultural production. Yet Propaganda crafted precisely these kinds of narratives to build the marketability and branded reputations of its directors by positioning them as struggling artists. Anne Marie Mackay, who was the head of Propaganda's music video division, and Juliana Roberts, who was in charge of Propaganda's rock metal music video division The Foundry, for example, claimed that Propaganda 'pushed' record labels to commission videos with original concepts and dramatic narratives despite the labels and recording artists preferring 'formulaic' and 'unimaginative' performance-centred videos.[23] Although Mackay's and Roberts's comments seem to be merely statements about creative preferences, they are examples of rhetorical manoeuvring that depicted Propaganda and its directors as creative innovators. Such rhetoric hides the commercial imperatives underpinning talent management and media production strategies.

As I show through an analysis of client Spike Jonze's music videos in the next chapter, Propaganda preferred concept videos because they helped to promote the company and its directors. Specifically, concept videos enabled the directors to exhibit their technical and creative skills, differentiate their work, and position themselves as artist-innovators. Understood in these terms, the notion of creative conflict between record labels and music video producers can be better understood as a tension between two parties with different investments in music video's promotional possibilities. That is, whereas record labels prioritise promoting musicians and their songs, integrated production and talent management companies want to promote the directors. As a result, MTV's vertical integration and relationship with mass culture can be understood as having offered Propaganda's directors greater exposure and as having created an industrial context that made the music video auteur increasingly valuable.

'A great training ground for new talent': Propaganda Films, PolyGram and consolidation

On one hand, PolyGram's acquisition of Propaganda was part of the major record label's strategy to reduce its music video production costs, and share in the profits of the music video production business, by taking ownership of the production companies. By 1991, PolyGram had taken majority stakes in music video production companies not just in the United States but across twenty-three other countries too.[24] On the other hand, PolyGram's acquisition was part of the company's ambition to become a major film and television studio as well. Between 1988 and 1994, PolyGram also acquired film production companies including Working Title, A&M Films, and Interscope Communications. PolyGram's acquisition of Propaganda and these other companies was thus symptomatic of a consolidation of ownership that was increasing across the cultural industries during the 1980s and 1990s.

As David Hesmondhalgh points out, corporate consolidation and interdependency threatens the 'relative autonomy, or creative freedom, that has traditionally been ceded to workers involved in making cultural products' and weakens the independent company's potential for producing alternative cultural work.[25] Hesmondhalgh also tells us that takeovers can be particularly perturbing for workers within independent media companies because they are more likely to mistrust corporate bureaucracies and '*feel* ... more autonomous of commercial pressures'.[26] With Hesmondhalgh's points in mind, it is significant that Golin and Sighvatsson reframed PolyGram's acquisition of Propaganda as a means for supporting its directors to fulfil their career ambitions and express themselves creatively. Indeed, despite political critique often being associated with independent film, Golin focused instead on claiming professional legitimacy as he described consolidation in the music video industry as a 'necessary evil' that created 'a much more professional way of doing business'.[27]

After PolyGram took a 49 per cent stake in 1988, *Variety* reported that Propaganda had secured finance for its feature film production but omitted any information about an exchange of equity.[28] Moreover, *Variety* paraphrased Propaganda's owners describing the deal as being 'Part of the company's policy ... to create opportunities for its music video and commercial [spot] directors to cross over into features'.[29] Hence Golin stated that Propaganda did not want to represent directors who could only make music videos and commercials but rather wanted to represent 'overall talent' and then sought to 'provide a means for them to express that talent in any one of a number of areas'.[30] Sighvatsson added that their directors needed to be 'flexible' creatively as he and Golin endeavoured to 'create an atmosphere where the guys [could] exercise their creative muscle without leaving the fold of Propaganda'.[31] Elsewhere, Sighvatsson stated that Propaganda's music video business functioned as 'research and development' that provided 'a great training ground for new talent'.[32]

On one hand, Propaganda's executives' comments about providing the infrastructure necessary for nurturing talent could be understood as an attempt to reassure potentially anxious clients that a partnership with a conglomerate would not jeopardise their creative freedom. Such comments are arguably indicative of how executives at independent production and management companies can feel anxious about their ability to retain clients as they become increasingly marketable. Working Title's co-chairman, Tim Bevan, conveyed this anxiety when explaining his production company's deals with PolyGram as well when he stated that 'The creative talent we've worked with are now on their second or third films so if we want to continue, we have to move up with them'.[33] Talent intermediaries' anxieties about their ability to continue working with key talent thus appears to be an important consideration that can play a role in facilitating industry consolidation.

On the other hand, company executives' efforts to frame the sale of their companies as if it is a means to grow with key talent can be understood as a form of rhetorical manoeuvring that masks their commercial imperatives and pursuit of greater profits. By making claims about the purportedly extraordinary creative talent of Propaganda's clients and their ability to succeed in many areas of media production, for instance, Golin and Sighvatsson depicted PolyGram's acquisition as a means for unlocking the talent management and production company's potential for significant growth. Doing so involved depicting Propaganda as an innovative company capable of exploiting new and varied markets and made PolyGram's acquisition appear to be a low-risk investment capable of offering investors high returns. Accordingly, Michael Kuhn, the then vice president of PolyGram, emphasised the potential for growth in 1989 after PolyGram, Propaganda and Working Title set up Manifesto Film Sales, a sales agent that was meant to exploit Propaganda's and Working Title's output internationally. Specifically, Kuhn stated that Manifesto was 'the beginning of an alliance of independents supported by a major company' and was capable of 'achieving a significant share of the independent movie market'.[34] Similarly, after PolyGram completed its 100 per cent acquisition of Propaganda and Working Title, Kuhn, who became the head of PolyGram Filmed Entertainment, described the deals as part of PolyGram's efforts to grow its 'film business through the development of a number of "label" production companies'.[35]

Kuhn, Golin and Sighvatsson's comments were symptomatic of a period when independence in film retained greater currency as an industrial label describing separation from conglomerates.[36] Their comments were also indicative of a discourse of entrepreneurialism that was gaining increasing currency at the time.[37] As Hesmondhalgh explains, this discourse places greater emphasis on the value of independence from powerful institutions as it presumes that smaller companies are 'more dynamic and able to innovate than the large conglomerates'.[38] This discourse, however, obscures interdependency and consolidation as it is taking place as well as the new realities that the subsidiary company often faces within its new corporate structure.

Although Kuhn's description of Manifesto as a form of 'alliance' indicated parity between members, for instance, the relationship between PolyGram, Propaganda and Working Title was inherently unequal. Kuhn highlighted PolyGram's more powerful position by referring to it as the 'major company' and, while profits from film sales were supposed to be shared, Manifesto was wholly owned by PolyGram. When PolyGram later partnered with Universal to establish Gramercy Pictures, a specialty film distributor, it made Manifesto practically obsolete and ended Propaganda's and Working Title's rights to share in profits.[39] Furthermore, 'An alliance of independents' depicted PolyGram, Propaganda and Working Title as collectively combating a larger ominous threat in the form of Hollywood. Yet Kuhn's rhetoric represented defensive posturing that masked PolyGram's aggressive behaviour and its own position as a subsidiary of Philips. In fact, Kuhn and PolyGram's ambitions to effectively dominate the independent film market were antithetical to the very concept of independent film in the first place. Following PolyGram's takeover of Propaganda and Working Title, Kuhn also stated that the production companies would operate as 'largely autonomous, creative units backed by a worldwide distribution network'.[40] Although PolyGram's CEO, Alain Levy, added that Kuhn would not 'become a studio chief' determining what movies its subsidiary production companies would make, Levy went on to state that Kuhn would give the production companies 'a strategic view' and make sure that they were being 'run within a budget'.[41] Levy's caveats undermined PolyGram's claims about its subsidiaries' continued autonomy because strategy and budgetary constraints imposed by parent companies clearly do shape the projects that any subsidiary production company can make.

In 1994, Propaganda's chief operating officer, Jim Tauber, confessed that PolyGram had encouraged them to produce films with 'some kind of edge ... along the lines of *The Crying Game* [Jordan, 1992] or *Reservoir Dogs*'.[42] This instruction probably meant that PolyGram wanted Propaganda to make films that were cheap to make but had the potential for crossover success and significant box-office returns as they were supposed to cohere to the new wave of purportedly edgy American independent films being produced at that time.[43] Propaganda gained a reputation for making such films as it co-produced *Kill Me Again* (1989) and *Red Rock West* (1993) with John Dahl, *Kalifornia* (1993) with Dominic Sena, and *Wild at Heart* (1990) with David Lynch.

After Propaganda failed to deliver a substantial 'edgy' breakout commercial success, however, PolyGram's executives instructed Propaganda to begin making films and nurturing directors with more mainstream commercial potential. As Golin confessed in 1994, Propaganda was beginning to focus on making 'movies that [were] more commercial'.[44] 'We're sitting down and saying ... "Is this a concept that [PolyGram] can market and sell,"' Golin added, 'We have that conversation now. We never used to have it'.[45] Golin also stated that the 'biggest misconception' that they encountered in Hollywood was that they 'only want to make small dark movies, and that's just not the case anymore'.[46] Likewise, Kuhn indicated that PolyGram's executives had grown impatient with lower than expected returns on their investment when he said that although Propaganda was 'making good commercial movies ... the next five years should be about reaping the benefits of the nursery of directing talent that is finally bearing fruit'.[47] Around the same time that this change of strategy was being made, Propaganda setup a new film and television management division as it began managing actors for the first time with its newly appointed head, Beth Holden, a former agent at William Morris, bringing along clients including Matthew McConaughey and Nicole Kidman.[48]

Golin's comments wrongly imply that the 'small dark movies' that they had been making were not commercial or made to sell. In spite of being an example of rhetorical manoeuvring that associates indie film with art over commerce, Golin and Kuhn's comments show how, under PolyGram's ownership, Propaganda went from being a company with a reputation for helping auteurs to create alternative work outside the studios, to one that sought to align itself with Hollywood and cultivated a reputation for managing directors and other top talent that were capable of making commercial mainstream films.

'It's not necessarily that we don't want to do business with the mainstream directors': Michael Moore, *Canadian Bacon* and Propaganda's mainstream (re-)orientation

Although Golin and his co-executives at Propaganda Films successfully cultivated reputations for offering auteur-directors the creative freedom that they need to innovate, any creative freedom that producers and producer-managers offer is always conditional and varies according to their tastes, the working environment in their companies, their business imperatives and wider market conditions. PolyGram's control of its subsidiaries' budgets and strategic oversight, for instance, appeared to have significant consequences for several of its employees and executives and their projects. After exiting Propaganda in 1994, for example,

Nigel Dick claimed that after 'the PolyGram bean counters came in' he and the company's other directors no longer got the budget necessary to express themselves as they were scrutinised for spending 'the markup'.[49]

PolyGram's oversight appeared to especially rankle with Sighvatsson. After PolyGram acquired Interscope, a company with a reputation for making 'entertainment with mass appeal' in the form of *Cocktail* (Donaldson, 1988) and *Three Men and a Baby* (Nimoy, 1987), for instance, Sighvatsson stated that the parent company should begin looking to its new production company for commercial films and let Propaganda do 'what we do best', which was focus on niche specialty production.[50] In the same article, Sighvatsson insisted that he viewed Propaganda as 'more of a research and development center than a profit center'.[51] Here, Sighvatsson appeared to be in denial about his more subservient role within Propaganda's new corporate structure and about PolyGram's expectation for a return on its investment. In 1994, PolyGram announced what was meant to be a 'temporary' restructuring of Propaganda by placing Golin in charge of the company's film and television businesses and Sighvatsson in charge of its music video and commercial spot divisions as well as its newly launched video games division. Sighvatsson initially appeared enthusiastic about his new role as he commented, 'If there's a natural step for music video and commercials directors, it's definitely games ... They're the best special effects people in the business'.[52] While ignoring the differences that exist between games and commercials production, Sighvatsson's comment epitomised just how malleable and focused on style the producer regarded Propaganda's auteur-directors to be. Yet the restructuring ultimately heralded Sighvatsson's exit from the company.

Arguably no project demonstrated the impact that PolyGram's ownership and strategic oversight had on Propaganda's projects more than *Canadian Bacon*, a satirical feature film about a group of working-class US civilians who invade Canada after their president (Alan Alda) fabricates a conflict between the two countries to grow his approval ratings. On one hand, *Canadian Bacon* appeared incompatible with the Hollywood mainstream and Golin and Sighvatsson's decision to produce it appeared to be proof of their commitment to taking risks by supporting alternative works made by 'directors who [didn't] want to take a project to a studio'.[53] For instance, the film was a leftist critique of government corruption, American cultural imperialism, and big business made by the activist documentary filmmaker Michael Moore in what was his first foray into fictional filmmaking. Moore had also failed to secure finance through Warner Bros. where he had a first-look deal because, he claimed, Warner asked him to reduce the film's politics and accentuate the romance between the film's leading vigilantes, Sherriff Bud Boomer (John Candy) and Honey (Rhea Perlman). Moore claimed that his inability to secure a production deal with a major studio showed that Hollywood was averse to making 'films that are funny, that deal with contemporary political issues and are accessible to a mass audience'.[54]

On the other hand, Moore *did* want to work with a major studio, but the studio chose not to work with him. Despite its leftist critique and the 'working-class hero' reputation that Moore attained,[55] *Canadian Bacon* also shared several properties with mainstream feature film. For example, *Canadian Bacon* starred John Candy, who found mainstream success in several comedies, including *Planes, Trains and Automobiles* (Hughes, 1987) and *Uncle Buck* (Hughes, 1989), alongside other recognisable actors such as Rhea Perlman, Alan Alda and Kevin Pollak. In fact, Candy's participation was key to Propaganda's backing with the company's executives reportedly expecting the film to be a broad comedy.[56] Hence, Moore asserted that Propaganda's producers repeatedly requested script changes during production that were meant to make Candy's role more like that in *Uncle Buck*; requests that Moore said he resisted because, he claimed, *Canadian Bacon* was meant to return the actor to edgier work akin to his role in *SCTV Network* (NBC, 1981–3).[57] Notably, even though Moore's comment positioned *SCTV Network* and *Canadian Bacon* as superior to network television and Hollywood genre film, it was a reversal of rhetoric that I analyse in Chapter 4 where television programmes involving indie-auteurs are elevated through comparisons to their film projects. Instead of seeking to work with independent directors due to their potentially progressive cultural and social agendas, therefore, Propaganda more likely did so because of the economic barriers that it faced. As Sighvatsson himself admitted, 'It's not necessarily that we don't want to do business with the mainstream directors, but we can't compete with the studios. We can't pay the $5 million fees or gross deals or whatever'.[58]

Following *Canadian Bacon*'s completion, Moore's relationship with PolyGram and Propaganda's executives began to deteriorate after the distributor MGM/UA, with which PolyGram had signed a distribution deal for the release of its most expensive pictures,[59] dropped the film from its slate. Moore claimed that he was 'caught in the middle' of a dispute between PolyGram and MGM/UA after the former had failed in its promise to deliver films to the distributor.[60] Moore also accused Propaganda and PolyGram of stopping him from screening his film at Sundance because they feared a political backlash and denounced PolyGram for being a 'purportedly liberal company'.[61] In contrast to the praise that Golin has received from many other filmmakers, Moore also suggested that the producer lacked the taste necessary for recognising his work's quality as he denigrated Propaganda's co-founder's previous film credits, *Daddy's Dyin' ... Who's Got the Will* (Fisk, 1990) and *Kalifornia*.[62]

Moore's claims about PolyGram's distribution deal and its assessment of *Canadian Bacon*'s politics were, however, refuted by the companies involved. With Moore's comments going uncorroborated, it is possible that he was simply disappointed and bitter about Propaganda's and PolyGram's reluctance to support *Canadian Bacon* after its completion. Moore's comments were arguably intended to retain his professional legitimacy and the value of his brand by making him appear to have better taste than Propaganda's executives, and meant to sustain his reputation as an indie-auteur and 'working-class hero' by making him appear to be caught in the middle of corporate battles. By remaining vocal about *Canadian Bacon*'s treatment, Moore also drew attention to his film in a way that arguably made it more marketable and thus more likely to eventually be distributed. Hence, when PolyGram finally arranged to give *Canadian Bacon* a limited release via Gramercy, Moore rowed back on his earlier criticisms by enthusiastically calling the specialty distributor 'the perfect company to release [his] film', one that would 'appreciate its subversive nature'.[63] While producer Kathleen Glynn, Moore's wife at the time, stated that Hollywood executives wanted to 'make him into a commodity for a comedy vehicle',[64] it was the filmmaker himself who was arguably mobilising notions about corporate and mainstream Hollywood to build his brand as an indie-auteur.

Canadian Bacon was most likely dropped from MGM/UA's release slate because it tested poorly with audiences.[65] Moore asserted that PolyGram and Propaganda wrongly tested *Canadian Bacon* with teenage audiences in shopping malls because they expected a broader comedy.[66] These comments were corroborated by David Brown, one of the film's producers at Propaganda, who said that the distributor should have targeted a 'grown-up' audience with greater awareness of political news.[67] Likewise, Peter Graves, PolyGram's marketing consultant, acknowledged that test-screenings fared better with 'smarter audiences' than teenagers.[68] Despite PolyGram's questionable market research and product testing, however, the company responded to *Canadian Bacon*'s poor test-screening results by deciding that the film no longer warranted the $10 million marketing costs needed to release it widely via its pact with MGM/UA. Disappointed with *Canadian Bacon*'s final cut, and possibly exasperated with Moore, Golin removed his name from the film's credits. Golin's decision to do so was arguably a move of symbolic significance as it suggested that the producer no longer unequivocally supported the alternative expressions of independent filmmakers. Sighvatsson, meanwhile, left Propaganda the same day that *Canadian Bacon* was dropped from MGM/UA's release slate. Accordingly, the case of *Canadian Bacon* highlighted Propaganda's executives' confusion about their roles under PolyGram's direction, and highlighted the challenges that changing business strategies enforced by a parent company can create for a single talent management and production division.

'I'm really a mom-and-pop businessman': Anonymous Content, expansion and quality control

In 1998, Philips Electronics sold PolyGram and its subsidiary divisions, including Propaganda, to Seagram. Seagram acquired PolyGram for its music businesses and, since it already owned Universal, sold PolyGram Filmed Entertainment to Barry Diller's USA Networks, which absorbed the company to create USA Films. In turn, Propaganda was broken up with USA Networks also absorbing Propaganda's film and television production divisions while Propaganda's more lucrative talent management and music video and commercial divisions were sold to an investment group named SCP Private Equity Partners. Yet Propaganda's future under SCP, which had no other media holdings, was marked by instability, and key management either resigned or were made redundant. In 1999, Golin exited Propaganda to create Anonymous Content and was soon joined by directors including Fincher, who became a partner, Gore Verbinski, David Kellogg and Mark Romanek. In 2001, after a series of management changes, the exit of key directors, and declining revenues, SCP closed Propaganda.

For some commentators summarising Propaganda's collapse, SCP represented a corporate culture and the antithesis of creative freedom. Jim Hanas, for instance, stated that Propaganda's 'revolution' had ultimately failed because 'A shop run by directors, became a shop run by venture capitalists'.[69] Dick concurred as he said of Propaganda's demise: 'You set out to reinvent the business, and by the time you're done, you are the business'.[70] While such narratives were typical of some commentators' efforts to identify authentic forms of rebellion in cultural production,[71] they also benefited many of Propaganda's producers and directors who were part of the company's success prior to SCP's takeover by making them seem to be genuine artists and mavericks. After founding Anonymous, Golin thus described his regret over losing Propaganda by stating, 'If I was smarter, if I was politically more savvy then, I could have kept Propaganda ... I'm really a mom-and-pop businessman. I'm not very sophisticated, I don't have relationships with investment bankers'.[72]

As a result, Golin sought to retain his reputation as an ideal producer welcoming autonomous expression. In doing so, however, Golin ignored the fact that he had founded Anonymous with funds from a retail investor, Herb Miller, and downplayed the sophistication of his company's revenue streams and integrated production and management business model.

After establishing Anonymous, Golin explained that the company would focus on making music videos, commercial spots and 'new media' or 'interactive product' while scaling back feature film production.[73] In doing so, Golin suggested that the company would concentrate on short-form production, which had proven lucrative for Propaganda, while avoiding becoming overstretched with feature film production. Seeking to increase Anonymous's share price, Golin suggested that 'new media' represented a sizeable opportunity for growth. 'There's huge potential in e-commerce', Golin stated, conflating e-commerce with new media.[74] As I discuss in the next chapter, Anonymous made *The Hire*, a form of branded content made for BMW and distributed online, its first significant production and the one designed to build the company's brand and position it as an innovative business that was at the forefront of a new market trend. Meanwhile, Golin commented that Anonymous would consider partnering with the Hollywood studios on the one or two feature films that it would make per year.[75] Accordingly, Golin revealed that Anonymous was to be more like Propaganda during its post-1994 years, when the company became more closely aligned with Hollywood. In these terms, Golin's new company remained indicative of intensifying interdependency between conglomerates and independent companies.[76]

During its first few years, Anonymous established itself as a leading short-form production and management company by not only securing the commission to make *The Hire* but also by making many other acclaimed commercials and music videos. In 2002, for example, Anonymous received six awards from the Association of Independent Commercial Producers and collected the Grand Prix, the top honour at the Cannes advertising awards, for *Tag* made for Nike, which was directed by Frank Budgen and produced in partnership with London-based Gorgeous Enterprises. In 2003, Romanek won the director of the year award at the Music Video Producers Association and, in 2004, the company increased its honours at the Association of Independent Commercial Producers to eight. In 1999, Anonymous also struck a deal with USA Films, which later became Focus Features, to produce features, including *Eternal Sunshine of the Spotless Mind*, which Golin had been working on at Propaganda before the rights were acquired by Seagram. In 2004, Universal released *Eternal Sunshine* under a first-look pact that Anonymous signed with the studio in 2002 in what represented the fruition of Anonymous's willingness to partner with the studios on feature films.

By the mid-2010s, Anonymous had successfully cultivated a reputation for being committed to making quality productions with auteur-directors. The Karlovy Vary International Film Festival contributed to this reputation, for example, when its organising committee paid a special tribute to the company in 2014 with screenings of *Eternal Sunshine*, *Winter's Bone* (2010) directed by Debra Granik, and an episode of Anonymous's recently released television production *True Detective*, which was directed by client Cary Fukunaga. Despite this reputation, however, Anonymous's productions included not only specialty auteur-directed features but also many more mainstream genre films. In addition to *Eternal Sunshine*, for instance, the feature films that Anonymous produced in the 2000s included *Babel* (2006) directed by Alejandro G. Iñárritu and *Smiley Face* (2007) by Gregg Araki, as well as romantic and teen comedies in the form of *50 First Dates* (Segal, 2004) and *In the Land of Women* (Kasdan, 2007), and action films and thrillers such as *Rendition* (Hood, 2007), *Cleaner* (Harlin, 2007) and *44 Inch Chest* (Venville, 2009). After Anonymous increased its feature film production, the company made indie-auteur–directed features such as *Winter's Bone*, *Spotlight* with Tom McCarthy, *The Revenant* with client Iñárritu, *Don't Worry, He Won't Get Far on Foot* (2018) with Gus Van Sant, *The Laundromat* (2019) with client Steven Soderbergh, and *The Beach Bum* (2019) with Harmony Korine, as well as action films such as *Bastille Day* (Watkins, 2016) and *Triple 9* (Hillcoat, 2016), teen comedies such as *Seeking a Friend for the End of the World* (Scafaria, 2012) and *Fun Size* (Schwartz, 2012), and a family film in the form of *Big Miracle* (Kwapis, 2012). Likewise, after Anonymous expanded substantially into high-end drama television production in the 2010s, it made several shows with auteur clients, including *The Knick*, *Mr. Robot* and *Maniac* as well as *True Detective*, which, as I discuss in Chapter 4, the company promoted as quality cinematic innovations, but also made several shows that were targeted at teen audiences, including *13 Reasons Why* (Netflix, 2017–20), *Dickinson* (Apple TV+, 2019–21) and *Home Before Dark* (Apple TV+, 2020–).

On one hand, this relative variety in Anonymous's productions could be partly explained by a substantial growth in its talent management divisions, which came to have a roster of roughly 500 clients by the mid-2010s, including a substantial number of writers and several high-profile actors including Samuel L. Jackson, Ryan Gosling and Emma Stone, many of whom had different interests and intentions about the projects that they wanted to work on. For example, *44 Inch Chest* and *Rendition* were directed by clients Malcolm Venville and Gavin Hood, respectively, while clients

Jack Amiel and Michael Begler wrote *Big Miracle* and *The Knick*, and Josh Singer wrote *Spotlight*. While Anonymous's brand centred around impressions that it offered auteur-directors creative freedom to create quality specialty works, then, its operations had become much broader and did not adhere to a single genre. The operations of talent management companies thus complicate simplistic notions of specialty production such as indie film that often involve labelling particular works as authentic, pure and organic, and others as manufactured commercial products. With Golin admitting that the diversification of Anonymous's business and its expansion into more mainstream genres made 'quality control' a challenge,[77] though, this also indicates how larger talent management companies may sometimes attempt to compartmentalise their projects to differentiate between so-called quality works and more mainstream productions. On the other hand, however, narratives of Anonymous's diversification and questions about genre and quality arguably obscured a broader truth about Anonymous's business; that is, that the company was part of the upper echelons of Hollywood and that, as such, the vast majority of its productions were closely aligned with the mainstream despite variations in genre.

Just as Propaganda and Anonymous had leveraged the auteur brands of many of its director clients to secure lucrative commissions for music videos and commercial spots, Anonymous did the same in television with *Variety* reporting that the company 'usually command[ed] higher-than-average fees upfront and a big slice of profit participation'.[78] In the mid-2010s, Golin was predicting that the revenues Anonymous would make from television would surpass those being made from commercials.[79] Moreover, many of Anonymous's shows were critically acclaimed and were nominated for, and sometimes won, awards at various festivals and ceremonies. *Mr. Robot*, for instance, collected honours from the South by Southwest Film Festival, the Gotham Awards, the Golden Globes, the Peabody Awards and the American Film Institute. Fukunaga won an award for Outstanding Direction for a Drama Series at the Emmy Awards for his work on *True Detective*'s season one episode 'Who Goes There', while the show was also nominated for awards at the Golden Globes, the Television Critics Association Awards, and the Writers Guild of America Awards. The twenty-fifth Gotham Awards (2015), which was when the event, run by the Independent Film Project (IFP), branched out into television and gave *Mr. Robot* the award for Best Long-Form Drama, also presented Golin with a lifetime achievement award. Notably, the critical acclaim for Anonymous's series was made possible in part due to the decisions made by certain festivals associated with indie films to rebrand themselves to include high-end television.[80] The IFP stated at the time, for instance, that 'the spirit and vision of the best of "independent film" is also realised in content created for a variety of platforms in a variety of lengths and formats'.[81] Likewise, the Sundance Institute's director commented, 'We try to track what the independent film world is doing, and then by following them, we follow the audience'.[82]

Golin claimed that the company did not pursue awards success but rather naturally gravitated towards making projects that, 'when they're done well, have a chance to be in contention for awards'.[83] Golin's comment was of course rhetorical manoeuvring as he implied that the company's works are worthy of awards even if they do not pursue them. This rhetorical manoeuvring was designed to cultivate the economic benefits that markers of prestige such as awards provide while distancing Anonymous from the commercial logic that is sometimes associated with campaign strategies. As Paul McDonald argues, achieving artistic legitimacy is sometimes dependent on appearing to reject commercial success but the prestige bestowed by awards 'still exists in a market context and in that respect retains a branding function'.[84]

In the mid-2010s, Anonymous also found its greatest critical successes to date in feature film with *The Revenant* and *Spotlight*. Both films were highly successful on the 2015–16 awards circuit with, for instance, *The Revenant*, Iñárritu, and Leonardo DiCaprio, winning Best Drama Film, Best Director and Best Actor, respectively, at the 2016 Golden Globes, before *Spotlight* collected Best Picture and Iñárritu and DiCaprio took the same honours for *The Revenant* at the 2016 Academy Awards. In turn, Anonymous's executives leveraged the hot streak that the company appeared to be on in film and television by hiring an investment bank, Guggenheim Partners, to help them to find a minority investor.[85] Eventually, a minority stake was acquired by Emerson Collective, a private limited company founded by Laurene Powell Jobs, the billionaire widow of the former Apple CEO Steve Jobs, that brands itself as a philanthropic organisation working towards creating a more just and equal society by investing strategically in certain businesses working in the realms of media, education, immigration and the environment. In 2020, Emerson took complete control of Anonymous after Golin died from Ewing's sarcoma at the age of sixty-four. According to Emerson's own website, the organisation has a mission to remove barriers to enable people to 'live to their full potential' and 'spur change and promote equality' through a range of strategies, including partnership with entrepreneurs.[86] Hence, Anonymous and Emerson Collective described the initial deal as being designed to allow the company and its clients to create more diverse content aimed at promoting social change and equality.[87] Powell Jobs said that Emerson would partner with Anonymous's 'talented team ... to create films, television and digital content that [could] inspire change', while Golin stated that the deal would 'expand opportunities' for Anonymous and its clients 'to highlight issues of social justice'.[88]

Emerson and Anonymous's purported commitment to shedding light on issues of social justice was reflected in some of the projects that Anonymous went on to make. These projects included: *Carne y Arena* (2017), a short virtual-reality experience co-financed by Emerson and written and directed by Iñárritu that was meant to allow audiences to experience what it was like for refugees crossing the border between Mexico and the United States; *What Do You Care About? #VoteYourFuture*, a social media campaign and three-minute compilation video that was partly directed by Anonymous clients including Iñárritu, Armando Bo and David O. Russell that saw star actors, including several clients, encouraging people to vote in the 2016 presidential election; *The Laundromat*, a feature that was written for the screen by client Scott Z. Burns, and directed by Soderbergh, that focused on the 'Panama Papers' scandal involving revelations about how wealthy individuals exploit a network of off-shore accounts and tax havens to maintain their wealth; *Worth* (Colangelo, 2020), a feature that starred Anonymous clients Michael Keaton and Stanley Tucci, and depicted how attorney Kenneth Feinberg handled the September 11th Victim Compensation Fund on behalf of the US congress; the second season of *Random Acts of Flyness* (HBO, 2018–), a sketch show created by client Terence Nance for HBO that Herman Gray and Maya Iverson-Davis have described as 'one of the few shows on television to explicitly render Black characters and their social relations complexly and compassionately, and to do so without sentimentalism or exoticism';[89] and *Eyes on the Prize: Hallowed Ground* (2021), a one-hour documentary special for HBO Max that explored the cultural and social impact that *Eyes on the Prize*, a documentary series about the American Civil Rights Movement that ran between 1987 and 1990, had for African Americans. *Carne y Arena* especially was perceived by some commentators as being indicative of Emerson and Powell Jobs's mission. In a *New York Times* article titled 'Can Laurene Powell Jobs Save Storytelling?', for example, Kara Swisher described *Carne y Arena* as a 'jarring and disturbing' virtual-reality piece that 'made a deeper impression about the vicissitudes of immigration than any news story could ever provide'.[90]

On one hand, therefore, Powell Jobs's investment in Anonymous could be understood as part of what Sherry Ortner describes as a wave of investment in independent film by a new group of wealthy individuals who have often made their money from the dotcom boom, are interested in art and have liberal progressive politics.[91] For Ortner, such liberal-leaning investors contribute to a 'political awakening' and a challenge to the neoliberal hegemony that she argues is reflected in many independent films.[92] On the other hand, Emerson's investment in Anonymous may be understood as symptomatic of neoliberalism itself. As David Harvey explains, discussing non-governmental organisations specifically but in terms that are applicable to Emerson, philanthropic organisations are often founded by very wealthy individuals who step into the void created by governments' withdrawals of social provision, and they tend to be undemocratic organisations that are usually accountable only to their donors and often presume to speak for and define the requirements of those in need of help.[93]

While Anonymous and Emerson portrayed their deal as being a force for social change, this rhetoric masked the fact that Powell Jobs's investment brought about co-ownership between Anonymous and a range of other media and technology companies in which Powell Jobs or Emerson were also shareholders, including Apple, Gimlet Media, The Atlantic Magazine, online magazine Ozy Media, news website Axios, and even another production company that later branched out into talent management named Macro (which I discuss in the final chapter). Since Emerson's investment in Anonymous, the company has produced a television adaptation of Gimlet's podcast *Homecoming*, signed a first-look agreement to produce content based on *The Atlantic*'s journalism, and has made several shows, including *Dickinson*, *Defending Jacob* (2020), *Shantaram* (2022), *Home Before Dark*, *The Last Days of Ptolemy Grey* (2022) and a feature film, *Swan Song* (Cleary, 2021), all for Apple TV+. Anonymous client Alfonso Cuarón has also signed a multiyear distribution deal with Apple TV+ under which he has produced and directed the series, *Disclaimer* (expected to air in 2024).[94] As well as being indicative of further consolidation in the media industries, the fact that Anonymous has made many of these projects with clients including not only Cuarón but also Sam Esmail, Morten Tyldum, Mahershala Ali and Samuel L. Jackson, prompts some questions about the ability of a talent management company that shares ownership with a major distributor to offer impartial management advice and guidance.[95]

'An atmosphere where the guys can exercise their creative muscle': indie-auteurism, gender and race

Throughout Propaganda's and Anonymous's histories, the companies have privileged hiring and collaborating with White male directors. For example, in 1990 Propaganda's most prolific music video directors were all White men who were under 45 years old, with several, including Fincher and Michael Bay, still in their twenties.[96] When the company's music video and commercial spot divisions closed in 2001, Antoine Fuqua was the only music video and commercial spot director of colour that it ever represented.[97] Most of

Propaganda's feature films and television series were also directed by White men. Exceptions among its feature films included *Heat Wave* (1991), a made-for-television movie about race riots that occurred in Los Angeles in 1965 directed by African American Kevin Hooks, *Portrait of a Lady* (1996) directed by Jane Campion and *A Thousand Acres* (1997) directed Jocelyn Moorhouse. The anthology series *Fallen Angels* (Showtime, 1993–6), meanwhile, had only one director of colour, Cuarón, and only one female director, Agnieszka Holland, from a total of fourteen. In fact, Propaganda preferred to give White male stars such as Tom Cruise and Tom Hanks opportunities to direct its episodes over other women and people of colour.

As Figure 2.3 shows, the percentage of female directors and male directors of colour among Anonymous's clients for commercial spot representation has gradually improved over time. In 2010, White men made up 73 per cent of Anonymous's clients for commercial spots compared to 24 per cent for men of colour, 2 per cent for White women (just one client), and 0 per cent for women of colour. In 2015, White men comprised 63 per cent, men of colour 30 per cent, White women 7 per cent and women of colour 0 per cent. In 2020, White men comprised 45 per cent, men of colour 34 per cent, White women 18 per cent, and women of colour 3 per cent. White men have also received greater opportunities to shoot

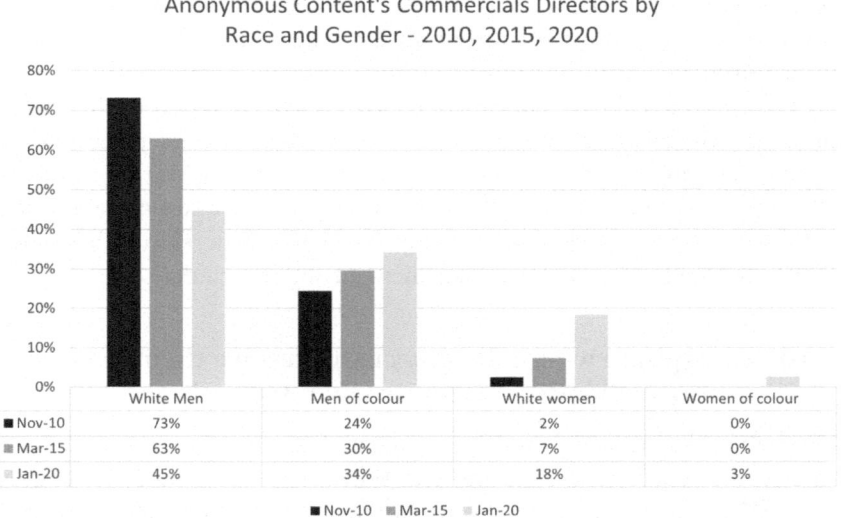

Figure 2.3 Anonymous Content's commercials directors by race and gender at five-year intervals from 2010 to 2020. (Source: Author's own, drawing on data collected from Anonymous Content's website for the requisite years)

Anonymous's film and television productions, although the company has given male directors of colour including Iñárritu, Fukunaga, Nance, Wong Kar-Wai and Ang Lee, all of whom have been clients, greater opportunities to make projects on larger budgets, including on branded content, feature films and television series. Meanwhile, Anonymous has collaborated with White female directors, namely Granik, Jodie Foster, Lorene Scafaria and Lynn Shelton, on feature films including *Winter's Bone*, *The Beaver* (Foster, 2011), *Seeking a Friend for the End of the World* and *Laggies* (Shelton, 2014), respectively. Although Anonymous co-financed *I Am the Night* (TNT, 2019) with client Patty Jenkins and hired client Dee Rees to direct one episode of *Electric Dreams* (Channel 4, 2017–18), however, the company has, as I discuss in Chapters 3 and 4, severely neglected women when deciding who to hire to direct its most high-profile commercials and especially its television series.

Despite the improvements for women among Anonymous's roster for commercials, the increases were made from awfully low numbers in 2010, and the percentages in 2020 still fall significantly short of being reflective of the American population. The extremely low improvement in the number of female directors of colour among Anonymous's commercial spot roster between 2010 and 2020, from 0 per cent to 3 per cent after the company took on African American Rees, confirms Kristen Warner's finding that women of colour are doubly discriminated against; that is, both in terms of gender and race.[98] Moreover, instead of contributing to social mobility, Propaganda's and Anonymous's infrequent work with clients of colour and women can be understood as part of their response to cultural shifts and efforts to tap into particular market trends. On one hand, for instance, the increase in the number of female directors among Anonymous's roster may be explained by a shift in its hiring practices following Powell Jobs's investment. Indeed, as well as leading to gains for female directors among Anonymous's client roster, Powell Jobs's Anonymous has also promoted women into key executive roles, most notably by hiring Dawn Olmstead as CEO in 2020 after Golin's death when Emerson took total control. Under Powell Jobs's ownership, there have also been signs that Anonymous's workplace culture has begun to change. When Anonymous terminated producer Keith Redmon's contract following findings of sexual misconduct, for instance, the company announced that it did not tolerate harassment or toxic behaviour.[99] Redmon confessed to 'consensual dalliances' and infidelity but denied all other forms of sexual misconduct, while he also admitted to having an 'intense management style' and sometimes speaking with a raised voice in a manner that he said was not unusual at Anonymous under Golin's leadership.[100]

On the other hand, the increase in Anonymous's female director clients among its short-form roster can be understood as a response to the increased public attention paid to gender inequalities in Hollywood following the #MeToo Movement. As I discuss in Chapter 3 in relation to Rees, such responses were not simply altruistic, for #MeToo created certain market opportunities in terms of advertising products and brands that Anonymous and other companies exploited. As I also discuss, Anonymous's hiring of auteurs from World Cinema is part of a strategy designed to help it to market products to international audiences.[101] Of the eight male directors of colour in Anonymous's roster for commercials in 2015, seven of those were listed as part of a more privileged group under the heading 'feature-film directors for commercials'. In contrast, only five out of the sixteen White men among Anonymous's commercial spot roster were listed in this more privileged group. This imbalance indicates that Anonymous has usually been inclined to work with directors of colour providing that they have already found substantial success in feature filmmaking and have established brands that the company could readily exploit. Similarly, Anonymous represents commercials directors who are already established in foreign countries, such as Pantera, an Argentinian directing troupe composed of Brian Kazez, Pato Martinez and Francisco Canton, in the United States only. In these cases, Anonymous increases its commissions without having to exert significant resources into building their reputations because its managers can point to the directors' success in their home countries. While Anonymous has effectively imported auteurs from World Cinema, therefore, the company has also historically done very little to enhance social mobility in the United States and, conversely, may contribute to draining other countries' media industries of their most marketable and financeable figures. Evidently, Anonymous's importing of male directors of colour also reinforces gender hierarchies by drawing on World Cinema's historic privileging of male auteurs.

Propaganda's privileging of young White male music video directors, meanwhile, was symptomatic of its tendency to mobilise auteur brands that mirrored the target audience, as well as of racial inequalities in music video production more generally. As Kevin Williams explains, MTV began by targeting young White audiences and excluded Black music, Black recording artists and Black audiences.[102] In turn, African Americans were denied opportunities to make videos for the major record labels,[103] and, in light of Propaganda's purported efforts to use music video as a means for nurturing talent, were arguably deprived of an important platform to promote their work and attain career progression. Mackay commented that Propaganda's disproportionately low representation of Black directors was a consequence of a dearth of African American directors in the music industry more generally.[104] Yet Mackay's comment undermines Propaganda's executives' claims that the company sought to use music video to 'nurture' directors.[105] Hence, Mackay revealed how talent intermediaries claim to nurture talent only when it suits them to do so and that the discourse of nurturing talent is flexibly deployed to suit business agendas.

After MTV began playing Black music following the astronomical success of Michael Jackson's album *Thriller*,[106] record labels started increasingly commissioning Black directors to make videos for their Black artists and so Propaganda took on Antoine Fuqua. As Fuqua has subsequently explained, he was only offered opportunities to direct R&B and rap videos, which at that time still had relatively low budgets, because record labels perceived him to be a specifically 'Black filmmaker' who was not capable of directing more expensive videos for White rock and pop artists.[107] Although Fuqua eventually went on to direct feature films, he says that it took the support of African American movie star Denzel Washington to make this happen and that he initially struggled to get jobs directing films with White leads as studio executives continued to pigeonhole him as a Black filmmaker.[108] Fuqua's pigeonholing by record labels also carried implications for the types of feature films that Black music video directors could go on to make as they were deemed more capable of directing mainstream Hollywood action and comedy films and less capable of directing indie and speciality films.[109] In contrast, and as I show in the next chapter, Spike Jonze's role directing concept music videos, often for indie artists, made his transition to indie film directing appear to be very natural.

Golin and Sighvatsson's focus on creating edgy indie features such as *Kill Me Again* and *Red Rock West* during the company's early years was also more likely to provide opportunities for White male directors who could be marketed as maverick auteurs. Noting the pre-eminence of this masculinised discourse across indie film production, Kathleen McHugh explains that the idea of the indie-auteur maverick clearly invokes the White, masculine and imperialist image of the Western outlaw hero.[110] 'The brilliant facility of this mythic and longstanding archetype', McHugh explains, 'is that it articulates the new, the edgy, the artistic, and the innovative within a familiar White, male, patriarchal order, where the outsider is, by definition, the most privileged insider'.[111] As I mentioned earlier, Sighvatsson said of his and Golin's strategy to grow the company and retain its clients that they would 'create an atmosphere where the guys [could] exercise their creative muscle'.[112] Sighvatsson's comment epitomised how the company's executives conceptualised the embodiment of alternative innovative expression in the form of the autonomous maverick White male auteur who exercises their minds and visions like the outlaw sometimes exercises his wit and brawn. In these terms, gender and racial inequalities amongst the talent management company's roster did not come about despite its purported dedication to supporting alternative visions, but because of it.

Considering Propaganda's privileging of a masculinised conception of auteurism, it is disconcerting that *Portrait of a Lady* and *A Thousand Acres* were reportedly marred by creative conflict between the producers and their female directors. Speaking with the *Ottawa Citizen* prior to the release of *A Thousand Acres*, Golin claimed that creative tensions emerged on both films due to the different perspectives that the films' producers and directors had about adapting the acclaimed novels on which they were based for the screen.[113] Golin stated that creative conflict is always a potential pitfall of adapting works for the screen because different individuals can feel very strongly about how the work should be adapted.[114] In the case of *Portrait of a Lady*, Golin said that Campion 'loved the novel so much that she didn't want to stray from it too far' and was 'very, very clear about her vision'.[115] Although Golin claimed that he was very proud of the movie and sought to work with directors with a clear vision despite 'the possible rockiness of the relationship', he commented that the film might not have flopped at the box-office if it had been shot differently.[116]

In the case of *A Thousand Acres*, though, Golin stated that the creative differences between its producers, which also included Sighvatsson and one of the film's stars, Michelle Pfeiffer, and its director were more intense because Moorhouse 'was very emotional'.[117] 'Some of the changes that we [the producers] wanted to make she [Moorhouse] couldn't go along with', Golin explained, 'and there was a period for a couple of days when she wanted her name removed from the picture'.[118] Although Moorhouse retained her screen credit, the film's producers hired editor Donn Cambern to recut it without Moorhouse being involved.[119] Writing in her biography, *Unconditional Love: A Memoir of Filmmaking and Motherhood*, released in 2019, Moorhouse said that she felt like the new editor was 'a stranger who had come to kidnap [her] movie', that they had 'total authority' over her, and that, after a week of watching her scenes being recut, she 'had no role on the film anymore'.[120]

While Golin described Moorhouse as becoming 'very emotional' during the production of *A Thousand Acres*, his comments on *Portrait of a Lady* made him seem to be a passionate but pragmatic producer who sought to balance creative and commercial imperatives. In eliding any concrete examples or evidence, Golin made Moorhouse's emotion appear irrational, even as he positioned his own passion as worthy of celebration. In contrast, Golin depicted himself as being if not aligned with the purported logic of the market then at least capable of predicting what sells and what does not. These depictions are highly problematic because they adhere to a cultural model of 'hegemonic masculinity', which, as Virginia Wright

Wexman explains by drawing on the work of Karen Ward Mahar, 'defines itself in terms of hierarchy, rationality, the repression of emotions other than anger', and even 'a propensity toward violence'.[121] With Moorhouse going eighteen years before making another feature film, her experience illuminates how the management of indie-auteurism can contribute to the underemployment of women in the film industries.

As *Canadian Bacon* shows, of course, conflict can occur between male directors and purportedly ideal producers too. Yet what is pertinent is the differences in the language that is used to describe the conflict when it involves a male auteur instead of a female one. For example, just four weeks before Anonymous was due to begin production on three more instalments for a second edition of *The Hire*, the company lost the commission reportedly because of a struggle over creative control and credit between Anonymous and Fincher, who acted as executive producer the first time around.[122] After initially refusing to comment, Golin eventually explained:

> I was upset [with Fincher] ... I was very unhappy with the way [*The Hire*] came down. I think Fallon [the advertising agency] could have behaved better, but we blew it ... Fincher and I have had massive fights over the seventeen years we have worked together. Dave is a brilliant filmmaker and I admire him so much. But he is a difficult guy. I love him but, we were in a place where his agenda and the company agenda were not completely lined up. He's in a place in his career where that's OK, and we were in a place with the company where we were trying to build a brand and it's important to us. And it got fucked up.[123]

Golin's comment provides a reminder that the brands of maverick filmmakers and those of the talent management companies contributing to constructing their image exist separately and in ways that can sometimes create tension. At the same time, Golin's description of Fincher as a 'brilliant filmmaker' and 'difficult guy' bolsters Fincher's reputation as a maverick and creative genius; a reputation that Fincher himself has often cultivated, doing so in part by emphasising his disagreements with studio executives.[124] Standing in marked contrast to Golin's depiction of Moorhouse as becoming 'very emotional', this all demonstrates how even narratives concerning instances of conflict in the media industries may be framed by gender dynamics and inequalities, and, while they may hinder the career progression of female directors, they can boost the reputations and facilitate the continued career progression of maverick male auteurs.

Conclusion

This chapter has taken a broad look into Propaganda's and Anonymous's changing business models, operations and ownership. It explored how

PolyGram's acquisition of Propaganda, which was symptomatic of consolidation in the media industries more widely, led to the talent management company being rebranded from one that sought to support independent filmmakers outside the studio system to one that was more closely aligned with the mainstream that sought to make commercial movies with marketable talent. The chapter demonstrated that Anonymous followed Propaganda's second-phase model and that, although the company's substantial growth saw it become involved with a wider range of projects spanning several different genres, the talent management company ultimately belonged to the upper echelons of Hollywood and made mostly mainstream productions.

This chapter has, however, scrutinised extratextual discourse perpetuated by figures such as Propaganda's founders and PolyGram's executives that distinguishes between artistically inclined independent talent management companies and commercially driven non-independent ones. As my discussion of Propaganda's operations in music video showed, its talent management and production strategies were underpinned by commercial imperatives and attempts to dominate markets even before its acquisition by PolyGram. Moreover, the chapter has argued that Golin's, Propaganda's and Anonymous's efforts to cultivate branded reputations for supporting alternative visions did not contribute to improving diversity in media production but instead contributed to gender and racial inequalities as the companies conceptualised indie-auteurs mostly as White, male mavericks. The next three chapters build on this overview of Propaganda's and Anonymous's talent management and production businesses by homing in on the companies' work with indie-auteurs in short-form, television and feature film production.

Notes

1. Goldstein (2004).
2. Ibid.
3. Ibid.
4. Ibid.
5. Jurgensen (2016b).
6. See, for example: Tzioumakis (2013); Pearson (2011); Jenner (2016).
7. Lury (2004) p. 7.
8. Johnson and Gray (2013) p. 2.
9. Richardson (1990a).
10. Banks (1996) p. 86.
11. Ibid. pp. 63–9, 86.
12. Ibid. p. 168.

13. Rohter (1990).
14. Richardson (1990a).
15. Banks (1996) p. 156; Dupler (1989).
16. Rohter (1990).
17. Ibid.
18. Ibid.
19. Richardson (1990a); Dupler (1989); Rohter (1990).
20. Banks (1996) pp. 4–5.
21. Olsen (2000); Wartofsky (1999); Kaplan (2016).
22. Banks (1996) p. 195.
23. Dupler (1989).
24. Eller and Dawtrey (1991).
25. Hesmondhalgh (2013) pp. 212, 216.
26. Ibid. pp. 212, original emphasis.
27. Dupler (1989).
28. Dawes (1988).
29. Ibid.
30. Dupler (1989).
31. Ibid.
32. Rohter (1990).
33. Groves (1989).
34. Ibid.
35. Eller and Dawtrey (1991).
36. Tzioumakis (2006) p. 266.
37. Hesmondhalgh (2013) p. 209.
38. Ibid. pp. 209, 212.
39. Eller and Dawtrey (1991); Fabrikant (1992).
40. Eller and Dawtrey (1991).
41. Ibid.
42. O'Steen (1994).
43. See, for example: Tzioumakis (2013) p. 32.
44. Chagollan (1994).
45. Ibid.
46. Brodie (1996).
47. Ibid.
48. Ibid.
49. Linnet (1999).
50. Brennan (1992).
51. Ibid.
52. Chagollan (1994).
53. Rohter (1990).
54. Fine (1993); Keogh (1993).
55. Goozner (1998); Clark (1998); Georgakas and Saltz (1998).
56. Natale (1995).

57. Ibid.
58. Rohter (1990).
59. Bridges (1993).
60. Persall (1995).
61. Persall (1995); Natale (1995).
62. Anon (1995); Busch (1994).
63. Natale (1995).
64. Fine (1993).
65. Natale (1995); Busch (1994).
66. Natale (1995).
67. Ibid.
68. Ibid.
69. Hanas (2001).
70. Ibid.
71. Merritt (2000) p. xiii.
72. Hatfield (2003).
73. Harris (1999); Geier (1999).
74. Harris (1999).
75. Ibid.
76. Hesmondhalgh (2013) p. 212
77. Jurgensen (2016b).
78. Littleton (2015a).
79. Jurgensen (2016b).
80. See also Sinwell (2023).
81. Luers (2015).
82. Galuppo (2016).
83. Kay (2014).
84. McDonald (2017) p. 495.
85. Jurgensen (2016b).
86. Emerson Collective (2016).
87. Belloni (2016); Fleming (2016).
88. Anon (2016a).
89. Gray and Iverson-Davis (2023) p. 22.
90. Swisher (2018).
91. Ortner (2013) pp. 101, 116–19.
92. Ibid. pp. 270.
93. Harvey (2005) p. 177.
94. Otterson (2019).
95. For discussions of potential conflicts of interest due to talent intermediaries engaging in production and the representation of talent simultaneously, see: Zelenski (2003); Shope (2006).
96. Fine (2010).
97. Anon (2020); Fine (2010).
98. Warner (2016) p. 172.

99. Belloni (2021).
100. Lang (2022); In 2023, Redmon, who claimed that he was the subject of a smear campaign conducted by Anonymous's new leadership, sued the company for breach of contract. After Anonymous's board agreed to a settlement out of court, the company and Redmon released a joint statement that recalled the 'significant contributions' that Redmon had made to the company during a 16 year period. After the settlement, however, Olmstead and her recently appointed COO, Heather McCauley, resigned, reportedly in protest (D'Alessandro, 2023).

    As I discussed in the book's introduction, it is very difficult to make conclusions based on behind-the-scenes events when they are obscured by non disclosure agreements and PR rhetoric. The settlement does not necessarily exonerate Redmon, though the whole event does point to problems of leadership at Anonymous following Golin's death and calls into question the extent to which Anonymous's board under Powell Jobs is really committed to changing its corporate culture.
101. David Andrews (2013, p. xi) describes European art cinema, Asian art cinema, indie cinema and New Hollywood as collectively comprising 'art cinema' as a flexible category.
102. Williams (2003) p. 30.
103. Banks (1996) p. 170.
104. Ibid. p. 172.
105. Dupler (1989).
106. Williams (2003) p. 32.
107. Anon (2020); Fine (2010).
108. Anon (2020); Fine (2010).
109. On quality aesthetics and Whiteness, see Nygaard and Lagerwey (2020) p. 155; on indie and Black exclusion, see: Sexton (2022).
110. McHugh (2016) p. 142.
111. Ibid. p. 143.
112. Dupler (1989).
113. Portman (1997).
114. Ibid.
115. Ibid.
116. Ibid.
117. Ibid.
118. Ibid.
119. Maslin (1997) p. 12; Moorhouse (2020) p. 160.
120. Moorhouse (2020) p. 160.
121. Wexman (2020) p. 60; Mahar (2006) pp. 196–9.
122. Graser (2002); Takaki (2002); Mallore (2002).
123. Hatfield (2003).
124. Weintraub (2010).

CHAPTER 3

Propaganda/Films

The Indie-Auteur and the Legitimation of Short-Form Production

Throughout most of their histories, Propaganda Films and Anonymous Content earned, and in the case of the latter, continue to earn, most of their revenues from making short-form productions including music video, branded content and commercials. As integrated production and talent management companies, Propaganda's and Anonymous's revenues in these realms have come from securing fees with sizeable markups on production costs as well as from taking a percentage of their clients' fees. Propaganda's and Anonymous's success in these areas has also hinged on a marketing strategy that has involved both companies leveraging their reputations for offering auteur-directors substantial creative freedom to express their purportedly innovative cinematic visions. Doing so differentiates their productions from most other commercials, advertising and mass culture. During Propaganda's earlier years, this strategy involved constructing its short-form clients as effectively feature film auteurs-in-waiting by claiming to be using its music video and commercial spot divisions as a means of nurturing talent and a form of research and development.[1] During Propaganda's later years and at Anonymous, the strategy more often hinged on hiring directors with an established track record in feature filmmaking and mobilising their existing brands as film auteurs.

This chapter thus explores how Propaganda and Anonymous mobilised auteurism and indie-auteurism to promote their projects as innovative short films through an analysis of three case studies. First, the chapter analyses Spike Jonze's Propaganda-produced music videos, considering especially the role that the company played in constructing Jonze's auteur brand and creating an impression that he was destined to become a feature film director. Second, the chapter analyses Anonymous's production of the first series of *The Hire*, which was a form of branded content comprising five roughly ten-minute episodes or short films each featuring a recurring character directed by five different auteurs and executive produced by Anonymous partner David Fincher. Third, the chapter analyses two collections of commercials, *The Receipt* (2017) and *The Box*, that were commissioned by the retail giant Walmart as part of its sponsorship of the 2017 and 2018 Academy Awards and homes in especially on one commercial produced by Anonymous and directed by its newest client, African American Dee Rees.

By analysing three case studies made during three different decades, the chapter aims to draw out continuities in Propaganda's and Anonymous's short-form production and talent management strategies. The chapter scrutinises claims made in the promotional, extratextual and critical discourse surrounding the projects that they are innovative and of exceptional quality. While Newman and Levine have explored how 'cinematization' functions as a legitimising discourse for certain forms of high-end scripted television,[2] this chapter investigates how Propaganda's and Anonymous's marketing strategies positioned their productions as short films to distance them from advertising as well as television. The chapter also considers to what extent advertisers, producers and talent management companies conceptualise screen authorship in racial and gendered terms as they mobilise it to legitimate their productions to appeal to specific audience constituencies. In doing so, the chapter considers whether Propaganda's and Anonymous's marketing strategies hinged on and reinforced simplistic and old-fashioned cultural and social distinctions privileging art over commerce, film over television and advertising, indie film over more mass modes of entertainment, new modes of consumption over more traditional ways of watching, niche middle-class sophisticated audiences over working-class audiences, and masculinity over femininity. As a result, the chapter argues that short-form production, which has often been neglected in studies of cultural production and indie film, is a space of great importance for understanding how indie-auteurism is constructed, is mobilised and evolves.[3]

'Overwhelm[ing] the cultural products they are meant to pimp': Spike Jonze, music video and the construction of an indie-auteur

Arguably, no director was more a product of Propaganda's talent management and media production strategies than Spike Jonze. Jonze joined Propaganda's subsidiary division, Satellite Films, in 1992, and made music videos and commercials for the company until 2001 when it collapsed after PolyGram was sold by Philips. Established in 1990, Satellite was dedicated to managing directors with limited experience of finding work and concentrated entirely on music video and commercial spot production and talent management. The division was both a manifestation of Propaganda's expansion and indicative of its owners', Steve Golin and Joni Sighvatsson's, mission to 'nurture' talent through music video and commercial spot production.[4] While Jonze had no experience as a music video and commercial spot director before joining Satellite, he became one of its star directors by cultivating an auteur brand, winning several awards, and seeing his fees increase substantially. Jonze remained at Propaganda after SCP Private Equity acquired it and its founders and other major directors exited. Thus, Propaganda's new owners described Jonze's decision to renew his contract with the company as evidence that it remained committed to maintaining its 'high level of creativity and ideal creative working environment'.[5] The fact that Propaganda was becoming increasingly unstable under SCP's ownership and would soon be folded demonstrates clearly how indie-auteurism can be mobilised to mask problems created by corporate consolidation.

Jonze also made his feature film directing debut on *Being John Malkovich*, which Propaganda and Golin produced with finance provided by PolyGram, as he joined Dominic Sena, who helmed *Kalifornia*, and David Fincher, who helmed *The Game* (1997), as one of only three of Propaganda's short-form directors who ultimately shot features for the company. Critics called *Being John Malkovich* 'predictably quirky' and 'offbeat' and placed Jonze alongside indie-auteurs such as Wes Anderson and Paul Thomas Anderson.[6] In turn, critics retrospectively searched Jonze's music videos for similarities to *Malkovich*. *Film Quarterly* noted that *Being John Malkovich* and Jonze's music videos 'blend[ed] several layers of intertextuality' and 'played with identity issues'.[7] *Film Comment* reported that Jonze had 'rise[n] from the relative anonymity of commercial and music video directing with a voice and vision so astonishing as to overwhelm the cultural products [that he was] meant to pimp'.[8] Accordingly, critics provided an impression that Jonze's works cohered under a single authorial vision and that his short-form productions warranted more attention than most others. In doing so, these critics implied that Jonze was a naturally talented artist who transcended the apparent commercial constraints and promotional functions of music video and commercial spot production. According to these critics, Jonze had progressed from music video to film, and this progression was organic, inevitable and deserved.

These narratives of Jonze's organic progression chime with the broader culture surrounding indie film that privileges indie's supposedly organic qualities and its distance from Hollywood's manufacturing of commercial products.[9] Notions that Jonze had overcome commercial constraints, however, were indicative of tendencies for music videos and commercials to be perceived as an inferior media form compared to film. The critics suggested that whereas music videos and commercials were designed to 'pimp' products, film provided a platform for much more authentic individual artistic expression. Yet Propaganda's and Satellite's roles in producing Jonze's music videos, managing his career and constructing his authorial brand shows that Jonze's 'progression' to feature film directing and his emergence as an indie-auteur was far from organic and inevitable. Considering, as I discussed in Chapter 2, how Propaganda benefited from MTV's emergence and consolidation in the music video sector, Jonze's work with the company also demonstrates that he was part of a highly industrialised and commercialised media industry sector.

Although hardly any news coverage exists of Jonze's first few years at Satellite, evidence of how Propaganda and its subsidiary division constructed him as an auteur can be found in the 2003 'Directors Label' DVD on Jonze, which was part of a series that Jonze created alongside former Propaganda producers, Vincent Landay and Richard Brown. The Directors Label DVD series, which contains additional entries dedicated to celebrating the work of other mostly White male music video directors, including Mark Romanek, Michel Gondry and Chris Cunningham, creates an impression of certain directors from the late 1980s and early 1990s scene as having been free to express themselves and experiment.[10] As Carol Vernallis has pointed out, director-focused DVD compilations 'enhance our sensitivity to music video directors as auteurs'.[11] Released after Jonze's emergence as a feature film director, the DVD, which includes a booklet featuring an interview with Jonze interspersed with stills from his music videos, must be understood in these terms as a paratext designed to reappraise and canonise Jonze's music video work and position it within a broader indie-auteur oeuvre.

In the DVD booklet, Jonze recalls that before signing with Propaganda his reel only included 'a couple of super low-budget videos', some 'skateboarding footage'[12] and a collection of photos.[13] Jonze says that Satellite's head, Danielle Cagaanan, reviewed his reel and agreed to sign him if he could get 'the energy, personality and point of view' from his photos into his music videos.[14] Jonze says that Cagaanan's instructions left him confused because his photos looked nothing like 'all the videos that [were] on TV'.[15] 'Everyone knows what a video is *supposed* to look like', Jonze asserted.[16] Yet Jonze says that he started figuring out what Cagaanan meant one year later when he began drafting treatments for 'If I Only Had a Brain' by MC 900 ft. Jesus. Jonze explains that he drafted two treatments, one depicting a young boy discovering MC 900 (Mark Griffin) operating a spooky TV shop from its basement, and the other depicting MC 900 being transported inside a cardboard box to a factory producing his new brain.[17] Jonze says that although he preferred the first treatment, Cagaanan encouraged him to submit the second one because it better reflected his personality.[18] 'She just thought it was more original', Jonze stated before adding, 'She could see other people writing the treatment with the image on the TVs, but she couldn't see anyone else writing that other one'.[19] Moreover, Jonze says that in retrospect the first treatment was 'pretty much just like a "music video" idea'.[20]

In these accounts, Jonze depicted himself as an indie-auteur-in-waiting. Jonze conjures up an image of a homogeneous music video sector and positions himself outside it. He claims to be unaware of his supposedly individual creative style, which he suggests is inherently incompatible with popular music video conventions. Doing so functions to reappraise Jonze's music video work by positioning it as part of his indie-auteur oeuvre. Jonze's depiction of himself as an authentic artist is an example of rhetorical manoeuvring, however, since he contradictorily claims to be unaware of a style that he simultaneously recognised as being different. Moreover, Jonze's admission that he preferred the first treatment undermines his own claims that the second always better represented his personality. Of course, it is impossible to align one treatment, from two created by Jonze, with some more authentic version of himself. While Jonze's description of Cagaanan's role in nurturing his creative identity risks undermining depictions of him as an autonomous artist, this represents a rhetorical sleight-of-hand as Jonze makes his creativity appear essentially organic and only in need of being nurtured. As a result, Jonze downplays Satellite's broader industry contribution in building his career, including the company's role in helping him to secure commissions by mobilising its relationships with record labels, and in developing and producing his videos.

As I discussed in the previous chapter, Propaganda favoured concept music videos to promote its directors as auteur filmmakers. Propaganda's preference for concept videos served a rhetorical function by positioning its directors as artists struggling against 'conservative' record labels, and they let Propaganda's directors incorporate dramatic narratives to give them greater leeway to play around with style and form. Hence, Propaganda's co-owner, Joni Sighvatsson, said in an interview conducted by Jonze that stylistic and formal experimentation allowed Propaganda's directors to exhibit their 'filmic background[s]' and 'command of the visual language'.[21] Similarly, Jonze expressed a preference for concept music videos during an interview with *Mirrorball* (25 April 1999), a documentary series broadcast on the UK's Channel 4 that celebrated the work of various music video directors, including Jonze's own. In the Directors Label DVD booklet, Jonze also described his video for Daft Punk's 'Da Funk', which sees a human-sized dog struggle with identity issues as he wanders the streets of New York in what is surely his most high-concept video, as 'a predecessor to [*Being John*] *Malkovich*'.[22] Notably, Jonze also explains that he frequently visited Fincher in his office to 'pick [his] brain about stuff' and 'learn how effects were done'.[23] Jonze's comment shows how management firms can function as hubs in the exchange of knowledge and skills. It also demonstrates how instead of exchanging critical political ideas as part of a social activism in a manner associated with the more radical end of independent film, Propaganda's directors sought to collectively develop their skills as visual storytellers.

With all of this in mind, Jonze's videos warrant closer inspection. Jonze incorporates stylistic flourishes, special effects and visual effects repeatedly across his music videos. Jonze's video for MC 900 ft. Jesus's 'If I Only Had a Brain', for example, includes point-of-view shots from inside the cardboard box, very low-angle shots of the box being collected and dropped off, and fast-paced tracking shots following the box rolling down a hill on a child's trailer. Jonze's video for Dinosaur Jr.'s 'Feel the Pain' includes a point-of-view shot from inside a golf hole with the ball teetering above, very low-angle shots of J Mascis (Joseph Donald Mascis Jr) teeing up, and a fast-paced tracking shot following J Mascis's golf buggy swerving around Manhattan. Jonze's video for the Beastie Boys' 'Sure Shot' has several low-angle shots, including its opening shot of a dog approaching the camera, close-up crane shots with the rappers hanging from the crane, sped-up tracking shots, montages created from archive footage, and transitions between colour and black-and-white. Jonze's video for Weezer's 'Undone (The Sweater Song)' is a single long-take tracking shot that begins upside down and in black-and-white before floating towards the stage where Weezer are performing, rotating 180 degrees, and transitioning to colour. Other examples of Jonze's use of visual and special effects include: the band Elastica chasing a digitally created ghost and firing laser guns at an animatronic Godzilla in 'Car Song'; Mike Watt riding a model train in 'Big Train'; a man running down the street alight for the duration of Wax's 'California'; the lead singer of Pavement, Steven Malkmus, performing with an invisible head in 'Shady Lane'; and the actor Christopher Walken flying around a hotel lobby in Fatboy Slim's 'Weapon of Choice'.

While Jonze's use of stylistic flourishes and special and visual effects draw attention to the visual storyteller, however, they gain value when perceived as cohering under a broader artistic vision. Thus, many of Jonze's videos combine stylistic flourishes and special and visual effects with formal play. Jonze's video for The Pharcyde's 'Drop' and Fatboy Slim's 'Praise You' provide particularly clear examples. The video for 'Drop' is played in reverse throughout, giving the impression of The Pharcyde's members flying up from the ground, balls bouncing up stairs and puddles of water rising into the air. The video ends with Fatlip (Derrick Stewart) pulling a hammer out of the air like Thor. A glass pane featuring a painting of four figures in black with red outlines symbolising The Pharcyde, which Fatlip had shattered with the hammer that he had thrown away, is subsequently reassembled. A figure then emerges in the space between the glass pane and the camera to complete his painting with the paint disappearing since the video is still playing in reverse (Figure 3.1). Once reassembled, the pane acts as a fourth wall separating The Pharcyde from the camera and audience. Its insertion functions as a framing device that gestures to Jonze's authorship as the painter parallels Jonze's position behind the camera. As a result, Jonze is positioned as the auteur with a unique artistic vision who operates outside convention. While the glass's shattering serves as a metaphor for Jonze's breaking of convention, however, the video merely reworks convention.

Like 'Drop', Jonze's video for Fatboy Slim's 'Praise You' is designed to create an impression of Jonze as breaking convention. The video begins with grainy handheld footage of Torrance Community's amateur dance troupe travelling to perform, with one of its members thanking Richard Koufey (played by Jonze) for training them. The brief opening scene is followed by a wipe transition to a title insert featuring garish

Figure 3.1 A still from Spike Jonze's music video for 'Drop'. (Source: Author's own screengrab)

green and pink font calling the video a 'Torrance Public Film Production' (Figure 3.2). Richard and his troupe subsequently perform in a theatre foyer to Fatboy Slim's 'Praise You' surrounded by bemused passers-by. Ambient sound and background dialogue plays throughout the performance to give the impression that we are watching an amateur recording. After performing, the troupe again discuss their performance and one member thanks Richard for his 'original' choreography, which Richard compares to 'B-boy posse' moves. Richard's comparison is ridiculous, since the choreography appeared amateurish, improvised and rigid, and was performed by White middle-aged men and women wearing button-up T-shirts and yoga pants.

The video for 'Praise You' is thus designed to draw comparisons between two authorial figures, Richard and Jonze, who appear to break convention. This comparison was underlined by critics who played along by crediting Richard as director.[24] Creating comparisons between Richard and Jonze, however, was intended to emphasise their difference. Whereas Richard's breaking of convention stems from his amateurism, Jonze's breaking of convention appears to be the work of a highly skilled and visionary auteur. As a result, 'Praise You' neatly captures the legitimation process underpinning Jonze and Propaganda/Satellite's music video work. While 'Drop', 'Praise You' and other videos directed by Jonze seem to be innovative artworks breaking music video convention, most other videos are positioned as standardised works made by inferior music video directors.

Many of Jonze's videos also recreated popular media programmes or

Figure 3.2 A still from Spike Jonze's grainy music video for 'Praise You' made in the style of an amateur production. (Source: Author's own screengrab)

genres. Jonze's video for Weezer's 'Buddy Holly' resembles a *Happy Days* (ABC, 1974–84) episode, his video for Beastie Boys' 'Sabotage' parodies 1970s TV cop shows, and his video for Bjork's 'It's Oh So Quiet' imitates Classical Hollywood musicals. Again, Jonze designs each of these videos to position himself as the reinventor of these popular media forms. For example, 'Buddy Holly' begins with an opening title sequence crediting Jonze as the *Happy Days* episode's director (Figure 3.3) and 'Sabotage' signals its mock-design and deliberately emphasises its low-budget production with the Beastie Boys members wearing ridiculous 1970s style wigs, doing hammy performances and stunts, and text reading 'for screening purposes only' appearing over archival footage used in place of a real explosion. As Michael Newman points out in his analysis of the Coen brothers, formal and generic play can encourage authorial readings by catering to middle-class and educated audiences who find pleasure in noticing the way that conventions are being played with.[25] Jonze's play with genre is not unique among Propaganda's directors, as Sena's and Fincher's music videos referenced canonical films including *Casablanca* (Curtiz, 1942), *8½* (Fellini, 1963), *Citizen Kane* (Welles, 1941) and *Metropolis* (Lang, 1927).[26] While Jonze's videos signalled his ability to recreate and potentially improve pop culture, Sena's and Fincher's referencing of canonical films aligned them directly with Classical Hollywood and World Cinema auteurs including Michael Curtiz, Federico Fellini, Orson Welles and Fritz Lang. While their specific references may have been different, however, the effect was the same: referencing made Jonze,

Figure 3.3 A still from Spike Jonze's music video for 'Buddy Holly'. (Source: Author's own screengrab)

Sena and Fincher seem to be directors who could create quality screen media beyond music video.

Critics responded to Jonze's videos by praising what they perceived to be his quirky style and reworking of media conventions. *Newsweek* described Jonze's video for 'Sabotage' as 'a parody of *The Streets of San Francisco* [ABC, 1972–7]';[27] the *Atlanta Constitution* reported that Jonze's 'Buddy Holly' video displayed a 'goofily self-conscious appreciation' of pop culture';[28] the *Boston Globe* called his video for Wax's 'California' 'quirky wicked fun';[29] the *Los Angeles Times* described the video for Daft Punk's 'Da Funk' thus: 'Another bizarre gem from director Spike Jonze';[30] and the *Ottawa Citizen* reported that his 'Praise You' video was 'a devastatingly funny spoof of music video conventions'.[31] In turn, critics interpreted the videos as highly artistic manifestations of Jonze's individual authorship. They called Jonze an 'auteur',[32] 'artist',[33] 'video savant',[34] and 'genius'.[35] *The Gazette* said that Jonze's 'Da Funk' video was 'much closer to a short movie than a music video',[36] The *New York Times* reported that his 'Praise You' video was 'more like a guerrilla art attack than a commercial for a pop song',[37] and the *Ottawa Citizen* claimed that Jonze's 'high-concept videos are smart in idea and execution' and that he spares viewers 'the jiggling booties and well-oiled bodies that characterize so much MTV fare'.[38] As a result, these critics reproduced problematic cultural and social hierarchies elevating apparently legitimate authored work meant for purportedly sophisticated (and mostly White) viewers over mass media and its supposedly undiscerning audience. While critics did so by depicting Jonze as an autonomous artist, Jonze's collaborations with Propaganda and major record labels and the exposure of his videos on MTV show that he was not independent after all.

'Think cinematic': *The Hire* as pioneering achievement or advertising rhetoric

Shortly after Golin exited Propaganda to launch Anonymous, the new talent management and production company was commissioned by Fallon Worldwide, an advertising agency, to produce *The Hire*, a form of branded content intended to promote Fallon's client, the luxury automobile manufacturer BMW. According to a summary of the project that was published in *Shoot* after *The Hire*'s release, Fallon had commissioned Anonymous after BMW gave them a brief to create an innovative and non-traditional campaign.[39] After BMW reportedly rejected Fallon's first and 'more traditional' campaign idea, Fallon successfully pitched what they described as a forty-five-minute 'serialized film'.[40] Fallon did so,

Shoot reported, after its creative director, Bruce Bildsten, instructed the company's art director, David Carter, and copywriter, Joe Sweet, to 'Think cinematic'.[41] Bildsten reportedly encouraged Carter and Sweet to draw inspiration from their earlier work on two commercials for watchmakers Timex shot by Tim Burton for Quentin Tarantino's advertising agency, A Band Apart .35mm.[42] With Carter confessing that making the Timex commercials had left him and Sweet reminiscing about 'Hollywood cool', Fallon contacted 'famous' Hollywood filmmakers including Fincher, who had become a partner in Anonymous, to direct.[43]

Although Fincher was reportedly unable to commit to directing *The Hire* because he was scheduled to shoot *Panic Room* (2002), Bildsten stated that he 'really embraced the idea' and asked if he and Anonymous could produce.[44] With Fallon accepting Fincher's proposition, Fincher reportedly then suggested that they should create a collection of 'short films' featuring one recurring character, The Driver, instead of a single serialised one.[45] Bildsten stated that making this change was 'a stroke of brilliance' because it gave Fallon and Anonymous access to 'much better and more diverse talent' who might not have wanted to have made a substantial commitment to shooting a feature.[46] After BMW approved five scripts written by Carter, Sweet and *Se7en* (Fincher, 1995) screenwriter Andrew Kevin Walker, Fallon and Anonymous hired auteurs John Frankenheimer, Guy Ritchie, Wong Kar-Wai, Alejandro González Iñárritu and Ang Lee to direct, as well as Clive Owen to play the lead role, and Mickey Rourke, Forest Whitaker, Stellan Skarsgård and Madonna for supporting roles. Of the production, Bildsten stated that while BMW made sure that they had the right scripts in place, the car company was 'hands-off with the directors'.[47] Meanwhile, Carter said that witnessing the directors' different approaches first-hand was like taking 'five semesters of film school'.[48]

This narrative of *The Hire*'s production epitomises how BMW, Fallon and Anonymous produced and promoted it as a form of cinematic and innovative autonomously authored art. The companies' executives repeatedly called *The Hire* a collection of short films, accentuated the feature film pedigree of the talent involved, and described the auteur-directors as having exceptional levels of autonomy that enabled them to express their purportedly individual and innovative cinematic visions.[49] BMW, Fallon and Anonymous also positioned *The Hire* as a collection of short films by distributing them on BMW's website alongside bonus features such as directors' commentaries, running trailers for the 'short films' on television, placing posters in hip urban venues, screening three of the instalments at the Cannes Film Festival, and encouraging newspapers and magazines to review them as movies. Thus, BMW's spokesperson,

Karen Vonder Meulen, said that *The Hire* was a 'non-traditional way to do something' that reflected consumers' expectations that BMW 'be innovative'.[50] Likewise, Golin portrayed *The Hire* as a new invention and Anonymous as its inventor as he stated, 'We call these films an example of "brand-integrated content"' before adding that 'To be successful in our business ... you have to think beyond the music video and the commercial'.[51] Journalists, too, played along. Erika Milvy called *The Hire* 'advertainment, [a] seamless synthesis of advertisement and entertainment' and described it as 'a crash course (as it were) in auteur theory, up close and interactive'.[52] Karl Greenberg wrote in *Brandweek* that *The Hire* was a 'Web-based film festival of eight-minute shorts featur[ing] the very hippest in celluloid auteurs'.[53]

The Hire was a manifestation of increasingly close relationships between Madison Avenue's advertising agencies and Hollywood, and symptomatic of talent intermediary companies and advertising agencies' tendencies to position themselves as discovering new markets.[54] Indeed, Golin's attempt to differentiate Anonymous's 'brand-integrated content' from its music video and commercial spot production was designed to build the new company's brand by positioning it as a leader in a new market. *The Hire* was, however, not as innovative as the promotional and critical discourse around it tended to claim. Katherina Stolley, Finola Kerrigan and Cagri Yalkin, for instance, point out that branded content is an extension of product placement and that the latter can be traced back to Classical Hollywood.[55] By mobilising the auteurs' brands to position the projects as short films, meanwhile, Golin and Anonymous were using the same production and talent management strategies that Golin and his co-executives used at Propaganda. Bildsten's admission that Fallon was inspired by their work with Tim Burton on two Timex commercials demonstrates how the mobilisation of auteur brands to position projects as cinematic and sell goods as 'cool' was not exclusive to Anonymous nor new and innovative in the case of *The Hire*. Even more broadly, journalists' comments about *The Hire* being a crash course in auteur theory reveal how old-fashioned ideas about cinema that attribute great works to an individual artist were being renewed to make the project appear innovative. While BMW, Fallon and Anonymous sought to associate *The Hire* primarily with new digital media, they simultaneously associated it with celluloid, and marketed it through traditional and analogue channels.

Fallon and Anonymous's promotional strategy also led to rhetorical manoeuvring that paradoxically involved creating associations between *The Hire* and film while distancing it from, and positioning it above, most filmmaking at the same time. Describing how each of the auteurs brought their own perspectives, Clive Owen declared that *The Hire* demonstrated that filmmaking has 'no rules'.[56] Golin likewise asserted that their 'creative freedom was unbelievable' and said that *The Hire*'s instalments were thankfully not commercials before he contradictorily stated that the budgets were equivalent to 'high-end commercials'.[57] Ang Lee also said that *The Hire* offered 'more freedom' than Hollywood, or any other filmmaking, before adding that he worked on *The Hire* as a 'creative break from all the social and publicity obligations that followed the success of *Crouching Tiger* [*Hidden Dragon* (2000)]'.[58]

While Golin, Lee and Owen emphasised the freedom that BMW offered, they elided the control that the company exerted. As well as having insisted on approving the scripts, BMW exercised economic control by approving the budgets, and placed limitations on how its cars could be depicted by stipulating that no passenger could die in one in a crash. Lee's efforts to distance himself from the publicity obligations surrounding *Crouching Tiger* are also contestable given that he was simultaneously participating in promoting *The Hire*. Collectively, these comments demonstrate how the Hollywood creatives involved in making *The Hire* sought to preserve their reputations as artists as they contributed to BMW's efforts to position itself as a benefactor of quality innovative work. The comments are symptomatic of filmmakers' tendencies to reframe their commercial spot work as a liberating experience, an opportunity to hone their skills, or merely as a means for funding their feature film work. Such rhetorical manoeuvring, however, ultimately reveals the auteur-directors' anxieties about doing commercial spot work in the first place.

BMW's, Fallon's and Anonymous's claims about innovation in the case of *The Hire* is particularly problematic because it contributed to reinforcing and masking class and gender hierarchies. Specifically, BMW commissioned *The Hire* to target young, predominantly male middle-class and upper-middle-class consumers who could afford to purchase their cars, who they described as being technologically savvy, ambitious and high achieving.[59] BMW's market research reportedly indicated that these consumers were averse to marketing and hard to reach through traditional channels, especially through television where new technologies, such as the DVR, allowed audiences to skip commercials.[60] BMW's vice president of marketing, Jim McDowell, explained, 'we asked ourselves, "What if we throw out some of our core assumptions – for instance, that we have to do brand image advertising on network TV?" We challenged Fallon to be wildly creative, if that's what it took'.[61] Conversely, Vonder Meulen commented that BMW's research showed that 85 per cent of people who buy BMWs, who she described as 'high-energy, type-A personalities', do research online before making the purchase.[62]

In these terms, BMW, Fallon and Anonymous mobilised ideas about the auteurs' cool and presented *The Hire* as manifestations of their purportedly cinematic and innovative visions to connect with consumers who desired a feeling of sophistication, luxury, innovation and hipness from their car brands. Even though Fallon placed trailers for *The Hire* on television, they positioned it and its audience against the audience for traditional television. Fincher and Fallon's decision to make *The Hire* a collection of short films instead of a single serialised one is pertinent in this regard because serialisation is more commonly associated with television than film. This change, which is ironic in light of the increasing legitimation of high-end television series in the new millennium, simultaneously bolstered Anonymous's brand, because it positioned the talent management company as a curator with the expertise capable of determining which artists and artworks deserved to be included. By positioning *The Hire* as innovative short films, however, BMW, Fallon and Anonymous contributed to legitimation discourses denigrating traditional television and implicitly denigrated working-class audiences who are unable to afford new technologies and consumer goods, which they effectively framed as old-fashioned and antithetical to progress.[63] These cultural and social hierarchies were reinforced by the critical discourse around the production. Gayle Macdonald described television as ephemeral, mundane, undesirable and even dirty when he reported that BMW 'believes traditional media is continuing to decay. God knows, everybody these days is looking for new avenues to place their product – there's TVs in elevators, screens above urinals'.[64] As a result, BMW, Fallon and Anonymous reinforced cultural hierarchies by bolstering impressions about their middle-class and upper-class consumers' superiority in a neoliberal and increasingly unequal classed society.

Bildsten's claims that Fallon and Anonymous had hired 'diverse talent' and looked for 'diversity in style' are also problematic.[65] The directors were fairly racially diverse for they included American (Frankenheimer), British (Ritchie), Mexican (Iñárritu), Taiwanese (Lee) and Hong-Kong Chinese (Wong) filmmakers. Yet these filmmakers were not hired for their ability to provide diverse social commentaries but for their potential to appeal to more consumers globally and to boost sales of BMW's cars internationally. Hence, it is unsurprising that *The Hire*'s production did not include any director from the Global South or African diaspora as consumers from these groups are also more likely to be paid significantly less and often have far less access to broadband internet.[66] Moreover, all *The Hire*'s directors and writers were men. Given Golin's and BMW's claims about the innovativeness of the project, this gender inequality confirms

Christina Lane's finding that women's involvement in developing new technologies often gets erased from the public narrative as men take the credit and the jobs during the marketing of them.[67] Each instalment of *The Hire* also exhibited the male auteur's cinematic sensibility and cool perspectives. As Stella Bruzzi discusses, 'men's cinema' sees style and mise-en-scène convey masculinity and place spectators in a position of quasi-identification with it.[68] Given that BMW, Fallon and Anonymous mobilised the auteurs' sensibilities to offer BMW consumers the feeling of freedom, cool and superiority that they expect from their cars, Bildsten's comment that Fallon and Anonymous had looked for 'diversity in style' when selecting their directors may be better understood, as Claire Molloy argues, as being indicative of how the indie-auteur sensibility has become less about independent thought and more a brand cohering to and reinforcing neoliberal ideals of consumer freedom.[69]

Each of *The Hire*'s instalments opens with a brief credit sequence that helps to position them as films. Each credit sequence includes a title, lists Anonymous Content as producer, and names the starring actors and director. 'Ambush' also credits Andrew Kevin Walker as its writer. Each instalment subsequently sees The Driver carrying out missions for clients, often while evading antagonists. 'Ambush' has The Driver protect a passenger (Tomas Milian) who is carrying diamonds from armed thieves; 'Chosen' sees The Driver protect an East Asian Holy child (Mason Lee) from kidnappers; 'The Follow' has The Driver conduct surveillance on the wife of a famous actor; 'Star' follows The Driver driving recklessly to punish a petulant celebrity (Madonna) on behalf of her manager; and 'Powder Keg' sees The Driver rescuing a war photographer (Skarsgård) after he witnesses a massacre in Nuevo Colón, Columbia. As a result, chases and stunts involving different BMW vehicles feature prominently and are given precedence over dialogue and character development. In keeping with BMW, Fallon's and Anonymous's efforts to position *The Hire* as a collection of short films, each of its instalments also has a different tone and style that conforms to the auteurs' oeuvres and mobilises their masculine cool auteur sensibilities. *The Hire* also features only three female characters, each of whom have stereotypical roles as the mother, wife/love interest and diva. Of these three, the wife has no dialogue and the mother has very little dialogue, while the wife and diva are shown to be the victims of abuse. Singling out three instalments, 'Powder Keg', 'Star' and 'The Follow', I consider how the auteurs' sensibilities and masculine cool are mobilised to help to sell BMW cars but perpetuates problematic representations of women.

'Powder Keg' is shot on location in a guerrilla filmmaking style with grainy handheld footage, natural lighting and ambient sound. It begins with its protagonist, a White male photographer, hiding in long grass, taking images of soldiers before they massacre their prisoners, and running away after he is spotted. Iñárritu and his co-editors, Luis Carballar and Gabriel Rodríguez de la Mora, cut between long establishing shots and point-of-view shots, while the slight sounds of the photographer's heavy breathing, the distant chatter and radio communication provide a naturalistic feel. As The Driver escorts the photographer to Colombia's border, the photographer looks outside the car window to see civil unrest, poverty and population displacement. These sights prompt the photographer to despair over what 'we' are doing to the country and the photographer anguishes over the value of his work, which he says has only helped to sell newspapers. The Driver offers reassurances about the value of his work and asks why the photographer chose his occupation in the first place. The photographer responds, 'I don't know, because my mother taught me to see'. After the photographer dies from injuries that he sustained from escaping the massacre, The Driver returns a necklace to the photographer's mother and lets her know that her son was posthumously awarded a Pulitzer Prize.

On one hand, the war-torn setting of 'Powder Keg', images of civil unrest and reference to global inequalities may be interpreted as Iñárritu's efforts to grapple with social changes brought about by neoliberalism.[70] According to Sherry Ortner, dark, angry and violent independent films can prompt social critique by encouraging audiences to reassess their own values and assumptions.[71] On the other hand, 'Powder Keg' can be understood as an example of how the indie-auteur sensibility is mobilised to sell consumer goods and reinforces neoliberal ideals of consumer freedom. For instance, 'Powder Keg' makes the photographer an on-screen representation of Iñárritu's authorship. Not only does Iñárritu take pictures like a photographer, but the guerrilla style of 'Powder Keg' also invokes his auteur vision by recalling his work on *Amores Perros* (2000). Moreover, the photographer's comment that his mother taught him to see suggests that she taught him to see *differently*, which can be read as a variation on the notion of the auteur's diverse vision. Thus, the photographer's and auteur's different ways of seeing are positioned implicitly and problematically as a superior way of seeing. Even though Iñárritu was a veteran director of commercials in Mexico before he shot *Amores Perros*, the photographer's contemplation over the value of his work may be understood simultaneously as a manifestation of Iñárritu's anxiety about migrating from making film in Mexico to directing BMW commercials in the United States; that is, his own questioning about the choices he has made and the value of his work. As a result, the potential of 'Powder Keg' for social critique is severely compromised as it does not properly interrogate the causes of the conflict and instead redirects our focus to questions about the value of the photographer and Iñárritu's work.

Unlike the naturalistic guerrilla style of 'Powder Keg', 'The Follow' has a non-linear narrative that creates a mystery from The Driver's surveillance as it cuts between scenes sometimes shot with a blue filter of The Driver following the movie star's wife (Adriana Lima) and his interactions with the movie star (Rourke) and his manager (Whitaker), which take place both before and after. 'The Follow' also has The Driver narrate his surveillance work in voice-over. As The Driver follows the wife along a dark highway at night, for instance, he says, 'Out in the open, distance is subjective. You can let the target ride the horizon, so long as you know their patterns'. After the wife falls asleep at the airport where she is seeking to board a plane to flee, The Driver takes the opportunity to look at her eyes, which she had been covering with sunglasses. An extreme close-up reveals that her eyes are bruised (Figure 3.4), and, deducing the abuser to be the husband, The Driver returns his payment. 'The Follow' ends with a medium-close shot of The Driver lit with green and blue light as he drives away down a long inner-city tunnel. The Driver makes one final comment: 'There's always something waiting at the end of the road. If you're not willing to see what it is, you probably shouldn't be out there in the first place'.

The fragmented narrative in 'The Follow', the voice-over narration, mixing of detective and romance themes, and evocative use of colour invoke Wong's authorship by recalling his work on critically acclaimed art-house features including *Fallen Angels* (1995), *Happy Together* (1997) and *In the Mood for Love* (2000). The fragmented narrative also places 'The Follow' alongside 'puzzle films' from the 1990s and early 2000s,

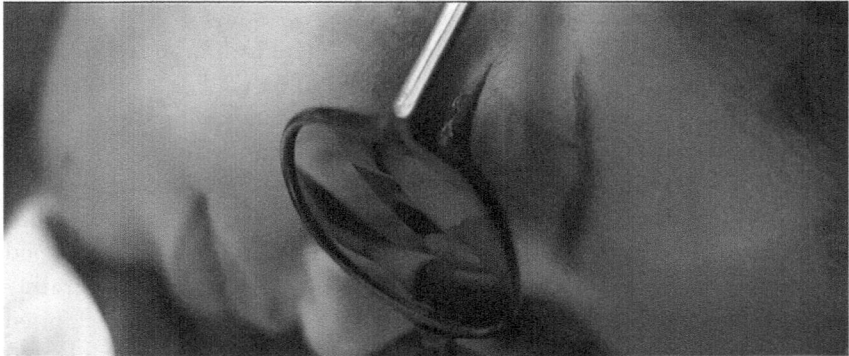

Figure 3.4 A still from Wong Kar-Wai's 'The Follow'. (Source: Author's own screengrab)

including Wong's *In the Mood For Love* and *2046* (2004), Iñárritu's *Amores Perros* and *21 Grams* (2003), Fincher's *The Game* and *Fight Club* (1999), as well as other features such as *Lost Highway* (Lynch, 1997), *Memento* (Nolan, 2000) and *Eternal Sunshine of the Spotless Mind*.[72] The Driver's commentary epitomises how *The Hire* functions as a puzzle film to offer pleasure. The Driver's commentaries, for instance, are vague and can be read as reflections on romance and life, while the final comment can be interpreted as a metatextual commentary on the storytelling that gestures to the pleasures that its purportedly more daring audiences may find from solving the narrative's puzzle. At the same time, The Driver's comments function as metaphors for driving, which shows how *The Hire* connects the auteur's apparently innovative storytelling and vision to the sense of adventure that BMW is offering.

In her analysis of Christopher Nolan's films including *Memento*, *The Prestige* (2006) and *Inception* (2010), Molloy argues that Nolan provides no critique of the abuse towards women in his films because his puzzle narratives instead prioritise offering pleasure from ambiguity.[73] As Molloy points out, this form of pleasure encourages consumerism by promoting repeat viewings on different formats.[74] Likewise, the fragmented narrative of 'The Follow' and its single extreme close-up of the wife's bruised face takes the abuse out of context and restricts audience empathy with the victim. Instead of prompting any serious questions, 'The Follow' uses domestic violence as a narrative device that facilitates The Driver's moralising about his work, allows Wong to showcase his storytelling talents, and helps to sell BMW cars.

Finally, 'Star' marks a significant departure in tone and style from 'Powder Keg' and 'The Follow' with its inclusion of dark and slapstick comedy. 'Star' begins with The Driver introducing the Diva as a beautiful, strong and talented woman before beginning to say that she is an 'absolute cunt' as Ritchie and his editor, Tom Muldoon, elide the profanity by cutting to her coughing. As The Driver subsequently drives around the city at speed to Blur's 'Song 2' to throw the Diva around in the BMW's back seat, he makes daft faces as he taunts her bodyguard, recklessly takes his hands off the steering wheel, and gains lift-off over a bridge with the soundtrack briefly cutting to 'Ride of the Valkyries', a piece of music that was originally composed by Richard Wagner and which also featured during a comedic car chase in *Blues Brothers* (Landis, 1980).[75] At one point, the Diva attempts to steady herself by grabbing The Driver's face only for him to accelerate and throw her back again. 'Star' ends with The Driver screeching to a halt at the Diva's destination to eject her onto the red carpet outside her venue (Figure 3.5). The Diva lies humiliated on the

Figure 3.5 A still from Guy Ritchie's 'Star' showing the Diva cowering from paparazzi on the red carpet. (Source: Author's own screengrab)

floor, her crotch stained with coffee which the awaiting paparazzi hurry to take pictures of after mistaking it for excrement.

'Star' invokes Ritchie's authorship because its dark and slapstick comedy recalls the director's work on *Lock, Stock and Two Smoking Barrels* (1998) and *Snatch* (2000), and because Madonna was his wife at the time. As in 'The Follow', the narrative of 'Star' centres around the abuse of a woman. While the wife's abuse in 'The Follow' facilitates The Driver and audiences' journeys of (self-)discovery, The Driver's physical and mental abuse of the Diva in 'Star' is made to appear justified by the Diva's own mistreatment of him and her staff. 'Star' encourages the audience to enjoy and laugh at the Diva's abuse and mistreatment, but its comedy is problematic because notions that it is 'just a joke' deflects scrutiny of it. The abuse of women, including petulant celebrities, however, is no laughing matter. In fact, *The Hire* becomes even more problematic as it reinforces the car's status as a symbolic object of 'masculinity, male identity and virility' as recent findings suggest that bad driving stemming from toxic masculinity causes as many crashes as alcohol, illegal drugs and fatigue.[76]

As I discussed in Chapter 2, Anonymous lost the commission to produce the second season of *The Hire* just a few months before production was due to begin following a struggle over creative conflict between Fincher and Anonymous. While the first season of *The Hire* demonstrated Fincher's ability to leverage his auteur reputation to secure work for Anonymous, the second evidenced the opposite. While Anonymous was reported to have lined up Jonze, Nolan and Lars von Trier to direct the second season, Tony and Ridley Scott's advertising company, RSA, which replaced Anonymous as producer, passed directing duties to Tony Scott, John Woo and Joe Carnahan. Although the production company and personnel changed, therefore, *The Hire*'s second season continued to demonstrate marketeers' and production companies' tendencies to conceive of indie-auteurs as men. While some male indie-auteurs such as Richard Linklater have actively resisted featuring images of the abuse of women in their films,[77] this section has demonstrated how financiers' and intermediaries' privileging of the indie-auteur's sensibility and masculine cool reinforces gender inequalities in media production, and perpetuates problematic screen representations, while simultaneously masking them by encouraging consumerism over social critique.

'Pretty radical ... for a Walmart commercial': Walmart, the Academy Awards and Dee Rees's cultural legitimation

The final section of this chapter explores two collections of commercials, *The Receipt* and *The Box*, that were commissioned by the retail giant Walmart and debuted during ABC's broadcast of the 2017 and 2018 Academy Awards as part of the retail giant's three-year sponsorship of the event. Like BMW's promotion of *The Hire*, Walmart marketed *The Receipt* and *The Box* commercials as innovative short films and manifestations of each of the directors' autonomous cinematic visions. To do so, Walmart and its advertising agency, Saatchi & Saatchi, hired filmmakers Antoine Fuqua, Marc Forster, and Seth Rogan and Evan Goldberg, to direct one commercial each for *The Receipt*, and Nancy Meyers, Melissa McCarthy and Anonymous client Dee Rees to direct a commercial each for *The Box*. While *The Receipt* marked a continuation of advertisers' tendencies to conceive of the auteur as male, therefore, Walmart's hiring of three women to direct *The Box* a year later seemed to mark a break from these prevailing production norms. After exploring the productions generally, the section turns specifically to Dee Rees's contribution. Doing so, it considers to what extent *The Box* provided an opportunity for its female auteurs to depart from earlier manifestations of masculine cool or whether they remained constrained by neoliberal impulses prioritising consumption over social critique.

After striking its sponsorship deal with the Academy Awards, Walmart executives reportedly decided to challenge various filmmakers to create a 'short film' based on an imagined customer's Walmart receipt. To do so, Walmart reportedly gave Fuqua, Forster, and Rogan and Goldberg significant autonomy with the only stipulation being that each commercial needed to feature the same six items featured on the receipt.[78] Positioning the project as highly innovative, Walmart subsequently boasted that it sought to create something 'as inspiring' as the Academy Awards itself, that the 'short films ... blurred the lines between *the* movies and *our* movies' and, as if there was a great hunger for it, that although everyone has 'seen a film based on a book, a play, a real event ... we've never seen a film based on a receipt'.[79] The filmmakers too described the autonomy that Walmart had supposedly given them and made claims about the innovativeness of the project. For example, Goldberg claimed that his first reaction to being offered the project was an utter disbelief that Walmart would 'follow through with this whole thing', while Fuqua explained, 'Walmart called and said, "We're going to let you make a little mini-movie." You don't get those calls that often for commercials'.[80]

Like *The Hire*, Walmart's promotion of *The Receipt* involved contradictions and significant rhetorical manoeuvring. Fuqua's description of *The Receipt* as both a mini-movie and a commercial in the same sentence, for instance, demonstrates how the project was actually a form of advertising that executives framed as cinematic. Walmart's sponsorship of the Academy Awards, an event associated with Hollywood glamour, Hollywood A-listers and prestige that appeals mostly to middle-class audiences, at first seemed surprising given that the company is known for operating supermarkets selling mass-produced goods often at discount prices. Yet its sponsorship of the Academy Awards was part of the company's response to Amazon, which was taking market share by encouraging consumers to make more purchases through the company online, including by getting them to subscribe to its Prime Instant Video and one-day delivery service. The range of items listed on the receipt featured in the commercial – bananas, batteries, paper towels, scooters, wrapping paper and a video baby monitor – were intended to show that consumers could complete all their purchases at Walmart rather shopping with its rival online. Walmart also commissioned *The Receipt* as part of its broader efforts to bolster consumer loyalty by making personalisation in the form of 'storytelling and creativity' central to its brand and ethos.[81] Referring to the campaign, Megan Kring, a Walmart spokesperson, stated, 'Every receipt tells a story ... so this is a bit of a homage to our customers'.[82] Likewise, Walmart's vice president of marketing, Kristen Evans, said that the company hired multiple directors to see how 'a single receipt seen through an artistic lens can tell an infinite number of stories'.[83] Walmart's executives' comments clearly recalled Anonymous's and Fallon's rhetoric surrounding *The Hire* in that they too were seeking to bolster and expand their appeal to consumers by mobilising notions of consumer choice and individuality, which they tied to the auteurs' cinematic visions and diversity in style.

Walmart's claims that *The Receipt* was a homage to its customers was hypocritical, however, because, around the same time, Walmart was angering its customers and allegedly breaching their consumer rights by insisting on checking their bags against their receipts as they exited the stores to deter and detect theft.[84] Fuqua's admission that Walmart *let* him make a mini-movie undermines notions about his transcendent individuality that underpin his auteur brand and the promotion of *The Receipt* as cinematic in the first place. Walmart's claims about *The Receipt*'s innovativeness are also undermined by the company's use of a familiar strategy that saw it hiring male directors and mobilising auteur cool to appeal to mostly middle-class and upper-class audiences. The 2017 Academy Awards also saw no woman nominated in its Best Director and Best Cinematography categories, while no woman helmed any of the feature films nominated for Best Picture. Of course, the absence of female directors in these award categories was not new but marked a continuation of the tendency of Hollywood studios to overlook women when making hiring decisions, and of the Academy and many other prestigious film institutions to neglect women when making their pronouncements of artistic merit in behind-the-scenes categories.[85] Thus, *The Receipt* and the 2017 Oscars demonstrated that advertisers and Hollywood's institutions continued to overwhelmingly conceive of the auteur as male into the late 2010s.

Despite Walmart's self-aggrandising over their production of *The Receipt*, audience response to the commercials was mixed. Walmart's omission of women directors in the making of *The Receipt*, for instance, prompted critic Ann Hornaday of the *Washington Post*, which is perhaps not uncoincidentally owned by Amazon's founder Jeff Bezos, to tweet the company about her disappointment. Walmart responded to the tweet by stating that it 'did reach out to women directors and it didn't work out, mainly due to scheduling'.[86] Yet Twitter users rightly rejected Walmart's excuse, with several asking Walmart to reveal how many female directors they approached, while one user astutely commented that it was unbelievable that the company had managed to hire in-demand male directors but was unable to hire any woman at a time when women directors are underemployed.[87] Walmart's omission of female directors and its exchange with audiences on Twitter was picked up by the mainstream press and brought the company negative publicity.[88] As Jeff Beer wrote in *Fast Company*, Walmart's omission of women did not support its purported claims that 'each receipt tells a story as diverse as the customers who shop us'.[89] Rather than providing practical and meaningful support to enhancing diversity in media production, therefore, Walmart followed BMW in tapping into a neoliberal ideology that values diversity in terms of profit-making.

Before Walmart set about developing another series of commercials for its second year of sponsoring the Academy Awards, late 2017 saw major revelations emerge about decades of sexual assaults committed by the indie producer Harvey Weinstein. These revelations prompted the #MeToo movement and a series of disclosures revealing many cases of sexual abuse committed mainly by men in positions of power both in Hollywood and in society in general. Consequently, gender inequality and sexual abuse in Hollywood dominated much of the conversation in the lead up to the 2018 Academy Awards and became topics that the event needed to address and navigate.[90] Although Walmart executives made the dubious claim that they were not trying to exploit the #MeToo movement for commercial gain,[91] the company commissioned three women, Rees, Meyers and McCarthy, to direct its three commercials for *The Box* to debut during ABC's 2018 Oscars broadcast. Walmart's decision to hire Rees was particularly astute as she had just become the first Black woman ever to be nominated by the Academy of Motion Picture Arts and Sciences for Best Adapted Screenplay for *Mudbound* (Rees, 2017), while *Mudbound*'s director of photography, Rachel Morrison, became the first woman ever to be nominated for Best Cinematography. These historic firsts gave Rees and *Mudbound* significant press attention and led to her being signed by Anonymous for commercial spot representation before she was commissioned by Walmart.

As with *The Receipt*, Walmart purported to give the directors complete autonomy as it promoted the commercials as short films exhibiting the auteurs' individual visions. Discussing the project, Rees stated:

> the whole proposal was, "We want you to do a short story about a box. You can do whatever you want with it. The only parameters are that the box has to arrive." It was a fun chance to do a little short film'.[92]

As well as emphasising her autonomy, Rees described the project as an opportunity to challenge herself creatively. 'I've never done a 60-second piece', Rees stated before adding, 'It's a real challenge – what can you do in a minute? I really wanted to push that. I wanted to go to the maximum'.[93] Like the rhetorical manoeuvring around *The Hire* and *The Receipt*, promotional discourse surrounding *The Box* elided the control that the commissioning company exerted. In this case, Walmart stipulated that each commercial must feature its blue delivery boxes, and that the boxes must be shown arriving on time, as it sought to promote itself as an alternative to Amazon in online retail. While Rees reframed *The Box* as an opportunity to challenge herself creatively as she too sought to retain her auteur brand, she also emphasised her ongoing collaboration with Morrison and *Mudbound* star Mary J. Blige, both of whom joined her in making the commercial. Rees's doing so adhered to broader findings that female auteurs emphasise collaboration more often than their male counterparts.[94]

The Box's critical reception stood in stark contrast to *The Receipt*'s with critics particularly praising Rees's Anonymous-produced commercial. Writing in *The Mary Sue*, Vivian Kane called Rees's commercial 'One of the year's best movies' and said that it surpassed much of what was being honoured at the Oscars itself.[95] Jude Dry wrote in *IndieWire* that Rees's work was 'pretty radical ... for a Walmart commercial'.[96] These and other critics celebrated Rees's commercial for two main reasons: because its protagonist was a little Black girl and because the girl appeared to have lesbian mothers who were both women of colour. Rees's commercial cuts between the home where the little girl plays inside the Walmart box while her mothers watch a movie, and the fantasy world that the girl imagines. In the fantasy realm, the girl imagines a space captain (played by an uncredited young Black female) battling an evil intergalactic commander (Blige) before the captain's spacecraft is shot down and crash lands on an alien planet where the space captain fights an alien monster and hides in an underground bunker. At one point, Rees cuts between the little girl reaching outside the Walmart box to grab some popcorn and the pilot reaching outside the bunker for provisions. After Rees returns us to the fantasy realm, her mother is heard informing the child that it is getting close to her bedtime, which prompts the girl to respond through the character of the pilot that 'Space captains don't have bedtimes'. As the mother remains resolute, Rees cuts back to the fantasy world to show the girl adopting the persona of the angry monster shouting 'No' and the emperor insisting that 'Evil commanders most certainly do not have bedtimes'. After reluctantly giving in, the girl and commander vow that 'This isn't over' before Rees and Morrison pan to both mothers on the sofa amused and chuckling.

Rees's commercial does not explicitly state that the two women are the girl's lesbian mothers, but it is implied by the presence of both women in the home at the girl's bedtime as well as Rees's pan to a two-shot and the women's affectionate smiles and laughter. Moreover, Rees herself is a proud lesbian who is known by some critics and audiences for having created *Pariah* (2011), a semi-autobiographical feature about a young Black woman embracing her identity as a lesbian while struggling to come out to her parents. Rees's brand thus prompts critics and audiences in the know to read *The Box* commercial as a lesbian text too. Rees's commercial also gestures to themes of identity, creativity and empowerment, as the little girl imagines her own fantasy world and adopts the persona of three different characters to speak to her mother. The Black female space captain also breaks from typical conceptions of astronauts as White and male. On one hand, therefore, the girl's adoption of three personas can be read as highlighting the multidimensionality of character. This multidimensionality can be interpreted as cautioning against narrow readings of character where marginalised identities are too often understood in very narrow binary terms as the opposite of a White male heterosexual norm. As Michael Gillespie argues, Black film is too often interpreted as a form of cinema that has a responsibility to authentically 'embody the black lifeworld or provide answers in the sense of social problem solving'.[97] Such readings are problematic, Gillespie argues, because they involve drawing on and reinforcing predetermined notions about a singular Black experience.[98] These predetermined notions of Blackness are also frequently underwritten by traditional ideas of masculinity and heterosexuality.[99] Thus, Rees's commercial arguably disrupts narrow readings by foregrounding the process of creativity and subjectivity. In doing so, Rees's commercial arguably supports Cynthia Baron's finding that Rees is one Black female filmmaker, alongside Ava DuVernay and Kasi Lemmons, who has taken back control of her history and representations in her productions.[100]

On the other hand, gesturing to themes of identity and creativity directs audience attention to Rees as an auteur. The girl's literal play mirrors Rees's own play with genre and form and recalls the framing devices that Jonze used in his music videos and the strategies that Iñárritu and Wong used in making 'Powder Keg' and 'The Follow'. Comparisons to *The Hire* are apt because, like BMW, Walmart developed its commercials using notions of 'diversity in style' as a metaphor for consumer choice. Walmart's mobilisation of discourses of authorship and the commercials' debut during the prestigious Academy Awards also positions *The Box* as legitimated culture. Rees's commercial provides a positive image of a respectable, albeit non-traditional, middle-class Black family who are non-threatening to the middle-class and upper-class audiences to whom it is designed to appeal. Hence, the characters shop at Walmart just as, the company wants us to believe, good consumers are supposed to, and they value quality family time together and movie watching like the Oscars' audience (Figure 3.6).

Walmart's positioning of *The Box* commercials as legitimated works and Rees's positive representations can thus be understood as a kind of strategic move that sees Rees navigating an American cultural terrain that, as Herman Gray has argued, 'remains deeply ambivalent about black

Figure 3.6 A still from Dee Rees's *The Box* commercial. (Source: Author's own screengrab)

cultural presence'.[101] Although Rees's collaboration with Walmart and the Academy Awards helps her as a Black woman to secure exposure, however, *The Box*'s legitimation and Rees's positive images also risk contributing to a further denigration of less respectable Black images and culture. As Raquel J. Gates elaborates, 'the burden of respectability places limitations on the forms that certain types of discussions can take' and the veneration of positive images can reinforce racist ideologies by further marginalising Black behaviours and people that deviate from White middle-class norms.[102] Although Rees has only sixty seconds of screen time, her adherence to the politics of respectability sees her present an aspirational image of Black people and scrub from her commercial spots any significant engagement with issues of prejudice or socioeconomic barriers. Indeed, these issues are present in *Pariah* but not in Rees's other commercials, including *Make It Yours* for Samsung, which debuted the same night during the Oscars broadcast and made consumption appear to be a means for expressing one's individuality, and *Never Stop Arriving* for Cadillac, which made consumption a means and outcome of Black success. While Rees's *The Box* commercial expands ideas of Blackness by representing lesbian parents and foregrounding multidimensionality of character, therefore, it simultaneously risks constraining representations by reinforcing negative attitudes towards Black people who do not conform to ideas about what is respectable.

Conclusion

This chapter has analysed iterations of short-form productions made during three different decades to draw out several continuities in Propaganda,

Anonymous and their commercial partners' advertising strategies involving indie-auteurs. The case studies demonstrate how the companies repeatedly mobilised indie-auteurism to promote their short-form productions as short films, while Propaganda's music videos, *The Hire* and *The Receipt*, demonstrate how advertisers have long tended to conceptualise auteurs as men, and often White men at that, to sell products to a mostly White and middle-class audience by invoking an aura of masculine cool. Hence, this chapter has shown that the impressions of innovativeness surrounding the productions that these strategies create obfuscate very problematic industrial, cultural and social hierarchies elevating auteur-driven filmmaking over mass modes of entertainment, educated middle-class audiences over mass audiences, masculinity over femininity, and male over female directors. While *The Box* saw Walmart and its partners hire three women, including one African American, to direct its commercials, the fact that they sought to avoid increased scrutiny and capitalise on the #MeToo Movement indicates that the project was merely a temporary respite from prevailing production norms. Given BMW and Walmart's mobilisation of artistic diversity as a metaphor for consumer choice, social critique and action is arguably quelled and *The Hire* and *The Box* commercials join certain other media industry PR strategies in creating a misleading impression that companies are doing enough to address gender and racial inequalities in front of and behind the screen.[103]

While commercial spot productions are often denigrated because of their associations with commerce, the brevity of short-form production is also often interpreted to mean that it lacks depth and does not warrant serious consideration.[104] Such notions appear in reverse in the increasing legitimation of serialised television, which various cultural and industry commentators, along with the growing number of indie-auteurs who have migrated to the sector in the 2010s, regularly champion for offering greater depth of story and character. Though I explore the indie-auteurs' migration to television to work on high-end series in the next chapter, this chapter shows that short-form productions that air on television, including music videos and commercial spots, may be understood as less privileged forms of indie TV. Thus, this chapter has made the case that short-form production warrants greater consideration as it is an important space where talent management strategies are developed and enacted, screen authorship is constructed, mobilised and shaped, and problematic cultural distinctions are disseminated.

Notes

1. Dupler (1989); Rohter (1990).
2. Newman and Levine (2012) pp. 5–6.
3. David Zelenski argues that a talent manager's right to 15 per cent commissions is based on the idea that they provide longer-term support to unproven clients whom agents have no incentive to represent because they have no track record of successfully securing work. Zelenski argues, however, that a talent manager's 15 per cent commission becomes suspect when they represent 'bankable' clients (Zelenski (2003) p. 996). Yet his tendency to see 'bankable' clients as A-list feature film stars ignores the fact that, in today's era of convergence, proliferation of distribution channels and media fragmentation, there are now more ways of monetising emerging talent than ever before.
4. Dupler (1989); Rohter (1990).
5. Goldrich (2000).
6. Graham (1998); Willens (1998).
7. Repass (2002).
8. Olsen (2000).
9. King (2017).
10. Vernallis (2013) p. 263.
11. Ibid. p. 263.
12. Jonze had previously founded *Dirt*, a quarterly skateboard and dirt-bike magazine targeting teenage boys.
13. Palm Pictures (2003).
14. Ibid.
15. Ibid.
16. Ibid.
17. Ibid.
18. Ibid.
19. Ibid.
20. Ibid.
21. Jonze (1994).
22. Palm Pictures (2003).
23. Ibid.
24. Dolan (1999).
25. Newman (2011) pp. 141–81.
26. Sena's video for Janet Jackson's 'Let's Wait Awhile' and Taylor Dayne's 'I'll Be Your Shelter' referenced *Casablanca* and *8½*, respectively. Fincher's videos for Madonna's 'Oh Father' and 'Express Yourself' referenced *Citizen Kane* and *Metropolis*.
27. Marin (1994).
28. Dollar (1995).
29. Graham (1995).

30. Ali (1997).
31. Wartofsky (1999).
32. Weisbard (1997).
33. Strauss (1995).
34. Marin (1994).
35. Wartofsky (1999).
36. Kronick (1997).
37. Powers (1999).
38. Wartofsky (1999).
39. Gaylin (2001).
40. Ibid.
41. Ibid.
42. Ibid.
43. Ibid.
44. Ibid.
45. Ibid.
46. Ibid.
47. Ibid.
48. Ibid.
49. Greenberg (2002).
50. Bouw (2001).
51. Silberg (2001).
52. Milvy (2001); see also Taubin (2001).
53. Greenberg (2002).
54. Grainge (2008) pp. 27, 35–6.
55. Stolley, Kerrigan and Yalkin (2022) p. 373.
56. Milvy (2001).
57. DeSalvo (2001).
58. Milvy (2001).
59. Gaylin (2001); Greenberg (2002); Bouw (2001).
60. Macdonald (2001).
61. Greenberg (2002).
62. Bouw (2001).
63. Newman and Levine (2012) pp. 132–5.
64. Macdonald (2001).
65. Gaylin (2001); Greenberg (2002).
66. Miller (2016).
67. Lane (2016) p. 72.
68. Bruzzi (2013) p. 5.
69. Molloy (2013).
70. See Ortner (2013) p. 3.
71. Ibid. p 3.
72. Buckland (2014).
73. Molloy (2013).

74. Ibid. pp. 45–8.
75. The song used in 'Star' is actually a cover of 'Ride of the Valkyries' called 'Space Machines' by composer William Kingswood.
76. Chrisafis (2023).
77. Bettinson (2015).
78. Atkins (2017).
79. Anon (n.d.).
80. Ibid.
81. Jones (2017).
82. Jones (2017); Atkins (2017).
83. Beer (2017).
84. Harris (2019).
85. See, for example, Peplow (2023); Daniels (2023); Omar (2020).
86. Hornaday (2017).
87. Ibid.
88. Beer (2017); Steinberg (2018).
89. Beer (2017).
90. North (2018).
91. Steinberg (2018).
92. Hayes (2018).
93. Ibid.
94. Columpar (2016); Badley, Perkins and Schreiber (2016).
95. Kane (2018).
96. Dry (2018).
97. Gillespie (2016) p. 2.
98. Ibid. p. 6.
99. Hall (1993) p. 112; Gray (1995); Gates (2018) p. 113.
100. Baron (2016) p. 217.
101. Gray (2005) p. 15.
102. Gates (2018) pp. 8, 12; see also: Gray (2005) p. 15.
103. Nygaard and Lagerwey (2020) p. 55; Nwonka (2019).
104. Westrup (2016); Felando (2015).

CHAPTER 4

Packaging Indie-Auteur Television

The Single-Director Model, Cinematization and the Pursuit of Legitimacy

This chapter analyses Anonymous Content's expansion into television in the mid-2010s and focuses especially on its role in packaging and producing high-end scripted series with indie-auteur directors who the company often hired to shoot entire series and seasons. While several critics perceived the indie-auteurs' migration to be a manifestation of their autonomous innovative sensibilities,[1] the chapter explores how the migration of indie-auteurs to the sector was a response to changing industrial, technological and cultural conditions occurring across film and television during the 2010s. Specifically, the chapter argues that Anonymous packaged its shows to stand out within an era of 'Peak TV' that saw an increased number of original high-end scripted series being commissioned by cable channels and streaming services. Shows packaged with a single auteur-director stood out because they represented a break from most American television drama production, which has usually involved writer-producer showrunners overseeing them and being granted authorial status in promotional and critical discourse, while directors have usually been hired to shoot just one or two episodes.[2] Moreover, Anonymous's practice of developing productions in-house, often before securing orders for full seasons, created an impression of them as being independently created outside of television's usual corporate structures and away from meddling network executives.[3] Thus, the chapter explores how the packaging technique enabled Anonymous to promote its shows as innovative manifestations of the auteurs' independent and unique cinematic visions.

The first section provides a brief history of Anonymous' expansion and points to some continuities and differences between Propaganda's production of *Twin Peaks* (ABC, 1990–1) and that company's efforts to enter the television market. The second section explores how Anonymous's strategy appealed to its indie-auteur clients and Hollywood's movie stars, while the third section explores the promotional function that the indie-auteur-directed series had for pay-TV and streaming services as I explore to what extent the indie-auteur and the single-director shows were ideally suited to an era of convergence. The fourth section homes in on two Anonymous productions, *True Detective* and *Mr. Robot*, and explores how Anonymous's clients' brands were mobilised, intersected and reshaped around each, considering longer-term struggles between writers and directors for creative credit and reflecting on whether the indie-auteur brand can retain long-term currency in television. In the absence of any series packaged by Anonymous with a single woman indie-auteur as director, the fifth section analyses *The Girlfriend Experience* (Starz, 2016–21), which was executive produced and packaged by client Steven Soderbergh, who appropriated and adjusted Anonymous's packaging technique by hiring Amy Seimetz and Lodge Kerrigan to share writing and directing duties.

Overall, the chapter considers how Anonymous's packaging technique differentiated its auteur-branded productions from most other television and what it meant for its clients' professional legitimacy and authorial brands. On one hand, the chapter scrutinises notions of innovation surrounding its shows as it posits that Anonymous's packaging technique represents a continuation of television legitimation discourses that reinforce cultural and social hierarchies by elevating new purportedly cinematic shows over traditional television. As Michael Newman and Elana Levine have discussed, television legitimation discourses that privilege so-called cinematic programming and new modes of consumption denigrate traditional television in the form of conventional programming and feminised genres such as the soap opera, low-tech viewing, and the 'elite conception of a mass audience too passive or stupid to watch differently'.[4] On the other hand, the chapter scrutinises narratives about the auteurs' creative autonomy considering Anonymous and its clients' collaborations with major media companies, including NBCUniversal, WarnerMedia,[5] Netflix and Amazon Instant Video. Bearing in mind Anonymous's efforts to position its shows as improvements on traditional television, the chapter considers how Anonymous's packaging technique may reinforce or redraw industrial, cultural and social hierarchies and relations between auteur-directors and so-called directors-for-hire, television's writers and directors, and male and female directors and auteurs.

Breaking 'the rules of television': Anonymous's expansion, origin narratives and high-end television's changing market

During the mid-2010s, an increasing number of indie-auteurs began migrating to television, with many directing the entirety or majority of full series or seasons of high-end scripted shows. In turn, indie-auteurism gained greater currency in television as television began to be seen increasingly as a space where indie-auteur figures could work with significant creative freedom on innovative and indie-orientated productions. Anonymous Content became a major player in facilitating these shifts as it began packaging high-end television series often with its indie-auteur clients. Specifically, Anonymous packaged and produced *True Detective*, which was created by client Nic Pizzolatto with indie-auteur client Cary Fukunaga as the director of its first season; *The Knick*, created by clients Jack Amiel and Michael Begler and directed in entirety by indie-auteur client Steven Soderbergh; *Maniac*, which was co-created and directed by Fukunaga; and *The OA*, which was co-created by client Brit Marling, who also played the lead role, and was mostly directed by her long-time indie-auteur collaborator, Zal Batmanglij. The company also packaged and produced *Mr. Robot*, which was created by the one-time indie film director and client Sam Esmail before he took on the directing responsibilities for all of seasons two to four, and *Homecoming* (Amazon, 2018–20), which had a first season written for the screen and directed by Esmail and a second season directed by client Kyle Patrick Alvarez.

In a 2015 article titled 'Anonymous no More' that was published after several of Anonymous's television and film productions, including *True Detective*, *The Knick* and *Mr. Robot*, and *Spotlight* and *The Revenant*, respectively, had found significant critical success, *Variety* reported that the company had scored big 'by bringing feature talent into TV on unusual terms'.[6] In the same article, Anonymous's founder, Steve Golin, claimed that he instructed the company's producers to focus increasingly on creating television series after witnessing Media Rights Capital (MRC) and David Fincher, who had recently exited Anonymous to establish his own short-form production company named Reset, selling *House of Cards* (2013–18) to Netflix for $100 million.[7] Golin claimed that he blasphemed in astonishment at witnessing MRC and Fincher, who committed to direct the pilot episode and executive produce, essentially using the same auteur-packaging technique that he and Fincher had used during their time together at Propaganda and Anonymous.[8] This narrative about the influence that *House of Cards* had on Anonymous's expansion was reiterated elsewhere by the company's other executives and producers. Anonymous and *True Detective* producer Richard Brown, for instance, claimed that Netflix's decision to give Fincher $160 million for two seasons 'sent an earthquake through the industry'.[9] Anonymous partner, producer and manager, Michael Sugar, called *House of Cards* a 'paradigm shifter', the 'evolution' of which, he claimed, was *True Detective* and *The Knick* because not only were they sold straight-to-series with movies stars attached but because they also had single-series directors, or as he described them, 'a singular director', in the shape of his clients, Fukunaga and Soderbergh, respectively.[10]

Certainly, there was evidence to support *Variety*'s and Anonymous's claims about the company's role in the migration of indie-auteurs to the sector. After Soderbergh and Fukunaga directed *The Knick* and the first season of *True Detective*, a wave of other shows that were not produced by Anonymous but had indie-auteurs attached as season or series directors began to be commissioned. Included, among others, were Mark and Jay Duplass directing all but one episode of *Togetherness* (HBO, 2015–16), Paul Haggis helming all episodes of *Show Me a Hero* (HBO, 2015), Seimetz and Kerrigan sharing directing duties for the first two seasons of *The Girlfriend Experience* before Anja Marquardt took over to direct the third season, Joe Swanberg helming *Easy* (Netflix, 2016–19), Woody Allen directing *Crisis in Six Scenes* (Amazon, 2016), Jean-Marc Vallée and Andrea Arnold helming one season each of *Big Little Lies* (HBO, 2017–19), Spike Lee directing every episode of *She's Gotta Have It* (Netflix, 2017–19), David Lynch directing all episodes of *Twin Peaks: The Return* (Showtime, 2017), Vallée shooting all of *Sharp Objects* (HBO, 2018), Ava DuVernay directing *When They See Us* (Netflix, 2019), Greg Araki helming *Now Apocalypse* (Starz, 2019), and Nicolas Winding Refn directing *Too Old to Die Young* (Amazon, 2019). The practice has also continued into the 2020s as Barry Jenkins directed *The Underground Railroad* (Amazon, 2021), Craig Zobel shot *Mare of Easttown* (HBO, 2021), Soderbergh directed *Full Circle* (Max, 2023), Batmanglij and Marling shot *Murder at the End of the World* (FX Network, 2023), Gus Van Sant has helmed the majority of *Feud: Capote vs. The Swans* (FX Network, 2024) and Alfonso Cuarón is directing *Disclaimer* (expected to air in 2024).

Anonymous's expansion into television during the 2010s, its strategy of packaging shows with single-series indie-auteur directors, and the number of similar shows that were subsequently commissioned, arguably indicates how a single talent management company can genuinely play a significant role in expanding indie as a discourse to television and reshaping indie as a field of cultural production. Yet the narrative of this seismic shift in indie and television production elided certain significant continuities and carried some problematic connotations. Notions about the improvement of television were a continuation and intensification of legitimation discourses and promotional strategies that could be traced back to at least the 1950s when advocates of pay-TV claimed that it could elevate programming standards and tastes.[11] As cable became widespread by the end of the 1980s, content producers and channels increasingly used authorship as a branding strategy too, doing so especially to target niche, young and middle-class audiences.[12] After HBO 'imposed itself as a model for producing the highest quality television possible',[13] premium cable channels such as Starz, basic cable channels such as FX and AMC, and, arguably to a lesser extent, streaming services such as Netflix, Amazon Instant Video and Hulu, followed suit.[14] While television authorship has usually been attributed to the writer-producer showrunner, cable channels including HBO sometimes hired indie-auteurs to launch their shows, while channels and platforms began commissioning programming exhibiting a quirky style associated with indie film to draw acclaim and bolster their brands.[15] While the Public Broadcasting Service had provided important sources of finance for the more socio-political film associated with the minority voices of the independent period,[16] therefore, the model of indie and indie authorship that gained currency in television during the 2000s and 2010s was mostly of the less radically political kind, associated with innovations in style and form and highly valued for its promotional function.[17] Hence, although Anonymous's model of production foregrounded the role of the auteur-director rather than the writer-producer showrunner, the author function remained the same as it served to differentiate auteur productions from the rest of television.

Although Anonymous's executives pointed to *House of Cards* as essentially creating a new epoch, arguably no show demonstrated the continuity underpinning the company's work more than *Twin Peaks*, which originally aired on ABC in 1990 and 1991. Not only had the show been rebooted in 2017 with David Lynch directing the entirety, but Golin's former company, Propaganda Films, also co-produced the original two seasons alongside the show's co-creators, Lynch and Mark Frost. Although Propaganda's co-founder, Joni Sighvatsson, confessed that the company was not involved in actually developing *Twin Peaks*, Sighvatsson and Golin still used their association with the show to improve their company's brand.[18] In doing so, Propaganda's co-founders depicted *Twin Peaks* as a programming innovation and described it as facilitating a market shift. Following *Twin Peaks*' release, Golin described the show as ABC's attempt to 'do something different' when faced with declining ratings, while Sighvatsson claimed that the show 'broke the rules of television' and created 'a much more open market'.[19] By implying that *Twin Peaks* was an improvement on television's usually safe programming, therefore, Propaganda's co-founders used rhetoric that anticipated Anonymous's executives' claims about their television productions in the 2010s as well as wider convergence-era discourses of legitimation.[20]

Propaganda subsequently sought to capitalise on *Twin Peaks*' success by producing two anthology series, *Hotel Room* (HBO, 1993), which Lynch also co-wrote and co-directed, and *Fallen Angels*, which had episodes helmed by a peculiar mix including directors such as Soderbergh, Cuarón, Peter Bogdanovich and John Dahl, as well as film stars Tom Cruise, Tom Hanks and Kiefer Sutherland. Because the demand for high-end television had not yet reached the same levels that it would in the so-called era of Peak TV in the 2010s, however, Propaganda was ultimately unable to expand into television to the same extent that Anonymous has since. Conversely, indie-auteur figures were finding greater opportunities in the indie film sector during the 1990s, as the sector was strong and growing. Moreover, and as I discuss more in the next section, Propaganda's ability to leverage the indie-auteur brand in television during the 1990s was limited by the fact that the indie-auteur brand held only minor currency in television at that time.

Finally, *Variety*'s report could also be understood as part of a wider public relations strategy and sales pitch as it was published after Anonymous's executives had hired the investment bank Guggenheim Partners to find a minority investor in the company. Anonymous's executives were crafting a narrative of a seismic shift in television production, one that, they implied, the company was expertly positioned to exploit. As a result, Anonymous's executives were positioning the company as a market leader much as Golin and his co-executives had done earlier in music video and branded content. Hence Sugar described Soderbergh as a 'pioneer' for making the move to television to direct *The Knick* and asserted that Anonymous had many more single-director productions 'in the pipeline'.[21] While mobilising Soderbergh's reputation for pioneering achievements, Sugar's rhetoric was meant to boost the currency of Anonymous's indie-auteur brands in television by positioning Soderbergh as the first of many indie-auteurs to migrate to the sector. In these terms, the migration of the indie-auteur to television may be understood as an exaggerated trend stemming from talent intermediaries and their clients' individual and collective business agendas.

'I don't need that on my resume': television (de)legitimacy, the single-director model and professional hierarchies

According to Violaine Roussel, packaging is about 'enticing others and engaging them in the process'.[22] 'What is at stake', Roussel argues, 'is "the value" of a package as the agent *anticipates it to appear* to production counterparts'.[23] In the first instance, then, Anonymous's executives, managers and producers needed to convince auteur-directors and movie stars to accept work on their television projects. Doing so was potentially no small feat, for Roussel tells us that despite improvements in television's reputation over the previous couple of decades, talent intermediaries continue to experience difficulties convincing clients who are used to working in film to take a job in television.[24] In terms of the indie-auteur, this involved not only overcoming perceptions that television work was inferior to feature film work, but also reassuring them that their brands could remain valuable in television, where indie held only limited currency and writers rather than directors had won the right to claim creative credit.[25] Anonymous's efforts to convince its indie-auteurs to migrate to television, therefore, helps to reveal how its promotion of its single-director model was directly tied to its clients and their collaborators' pursuits of professional legitimacy and efforts to retain auteur and star brands.

Several of Anonymous's indie-auteur directors who went on to helm one of its series expressed a reluctance about entering television in the first place. After announcing his ultimately short-lived retirement from feature filmmaking, for example, Soderbergh said that he turned down lucrative opportunities to direct pilot episodes because he did not want to take jobs away from directors who rely on television work for their livelihood, whom he called 'lifers'.[26] 'I don't need that on my resume', Soderbergh stated.[27] Soderbergh also said that he turned down opportunities to direct pilot episodes because he did not want to merely direct pilot episodes and attach his name as an executive producer without being involved in a show's longer-term development and production.[28] In a telling line that concluded the interview though, Soderbergh gestured to his future television work by saying, 'If it was something I originated, if it was something I came up with, that wouldn't exist if I didn't exist, that's different'.[29]

While portraying himself as being unwilling to sacrifice his professional integrity for profit, Soderbergh's comments were designed to retain the value of his brand by reminding audiences that his name meant something of value because it signified his authentic creative contribution to a project. Here, Soderbergh's comment recalled the Coen brothers' assertion that they resisted putting their names on products that they do not control. Simultaneously, Soderbergh was positioning himself as an elite director because he had a track record of success in film, rather than television. Hence, Golin sought to boost impressions of television as a space where auteur-directors could achieve visibility as he made the dubious claim that he 'only knew who [Alfred] Hitchcock was because he had a TV show'.[30] Golin's rhetoric elided the fact that Hitchcock was arguably able to achieve visibility in television because his role as a producer, rather than a director, of *Alfred Hitchcock Presents* (CBS, 1955–62) enabled him to leverage his auteur brand in the sector.[31] More specifically, Anonymous's single-series director model was designed to address the indie-auteurs' anxieties by creating an impression of their authentic and personal investment in the project. As Sugar put it, the single-director model was 'sexy for a film director' because it was 'very unusual' and 'a movie thing'.[32] Hence, although Soderbergh did not 'originate' *The Knick*, which was written by Amiel and Begler before Soderbergh was hired to direct, Anonymous's production model convinced Soderbergh to relax his own rules about directing television.[33]

Sugar's claim about the desirability of Anonymous's model appeared to be backed up by Batmanglij and Esmail. Batmanglij said that he and Marling converted their script for *The OA* into a series after struggling to get it made in film because they were impressed by Fukunaga's work on *True Detective*, which Batmanglij described as an '8-hour movie', and because television's longer format enabled them to build a more elaborate world.[34] Esmail claimed that, despite initially intending to make *Mr. Robot* as a feature film, he turned his script into a pilot episode after seeing how 'cinematic' *True Detective* looked.[35] According to Esmail, Fukunaga's role and *True Detective*'s 'cinematic' aesthetics encouraged him to consider moving to television because, he says, 'directing was [his] first and foremost goal'.[36] While some critics have perceived the migration of indie-auteurs to television to be a sign of their autonomy, Batmanglij's comment highlights that they often moved to television after experiencing difficulties getting feature films made. Such narratives need to be treated with caution, however, because they can be designed to boost the director's brand by creating an impression that they are artists-at-heart who struggle against commercial imperatives and trends instead of pursuing them. The tendency of auteur-directors to claim that their projects were initially conceived as movies may also be part of their legitimation by imbuing them with an aura of the cinematic from conception.

As Roussel explains, packaging involves creating belief in the quality of a project to aggregate clusters of talent.[37] Brown thus admitted that attaching a single director to shoot *True Detective*'s first season was a tactic used to attract movie stars Matthew McConaughey and Woody Harrelson.[38] Several of Anonymous's other productions with single-series and single-season directors had movie stars attached too. *The Knick* starred Clive Owen, *Maniac* starred Emma Stone and Jonah Hill, and *Homecoming*'s first season starred Julia Roberts and its second Janelle Monáe. On one hand, the tactic of attaching a single director offered feature film actors the consistency that they are used to in film, and, on the other, mobilised the auteur's brand to create an impression of the project's likely exceptional cinematic quality.[39] McConaughey, for example, said that he was a 'big fan' of Fukunaga's debut feature, *Sin Nombre* (2009), and that Fukunaga's involvement reassured him that he would be 'in the hands of a good storyteller'.[40] Referring to her work on *Homecoming*, Roberts stated that she 'chose to be working with Sam [Esmail] more than choosing to do TV' and said that in the last five years television had 'come into its stride'.[41] The important role that attaching a single director has played in enticing feature film actors to television productions was also articulated very clearly by Nicole Kidman in a conversation with Ewan McGregor for *Variety*. After both actors assert that more movie stars began migrating to television after McConaughey and Harrelson worked on *True Detective*, Kidman explained that she moved to television to work on *Big Little Lies*, with its full seasons helmed by Vallée and Arnold, because she is 'interested in auteurs ... interested in filmmakers'.[42]

In reality, it was not actually new for Hollywood talent to cross between film and television. Several of Anonymous's shows that featured so-called movie stars, such as the first season of *Mr. Robot* with Christian Slater, *I Am the Night* with Chris Pine and *The Last Days of Ptolemy Grey* with Samuel L. Jackson, also did not have single-series directors thereby highlighting the fact that a range of factors, not least the quality of the script, influence actors' decisions about which projects to take on. Yet these actors', directors' and producers' comments show how Anonymous's strategy of packaging productions by attaching a single-season or single-series director was intended to make their shows appear to be innovative manifestations of the auteurs' autonomous and cinematic visions. As Deborah Jaramillo explains, 'cinematic' is an 'inherently positive, even boastful word that many people rally around and ascribe to the best of the best on TV'.[43]

By seeking to retain and enhance their professional legitimacy and associations with feature film, these directors and actors contributed to cultural hierarchies that see film being elevated and most television denigrated. These cultural hierarchies are particularly problematic as they often involve implicitly and explicitly denigrating the work and tastes of most others. For instance, Sugar claimed that 'Some director doing a pilot has usually been about the money. Just do a job, do a pilot, you're in and out in two months'.[44] Sugar implied that most television directors work for money and are not really invested in the overall quality of a series. Soderbergh's comment about television's 'lifers' is more sympathetic to directors who need to make a living, but he still builds his brand off denigrating others by suggesting that most television directors are effectively stuck doing undesirable work of a kind that he does not need to accept. Just as Roberts claimed that television had 'come into its stride', so too Harrelson remarked that, because 'television is just so good now', he had been watching a lot of it and it made him more open-minded about working in the sector.⁴⁵ Yet Harrelson also implicitly distinguished between so-called cinematic television and its more traditional genres as he clarified that he 'obviously' did not mean that all of television was good now.⁴⁶ Premised on an assumption that they have the taste necessary for distinguishing good from bad, the auteur-directors, talent managers and star actors contributed to television legitimation discourses that elevated new indie-auteur work over more conventional programming. By aiming to position its clients as indie-auteurs who could improve television quality, then, Anonymous also positioned most television directors as directors-for-hire whose work was symptomatic of television's purported ills.

'The creative frontier': the single-director model in an era of convergence

To what extent is the migration of indie-auteurs to television during the 2010s and into the 2020s ideally suited to an era of media convergence? Anonymous's development of its productions in-house, its single-director model and the straight-to-series orders that it received created an impression that its shows were manifestations of the auteurs' visions that were unimpeded by the distributor-buyers. The model enhanced the directors' reputations as innovative auteurs who were determined to protect their autonomy and committed to quality and made the distributor-buyers appear to be exceptionally supportive benefactors who gave them the creative freedom to express themselves. For example, Batmanglij said that Netflix unequivocally supported his and Marling's 'unneutered' storytelling.⁴⁷ Fukunaga implied that HBO embraced his purportedly cinematic vision as he recalled asking HBO executives before production began on *True Detective* whether they wanted him to shoot it 'for television'.⁴⁸ Elaborating that he did not want to fight with the channel's executives on the shots he wanted, Fukunaga claimed that HBO executives ultimately told him to shoot it as he saw it.⁴⁹

Anonymous's packaging technique and the rhetoric surrounding its single-director shows also often involved promoting the productions as cinematic innovations enabled specifically by pay-TV models, including basic cable, premium cable and subscription streaming services. After announcing his so-called retirement from feature-filmmaking but before committing to making *The Knick*, Soderbergh praised Netflix's and HBO's subscription models by claiming that their 'guaranteed revenue streams' gave creatives with 'cool shit' significant autonomy and stated that streaming's departure from television's daily scheduling patterns meant that there were no longer any rules forcing creatives to work 'in a box'.[50] Batmanglij and Marling said that their purportedly 'unneutered' storytelling was enabled by Netflix's subscription model, which they stated gave them the freedom to make episodes of variable lengths due to its absence of commercials.[51] Marling thus claimed that Netflix was at the 'creative frontier' because it had been 'unfettered from marketing'.[52]

In some instances, the auteurs even portrayed the channel's or platform's rebranding initiatives as facilitating their own autonomy and innovation. Soderbergh and HBO executives claimed that it was the auteur who suggested that *The Knick* should air on HBO's sister-channel, Cinemax. Gesturing to his own interest in standing out within a crowded field, Soderbergh claimed that he said to Michael Lombardo, HBO's president of programming, 'This may sound a little weird, but I'd rather be the big kid at a really small school'.[53] Similarly, Esmail claimed that USA Networks' eagerness in the mid-2010s to overhaul the channel's brand gave him maximum autonomy. 'They're giving me as much control as I want on my show', Esmail stated, before adding that the broadcast networks would have 'tried to turn it into a procedural type of show'.[54]

On one hand, narratives surrounding indie-auteur single-director series and seasons has positioned them as being ideally suited to an era of pay-TV and streaming where audiences can enjoy the indie-auteurs' purportedly unique and individual visions in their entirety without commercial breaks and without having to wait for the next episode to air on linear television. Such comments elide the different models that streaming services have adopted, with some offering commercial spots as a means of revenue,[55] and contribute to a discourse that sees technological improvement in the form of cable television and then streaming services as offering indie-auteurs similar or greater levels of autonomy than they were used to getting in indie film. Writing in *Vulture*, for example, Adam Sternbergh collapsed distinctions between film studios and television platforms, and between different pay-TV businesses and models, as he commented that twenty-five years after *Sex, Lies, and Videotape* ushered in an indie film renaissance 'The same swashbuckling energy that gave rise to the indie film movement has migrated to TV programming online'.[56] 'Netflix is Miramax, Amazon is Fox Searchlight, and your laptop is the Sundance Festival – a clearinghouse for potential breakouts waiting to be discovered'.[57] Narratives about pay-TV and streaming offering auteurs greater autonomy to innovate, however, are highly problematic as they belittle audiences who continue to watch traditional television, including those who cannot afford pay-TV subscriptions.[58]

On the other hand, indie-auteur television has arguably been facilitated by the legacy media conglomerates' shifting priorities and investments across their businesses, as well as by the emergence of powerful streaming services such as Netflix and Amazon Instant Video. Notions about the indie-auteurs' unimpeded visions surrounding certain productions, however, risk boosting corporate agendas by obscuring industry horizontal and vertical forms of integration. Such narratives may, in turn, maintain unequal industrial relations that reinforce the precarious working conditions of most television labour and harm most independent producers.[59] In his 2013 study of the Federal Communications Commission's (FCC) reviews of media ownership during the 2000s, Josh Heuman found that the Writers Guild's 'economic' arguments, which emphasised objective issues of property ownership including copyright and profit participation, were more effective than its 'artistic' arguments, which invoked rhetorical and contestable notions of valuable artistic autonomous work against a devalued industrial heteronomy.[60] With the Guild calling for a mandate requiring the networks to reserve a quarter of their schedules for 'valuable independently produced programs', Heuman found that economic arguments drawing on the regulatory vocabulary of neoliberalism produced small incremental gains by framing workers as entrepreneurs or small businesses disadvantaged by unfair market conditions.[61] In contrast, the Guild's artistic arguments of independence often seemed 'suggestively congruent with aspirations for professional status' and obscured inequalities between labour.[62] They also risked reinforcing corporate agendas by presenting opportunities for the networks and their parent conglomerates to point to the value that they add to work in its distribution and promotion, as well as to examples of artworks produced in less regulated industrial contexts.[63] While Anonymous's talent management strategy may involve enhancing the marketability and remuneration of its clients by arousing the buying power of the channels and drumming up demand for auteur-directed productions, the fact that it is predicated on denigrating most television work and directors-for-hire, and favours the conglomerates by making them seem to be benefactors of autonomous labour, shows that the strategy is not about calling for improvements in television work in general. For Anonymous and its clients, therefore, indie-auteurism forms the basis of a transaction but it is hardly an instance of the 'economic' argument for independence endorsed by Heuman.

The auteurs' comments about their work and pay-TV models were, moreover, highly contentious and sometimes downright wrong. Soderbergh's claim that there are 'no rules' to subscription television ignored the many institutional and industrial models that pay-TV

130   THE TALENT MANAGEMENT OF INDIE AUTHORSHIP

channels and platforms use to inform their commissioning of shows and decisions about whether to keep them on the air, as their investment in productions associated with movie stars and indie-auteurs demonstrates. Such rhetoric also obfuscated the commercial realities around the channels' acquisitions and rebranding decisions. Contrary to Soderbergh's and Sugar's efforts to depict *The Knick*'s airing on Cinemax as symptomatic of the indie-auteurs' pioneering ethos, for example, HBO executives decided to air *The Knick* on Cinemax as part of a rebranding of the channel that was meant to position it as a home for high-end original programming to increase the value of HBO's offerings and reduce subscriber churn.[64] Similarly, USA Networks acquired *Mr. Robot* as part of a rebranding that saw the channel move away from its 'blue skies' programming comprising shows such as *Suits* (2011–19), *Burn Notice* (2007–13) and *Royal Pains* (2009–16), which focused on aspirational characters, including doctors and lawyers, took place in sunny idyllic settings, and had light-hearted and optimistic tones, and towards darker programming using the moniker 'We the Bold' (Figures 4.1 and 4.2). USA Networks did so because its

Figure 4.1 A season three poster for *Burn Notice*, part of USA's 'blue skies' programming. (Source: Photofest)

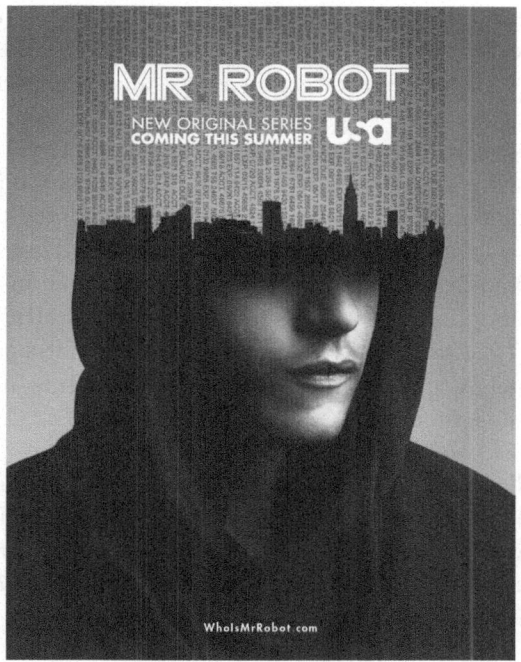

Figure 4.2 A *Mr. Robot* season one poster features a dark cityscape and displays the protagonist's introversion in what represents a break from USA's 'blue skies' programming. (Source: Photofest)

ratings among young and primetime audiences had begun to decline. These declines were particularly concerning for NBCUniversal as USA Networks made around one-third of the total advertising revenues generated by all the parent company's cable channels.[65]

Marling and Batmanglij's assertion that creatives were now 'unfettered from marketing' also ignored the fact that marketing has continued to play an important role in the operations of streaming services such as Netflix, not to mention Netflix's subsequent launch of a cheaper service with commercials.[66] Marling's claim about Netflix's absence of marketing merely adhered to the company's executives' own claims that Netflix does not have a brand as they try to stop the platform from being identified too closely with any one show.[67] In the case of *The OA*, Netflix adopted a deliberately minimal marketing campaign that involved posting very few and vague messages such as 'Have you seen death? Have you seen darkness? Have you seen the light?' on social media platforms leading up to its release. Instead of being evidence that Netflix had rejected marketing as Marling suggested, its minimal approach to promoting *The OA* was designed to create intrigue and build buzz online for its new show, and to differentiate the service from broadcasters which tend to be associated with broader campaigns targeting a mass audience over personalised approaches.[68]

For all the boasting about the innovation and quality of shows including *True Detective*, *The Knick*, *Mr. Robot* and *The OA*, the indie-auteur and single-director model also does not provide a guarantee that audiences will actually watch and stick with the shows. As Alisa Perren notes, many of the shows identified as examples of indie TV by the industry and critics 'proved to be disappointments to their distributors'.[69] HBO, for instance, did not renew *The Knick* for a third season because, Soderbergh confessed, the show did not successfully help to 'rebrand and draw new eyeballs to [Cinemax]' as was intended.[70] Netflix also cancelled *The OA* prematurely in 2019 after just two seasons.

The cancellation of indie-auteur shows, following especially the increasingly global focus of streaming services as they seek to distribute shows by exploiting intellectual properties that are highly marketable for luring mass audiences, such as *The Lord of the Rings: The Rings of Power* (Amazon, 2022–), *House of the Dragon* (HBO Max, 2022–), *The Sandman* (Netflix, 2022–), and *The Continental* (Peacock, 2023), thus suggests that television in an era of convergence may not be ideally suited to the indie-auteur after all. Such cancellations undermine notions that pay-TV services offer unequivocal support to auteur creators. Responding to Netflix's cancellation of *The OA*, Marling unsurprisingly reversed her stance on the prospects of storytelling in the contemporary era of streaming. She posted on Instagram that the show's 'unexpected cancellation begs larger questions about the role of storytelling and its fate inside late capitalism's push toward consolidation and economies of scale'.[71] Although presented as a critique of media under neoliberalism, however, Marling can be understood as having been attempting to recuperate her and Batmanglij's reputations as indie-auteurs purportedly opposed to corporate media. In doing so, Marling's rhetorical manoeuvring points to how indie-auteur brands are sustained as a point of distinction while confirming how the mobilisation of those brands to promote pay-TV series obscures the consolidation to which indie-auteurs are supposed to be opposed in the first place.

'I should be working on my own vision': *True Detective*, *Mr. Robot* and brand building

Anonymous and its clients' rhetorical manoeuvring was highly contradictory. Anonymous's productions, including *The Knick*, *True Detective*,

Mr. Robot, *Maniac*, *Homecoming* and *The OA*, were television shows and no amount of posturing about the supposedly cinematic visions of the auteur-directors could change that fact. Although Anonymous's executives portrayed their television productions involving single-series and single-season directors as an improvement, Anonymous has made many series, such as *13 Reasons Why* (Netflix, 2017–20), *The Alienist* (TNT, 2018–20) and *Berlin Station* (Epix, 2016–19), with multiple directors in a manner that is more typical of most drama production. Moreover, after Fukunaga helmed season one of *True Detective*, nine different directors shared directing responsibilities on its second and third seasons. Conversely, seven directors shared directing responsibilities on *Mr. Robot*'s first season before Esmail secured total directing responsibilities from season two onwards. *Mr Robot*'s pilot episode was directed by Niels Arden Oplev, the director of *The Girl with the Dragon Tattoo* (2009), despite Esmail's claims that USA let him be 'as creative as he wanted to be on his show', and Christian Slater, who played the eponymous character, crediting Esmail with making it cinematic following the pilot's screening at South by Southwest Festival.[72]

While all of these examples point to the hypocrisy in Anonymous's rhetoric and strategy, which hinges on elevating its single-director series and seasons above shows with directors-for-hire, *True Detective* and *Mr. Robot* provide particularly useful case studies for exploring dynamics between professional legitimacy and auteur branding. Indeed, changes in the directing responsibilities of *True Detective* and *Mr. Robot* demonstrate clearly that Anonymous's single-director model was not just about improving the quality of the series or advancing the directors' craft, as the talent managers, producers and clients implied, but was also about building the clients' auteur brands. They show how Anonymous's efforts to build its clients' brands in television has also had implications for the writer-producer showrunners who have usually been positioned as television's authorial figures. Moreover, *Mr. Robot* and Esmail's own production activities demonstrate how Anonymous's expansion to television has diversified Anonymous's business and contributed to further mutations in television authorship.

Changes in the directing responsibilities of *True Detective* from its first to second seasons were partly a consequence of a struggle over creative credit. The production of the show's first season was reportedly marred by creative conflict between Fukunaga and Pizzolatto, who gained a reputation for unrelentingly enforcing his ideas about the project and being unwilling to compromise.[73] Pizzolatto's unwillingness to compromise came across clearly when he explained why he left the writing team on

The Killing (AMC, 2011–13; Netflix, 2014) before making *True Detective*. Pizzolatto stated, 'I thought I could do it better ... I thought I should be working on my own vision. I want to be the guiding vision. I don't do well serving someone else's vision'.[74] As well as indicating Pizzolatto's inability to collaborate effectively, his repeated emphasis on his individual vision shows how he strived to position himself as *True Detective*'s solitary author. Pizzolatto simultaneously situated his work within a broader context that, he suggested, saw television drama supplant indie film in terms of quality and prestige. Pizzolatto stated that he aspired to break into the cable-television business because the 'writer stays in control' and that artists from the independent film movement were increasingly migrating to the sector because, for the previous ten years, 'American television [had] beaten out American movies in terms of overall intelligence and depth'.[75]

Pizzolatto thus sought to advance his reputation by situating his work within a field of production that many cultural commentators deemed to be on the ascendency, and over which television's writers had won the battle with directors to claim creative credit.[76] Although Fukunaga had progressed from making his low-budget feature debut *Sin Nombre* to shooting the mid-budget specialty film *Jane Eyre* (2011) for Focus Features, he had not yet received the level of critical acclaim that he would for shooting *True Detective*'s first season. With Pizzolatto implicitly attributing television's purportedly increased intelligence and depth to the writer's vision, he would undoubtedly have been irked therefore by reviewers' repeated claims that *True Detective*'s quality stemmed from Fukunaga's 'cinematic' vision.[77] Pizzolatto's efforts to establish himself as *True Detective*'s solitary author was also undermined when Fukunaga's reputation was bolstered after critics commented that the auteur-director's departure led to a decline in quality in its second series.[78] Even HBO's Lombardo confessed that the second season was one of the channel's 'biggest failures'.[79] Meanwhile, and as I discuss more in the next chapter, Netflix was promoting the acquisition of its first original feature film for its streaming service, Fukunaga's *Beasts of No Nation*, by releasing a trailer that described Fukunaga as the 'award winning director of *True Detective*'.

The critical discourse crediting Fukunaga with the show's quality was simplistic, particularly in light of Fukunaga's own assertions that the partnership between him and Pizzolatto was imbalanced and became increasingly so as Lombardo granted more power to Pizzolatto in post-production.[80] Yet reports of conflict between Fukunaga and Pizzolatto indicate how Anonymous's model of production can exacerbate old tensions between different above-the-line talent constituencies that compete for creative credit.[81] Praise for Fukunaga was undoubtedly symptomatic of

Anonymous's single-director model, which was designed to generate value around the productions by inflating impressions of the auteur-director's role. At the same time, *True Detective* demonstrated clearly how struggles for creative credit are often predicated on the denigration of the victor's more anonymous collaborators. While Pizzolatto strived to differentiate himself from his colleagues in the writer's room, Fukunaga was elevated above directors-for-hire to whom *True Detective*'s second season's perceived failings were implicitly and explicitly attributed.[82] Fukunaga subsequently strived to reassert his association with film and distance himself from too close an association with television during the promotion of *Beasts of No Nation*.[83] That Fukunaga did so provides a reminder that his brand was built around notions of his innovative cinematic vision, and his reputation boosted by notions that he enhanced the quality of *True Detective*, rather than an association with television in general.

While Fukunaga had established himself as a feature film director before shooting *True Detective*, Esmail had only shot one short film and a very low budget feature named *Comet* (2014), which was produced by Anonymous and Esmail's manager Chad Hamilton, before he created *Mr. Robot*. In fact, Esmail was better known in Hollywood as a screenwriter because, in addition to *Comet*, he wrote two screenplays that *The Black List* ranked among the best unmade screenplays of their respective years as well as several scripts that he wrote as a freelancer.[84] As a result, Esmail directed only three episodes of *Mr. Robot*'s first season and did not direct its pilot, traditionally a very important episode for establishing the look and tone of a series, despite Anonymous making a practice of installing its clients as directors and Esmail insisting that directing was his 'first and foremost goal'.[85] Moreover, Esmail says that he had already grown frustrated that producers would not let him direct his own scripts and made *Comet* to announce to the industry 'I'm a director, you can't say I can't direct anymore'.[86]

After *Mr. Robot*'s breakout first season was championed by critics as an 'Edgy, auteur-driven dark tale' and a 'daring risk' for a channel with a reputation for 'churning out' blue skies programming,[87] Esmail successfully negotiated to take on full directing responsibilities. In doing so, Esmail paid tribute to the 'great work' that the other season one directors had contributed.[88] Yet he said that by taking on full directing responsibilities he could make the production more efficient because he could shoot many scenes that take place across the season at the same location at once and asserted that he was very specific about the show's 'visual grammar'.[89] Elaborating on the purported efficiency of his approach Esmail stated, 'I'm not here to say that I want to change the TV industry ... [but] For shows that are hyper-serialized, it just seems to make more sense to follow a feature film model than follow a television model, which was set up more for a procedural type of show'.⁹⁰ While Pizzolatto drew clear distinctions between himself and his collaborators, and between the quality of contemporary film and television, Esmail took a more balanced and amicable approach that was less likely to offend his former collaborators or personnel working in one sector of the American media industries more generally. Esmail's comments were, however, an example of rhetorical manoeuvring that saw him still seeking to install himself as the show's solitary artist, differentiate *Mr. Robot* from traditional television, and position himself implicitly as an innovator.

Around the same time that USA renewed *Mr. Robot* for a second season, Esmail struck a long-term production deal with USA's sister company Universal Cable Productions (UCP)⁹¹ under his production banner Esmail Corp., which he cofounded with Hamilton. The deal was renewed in 2019 for $20 million to $25 million per year, which was reportedly UCP's most lucrative co-production deal ever and struck following competition from Amazon Studios for Esmail's services.⁹² Retaining Esmail was deemed to be particularly important for NBCUniversal as it was preparing to launch its own streaming service, Peacock, for which it needed content.⁹³ Under the deal, Esmail Corp., UCP and Anonymous have gone on to co-produce *Homecoming*, *Briarpatch* (USA Network, 2019–20), *Angelyne* (Peacock, 2022), and *The Resort* (Peacock, 2022–), and Esmail Corp. and UCP have produced *Gaslit* (Starz, 2022). In addition, Esmail took on the responsibility of overseeing the production of *Mr. Robot*'s transmedia extensions, including a mobile app and game, a virtual-reality experience, a book and a collection of comics. In doing so, Esmail has asserted that he continues to be committed to art over commerce by claiming to have insisted that all these extensions be created to add to the story rather than to serve as promotional vehicles for the show.⁹⁴ As a result, Esmail took on the role of being a 'brand manager' overseeing an array of products related to a single series as well as that of a 'mega-producer'.⁹⁵

According to Leora Hadas, the mega-producer is another rung on the authorship ladder, one that functions as a kind of brand ambassador authenticating and giving cohesion to multiple shows that are run on a day-to-day basis by different individual showrunners who sometimes lack the necessary brand names to market them on their own.⁹⁶ While Esmail wanted to become an auteur-director, therefore, he has become an auteur at a much larger scale, has done so chiefly in television, and contributed significantly to Anonymous's growing list of television productions. While Anonymous's strategy for expanding into television relied on boosting the currency of its auteur-directors' brands in television, the breadth of

Esmail's roles demonstrates that it also contributed to ongoing mutations in television authorship. Given the level of critical acclaim that Esmail has received, these mutations are potentially problematic as they may normalise expectations in a neoliberal economy that talent deserving of recognition, opportunities and reward should take on ever more roles.[97]

According to Hadas, the mega-producer is also a 'form of authorship suitable to an industry that thinks in terms of conglomeration, horizontal integration, and large-scale exploitation of assets' such as expensive franchises and intellectual properties.[98] In a context of consolidation and unequal labour conditions brought about by neoliberal policy, it is particularly concerning that Esmail's brand and the increases in his roles have been regularly framed in promotional, extratextual and critical discourse through reference to his purported independence and his loose associations with independent film. Reporting on Esmail becoming the director for *Mr. Robot*'s second season, *Variety* commented that 'Esmail comes from the world of independent film ... and he's approaching "Robot" with that mindset'.[99] Likewise, when Esmail Corp. and UCP struck their production deal, UCP's chief operating officer, Jeff Wachtel, commented that 'We put our faith in artists with a very independent vision ... We invest them with the authority to make the shows they want to make'.[100] Esmail, meanwhile, has sought to continuously reaffirm and even overstate his links to independent or indie film. He has described *Mr. Robot*'s shoot as like being on an 'indie film set', has repeatedly articulated an affinity with 1990s independent filmmakers, and described *Comet*, which is his only indie feature, as his 'first indie feature'.[101]

Given Esmail's increasing associations with television and distance from indie film production, he tests the limits of indie-auteurism as a discourse and branded identity. While Perren has argued that 'indie TV' has diminished as a discourse after 2017 as terms such as 'prestige', 'quality' and 'cinematic' television retained greater currency,[102] the case of Esmail points to how indie-auteurism continues to be mobilised paradoxically to frame overarching film and production deals in an era of convergence. Likewise, when Soderbergh signed an overarching deal with WarnerMedia to create feature films and television series for its then-recently launched streaming service, HBO Max,[103] in 2020, the *Hollywood Reporter* announced that 'The indie pioneer [had] signed a sweeping overall deal with the media giant' while HBO executives called him an 'indefatigable innovator' and 'groundbreaking filmmaker'.[104] Given Esmail's lucrative co-production deal with Universal and Soderbergh's with WarnerMedia, it is highly questionable how equipped they are to challenge consolidation in the media industries and fight for the rights of most of its workers.

Instead, it is more likely that their indie-auteur brands obscure the interdependency and consolidation that continues to disadvantage most of the industries' workers.

An 'arranged marriage': Steven Soderbergh, Amy Seimetz and cinematic television's gender dynamics

While Anonymous's independent feature packaging technique was predicated on elevating the work of the company's indie-auteur clients above that of most television directors, it also reinforced problematic gender dynamics between men and women. Though women occupy a disproportionately small number of directing positions across American film and television,[105] women directors also more often come to rely on television work for their livelihood after struggling to receive the same opportunities to continue making films as their male counterparts.[106] Linda Badley, Claire Perkins and Michele Schreiber conceptualise women's indie film as being marked by an 'in-betweenness' because their work is rarely ironic, popular or political enough to be easily absorbed into, and marketed using, pre-existing categories.[107] As a result, they argue, women directors have more often struggled to achieve visibility within the indie film marketplace.[108]

Jessica Ford builds on Badley, Perkins and Schreiber's conceptualisation of women's indie as an in-between space to argue that the evaluative criteria of television that privileges work perceived as cinematic undervalues and obscures women's work, including a recent cycle that Ford calls 'women's indie television'.[109] While notions of cinematic television tend to revolve around 'male-centric series that draw on hi-fi film aesthetics and style' and tend to be big in scale and scope, Ford argues that women's indie television, which includes shows such as *Girls* (HBO, 2012–17), *Insecure* (HBO, 2016–21), *One Mississippi* (Amazon, 2015–17) and *Better Things* (FX Network, 2016–22), mostly takes place in domestic settings, focuses on the everyday and mundane, adopts low-key production techniques, and flattens or dampens emotional spectacle.[110] Similarly, Newman and Levine point out that an even more denigrated form, the soap opera, is rarely referred to positively in discourses of legitimation.[111] This is, they argue, a very significant omission 'given the centrality of serialization to historical conceptions of feminized popular culture, and the centrality of feminized qualities in the constructions of pre-convergence television as mass culture'.[112]

Anonymous's executives, producers and managers have thus contributed to the underemployment of female directors in the American television industry by attaching only men as single-series and single-season directors on its productions. Anonymous's efforts to build its clients' reputations and differentiate several of its shows by emphasising the roles of these directors also disproportionately denigrates women directors who Sugar and Soderbergh framed as directors-for-hire or 'lifers' stuck 'just doing a job'. Moreover, Anonymous's strategy of promoting its shows as innovations drew from an old-fashioned masculinised discourse that sees innovation in indie production as stemming from the male maverick or renegade outsider.[113] This discourse is reinforced by Anonymous's packaging technique as its executives and clients claimed that the single-season director must have extraordinary stamina to create these apparently innovative eight-hour or twelve-hour movies. Sugar, for example, commented that Fukunaga's and Soderbergh's directing of the entirety of the first seasons of *True Detective* and *The Knick* 'like a movie' was 'horribly exhausting' for his clients and required them to have exceptional energy.[114] Batmanglij depicted making these 'eight-hour movies' as similarly exhausting when, recalling the steps that he took before committing to direct *The OA*'s first season, he explains that he asked Fukunaga what it was like directing all eight episodes of *True Detective*'s first season and said that Fukunaga responded, he 'couldn't have done 9'.[115] By implicitly connecting the single-director model of production to strength, stamina and masculinised conceptions of the maverick ethos, Anonymous's executives and clients simultaneously risk excluding female directors by presupposing that they are incapable of shooting television in this purportedly more innovative way. The number of women directing full seasons of these American television dramas is thus disproportionately low.

In the absence of a show produced by Anonymous with a woman as the single-season director,[116] this chapter's final section turns to the first season of *The Girlfriend Experience*, which was a show that Soderbergh executive produced and packaged. Adjusting the production strategy that was being used by his management company, Soderbergh packaged *Girlfriend* by hiring Seimetz and Kerrigan to co-write and co-direct in what he described as 'a sort of independent auteur director-driven approach'.[117] On one hand, Soderbergh's decision to hire Kerrigan and Seimetz could be understood as an example of his efforts to champion indie filmmakers who often fail to receive the recognition that he believes they deserve.[118] After Soderbergh briefly quit film in 2013, for instance, he advocated for a film industry that empowers filmmakers by asserting that if he was the head of a Hollywood studio he would 'call Shane Carruth or Barry Jenkins or Amy Seimetz and ... bring them in and go, ok, what do you want to do?'[119] On the other hand, Soderbergh's independent auteur approach positioned Seimetz *in between* two men in a patriarchal arrangement that Soderbergh tellingly described as an 'arranged marriage'.[120] Such dynamics are evident elsewhere in television in the work of female indie-auteur figures such as Pamela Adlon and Lena Dunham who have also relied on male 'allies' in the form of producers Louis C.K. and Judd Apatow.[121] Soderbergh's analogy becomes particularly problematic, however, given that, as Wexman points out, 'The conventions of credit attribution have played a significant role in marginalizing women, who have historically been socialized to relinquish their names at marriage and to act as unsung helpmates to men'.[122]

Commenting on this so-called 'arranged marriage', Seimetz said that making *Girlfriend* was like a 'social experiment' because, she explained, she had never before 'wanted to have to bend [her] vision or compromise or collaborate with somebody and write something together'.[123] Seimetz's admission about her reluctance to compromise or collaborate on her vision contradicts findings by some scholars that an emphasis on collaboration tends to be a more prominent feature of the discourse around women's film and television practice.[124] While collaboration should be celebrated, Seimetz's comment indicated that she was being expected to compromise in a manner that was not the case for her male counterparts on Anonymous's single-director series and seasons. Indeed, it is telling that Seimetz and Kerrigan divided duties more distinctly for *Girlfriend*'s second season as each one wrote and directed a separate story with episodes for each airing back-to-back. The idea of *Girlfriend*'s production as 'an arranged marriage' also indicated that Seimetz and Kerrigan were ultimately subservient to Soderbergh, who was positioned as a paternal authority figure. Hence, *Girlfriend* helped Soderbergh to continue to build his reputation as an elite director, 'indie-pioneer' and creative-entrepreneur, and was a step for him in becoming a mega-producer through his overarching deal with WarnerMedia.[125] In contrast, Seimetz's brand was mobilised to promote *Girlfriend* as innovative and deflect scrutiny of its sexually explicit representations.

A loose adaptation of the 2009 feature film of the same name that Soderbergh directed, *Girlfriend* is an anthology series that broadly focuses on the lives of high-end escorts. Season one focused on Christine Reade (Riley Keough), a talented law student who secures a prestigious internship at a law firm before beginning to work as an escort. The series cuts between Christine's legal and illicit activities and adopts conventions associated with the thriller genre as she is deceived and robbed, is threatened with exposure and discovers corruption in the law firm. After Christine is fired from the firm because an infatuated but jettisoned client exposes her escorting, Christine uses secret recordings that she makes of interactions with colleagues, including sexually explicit footage revealing her affair with her boss, to successfully sue the firm for $1 million on the grounds of creating a hostile working environment and enabling sexual harassment. By interweaving Christine's story with a conspiracy narrative and thriller conventions, *Girlfriend* adheres to the masculinised tradition of cinematic television that tends to be big in scope and scale rather than women's indie television.

Girlfriend also conforms to the masculinised tradition of cinematic television in terms of its mise-en-scène and aesthetics. The first season, for example, is predominantly set in office buildings, hotel rooms and upmarket restaurants where white, grey and beige feature heavily, has many long-shots of character interactions often with the camera set up in adjoining rooms, has very bright lighting to reduce shadows and contrasting colours, and regularly includes continuous ambient sound coming from the whirring, buzzing and beeping of air-conditioning systems, lift and electronic doors, and office communication devices. Conversely, close-ups on characters' faces foregrounding their emotions are rare and tend to be reserved to show Christine's distress or discomfort during her most unpleasant and fraught sexual encounters. In this way, the first season has a cold clinical aesthetic that creates an impression that it is offering a commentary on prostitution and power, restricts the pleasure that it may offer from its eroticism, and limits it from being read as purely voyeuristic. Its mise-en-scène also stands in direct contrast to women's indie film and television, which usually takes place in domestic settings and employs low-key styles emphasising everyday emotion over spectacle.[126]

With *Girlfriend* tending to explore the power dynamics between Christine and her male clients and boss, Seimetz's authorship and gender was made to be an important part of its promotion and critical reception. Starz's season one trailers and posters described *Girlfriend* as being 'From Executive Producer Steven Soderbergh' but did not mention Seimetz and Kerrigan, which reflected and reinforced the professional and authorial hierarchy that existed between the three of them (Figure 4.3). Soderbergh's decision to pair Seimetz with Kerrigan also supported an impression that the series was complex and did not adhere exclusively to a male or female perspective. In an interview with *W Magazine*, for example, Seimetz claimed that having two directors created an ambivalence to issues such as prostitution that made audiences uncomfortable.[127] While Jason Mittell argues that new and more 'complex' forms of television in the twenty-first century can be best understood through an analysis of television itself 'rather than holding onto cross-media metaphors

Figure 4.3 'It's personal': *The Girlfriend Experience*'s season one poster. (Source: Reproduced by kind permission of Canyon Design)

of aspiration and legitimation',[128] however, Seimetz described *Girlfriend* as more alike 'the best sort of cinema', which, she asserted, 'leaves you talking or thinking about it afterwards'.[129] In turn, Seimetz differentiated *Girlfriend* from traditional television, which she implied closes down space for critical thought, 'because in TV, although it's getting more and more interesting, you're still so used to the program telling you how to feel'.[130]

Consequently, critics including the *W* interviewer Fan Zhong suggested that Seimetz's role as the show's co-writer and co-director gave it an authentic feminist perspective that justified its representations.[131] Seimetz's role as co-writer and co-director was problematic in these terms because it contributed to reinforcing inaccurate postfeminist notions that women have achieved parity in American society. These notions ignore evidence of continuing gender inequalities just as they ignore Seimetz's subservience to Soderbergh and the lower value given to her brand in marketing. At the same time, Soderbergh's 'independent auteur-director' approach, Seimetz's comments, and critics' responses, reinforced the evaluative criteria that privileges masculinised cinematic modes of television and legitimation discourses that denigrate television forms associated with women creators and audiences, including not only 'women's indie television' but also the soap opera.[132]

Conclusion

Having explored Anonymous Content's expansion to television during the 2010s, this chapter has demonstrated that the company influenced television production by developing a single-series director model for dramas and prompting the migration of many indie-auteurs to the sector. Rather than bringing about improvements in television production, however, the chapter has shown that the single-director model and indie-auteurs' migration was symptomatic of and reinforced broader legitimation discourses elevating authored cinematic premium programming over mass media. Moreover, the chapter has contested notions about the innovativeness of Anonymous and its clients' operations and work as it has revealed that they ingratiated themselves to distributors by offering them a form of distinction to market their subscription services and sometimes did so unsuccessfully as their shows were sometimes cancelled prematurely.

Having drawn on Heuman's investigation into the relationship between industrial authorship and different conceptions of independence, the chapter has also demonstrated that Anonymous's mobilisation of indie-auteurism in television and its clients' efforts to retain their professional legitimacy serves powerful distributors' corporate interests and risks maintaining harmful labour conditions. As Anonymous's talent management strategies are predicated on elevating those figures that it brands as indie-auteurs above so-called directors-for-hire, the company contributes to sustaining unequal labour relations based on simplistic distinctions that offer a limited pool of practitioners a disproportionate level of reward. With Anonymous having failed to install a single woman as a single-series or single-season director of one of its own shows, Anonymous's model also disproportionately disadvantages women directors who have more often come to rely on television work for their livelihood after failing to receive equal opportunities in film.

Notes

1. Sternbergh (2014); Greenwald (2014); L.S. Miller (2015).
2. Mittell (2015) pp. 89–90.
3. Timothy Havens writes that:

    television tends to be corporately planned and authored far more than other media products, including films, music, and games, which are sometimes developed and produced with less direct involvement of corporate executives. But there is really no such thing as 'independent' or 'alternative' television, and there are very few instances of motivated, creative individuals producing 'surprise hits' outside of dominant, corporate structures, as there are in other industries. (Havens (2014) p. 41)

4. Newman and Levine (2012) p. 3.
5. During the period discussed in this chapter, WarnerMedia changed its name from Time Warner after AT&T acquired the company in 2018.
6. Littleton (2015a).
7. See also Stubbs (2020) p. 137.
8. Littleton (2015a).
9. Burnside (2015).
10. Thompson (2015).
11. McMurria (2007) p. 47.
12. Newman and Levine (2012) pp. 4, 42; Pearson (2011); Jancovich and Lyons (2003); Caldwell (1995) p. 105.
13. McCabe (2013) pp. 186–7; see also Santo (2008) pp. 20–1.
14. See: Akass (2015) pp. 744–6; Newman and Levine (2012) pp. 32–3; Santo (2008) pp. 38–9; Jenner (2016) pp. 261–3; Tryon (2015).
15. McCabe (2013) p. 189; Jenner (2016) p. 264; Newman and Levine (2012) pp. 61–72.
16. McCracken (2016).
17. *When They See Us* is arguably the most explicitly political of the indie-auteur directed shows, while others including *The Girlfriend Experience*, *Too Old to Die Young* and *The Underground Railroad* contain some elements of political critique too.
18. Rohter (1990).
19. Ibid.
20. As Newman and Levine (2012, pp. 26–9) explain, *Twin Peaks* anticipated convergence-era discourses of legitimation in part because Lynch's reputation for creating strange, violent and erotic thrillers differentiated it from corporate network television.
21. Thompson (2015).
22. Roussel (2017) p. 147.
23. Ibid. p. 148, original emphasis.
24. Ibid. p. 134.
25. Wexman (2020) pp. 38–60.
26. Smith (2013).
27. Ibid.
28. Ibid.
29. Ibid.
30. Jurgensen (2016b).
31. Schatz (2009) p. 524.
32. Thompson (2015).
33. In their book, *Seeing It on Television: Televisuality in the Contemporary US 'High-End' Series*, Max Sexton and Dominic Lees (2021, p. 59) wrongly

state that Soderbergh was responsible for hiring the writers of *The Knick* and do not mention Anonymous Content, which is indicative of the success of Anonymous's packaging technique, designed as it was to attribute authorship to Soderbergh, and of how the roles played by talent management companies have gone unacknowledged in most scholarly work.

34. American Film Institute (2019).
35. Swisher (2019).
36. Ibid.
37. Roussel (2017) p. 5.
38. Helmore (2014); Blake (2014).
39. Rizzo (2014); Idato (2014); Birnbaum (2017).
40. Idato (2014); Stern (2014).
41. Levy (2018).
42. Birnbaum (2017).
43. Jaramillo (2013) p. 67.
44. Thompson (2015).
45. Idato (2014).
46. Ibid.
47. SAG-AFTRA Foundation (2017).
48. James (2015).
49. Ibid.
50. Smith (2013).
51. Onstad (2017).
52. Ibid.
53. Ayers (2014); Ng (2014).
54. Pallotta (2016); Bauder (2015).
55. On different streaming models, see Johnson (2018); Lotz, Lobato and Thomas (2018).
56. Sternbergh (2014).
57. Ibid.
58. McMurria (2007) p. 58; Newman and Levine (2012) pp. 129–33.
59. Hesmondhalgh (2013) p. 203; Lotz (2007) p. 82.
60. Heuman (2013) pp. 131–3.
61. Ibid. pp. 120, 138.
62. Ibid. pp. 122, 131.
63. Ibid. pp. 131–4.
64. Anon (2014).
65. Villarreal (2014); Baysinger (2015).
66. Forristal (2022).
67. Havens and Stoldt (2023) p. 202.
68. Ibid. p.202.
69. Perren (2023) p. 72.
70. Sepinwall (2021).
71. Aurthur (2019).

72. Eyerly (2015).
73. Clarke (2021); Collin (2015).
74. Walker (2013).
75. Ibid.
76. Wexman (2020) pp. 46–53.
77. Hiltbrand (2014); Wollaston (2014); Harvey (2014).
78. Shepherd (2016); Rosenberg (2015).
79. Shepherd (2016).
80. Sharf (2021).
81. Wexman (2020) pp. 52–3.
82. Markowitz (2015).
83. Anon (2015a).
84. Swisher (2019).
85. Ibid.
86. Ibid.
87. Lowry (2015); Randee (2015).
88. Birnbaum (2016).
89. Ibid.
90. Ibid.
91. Universal Cable Productions has since been renamed as Universal Content Productions.
92. Andreeva (2019).
93. Ibid.
94. Film Independent (2016); Swisher (2019).
95. On the auteur as brand manager, see Newman and Levine (2012) p. 54; on 'mega-producers' see Hadas (2020) pp. 92–9.
96. Hadas (2020) p. 96
97. See also Graham and Gandini (2017).
98. Hadas (2020) p. 117.
99. Birnbaum (2016).
100. Malone (2016).
101. Swisher (2019); Littleton (2016); Ryan and Greenwald (2017).
102. Perren (2023).
103. WarnerMedia has subsequently renamed HBO Max to Max to retain HBO's 'quality' associations. Max distributes more mainstream genre productions of a kind that the cable channel, HBO, tended not to be associated with and often defined itself against.
104. Goldberg (2020).
105. Hunt and Ramón (2022) p. 3; Ramón, Tran and Hunt (2022) p. 4.
106. Lane (2016) p. 71; Schreiber (2013) p. 88.
107. Badley, Perkins and Schreiber (2016b).
108. Ibid.
109. Ford (2019); see also Ford (2018).
110. Ford (2019) pp. 932–4; see also Ford (2018) p. 18.

111. Newman and Levine (2012) p. 81.
112. Ibid. p. 81.
113. McHugh (2016) p. 142; Perkins (2016) p. 140.
114. Thompson (2015).
115. American Film Institute (2019).
116. At the time of writing, *True Detective: Night Country*, written and directed by Issa López remained in production. With two women, Jodie Foster and Kali Reis, also cast in the lead roles, the show is arguably symptomatic of a change in Anonymous's hiring decisions following Emerson's takeover.
117. Pierce (2016).
118. Gallagher (2013) p. 218.
119. Brody (2013).
120. Jurgensen (2016a); Hale (2016).
121. Nygaard and Lagerwey (2020) p. 151.
122. Wexman (2020) p. 71.
123. Hale (2016).
124. Badley, Perkins and Schreiber (2016b) p. 3.
125. Goldberg (2020).
126. Ford (2018) p. 18.
127. Zhong (2016).
128. Mittell (2015) p. 2.
129. Zhong (2016).
130. Ibid.
131. Zhong (2016); Seitz (2016).
132. Ford (2019) pp. 928–3; Newman and Levine (2012) pp. 80–2.

CHAPTER 5

Navigating Specialty Film's Decline and Disruption

Specialty Film, Studio Blockbusters and the Maverick Male Myth

During the 2010s, many cultural commentators described Hollywood specialty and indie film as going through a period of crisis and decline marked especially by several studios' moves to close, sell and restructure their specialty divisions, including Warner Independent, Paramount Vantage, Miramax and Focus Features.[1] Tino Balio explains that a downturn in Hollywood specialty filmmaking began partly as a consequence of the 2008 financial crash as studios began finding it more difficult to secure capital after Wall Street became more stringent in its borrowing.[2] At the same time, Balio explains that the emergence of video-on-demand led to a decline in the sales of DVDs and Blu-Rays, which were a major source of income for specialty films.[3] In the face of these challenges, the studios focused increasingly on financing and distributing 'event' pictures, including comic-book franchises and family films.[4] Where the studios remained involved with specialty film, Balio notes that they cut costs and spread risk by partnering increasingly with semi-independent production companies like New Regency, a company that was 20 per cent owned by 21st Century Fox.[5] Some trade press reporters also pointed to the growth of premium scripted television as a reason for declines in specialty film production.[6] These reporters argued that the specialty market shrank because its traditional adult audience was spending more time watching high-end cable series such as Anonymous's *True Detective*.[7]

These developments in the specialty film sector potentially impacted upon talent and their representatives in two main ways. First, by financing and producing fewer indie or specialty films, the studios created a buyer's market for talent that reduced their employment opportunities and diminished the positions held by their representatives in negotiations over fees and residuals such as profit participation.[8] Second, by becoming more reluctant to finance and distribute specialty films, studios limited the capital and resources that talent needed to make their projects and reduced the fees that they offered for acquisitions.[9] These circumstances risked being particularly acute for an integrated talent management and media production company such as Anonymous. Apparently confirming this difficult period, Golin said in an article pertinently titled 'No Country for Gold Men' that gestured towards the decline of the indiewood period that 'The movie business just sucks, especially for dramas'.[10] 'There's lots of downward pressure on budgets and producers' fees', Golin stated, before adding that the high risks and low rewards made producing specialty films 'a pretty scary way to make a buck'.[11]

While the 2010s saw a decline in studio specialty filmmaking, however, the decade also saw new opportunities emerge. The growth in premium television production, for instance, was partly created by the parent conglomerates' shifting investment priorities and indicates that there was hardly a decline in the overall production of so-called serious adult-orientated screen media fare. The 2010s also saw the growth of streaming services, including Netflix, Amazon Instant Video and Apple TV+, which expanded not only into television but also into the production and distribution of original feature film. At first at least, these streaming services seemed to concentrate on acquiring and financing lower-budgeted indie and specialty films such as *Beasts of No Nation, Manchester by the Sea, The Fundamentals of Caring* and *Tallullah* (Heder, 2016), doing so to appeal to passionate niche audiences who could afford to subscribe and would help to promote the services by spreading word-of-mouth.[12] Sarah Sinwell argues that streaming services have helped to widen indie films' exposure even if the significant role of major tech companies in the space brought indie production further into the realms of corporate interests and dampened hopes that online technologies might bring about a return to a more authentic independent filmmaking.[13]

This chapter thus explores how Anonymous and its auteur-director clients navigated these changing conditions in the 2010s. The first section explores Anonymous's response to these changing conditions in general and scrutinises the narratives that the company's executives crafted about the specialty film sector and its relationships to Hollywood's blockbuster filmmaking. The next two sections then focus in on two specialty feature films made by two of Anonymous's clients in reportedly very challenging industrial and production conditions. The second section in this chapter analyses specifically *The Revenant*, which was co-produced by Anonymous and New Regency and co-written and directed by client Alejandro G. Iñárritu for the Hollywood studio Twentieth Century Fox. The third section analyses *Beasts of No Nation*, which was written and directed by Anonymous client Cary Fukunaga before being acquired by Netflix and becoming the streaming service's first original feature. While the previous chapter demonstrated that Anonymous and its auteur-directors were able to take advantage of the increased spending by distributors in premium television, the section thus considers how indie-auteurs and their intermediaries found new, if not necessarily lasting, opportunities producing specialty feature films for these streaming services.[14]

While the third section also explores how Netflix used *Beasts* to continue crafting an image of itself as a disruptor of the established media industries, the back-to-back discussion of these two case studies indicates that the streaming service's investment in specialty film was not necessarily as disruptive as the company wanted audiences to believe. More specifically, the chapter considers how a version of indie or specialty film built around notions about the maverick male auteur struggling in difficult industrial and production conditions was maintained. This argument is made with recognition that the evaluation of authorship in relation to gender is complex and has been, in film studies historically, fraught with pitfalls.[15] Although masculinity and determination are not mutually exclusive, notions of rugged masculinity have been reproduced throughout cinema history since early western and adventure movies. Yet as Paul Sellors notes, conceptions of authorship that 'assert God-like control over meaning' must be rejected in favour of an approach that sees authorship discourses as being produced at specific moments in time.[16] Thus, this chapter considers how certain directors and their intermediaries' efforts to navigate changing industrial, economic and technological conditions contributed to ideas of the auteur as a maverick male.

'We don't have blockbuster taste': exaggerating specialty film's decline

While the studios' reduction of investment in specialty film may have had a real impact on talent and their representatives working in the sector, Geoff King argues that proclamations of studio specialty film's decline were greatly exaggerated and that notions of crisis are a permanent feature of indie film discourse.[17] In fact, King argues that the Hollywood studios and their remaining subsidiary companies continued to finance and distribute 'quality Hollywood films' such as *Inception*, *The Social Network* (Fincher, 2010), and *The Assassination of Jesse James by the Coward Robert Ford* (Dominik, 2007).[18] King argues that the studios have done so to preserve their relationships with name talent, whose passion projects they greenlight so that they may partner with them again on more commercial projects in the future.[19] Yet King's argument prompts consideration as to why figures working in the industry, such as Golin, would deliberately exaggerate specialty film's decline. One reason may be that notions about the determination of talent to create art within unfavourable conditions can be a form of rhetorical manoeuvring designed to boost their brands and enhance their leverage in negotiations. Notions that highly determined creative talent are the driving force behind interesting alternative film are precisely what makes indie-auteurs marketable. In these terms, the studios' reduction of investment in specialty film can be reframed as both a set of challenges that producers and talent working in the sector strive to overcome and a narrative for them to exploit.

Evidence of Anonymous's executives crafting and exploiting this narrative can be seen in comments made by Golin and Michael Sugar at the 2014 Karlovy Vary International Film Festival in 2014, where Anonymous was the subject of a special tribute. Golin said:

> We don't have blockbuster taste. We do movies we care about and TV we like ... We like drama, which is very, very difficult to do in the movie business right now. And that's what's so exciting about TV ... I would love to have a franchise, but I don't see myself doing what Marvel does. I just don't have the sensibility for it. I wish I did.[20]

Meanwhile, Sugar stated:

> The throughline of the movies and TV we make and even the clients we represent on the management side is a certain quality of storytelling, the canvas – its size, shape – is less relevant. If the first two episodes of *True Detective* were a movie, we would be very proud of it ... We are very driven by the quality of the filmmaker. The movies and television we are making are with what we feel are the best directors in the business.[21]

Here, Golin and Sugar depict Anonymous and its clients as being driven by an authentic artistic logic and struggling against studios increasingly prioritising extraordinary profits from the exploitation of intellectual properties. Although Golin attempts to portray Anonymous's prioritisations as illogical because it involves disavowing larger profits, his and Sugar's rhetoric nevertheless serves several economic functions. It enhances the value of Anonymous's film productions by making them appear to have been made by passionate artists in inhospitable conditions and positions them as exceptionally rare examples of quality of a kind that audiences should seek out.

As Tzioumakis has explained, indie or specialty cinema can be understood as 'a discourse that expands and contracts when socially authorised institutions ... contribute towards its definition'.[22] Although Golin's comment contributed to narratives of specialty film's decline, it also helped to keep attention on specialty filmmaking and more specifically on Anonymous's version of specialty filmmaking, namely projects built around its indie-auteur clients. While King noted that the closure of the studio specialty divisions was celebrated by some cultural commentators and practitioners as the demise of the indiewood[23] model and a possible return to a more authentic independent filmmaking,[24] Golin did not celebrate indiewood's demise but rather effectively mourned the closure of the specialty divisions and the changes that their loss brought upon the sector. Golin mourns them because of the interdependency that exists between Anonymous, as one of Hollywood's leading talent management companies, and the studio conglomerates. The studios are major employers of Anonymous's clients and are financiers of its projects capable of paying some of the largest fees. As the subsequent sections will argue, even following the emergence of new distribution channels, the studios were still excellently positioned to sustain, enhance and disperse the stardom of Anonymous's clients as they remained equipped with comprehensive theatrical distribution and marketing infrastructure and expertise.

Although Golin positions Anonymous's productions against Marvel, which was acquired by Disney in 2009, he is diplomatic as he empathises with the studios' turn to franchise filmmaking in the knowledge that Anonymous needs to retain the studios as trading partners. As Violaine Roussel explains, talent intermediaries think of relationships as a capital, that is, 'an asset that they possess and actively work at keeping'.[25] Yet Golin's comment that Anonymous does not have Marvel's sensibility is contestable in light of the fact that Anonymous has helped its clients to secure work on several big-budget franchise films. For example, Sugar helped Gavin Hood to secure work as the director of Twentieth Century Fox's *X-Men Origins: Wolverine* (2009), Patty Jenkins to secure work on Warner Bros./DC Comics' *Wonder Woman* (2017) and *Wonder Woman 1984* (2020), Marc Webb to secure directing duties on Sony's *The Amazing Spider-Man* (2012) and *The Amazing Spider-Man 2* (2014), and Cary Fukunaga to secure employment on the latest instalment in the James Bond franchise, *No Time to Die* (2021).

Sugar's comment that 'The throughline of the movies and TV [that Anonymous makes] *and even the clients* [they] represent on the management side is a certain quality of storytelling' (my emphasis) is particularly revealing. It shows how Anonymous's executives struggle to compartmentalise the company's productions from those of their clients as they seek to retain the company's reputation for quality alongside that of its clients' reputations as auteurs as they work across a fairly wide range of projects. On one hand, Anonymous's efforts to maintain their clients' reputations as auteurs might be conceptualised as a form of resistance to the studios in an era where the Hollywood majors started prioritising worldbuilding around intellectual properties often at the expense of a director's individual style.[26] On the other hand, Anonymous's executives' efforts to position the company and its clients' feature film work against studio blockbusters can be understood not as a measure of its auteur clients' actual independence, but rather as a strategy designed to build their brands, enhance their leverage and fees, and create maximum opportunities including often with those same employers from whom they are meant to be independent. As Roussel explains, talent intermediaries often encourage their clients to adopt a 'one for them, one for us' formula that has the client alternate between very commercial projects and so-called passion projects.[27] Doing so, Roussel says, sustains two measures of value simultaneously, as the big-budget project connotes that the client is a 'name talent' or 'big player', while the lower-budgeted specialty or indie productions signal quality.[28]

Explaining how he actively convinces studio executives to hire clients coming off modestly budgeted features for big-budget blockbusters, Sugar stated, 'I try to find the through line. I believe a storyteller is a storyteller and the canvas is dictated by the story, not the other way round ... There are not that many great storytellers'.[29] Creating an impression of solitary artists whose work transcends industry modes of production, Sugar's description of the blockbuster as merely a different canvas makes his clients appear to be innovative artists dedicated to pursuing quality regardless of which employers they work with. Sugar also points to the narrative similarities between his clients' specialty and big-budget work, such as the protagonists' 'existential angst' in Hood's *Tsotsi* and *X-Men Origins: Wolverine* and the romance between two young people in Webb's *500 Days of Summer* and *The Amazing Spider-Man*.[30] In doing so, he draws an equivalence between his clients' work that positions them as auteurs with a single oeuvre while obscuring the differences in scale and the role of the studio employers.

In some instances, Sugar's clients and the studios parted ways during development on big-budget blockbusters, reportedly due to creative differences. After this happened, Sugar worked to sustain his clients' reputations as auteurs and deflect scrutiny of what might have been perceived as his clients' failures on the biggest stages by framing their departures as a refusal to compromise on their visions. Referring to Marvel's decision to replace Patty Jenkins and Edgar Wright on *Thor: The Dark World* (Taylor, 2013) and *Ant-Man* (Reed, 2015), respectively, Sugar explained that 'Marvel is the kind of place that controls their product, their world, in a very specific way ... If you don't meet their vision, you're done'.[31] Sugar remained diplomatic by conceding that it is Marvel's right to control their product while he sought to retain his clients' reputations as auteurs by making them appear to be uncontrollable.

While Sugar suggests that Jenkins and Wright were unwilling to compromise on their visions in the making of *Thor* and *Ant-Man*, he also implicitly suggests that when his clients do complete blockbuster franchises that they must have, by extension, prevailed in asserting their visions. Hence, when Jenkins and Fukunaga, the latter of whom Warner Bros. reportedly replaced as the director of *It* (Muschietti, 2017) following creative differences,[32] went on to direct the blockbuster franchises *Wonder Woman* and *No Time To Die*, Sugar contributed to creating an impression in critical and promotional discourse of those films as being authentically of auteur quality. Reviewing *No Time to Die*, for instance, *Empire*'s John Nugent commented that 'Fukunaga, it seems, was an ideal choice of director, skilfully balancing the contradictions of the character and the franchise ... he has always been an intuitive filmmaker, deeply interested in the humanity of his characters'.[33] Meanwhile, A.O. Scott wrote in the *New York Times* that Jenkins and screenwriter Allan Heinberg successfully shook off the 'blockbuster branding imperatives' to make *Wonder Woman* 'a movie' instead of 'another installment in an endless sequence of apocalyptic merchandising opportunities'.[34] All of this points to how talent managers help to sustain their clients' reputations as indie-auteurs despite sometimes working through the channels of the corporate mass media.[35] By maintaining their clients' reputations as auteur mavericks to help the studios to differentiate their products, therefore, Golin's and Sugar's rhetorical manoeuvring and strategies are symptomatic of the depoliticisation of American indie film that sees indie-auteurism remaining valuable for branding while being disassociated from political critique.[36]

Golin's comment that television was a growth area for drama is indicative of Anonymous's expansion into premium drama production and provides a reminder that the proliferation of television channels and platforms opened new opportunities for Anonymous to exploit. By depicting Anonymous as being very driven by the quality of the filmmaker, Golin and Sugar sought to give Anonymous's brand coherence at a time when it risked being diluted by its expansion to television. As I discussed in the previous chapter, its executives' efforts to retain Anonymous's associations with high-quality production reinforced television legitimation discourses that implicitly denigrated traditional programming at the expense of purportedly cinematic fare. Sugar's comment that if '*True Detective* were a movie, [they] would be very proud of it' epitomises how the company sought to position its series as cinematic and distance them from most television fare. In the context of a declining specialty film market, however,

Golin and his co-executives were often quick to point to the substantial fees and profits that the company was making from premium television production.[37] By doing so, they not only maintained Anonymous's share price by creating impressions of it as a growing business but also invoked competition between media as they used television as leverage to coerce film financiers to pay to retain the company and its clients' services.

While Anonymous's executives' efforts to position themselves as being committed to quality in a period of specialty film decline may ultimately have been designed to stimulate consumption in the company and its clients' productions, doing so functioned, as I mentioned earlier, to sustain specifically Anonymous's *version* of specialty filmmaking. Given that Anonymous's specialty productions have mostly been built and marketed around male maverick auteurs, it is both disconcerting and unsurprising to find that most of Anonymous's directors who managed to continue finding work in this period on specialty films were men. As well as Iñárritu's role directing *The Revenant*, Anonymous made *Spotlight* (2015) and *Stillwater* (2021) both with Tom McCarthy, *Don't Worry, He Won't Get Far on Foot* (2018) with Gus Van Sant, *Boy Erased* (2018) with Joel Edgerton, *The Beach Bum* (2019) with Harmony Korine, and *The Laundromat* (2019) with Steven Soderbergh. As I shall show, this gender inequality is particularly problematic given that narratives about the auteurs' dedication to creating art in spite of the challenging conditions that they reportedly face can reinforce narratives about the maverick male auteur as the figure revitalising Hollywood from its margins.[38]

'A man-against-nature film': Iñárritu, *The Revenant* and ideas of artistic sacrifice

Arguably, none of Anonymous's clients have positioned themselves against Hollywood comic-book franchises more than Alejandro G. Iñárritu. As Paul Julian Smith discusses, Iñárritu criticised what he perceived as Hollywood's formulaic storytelling following the release of *Amores Perros*.[39] More recently, *Birdman or (The Unexpected Virtue of Ignorance)* (2014), which Iñárritu co-wrote, co-produced and directed, satirised the state of contemporary cinema with emphasis on Hollywood's turn to comic-book franchises. The film focuses on a former Hollywood star who was best known for playing the superhero, Birdman, as he struggles to relaunch his career as a serious actor by starring in his own Broadway play. Iñárritu and his co-producers drew comparisons with real-world Hollywood filmmaking by casting in the lead role Michael Keaton, an actor who was himself best known for playing Batman in *Batman* (Burton, 1989) and *Batman Returns*

(Burton, 1992) before similarly falling out of favour in Hollywood in the late 1990s and 2000s. Enhancing the comparisons with real-life Hollywood filmmaking further, Iñárritu and his collaborators cast Edward Norton, who played the eponymous character in a critically maligned adaptation of *The Incredible Hulk* (Leterrier, 2008), and Anonymous client Emma Stone who played Gwen Stacey in *The Amazing Spider-Man* and its sequel. *Birdman*'s narrative also makes many references to actors' roles in comic-book films including Michael Fassbender's performance as Magneto *in X-Men: Days of Future Past* (Singer, 2014) and *X-Men: First Class* (Vaughn, 2011), and Jeremy Renner and Robert Downey Jr's roles as Hawkeye and Ironman respectively in Marvel's Avengers films. In addition, *Birdman* references Hollywood promotional activities such as stars being interviewed on *The Late Show with David Letterman* (CBS, 1993–2015).

With *Birdman* creating an impression of a Hollywood that is obsessed with big-budget comic-book franchise films, it gave Iñárritu an opportunity to disparage the state of Hollywood filmmaking. Doing so simultaneously enabled Iñárritu to promote *Birdman* and enhance his auteur brand by positioning the film as a quality work made by an artist with integrity who had not succumbed to the trappings of commercialism. In a single interview with *Deadline*, Iñárritu described comic-book franchise films as 'poison' and 'cultural genocide' because, he said, the audience had become 'so overexposed to plot and explosions and shit that [mean] nothing about the experience of being human'.[40] Iñárritu also called comic-book films 'very right-wing' because they focus on people killing other people who do not share the same beliefs and because the heroes are usually rich and powerful.[41] In turn, Iñárritu claimed that Hollywood's obsession with comic-book films and extraordinary profits had destroyed any space to exhibit 'good nice films' and had created conditions where the people making them are forced to 'work for free'.[42] 'You have to do that [work for free] on a movie like this', Iñárritu stated, before adding that making *Birdman* 'was an act of love and passion and belief'.[43]

Iñárritu persisted with similar rhetoric during the promotion of his next film, *The Revenant*, which tells the story of Hugh Glass's survival at the American frontier during the early 1800s. Promotional and critical discourse surrounding *The Revenant* focused especially on its challenging production, which reportedly went substantially over budget and over schedule after the production moved from Canada to Argentina for snow-covered landscapes. While critics attributed *The Revenant*'s production issues to Iñárritu's 'mad' disposition and his insistence on filming the movie sequentially,[44] Iñárritu portrayed the move as part of his determination to create authentic works of art. In doing so, Iñárritu likened *The*

Revenant to 'organic produce' and contrasted his work against Hollywood's blockbusters, which he described as 'tasteless' genetically modified foods.[45] 'It's like biting a real apple instead of a GMO apple', Iñárritu stated, 'You're so used to the pixel world that we are fed from Hollywood'.[46] Asserting that Hollywood had 'lost the taste for the real', Iñárritu depicted himself as an authentic artist with very organic tastes. Hence, Iñárritu also recalled a recent visit that he and his family made to Cusco, Peru, where he said that he ate a corn-based street food that almost made him cry because it reminded him of how it tasted as a child in Mexico.[47]

Narratives about Iñárritu's commitment to authenticity were also epitomised by reports about the extreme sacrifices that the film's cast and crew made to fulfil Iñárritu's expectations during production. Several press outlets reported that Iñárritu's unwillingness to do anything in half measures, including his determination to shoot under limited natural light and refusal to use soundstages and greenscreens, meant that the cast and crew were forced to sleep in remote locations, travel long distances in freezing conditions, and work under intense pressure.[48] Press reports focused especially on the 'extreme sacrifices' that the film's star, Leonardo DiCaprio, was willing to endure.[49] These sacrifices included: DiCaprio 'working through sick days' after repeatedly catching flu due to the low temperatures; DiCaprio having to carry the heavy weight of his bear fur costume, which he says reached a hundred pounds when it became wet; DiCaprio's nerves being 'absolutely shredded' after shooting a highly choreographed action scene that Iñárritu wanted to capture in a single take; DiCaprio being covered in live ants; and, most widely reported of all, DiCaprio biting into a raw bison liver despite being a vegan because the replica organ that the prop department supplied did not look 'authentic enough'.[50]

To differentiate *The Revenant* from contemporary special-effects–heavy blockbusters, Iñárritu situated it within a tradition of 'man-against-nature' filmmaking where the 'directors went to places, and … risked challenges'.[51] *The Revenant* was 'a homage to the original cinema tradition', Iñárritu stated, before adding that he 'passionately believe[s] that that should be an example of how film should be committed'.[52] The 'man-against-nature films' that Iñárritu cited included Andrei Tarkovsky's *Andrei Rublev* (1966), Akira Kurosawa's *Dersu Uzala* (1975), Francis Ford Coppola's *Apocalypse Now* (1979) and Werner Herzog's *Fitzcarraldo* (1982).[53] In turn, press reports likened *The Revenant*'s troubled and very expensive production to that of *Apocalypse Now*, *Fitzcarraldo* and *Heaven's Gate* (Cimino, 1980), films that have been mythologised for nearly bankrupting their producers.[54] New Regency was reportedly particularly financially exposed to *The Revenant* going over production because, under the terms of its deal with Twentieth Century Fox, it was forced to supply most of the additional financing. This arrangement between Fox and New Regency captures how the studios rely on deals with independent or semi-independent production companies to limit their own exposure to risk.

Evidently, press reports and promotional discourse surrounding *The Revenant* crafted a narrative of the film's difficult and even perilous production in terms of both the economic industrial precariousness of its producers and the extremities of shooting a supposedly authentic specialty production. This narrative functioned to bolster the reputations of Iñárritu, the film's producers and its stars by positioning them as artists dedicated to making quality innovative work despite the immense challenges that they reportedly faced. The narrative served to enhance Iñárritu's auteur brand and gave Fox a means to differentiate *The Revenant* from mainstream Hollywood tent-pole comic-book pictures. Thus, Iñárritu's denigration of comic-book franchises did not deter Fox, which distributed *Birdman* through its specialty label Fox Searchlight, from working with him again on *The Revenant*, even though the parent studio was also heavily involved in financing and distributing comic-book franchise films such as those of the X-Men series. While Iñárritu and his films' stars may also reduce their fees to get their passion projects made, doing so may be a risk worth the rewards if they can mobilise their brand name to claim profit participation.[55] After *The Revenant* became successful at the box-office, where it earned $183 million domestically and $349 million internationally,[56] Golin contributed to the narrative of *The Revenant*'s troubled production by commenting that it was 'an amazing experience' but one that he never wanted to repeat and said that if the film had been unsuccessful then it 'would have been *Heaven's Gate*'.[57] Golin's comment is rhetorical manoeuvring as he implicitly reiterated that the film was a success while he boosted Anonymous's brand by positioning it within a filmmaking tradition that supposedly privileges art over commerce.

Fox adopted a platform distribution strategy that involved giving *The Revenant* a limited release in late 2015 to gain awards eligibility before expanding into more than 3,000 screens as the film gained momentum during the awards season.[58] Doing so was typical of studios' handling of specialty films as they sought to target mass and niche audiences simultaneously.[59] Fox's efforts to target niche and mass mainstream audiences was also evident in its promotional materials or paratexts. Fox targeted niche adult audiences by producing posters and a trailer that mobilised Iñárritu's auteur brand by attributing *The Revenant* to him. At the same time, Fox targeted more mass mainstream audiences by foregrounding the film's stars, DiCaprio and Tom Hardy, and its action and spectacle. For instance, Fox's two posters featured close-up portrait images of DiCaprio and Hardy with the actor's names at the top in a larger font than that of the director's, and a tagline, 'Blood Lost. Life Found', that gestured to the film's action film properties, placed prominently above the film's title.

Action and spectacle feature heavily in Fox's teaser trailer which opens with a low-angle shot behind the film's protagonist, Glass (DiCaprio), as he stands watching an avalanche beginning in the background (Figure 5.1). The camera pans slowly to Glass's side as he proclaims in voice-over, 'I ain't afraid to die anymore; I've done it already'. As the score begins to build, the trailer cuts to a battle scene where Glass rushes through a forest carrying his gun before he and his fellow soldiers fight with Native Americans in a highly choreographed battle sequence that Iñárritu and his cinematographer, Emmanuel Lubezki, shot as one long take. After being pinned down in the mud, blood splatters across Glass's face after the Native American man pinning him down is killed off-screen. Glass then stands back up, begins roaring and wipes the blood from his face as he continues to fight. After the camera pans around to reveal a troop of Native American reinforcements approaching along a hilltop on horseback, Glass and his fellow soldiers retreat in boats as they shoot at the Native Americans who rush at them through the water. After the trailer cuts to a title insert with big bold white font describing *The Revenant* as being 'From Academy Award-Winning Director Alejandro G. Iñárritu', the rest of the trailer continues in a similar vein to how it began with shots of Glass struggling for his survival and sometimes engaging in combat, always within spectacular environs, edited to match the rhythm of the score which is synchronised with the repetitions of Glass's heavy breathing.

By invoking Iñárritu's authorship and boasting about his award-winning credentials, Fox's paratexts complement the extratextual discourse sur-

Figure 5.1 A still from the trailer for *The Revenant*. (Source: Author's own screengrab)

rounding *The Revenant* to position it as a legitimated quality film. *The Revenant*'s legitimation, however, is problematic. Notions about *The Revenant*'s difference from the Hollywood blockbuster, for instance, are overstated given the film's significant budget, association with major stars, and rise to the top of the North American box-office. Indeed, the prominence of the film's stars in *The Revenant*'s paratextual materials is indicative of how the film was more aligned with the higher-end of Hollywood filmmaking than the commercial indie films that gained prominence in the 1990s. Yet some critics seemed to buy into Iñárritu's and Fox's efforts to distinguish *The Revenant* from most blockbusters. Prompted partly by *The Revenant*'s limited release and the promotional discourse about Iñárritu's 'struggle with nature' during production, Bob Strauss called it a film that tackles 'important subjects', encourages thinking and is meant for 'serious movie lovers' weary of 'pixilated fantasies' and 'escapist action brands'.[60] Likewise, Pamela McClintock responded to *The Revenant* replacing *Star Wars: The Force Awakens* (J.J. Abrams) at the top of the American box-office in the second week of January 2015 by calling it 'a surprise' and 'upset' considering the former's 'tough subject matter'.[61] Manohla Dargis rejected the notion that *The Revenant* was antithetical to the mainstream blockbuster however, as she stated that Iñárritu was attempting to 'amp up [the] art-house experience with blockbusterlike awesomeness'.[62]

The legitimation of *The Revenant* based on notions about Iñárritu's vision and commitment to authenticity also relied on and reinforced cultural and social hierarchies. Even though *Birdman* and especially *The Revenant* ended up being far from niche, Iñárritu's criticism of Hollywood blockbusters elevated specialty film's supposedly discerning and 'thinking' audiences while denigrating mass media and the tastes of mainstream audiences who, he suggests, can no longer distinguish between 'the real' and Hollywood pixilated fare. Iñárritu's criticism of comic-book films as 'right-wing' and poison also arguably serves to position him as a liberal artist but risks labelling the mainstream audience as a corruptible mob. The legitimation of Iñárritu's filmmaking is also problematic as it reinforces gender inequalities by privileging masculinity and 'men's cinema'. While I explored Iñárritu's contribution to 'men's cinema' in the case of his commercial for *The Hire* in Chapter 3, Iñárritu's labelling of *The Revenant* as a 'man-against-nature film' similarly places him within an overwhelmingly masculine and elitist filmmaking tradition. Glass's observation of the avalanche shown in the teaser trailer epitomises Iñárritu's position within this tradition as it was a sequence that he cited as evidence of his dedication to realism and *The Revenant*'s 'man-against-nature' themes by emphasising that he created the avalanche without using VFX.[63] While Iñárritu's shot of Glass watching the avalanche conveys the protagonist's relative powerlessness against the natural world, the camera setup and movement shows off Iñárritu's cool vision and encourages identification more with the auteur than the film's hero in a manner that Stella Bruzzi has described as being typical of 'men's cinema'.[64]

Without explicitly using the terms 'men's cinema' or masculinity, Dargis gestured to Iñárritu's auteur cool when she stated that blood in *The Revenant* 'doesn't just splatter, it also sizzles'.[65] *The Revenant* is, Dargis said, 'filmmaking as swagger'.[66] Carole Cadwalladr was more critical in her response, as she called *The Revenant* a form of 'meaningless pain porn' where the violence was pointless spectacle and said that it was 'the kind of tedious, emotionally vacant film that has certain critics and Academy Award judges wetting their pants'.[67] Perhaps most troublingly, Iñárritu responded to one reviewer's assertion that *The Revenant* would not appeal to women by describing such criticism as a 'cacophony of imbeciles'.[68] Although masculine cool can appeal to women as well as men,[69] Iñárritu's outright dismissal and disdain demonstrates how legitimation can serve to deflect criticism and stop filmmakers from engaging in a constructive dialogue about their work. Iñárritu's efforts to deflect criticism may be understood in these terms as confirming Bruzzi's finding that:

> the determining male 'anxiety' is not that masculinity is foolish or easily mocked, but that, having thought it was the identity position against which its 'Others' were defined, it discovers, in fact, that it is the most precarious and unstable of identity positions.[70]

Narratives about Iñárritu's self-sacrifice and tolerance of pain show how the so-called 'man-against-nature' filmmaking tradition regards rugged masculinity as extremely useful, if not essential, for creating innovative works of art. Hence, Iñárritu collected his award for Best Director of a motion picture at the Golden Globes by telling the audience that the quality of the film was 'not about the budget or the genre' before saying that although making the film was 'the most difficult journey ... pain is temporary, but film is forever'.[71] After thanking the film's producers, including New Regency's founder Arnon Milchan, and Anonymous executives Steve Golin and Keith Redmon, Iñárritu ended his speech by thanking DiCaprio, whom he called a 'hero', and, pointing to the star, declared, 'you are the guy, you made this fucking film my friend, I love you'.[72] This privileging of notions of rugged masculinity surrounding ideas about the pursuit of art is highly problematic because it underpins the masculinisation of auteurism that has for far too long restricted the job opportunities of women directors and sustained an industrial and cultural context where women producers and directors feel that they must resist exhibiting femininity to enhance their visibility and compete for positions.⁷³ The gendered language that Iñárritu used to credit DiCaprio, who he effectively positions as his on-screen surrogate, demonstrates how male bonds are frequently mobilised, exhibited and celebrated in both the development and promotion of Hollywood's products while financiers remain reluctant to back projects packaged with female stars occupying the lead roles.⁷⁴

According to Kathleeen McHugh, the maverick as an idea descended from the Western outlaw hero and is not only a male but also a White and imperialist character.⁷⁵ To what extent, then, do Iñárritu and *The Revenant* complicate the racial and imperialist components of the maverick myth? Certainly, there is evidence that they do complicate it, as Iñárritu describes the film as addressing the roots of capitalism in America where White men profited from destroying the environment, killing animals, and exploiting and devastating Indigenous communities.⁷⁶ Moreover, in interviews Iñárritu regularly speaks about Mexican culture, including spicy food, rancheros and bolero music, and telenovelas.⁷⁷ These kinds of cultural details are unsurprisingly rarely found in the critical discourse surrounding an indie culture that has historically privileged White male auteurs. They arguably gain a political resonance as Iñárritu also speaks about 'the fear of otherness' that exists in America.⁷⁸ As I noted in the case of Iñárritu's work on *The Hire*, his films, including *The Revenant*, may be understood as a form of cultural critique that encourages audiences to reassess their own values and assumptions.

One must, however, be wary of too simplistic a reading that sees Iñárritu breaking from the racial and imperialist components of the maverick myth. Iñárritu's claims that *The Revenant* critiques capitalism functions, like *Birdman* and its satirising of contemporary Hollywood, to bolster his auteur brand and differentiate his films from the mainstream. Iñárritu's reference to spicy food, bolero music and telenovelas is also consistent with his tendency to represent Mexico in his films in fairly archetypal ways as he positions himself as a World Cinema auteur and caters to an international audience.⁷⁹ Likewise, Iñárritu's comments about eating organic foods outside the United States, including corn in Peru and mango in Mexico, serve to validate his 'organic' tastes and invoke his Latin American heritage. Yet *The Revenant* is firmly rooted in the American capitalism that Iñárritu claims the film critiques, while his reported decision to relocate the production from Canada to Argentina was not only expensive but also increased the production's carbon footprint at a time when environmental change stemming from carbon emissions are widely reported to be a major threat to developing nations and Indigenous peoples.⁸⁰ Moreover, Iñárritu's tale about his trip to Cusco, which is the main hub for tourists in Peru for visiting Inca ruins and something that he conveniently ignores, provides a reminder of Iñárritu's privileged position in international production for he has earned much of his wealth, and the luxury to travel, after his labour and brand were imported from Mexico to Hollywood. Although the allure of Hollywood was evidently too great for Iñárritu to resist, Hollywood has nevertheless helped him to build his brand as a maverick auteur and to express his masculine cool vision. As a result, Iñárritu's indie-auteur brand arguably ends up obscuring Hollywood's power in the production and distribution of screen media globally.

'The hardest thing I'd ever done – physically, mentally, emotionally': *Beasts of No Nation*, disruption and the persistence of the maverick male myth

In 2015, Netflix acquired its first original feature film for its streaming service in the form of *Beasts of No Nation*, which was written for the screen, directed and produced by Anonymous client Fukunaga, starred Anonymous's then client Idris Elba, and told the story of a child soldier's (Abraham Attah) experiences fighting in an unnamed African country's civil war. Netflix's acquisition drew significant press attention because not only did it mark the streaming service's emergence as a distributor of original feature films, but the $12 million fee that Netflix paid also appeared to be extraordinarily generous since it was twice the film's budget and significantly greater than the $8 million that was reportedly offered by 'traditional' specialty distributors, Focus Features and Fox Searchlight.[81] Reporters described Netflix's acquisition as 'eye-popping', 'groundbreaking' and a 'game-changer'.[82]

Following Netflix's acquisition, critics noted that Fukunaga had been striving to make *Beasts* for almost a decade after he became interested in the subject of child soldiers while studying history at the University of California.[83] Although Fukunaga sold the rights to his already completed debut feature, *Sin Nombre*, and *Beasts*, in 2005, critics reported that Focus Features reneged on its agreement to finance the latter in 2008 after another film about child soldiers named *Johnny Mad Dog* (Sauvaire, 2008) failed to secure US distribution and 'spooked investors'.[84] *Beasts*' collapse at Focus came around the time that, as Tzioumakis has explained, production, distribution and marketing costs for specialty films ballooned and studios became even more risk-averse as they began looking increasingly for projects with wider box-office appeal.[85] After Fukunaga shot Focus's co-production of *Jane Eyre*, therefore, he found work in television on *True Detective* which, as I discussed in the previous chapter, boosted Fukunaga's reputation after he won critical acclaim and an Emmy for Best Directing.

Significantly, Fukunaga replaced Iñárritu as *True Detective*'s season one director after *The Revenant* got the green light to begin production, thereby evidencing the interchangeability of Anonymous's male indie-auteur clients. During Fukunaga's work on *True Detective*, an Anonymous producer suggested that he cast Elba to play The Commandant and leader of the child militia.[86] With his and Elba's stardom being on the rise, and Elba signing on as an executive producer, Fukunaga was then reportedly able to secure investment from Participant Media and Red Crown Productions to finally enter production.[87] Although Anonymous did not produce *Beasts*, the company played a significant role in getting it greenlit, thus illustrating that the producer-managers' influence in what A.T. McKenna calls 'reputation networks' goes well beyond the projects for which they take credit.[88]

Evidently, critical discourse surrounding *Beasts* and its lengthy development positioned it as Fukunaga's passion project. As well as boosting Fukunaga's reputation as a figure with significant creative integrity committed to making quality work, these critical narratives aided Netflix's efforts to position itself as a disruptive company by making it appear to be a willing benefactor of struggling artists and daring productions of a kind that Hollywood appeared increasingly reluctant to back. Ted Sarandos, Netflix's chief content officer, asserted that the company was 'trying to make the films that are not getting made' and 'picking projects that are exceptional ... and otherwise difficult to distribute'.[89] Fukunaga's manager, Sugar, who successfully sold his production of *The OA* to Netflix during the same week that the streaming service acquired *Beasts*, commented that the media landscape was 'changing quickly and drastically' and that 'old formulas [were] no longer relevant'.[90] Sugar added that 'web-based companies' had become 'just as worthy players as the major studios and networks', and that the sizeable fee that Netflix paid for *Beasts* would 'pave the way for other [independent] films like it'.[91]

Sugar's comment demonstrates how talent managers craft narratives to suit different purposes at the same time. While he created an impression of an upturn in specialty film production surrounding Netflix's acquisitions, his comments in the first section of this chapter show that he and his Anonymous co-executives were simultaneously describing the movie business as being in decline. Sarandos's assertion that Netflix would make and distribute otherwise neglected films created a false impression of Netflix's role in *Beasts*' production by eliding the fact that it was made without Netflix's participation. Such rhetoric contributes to the often-confusing label 'Netflix original', which can refer both to productions that the company acquires and ones that it produces.[92] Sarandos's and Sugar's comments also create a misleading impression about the size of the studios' withdrawal from specialty film since Focus Features and Fox Searchlight both tried to acquire *Beasts* but were outbid.

Netflix's efforts to position itself as a benefactor of neglected artists, and one willing to pay generous fees, is also contentious. Netflix paid a larger upfront fee than the studios in part because it needed to provide a greater incentive for the film's producers to work with the company. For producers and talent, choosing to work with Netflix at that time represented a risk because the streaming service did not yet have any track record in distributing original feature films. Like Netflix's earlier and more substantial $100 million acquisition of *House of Cards*, the above-average fee that Netflix paid for *Beasts* was designed to make waves in the industry to attract more talent to working with the company on future projects.[93] Moreover, Hollywood attorney Linda Lichter cautioned that Netflix would stop paying so much once everyone in Hollywood wanted to work there.[94] On one hand, this all indicates how Hollywood talent and their representatives could take advantage of Netflix's ascendency to attain immediate and substantial fees and to secure a form of leverage to sustain those fees in wider industry negotiations. On the other hand, Lichter's comment and the extratextual discourse surrounding *Beasts* created an inflated impression that everyone wanted to work at Netflix now.

Soon after acquiring *Beasts*, Netflix announced that it would release the film on its streaming service and in cinemas on the same day. To secure theatrical distribution, Netflix struck deals with New York–based distributor Bleeker Street and an exhibitor of specialty film, Landmark Theatres. Netflix's decision to adopt a day-and-date release, however, broke with the traditional practice of distributing films in theatres for an initial window before they are made available in other formats. This prompted the National Association of Theatre Owners (NATO) to announce that the major cinema chains that it represented would refuse to show the film.[95] Asserting that *Beasts*' release online would reduce audiences' willingness to pay to watch the film in theatres, NATO claimed that the boycott was necessary to protect the business of its members.[96]

NATO's decision to boycott *Beasts* was not entirely surprising given that the organisation and major cinema chains had threatened to boycott films on earlier occasions when they perceived the theatrical window as being threatened. Consequently, Netflix's executives may not only have anticipated NATO's move, they may even have hoped for it. Indeed, the boycott helped to generate a sense of controversy around Netflix's distribution of *Beasts* that its executives exploited to reinforce impressions that the company was a disruptor of traditional practices and industries. Netflix's executives and *Beasts*' producers incorporated the boycott into their promotion of the film. In addition to Sarandos's comment about Netflix releasing 'difficult to distribute films',[97] *Beasts*' co-producer, Amy Kaufman, asserted that Netflix's 'muscle' would enable *Beasts* to be seen by a larger and more diverse audience than if it had been released through 'a traditional platform'.[98] Kaufman claimed that Netflix's distribution of *Beasts* 'could be a game changer' with the potential to alter 'the way people perceive how movies and art are delivered to them'.[99] Fukunaga, meanwhile, called the boycott 'fake' and argued that the cinemas that belonged to NATO would 'never have shown the film anyway'.[100] Gesturing to Netflix's subscription model, Fukunaga argued that the company was not beholden to the same distribution model as the studios because the streaming service did not need to gain money back at the theatrical box-office.[101]

As the rhetoric surrounding NATO's boycott demonstrates, *Beasts*' producers and Netflix's executives promoted the film as one that was of an exceptional quality and deserved to be seen by a large and diverse audience. In doing so, they made the studios and mainstream theatrical distribution appear inhospitable to serious, impactful, quality and auteur-driven work. Although the promotional rhetoric created an impression of Netflix as an essentially altruistic company, these impressions boosted Netflix's brand and were designed to attract subscribers by making the streaming service appear to be a valuable proposition offering consumers a kind of specialty content that they could not find anywhere else. *Beasts*' legitimation also functioned to justify Netflix's practices, including its decision to release the film on its streaming service on the same day as in cinemas. As Gerald Sim argues by drawing on the work of Mareike Jenner, '"quality" is a shiny result that burnishes the company's achievements'.[102]

Netflix promoted itself as a disruptive cultural force by mobilising Fukunaga's brand in paratextual materials. Netflix's trailer for *Beasts* described Fukunaga as the 'award winning director of *True Detective*', and Netflix screened the trailer during press junkets as *True Detective*'s critically maligned second season, which Fukunaga did not direct, was airing on HBO. The *Washington Post* responded to the trailer by commenting that Netflix was 'thankfully' giving audiences more of Fukunaga's 'rich' and 'unnerving' vision, which, it said, was so badly missing from *True Detective*'s second series.[103] In turn, *Wired* magazine suggested that Fukunaga's purported autonomy, which it implied was manifested in his migration between sectors, was indicative of progress. *Wired* reported:

> He's [Fukunaga's] made indies, directed the first season of *True Detective* for HBO, and now he's distributing his passion project with a streaming service ... he's part of that wave of directors willing to take their wares anywhere they can do their best work – a wave that includes David Fincher, Steven Soderbergh, and Jason Reitman.[104]

Wired's comment captures neatly how cable channels and subscription streaming services were being positioned as offering auteurs autonomy and opportunities to innovate, just as indie cinema reportedly had during previous decades. *Wired* also commented that Netflix had disrupted more than one industry, from video-rental stores to cable TV and now theatrical distribution.[105] This narrative confirms Sim's finding that Netflix's brand and efforts to position itself as an individual agent of change work to validate neoliberal capitalism's promise that 'productivity and innovation arrive via an "invisible hand" that guides individualist effort'.[106] *Wired*'s grouping of four male auteurs, Fukunaga, Fincher, Soderbergh and Reitman, meanwhile, provides a pertinent reminder that these figures are not valued for their ability to challenge corporate authority but for their construction as indie-auteurs and impressions about their autonomy. Hence, Fukunaga's claims about the economics of Netflix's subsciption model, which recalls Soderbergh's claims about the 'guaranteed revenue streams' of subscription services from the previous chapter, contribute to misleading impressions that Netflix and other pay-television services are immune to fluctuations in the market. In these terms, notions about the auteurs' dedication to quality within difficult contexts arguably validates neoliberal capitalism during its periods of instability and uncertainty by creating impressions that art can prevail even in the most difficult of circumstances.

Fukunaga's and Kaufman's enthusiasm for Netflix's distribution of *Beasts* in response to NATO's boycott is also contentious. On one hand, their enthusiasm can be understood as being indicative of how Netflix's high-profile collaborators have often adopted the streaming service's rhetoric about its favoured modes of consumption.[107] After Netflix acquired *House of Cards*, for instance, Fincher claimed that he binge-watched all episodes of it because 'If you're making a show that's available to viewers on the same day ... you have to experience it in the way that they might'.[108] In doing so, Fincher effectively authorised and naturalised binge-watching and contributed to an impression that Netflix's programming was irresistible. On the other hand, Fukunaga's and Kaufman's enthusiasm for Netflix's distribution of *Beasts* was undermined by Fukunaga's admission that the producers hesitated before accepting Netflix's offer because they 'wanted the movie to be seen in movie theatres'.[109] Fukunaga says that, before signing over the rights, he and his co-producers stipulated that Netflix treat *Beasts* 'like a movie'.[110] When Netflix ended up giving *Beasts* only a limited theatrical distribution in the United States and United Kingdom, Fukunaga admitted to being disappointed that it was not being screened in more territories.[111]

For *Beasts*' co-producers, the film's screening in theatres mattered because it increased their opportunity to share in profits earned from theatrical distribution. Indeed, Netflix has tended to pay producers greater upfront fees to acquire productions in part because Netflix's tendency to take exclusive rights for its streaming service limits producers' opportunities to earn revenues through syndication or theatrical sales.[112] For Fukunaga, a theatrical screening was also part of his efforts to retain his reputation as a *filmmaker*. 'Of course you want to be considered a theatrical film-maker if you're making a two-hour film', Fukunaga stated before adding, 'perception is important: that's why we don't walk around naked'.[113] Conflating public decorum with his own professional legitimacy and marketability, Fukunaga's comment demonstrated his anxiety that *Beasts*' lack of theatrical distribution might see it be labelled derogatorily as a 'TV movie' and that, in turn, he might become known as 'just' a television director.[114] Likewise, Sugar stated that Fukunaga's television work 'turned out well for him' but emphasised that 'he's still doing movies'.[115] While Fukunaga's efforts to distance himself from television was contradictory given that his reputation was bolstered by his role directing *True Detective*, that show was, as I discussed in the previous chapter, positioned as cinematic and differentiated from television by the single-director model that Anonymous used in the production of its first season. While Fukunaga contributed to Netflix's rhetoric about its favoured modes of consumption, therefore, his emphasis on theatrical distribution also demonstrates how rupture can occur between distributors and freelance talent as the latter seek to protect their own brands and long-term employability.

Finally, notions that Netflix's acquisition of *Beasts* was indicative of old formulas becoming redundant and symptomatic of Netflix as a culturally disruptive force are highly contentious given that *Beasts* was another specialty film that was greenlit and marketed around its male indie-auteur and male star actor. As Sim has explained, Netflix has repeatedly mobilised ideas about the maverick or disruptor built around White male figures to promote its brand and business.[116] Examples include portrayals of Netflix's executives, Reed Hastings and Ted Sarandos, the characters Walter White and Don Draper following its acquisition of the rights to *Breaking Bad* (AMC, 2008–13) and *Mad Men* (AMC, 2007–15) respectively, and David Fincher and Kevin Spacey surrounding its promotion of *House of Cards*. Recalling extratextual and critical narratives around *The Revenant*, promotional and critical materials also crafted an impression of Fukunaga's passion and determination during production.

Specifically, *Beasts*' production was reportedly fraught with hazards and challenges after Fukunaga convinced his colleagues and financiers that they needed to shoot in West Africa to be 'authentic to the story'.[117] The problems that the production reportedly faced included: Fukunaga and crew members contracting malaria;[118] Fukunaga losing forty pounds in weight after he was infected by an intestinal parasite;[119] Fukunaga almost stepping on a deadly black mamba snake;[120] a camera operator pulling his hamstring and Fukunaga stepping in to replace him;[121] Elba clinging to a tree to avoid falling off a cliff;[122] equipment being stolen and local workers extorting for higher wages;[123] monsoon rains washing away sets;[124] and the Ebola pandemic breaking out in neighbouring countries.[125] Recalling the production in an interview with *Vogue*, Fukunaga described *Beasts* as 'the hardest thing [he'd] ever done – physically, mentally, emotionally'.[126] In turn, the *Vogue* interviewer, John Powers, commented that Fukunaga makes work that 'engages with the larger world' while his peers 'do superhero movies'.[127] As a result, these narratives contributed to positioning *Beasts* as a specialty work made by a purportedly determined and passionate auteur. Yet the film's legitimation was laced with a familiar masculine discourse that sees quality work being created by a maverick willing to work through pain for his art and transcend the barriers of more conventional filmmaking. While Fukunaga and Elba are both men of colour,[128] the narrative of *Beasts*' troubled production also carries a colonialist air as notions about its innovativeness hinge on the portrayal of the American production venturing into the more unknown and seemingly hazardous filmmaking territories of Africa.[129]

According to Fukunaga, *Beasts* was meant to be an interrogation of the 'patriarch system' and of the seductive power of the charismatic leader.[130] It was ironic, however, that *Beasts*' producers were only able to secure the finance after Elba signed on, that a central appeal in casting the actor was, Fukunaga admitted, his 'gravitas, intelligence and testosterone', and that, after Elba committed to the project, Fukunaga rewrote the script to make The Commandant a more central character and the 'father–son dynamic' that develops between him and the child soldier Agu a more prominent aspect of the story.[131] Consequently, Netflix's trailer emphasised Elba's masculinity and sex appeal. The trailer's first image of Elba, for instance, has him walking down a small hill flanked by child soldiers with a cigarette in his hand and his khaki camouflage jacket unbuttoned showing his very toned chest and abdomen (Figure 5.2). After two close-ups of The Commandant speaking to Agu, including one where Elba smokes his cigarette with significant style through the side of his mouth, he is shown for a second time in his military jacket again displaying his bare chest. A sense of masculine cool is also created through movement both by Elba's performance and the staging, with Elba regularly shown walking and on one occasion dancing, as well as by the camera as it pans around him. A low-angle medium shot of Elba looking defeated and turning slightly as he observes the environment around him burn also recalls the image of DiCaprio watching the avalanche

Figure 5.2 A still from the trailer for *Beasts of No Nation*. (Source: Author's own screengrab)

in *The Revenant* as it invokes the man-against-nature theme that Iñárritu referred to explicitly. Although the shot in *Beasts* is meant to convey The Commandant's turmoil and defeat, it is indicative of how the audience is ultimately encouraged to identify with the filmmaker rather than the hero. As a result, *Beasts*' promotional materials positioned the film as an intelligent and progressive specialty work even as they preserved and relied on images of masculine cool in the form of the auteur's vision.

Conclusion

After opening in thirty-one Landmark Theatres in the United States, *Beasts* took only $51,000 at the box-office. *The Hollywood Reporter* commented that this figure represented a dismal return that risked dooming *Beasts*' awards hopes.[132] This article and other negative press coverage about *Beasts*' disappointing box-office returns prompted Netflix, which does not usually disclose viewing figures, to report that *Beasts* received three million views in two weeks, although it did not specify how of many of these were complete viewings.[133] By releasing these viewing figures, Netflix sought to limit the damage that was being done to its brand and talent recruitment. Damage appeared to have been done, however, as *Beasts* went on to receive no Academy Award nominations and just a few months later, at the 2016 Sundance Film Festival, the actor-director-writer-producer and another Anonymous client, Nate Parker, and his co-producers, rejected a $20 million bid from Netflix for their feature film *Birth of a Nation* in favour of a $17.5 million bid from Fox Searchlight. While Sugar had declared that Netflix's $12 million acquisition of *Beasts* would 'pave the way for other [independent] films like it' to be released by 'web-based companies', therefore, *Beasts* had now become, according to critics, 'a cautionary tale' encouraging filmmakers to reject the streaming service in favour of 'the big screen', an awards campaign and 'a more familiar theatrical distributor of prestige titles'.[134] Although Netflix may tender different models for measuring success, these kinds of challenges and reported failures are worth remembering, as narratives of successful technological disruption usually involve selectively recounting achievements while simultaneously erasing failures.[135]

In contrast to Netflix's fortunes during the awards season with *Beasts*, Fox's success on the awards circuit with *The Revenant* and other features indicated at the time that the studios remained the best positioned to manage an awards campaign, while its acquisition of *Birth of a Nation* confirmed that the studios had not retreated from specialty filmmaking entirely. Since the mid- to late 2010s, of course, the environment has continued to shift somewhat as Fox was taken over by Disney, which has dropped the Fox name and used Searchlight to release its specialty pictures theatrically and later through its own streaming service, Disney+. Meanwhile, Netflix appeared to come close to winning a Best Picture Oscar for its features *Roma* (Cuarón, 2018) and *Power of the Dog* (Campion, 2021), which was a feat that Apple TV+ achieved in 2022 with *CODA* (Heder, 2021).

While the ownership of major media distributors may continue to be in a state of flux and the Academy Awards and other major ceremonies continue to be used as sites for cultivating favour from critics and audiences, however, Karen Petruska reminds us that 'Overinvesting in traditional industry discourses ... may unintentionally privilege hegemonic narratives and longstanding practices that might benefit from genuine disruption'.[136] As this chapter has shown, notions of competition between media sectors and employers may be created and exaggerated by talent intermediaries seeking to sustain their leverage and that of their clients. Talent intermediaries' efforts to do so arguably becomes increasingly challenging in an era of convergence when the opportunities for indie-auteurs and other talent to migrate between sectors and employers are reduced. As Peter Labuza explains, while independent filmmakers may continue hustling, doing so:

> becomes harder when digital distribution – and the need to access these primary platforms to make *any* profit – strangles the industry. Giants such as Netflix are positioned to control which films get made and how, without necessarily following the preferences of consumers.[137]

Arguably, this potential loss of leverage risks becoming increasingly challenging in the late 2010s and early 2020s when, as Mareike Jenner and Alisa Perren have both pointed out, streaming services have begun increasingly producing and distributing work based on intellectual properties aligned with more 'popular' genres to appeal to mass audiences.[138] Yet one must be wary of repeating the same narratives about a decline and crisis of specialty production around streaming services that have long existed around studio specialty film. As this chapter has demonstrated, the legitimation of specialty film is all too often underpinned by myths about the maverick male working autonomously to create quality work in seemingly inhospitable conditions. As these myths are likely to retain value for differentiating specialty productions and enhancing the streaming services' brands as disruptors, therefore, they are likely to preserve gender inequalities as male indie-auteurs benefit from being the ones seen to be hustling, while a disproportionately larger number of female filmmakers continue to struggle to build reputations as 'big names' and secure the same volume and quality of opportunities.

Notes

1. Balio (2013) pp. 25–33; Tzioumakis (2013) pp. 36–8.
2. Balio (2013) p. 40.
3. Balio (2013) pp. 25–33; Perren (2012) p. 231.
4. Balio (2013) pp. 25–33.
5. Ibid. p. 37.
6. Goldstein (2014).
7. Ibid.
8. Bart (2013).
9. Balio (2013) pp. 36–8.
10. Goldstein (2014).
11. Ibid.
12. Lang (2015); O'Falt (2016).
13. Sinwell (2020) p. 64.
14. As Mareike Jenner notes (2018, p. 139), streaming services such as Netflix invested heavily in specialty or quality productions of a kind that appealed to indie film and cable television's niche adult audiences as they sought to grow their subscriber base. As streaming services such as Netflix have grown and sought to appeal to wider audiences, however, they have increasingly ventured into more 'popular' genres. As an example, Jenner cites Netflix's co-production deal with the comedy actor Adam Sandler and its acquisition of the sitcom *Fuller House* (2016–20).
15. Sellors (2010) pp. 81–4.
16. Ibid. p. 83.
17. King (2016) p. 38; King (2013b) pp. 41–5.
18. King (2016) pp. 32–8.
19. King (2016) pp. 32–8; see also King (2009) p. 6.
20. Kay (2014).

21. Holdsworth (2014).
22. Tzioumakis (2006) p. 11.
23. Although Geoff King capitalizes indiewood, I write it with a lowercase i for consistency and because, like Yannis Tzioumakis, I regard it as a discourse that refers to a period that appeared to be marked by greater tendencies in terms of production that are associated with Hollywood.
24. King (2013b) p. 44.
25. Roussel (2017) p. 79.
26. D. Johnson (2012) p. 12; Uhlin (2020) p. 141.
27. Roussel (2017) p. 176.
28. Ibid. p. 176.
29. Mowe (2014); see also Schilling (2013).
30. Mowe (2014).
31. Thompson (2015).
32. Setoodeh (2015a).
33. Nugent (2021).
34. Scott (2017).
35. Newman (2009) p. 20; Newman (2011) p. 45.
36. Molloy (2017) pp. 368–9.
37. Jurgensen (2016b); Littleton (2015a).
38. McHugh (2016) p. 142.
39. Smith (2021) p. 13.
40. Fleming (2014).
41. Ibid.
42. Ibid.
43. Ibid.
44. Goldman (2015); A. Lee (2015).
45. Brady (2016); see also Romney (2016).
46. Brady (2016); see also Romney (2016).
47. Romney (2016).
48. Anon (2015d); J. Miller (2015); O'Connell (2015).
49. O'Connell (2015).
50. Anon (2015d); J. Miller (2015); O'Connell (2015).
51. Romney (2016).
52. Ibid.
53. Ibid.
54. Goldman (2015); Galloway (2016); Jurgensen (2016b).
55. As Phil Drake (2008, pp. 78–9) discusses though, Hollywood's 'creative accounting' practices often make profit participation deals an unreliable source of income for Hollywood talent.
56. BoxOfficeMojo (n.d.c).
57. Jurgensen (2016b).
58. McClintock (2016a).
59. Schatz (2017) p. 257; Tzioumakis (2012) p. 169; Perren (2012) p. 36.

60. Strauss (2015b).
61. McClintock (2016a, 2016b).
62. Dargis (2015).
63. Romney (2016); Brady (2016).
64. Bruzzi (2013) p. 5.
65. Dargis (2015).
66. Ibid.
67. Cadwalladr (2016).
68. Romney (2016).
69. Bruzzi (2017) p. 389.
70. Bruzzi (2013) p. 50.
71. Stone (2016).
72. Anon (2016b).
73. White (2016) p. 46; Perkins (2016) p. 138.
74. White (2016) p. 44.
75. McHugh (2016) p. 143.
76. Romney (2016).
77. Ibid.
78. Ibid.
79. Shaw (2013) pp. 108–11
80. Davis (2007); Filho et al. (2021).
81. McClintock (2015); Setoodeh (2015b).
82. McClintock (2015); Harwell (2015); Brownstein (2015).
83. Setoodeh (2015b); Watercutter (2015); Covert (2015); Egner (2015).
84. Setoodeh (2015b); Watercutter (2015); Covert (2015).
85. Tzioumakis (2012) p. 169; Tzioumakis (2006) p. 264.
86. Anon (2015c).
87. Coyle (2015); Anon (2015c).
88. McKenna (2012) p. 612.
89. Setoodeh (2015b).
90. Goldsmith (2015).
91. Ibid.
92. Jenner (2018) p. 9.
93. Coyle (2013).
94. Kilday (2015a).
95. Sacks (2015a); Greenberg (2015); Gee (2015).
96. Sacks (2015a); Greenberg (2015).
97. Setoodeh (2015b).
98. Gee (2015).
99. Ibid.
100. Sacks (2015b); Anon (2015a).
101. Anon (2015a).
102. Sim (2016) pp. 188–9; Jenner (2016).
103. Rosenberg (2015).

104. Watercutter (2015).
105. Ibid.
106. Sim (2016) pp. 188–9.
107. Sim (2016) p. 191; Jenner (2018) pp. 109, 126.
108. Garrahan (2013).
109. Watercutter (2015); see also Rose (2015a).
110. Watercutter (2015).
111. Anon (2015a).
112. Sandberg (2019).
113. Anon (2015a).
114. For a discussion of the denigration of TV movies, see Gomery (1983).
115. Thompson (2015).
116. Sim (2016) pp. 194–5.
117. Setoodeh (2015b); Anon (2015a).
118. Egner (2015).
119. James (2015).
120. Collin (2015).
121. Strauss (2015a).
122. Alexander (2015).
123. B. Lee (2015).
124. Collin (2015).
125. Coyle (2015).
126. Powers (2015).
127. Ibid.
128. In an interview with *The Guardian*, Fukunaga says that a lack of diversity is a problem for cinema. Fukunaga goes on to acknowledge that he may have benefited from his own skin colour, as he says that, although he is Japanese American, he is 'probably perceived to be white' (B. Lee, 2015).
129. Fukunaga's debut feature, *Sin Nombre*, which told the story of a Honduran girl's efforts to get into America, was also criticised for sensationalising poverty or being 'poverty porn'. Fukunaga has rejected this criticism (B. Lee, 2015).
130. Anon (2015c).
131. Anon (2015c); Buckley (2015).
132. Kilday (2015b); see also McClintock (2015); Harwell (2015); Brownstein (2015); Hamedy (2015).
133. Rottenberg (2016); Coyle (2015).
134. Lang and Setoodeh (2016); Coyle (2017); Rottenberg (2016).
135. Lepore (2014).
136. Petruska (2023) p. 242.
137. Labuza (2021), original emphasis.
138. Jenner (2018) p. 139; Perren (2023) pp. 72–3.

CHAPTER 6

Black Agents and Agency

Charles D. King, Macro and the Talent Management of Black Indie-Auteurs

In the 2010s and 2020s, the number of Black people working as talent intermediaries in Hollywood has remained disproportionately low.[1] Consequently, the few Black agents that are recruited are more likely to feel isolated and less likely to offer their opinions.[2] J.B. Fitzgerald of United Talent Agency (UTA), for instance, explains:

> In meetings or on calls, I still often am the only African-American in the room. In moments, where I wanted to express an opinion, I found myself struggling with an internal dialogue of 'how will my opinion be received?' I can recall a couple instances where I missed my window to speak up, because I was taking too much time struggling with that internal dialogue.[3]

If, as Denise Mann argues, that much of the control over careers passed to talent intermediaries in post-Classical Hollywood,[4] then the limited number of Black agents risks restricting the visibility of people of colour on screen and the authenticity of Black filmmakers' stories. Without enough Black agents, Black actors, directors and writers are also more likely to be represented by White agents. Although White agents can be important allies, White representation of Black artists because of a deficit in the number of Black agents has significant implications. White representation of Black artists arguably represents a manifestation of 'Hollywood's plantation scheme', which Monica White Ndounou describes as an ideology and pattern of production inherited from plantation arrangements where Whites, including slave owners, used Black bodies for White entertainment.[5] 'The lack of evolved representations of African Americans as individuals with emancipated consciousness, especially in their interactions with Whites, in theater and film', Ndounou argues, 'is symptomatic of the broader issue of plantation politics plaguing the development of African American characters and films past and present'.[6] Even if White producers see themselves as allies, Ndounou adds, their seeing themselves working according to a 'progressive ideology' can 'decrease the likelihood that producers question racist potential in production and reception'.[7]

The limited number of Black agents and agents of colour in Hollywood also risks reinforcing impressions that the ideal agent is White. In his study of the first Black attorneys in the United States, Kenneth W. Mack found that many early-twentieth century Black attorneys complained that 'local Black communities desired Whiteness in a lawyer'.[8] Black attorneys commented that Black prospective clients harboured the 'mistaken assumption that the White lawyer's influence in the White-dominated system was more valuable than the Black lawyer's skill'.[9] Mack's findings are echoed in the present-day by Black agents. Agent Tiauna Jackson, for instance, declares, 'I've had an instance where an unknown Black actress told me flat out that she wanted a White agent. She had no credits. But she knew that to succeed you needed to align yourself with someone White'.[10] This idea about the ideal agent being White in a White-dominated system creates problems for the Black talent intermediary who must strike a balance between being able to successfully work according to the rules of the system while depicting themselves as being capable of fulfilling the specific needs of their clients who are often, though not exclusively, Black. Drawing from Mack's finding, Black agents appear caught between the needs of the larger, White-dominated system, and those of their own racial group.[11] Black agents are required to appear exceptional, representing the highest aspirations and greatest potential of their social group, and authentic, someone as much like the masses of their social group as possible.

With these issues in mind, this chapter investigates the work of Charles D. King, a Black former agent and the first African American partner at WME (William Morris Endeavor), and now CEO and founder of an integrated production and talent management company named Macro. King and Macro have repeatedly collaborated with and championed Black on-screen talent and auteurs, including, in the case of the latter, Tyler Perry, Tim Story, Ryan Coogler, Dee Rees, Boots Riley, Shaka King, Steven Caple Jr, Ekwa Msangi, Issa López and Blitz 'The Ambassador' Bazawule. At WME, King has also negotiated deals for indie-auteur associated screen projects such as *Barbershop*, *Diary of a Mad Black Woman* and *House of Payne*. Macro and King have also produced indie features including *The Land* (Caple Jr, 2016), *Mudbound*, *Sorry to Bother You* (Riley, 2018), *Farewell Amor* (Msangi, 2020), *Nine Days* (Oda, 2020), *Judas and the Black Messiah*, and *They Cloned Tyrone* (Taylor, 2023) as well as the indie-inflected series *Gentefied* (Netflix, 2020–1). Upon founding Macro, King stated: 'The one underlying theme is "premium" … I'm looking for artistic integrity'.[12] King's comment linking artistic integrity to quality output clearly resembles the kind of rhetoric used by other talent intermediaries responsible for managing indie-auteurism that I have discussed in the book so far. As an integrated production and talent management company purportedly prioritising premium content and operating across screen media, Macro also resembles Propaganda Films and Anonymous Content. Indeed, it is significant in this regard that, since establishing Macro in 2015, King has secured Macro's largest source of investment from Laurene Powell Jobs's Emerson Collective, thereby giving the company a degree of co-ownership with Anonymous.

At the same time, however, King and Macro's championing of Black auteurs provides an exceptional opportunity to assess areas of divergence with their predominantly White counterparts. So far, this book has critiqued notions about autonomy and singular vision that have arisen in indie culture and which have been constructed and managed by White male intermediaries around mainly White male auteurs. One reason that the book has done so is because critiquing autonomy helps to correct myths about White male intermediaries and auteurs as 'great men' and maverick geniuses. When applied to the study of Black talent intermediaries and their clients, however, this critique takes on an additional resonance because in popular discourse the autonomy of Black people has too often been denied and called into question. On one hand, the denial of Black autonomy can be traced back to the social realities of slavery where Black people were put in chains and their freedoms removed. Hollywood's plantation scheme represents one manifestation of this denial of Black autonomy in contemporary society.[13] On the other hand, Black autonomy is questioned through suspicions expressed in popular discourse that the Black person, especially they who participate in mainstream culture and society, often does not behave authentically because they are being instructed by White people and culture. As Randall Kennedy explains:

> The specter of the 'sellout' haunts the African-American imagination. A long-oppressed minority situated in the midst of a dominant White majority, Blacks fear that Whites will favor and corrupt acquiescent Negroes who, from positions of privilege, will neglect struggles for group elevation. African Americans fear that Whites will empower 'Oreos' who 'look Black but think White.' African Americans fear that Whites will promote Black free riders and defectors who sap solidarity and discourage effective strategies for resisting subordination.[14]

In this wider context, this chapter seeks to shed light on the specific challenges that Black talent intermediaries face in managing auteurs of colour and the consequences that doing so has on their work. The aim is not simply to interpret Black agents as the opposite of White agents. As Stuart Hall stated, 'By definition, Black popular culture is a contradictory space. It is a site of strategic contestation. But it can never be simplified or explained in terms of the simple binary oppositions'.[15] Indeed, the chapter investigates how Macro and King at once adhere to the wider talent intermediary and Hollywood studio system, seek to differentiate themselves from Hollywood's established agencies and management companies, and endeavour to shift the conversation around the commercial and cultural possibilities for Black talent and Black-run intermediary businesses. The chapter considers how King builds his and his clients' reputations and promotes Macro's productions by constructing their director clients and director collaborators as autonomous individuals fulfilling their singular creative visions while often working towards filling a deficit in Black cultural expression. In doing so, the chapter explores how ideas about creative autonomy intersect with broader notions of Blackness.

'Amplif[ying] the voices of diverse talent': Charles D. King and 'thinking Macro'

King founded Macro in 2015 alongside his wife Stacey King, whose background is in fashion. To do so, Charles King exited WME, Hollywood's largest talent agency, where he had worked since 1997 when he joined the agency's trainee programme, before William Morris merged with Endeavor, and rose through its ranks to become its first-ever African American partner. Charles King announced that Macro would focus, first, on producing feature films, television series and digital content targeting 'multicultural audiences' and, second, on developing 'brands and new platforms at the intersection of content, lifestyle and technology'.[16] Since establishing Macro, King has taken on the role of being the company's figurehead and the face of its brand. King and Macro regularly invoke his agenting work to legitimate the company's purported socially driven mission and its credentials for spotting talent and mobilising brands in the screen entertainment marketplace. Upon founding Macro, for instance, King stated:

> There were two major catalysts that propelled me to move to L.A. and enter the industry over 15 years ago: my vision to build a media company one day and the knowledge that what I saw on screen did not fully reflect the spectrum of who we are ... It's clear to me now, as it was then, that there's a growing appetite for content that serves the more diverse world we live in.[17]

Elsewhere, King said of Macro's mission to create content with more diverse representation, 'I've been sitting in these [Hollywood] rooms for the last 15 years. The studios aren't focused on it; the packagers aren't focused on it ... There's a huge void and a huge opportunity'.[18] King's comments capture neatly how the former talent agent frames Macro's mission in terms of its social and cultural benefit while gesturing to its commercial potential.

In 2019, Macro expanded into talent management, launching Macro Management and UNCMMN. Macro Management was rebranded as M88 in 2020, when King's former colleague and WME partner Phillip Sun joined the company. While M88 focuses on managing clients in film and television, UNCMMN is dedicated to managing clients in procuring sponsorships and creating branded content. Upon rebranding Macro Management as M88, the company announced some headline client signings that included Coogler, Bazawule, Michael B. Jordan, Donald Glover, Riz Ahmed, Naomi Scott, Gemma Chan, and Idris Elba. King and Sun declared that M88 aimed to amplify 'the voices of artists and creators from the global new majority',[19] while Macro's website describes UNCMMN as 'amplif[ying] the voices of diverse talent through talent management and branded entertainment partnerships'.[20] In turn, King has stated that Macro was set up to be a 'disruptive' company that participates in shaping and lifting culture and economically empowering people of culture.[21] In these terms, Macro's operations represent an important break from industry and production norms. With a leadership team composed mostly of people of colour and many women, Macro represents a shift away from Hollywood's 'plantation' modes of production. By framing managing and producing projects with people of colour as an enormous global business opportunity, Macro's marketing discourse also departs from the conventional Hollywood logic that films and television series with mainly Black casts do not sell well internationally.[22] As a result, Macro is positioned as offering greater employment and business opportunities to people of colour in the media industries and as offering more diverse and authentic representations of people of colour on screen.

While Macro's mission appears highly commendable, it is necessary to scrutinise more closely King's efforts to use his agenting work to legitimise Macro's mission. Indeed, it is very significant that most publicly available information about King's agenting work has come from interviews that he has provided since establishing Macro. Such extratextual discourse represents an effort to retrospectively shape a narrative about his agenting work that fits with Macro's purported mission. At the same time, King's reported rise from the William Morris mailroom to agency partner and Macro CEO positions him as a visionary fulfilling his master plan.[23] On Macro's website and repeatedly in interviews, King tells of how he declared in his 1996 Howard Law School graduation yearbook that he would one day 'be the head of a diversified entertainment and media company'.[24] The website adds: 'a little over 15 years later, that proclamation became MACRO. As CEO, he casts the overall vision, mission and strategic goals for all things MACRO and its multiple business verticals'.[25] As I have already discussed, such ideas exemplify a 'great leader' and neoliberal entrepreneurial discourse that surrounds industry executives generally. It is thus unsurprising that King is celebrated by financial institutions such as Bloomberg, which ran a feature called 'Portrait: How This Black Mogul is Disrupting the Movie Business', and Morgan Stanley, which interviewed King and his wife to explore their 'Life as Entrepreneurs' as part of the 2021 American Black Film Festival.[26]

In a 2017 interview with *Complex*, King recalled that joining William Morris's 'legendary' trainee programme was 'a way to build relationships from the ground floor up, to understand the language'.[27] King added that William Morris effectively 'Dropped [him] into a pot of gold' and asked him 'How much gold do you want to mine?'[28] King said that, uncharacteristically for a trainee, he began signing clients and building relationships with William Morris executives during his time working in the mailroom. King emphasised that, as the only African American in William Morris's trainee programme, he had to work harder than his White counterparts. 'I had to read twice as many scripts, I came in early, I was the last one there, I came in every weekend, I was bringing in clients and cultivating business way before I was an agent'.[29] Asked what kind of conversations he had with the chief executive of William Morris, King recalled having sent 'proposals and charts about the shifting demographics in the country and how youth culture is impacted by urban culture and how that was pop culture'.[30] Cultural shifts that were already happening in fashion and music, King stated, were going to happen in film and television.[31] Asked how his memos were received, King asserted that 'they were well received, they [the CEO] understood'.[32] King reiterates these sentiments elsewhere when he states:

> The leaders at the top of William Morris and, frankly, the senior chairman level of a lot of the studios that I would interface with, they would usually get it ... A lot of times, you find it's the people in the middle that are less visionary. And so, yeah, of course, there were moments where I would be discussing things or bringing up concepts and meetings and literally got laughed at. And then a few years later, I was running the meetings because I was generating ten times more revenue than they were.[33]

On one hand, King's comments highlight the barriers and discrimination that many Black people experience in their working lives. King's comment about working harder highlights how Black agents are expected to prove themselves as exceptional, while his recollection of being laughed at is another example of the isolation that Black agents can experience in the White-dominated industry. King's mention of moderately successful but somewhat incompetent White agents could be a response to clients, including especially Black clients, who may mistakenly perceive the ideal agent to be White. On the other hand, King's crediting of studio chairman and William Morris executives with vision is conspicuous for repeating the 'great leader' discourse which, as the CEO of Macro, King cultivates. King may also be reluctant to criticise powerful media industry figures with whom, by his own admission, he has exerted significant time and energy building relationships.[34] Yet King's rhetoric is problematic as he generalises about and denigrates company employees and middle management. While appearing to have had the last laugh, King unfortunately presents commercial success and entrepreneurialism as tonics to inequality and contributes to neoliberal myths about meritocracy in the industry. These ideas are highly contentious when understood within a context where Black socioeconomic inequalities are too often regarded as a failure of Black people to work as hard as their White or Asian counterparts.[35] The 'great leader' discourse surrounding narratives of racial progress is problematic given that, as Catherine R. Squires explains, it underrepresents the contributions of more anonymous activists, including especially women, and suggests that equality agendas fail if he falls.[36]

King's reference to urban culture is vague.[37] King's linking of urban culture and youth culture brings to mind the 1990s' hip-hop gangsta cycle and its films such as *Boyz n the Hood* (Singleton, 1991), *New Jack City* (Peebles, 1991) and *Menace II Society* (Hughes, 1993). King went on to negotiate deals for features such as *Barbershop* and *Hustle & Flow* that would broadly fit within this cycle. Significantly, though, many of the films of the hip-hop gangsta cycle had been released before King became a William Morris trainee. King's recollection of sending the agency CEO charts predicting urban culture's influence on the mainstream, therefore, may be overstatement intended to position himself as having always been a disruptive figure in tune with cultural and market trends. Simultaneously, King's recollection indicates how he strategically navigated William Morris's corporate culture. Yet King's comments about being understood by William Morris's senior executives can be interpreted in reverse to mean that *he* understood what *they* wanted. King's comment about William Morris's training room providing an opportunity to 'understand the language' indicates how talent agencies create institutional cultures that function to socialise their agents.[38] Of course, King's training and early agenting was occurring in a context during the late 1990s and early 2000s when multiculturalism and diversity had already begun to be reconceptualised within the Hollywood industries as marketable properties valuable for appealing to different niche demographics.[39] As King defines urban culture as part of a market trend beginning to have mass appeal, it is hardly surprising that his memos would be well received by agency senior executives seeking greater revenues through expansion into new markets. King's memos showed William Morris's executives that he could speak the agency's language and adhere to its culture.

Rather than being a disruptive figure, King's emphasis on urban culture indicates how he adhered to White executives' narrow conceptions of Blackness. As Ndounou as well as Cherise A. Harris and Keisha Edwards Tassie argue, Hollywood executives have privileged hip-hop gangsta films due to their commercial potential derived from an appeal to Black urban audiences and young White males.[40] Hollywood executives have done so, they argue, at the expense of alternative stories and representations.[41] Yet Ndounou also acknowledges that hip-hop gangsta films provide important career opportunities for Black filmmakers as many directors who have helmed successful gangsta films have subsequently been offered opportunities to direct films with bigger budgets and White casts.[42] Ndounou contrasts these directors' career trajectories with that of Black independent filmmakers such as Haile Gerima, whose career she says stalled after prioritising cultural values over commercial appeal in the making of *Sankofa* (1993).[43] Broadly, this dilemma between choosing to pursue authenticity and remaining marginal or making compromises to expand appeal and opportunities is one that has existed for Black filmmakers throughout much of cinema history.[44] King's work at William Morris thus indicates how these dilemmas are manifested in the choices made by Black talent intermediaries who seek to advocate for Black artists while navigating industry and corporate expectations. King and Macro may seek to advocate for Black talent, but they do so within the restricted parameters created by the Hollywood agencies and studios.

At a 2015 New York Producers Guild panel on diversity, King described shepherding music video directors to features, and independent film directors into 'the mainstream marketplace and then back into smaller redemptive movies', as being akin to 'the underground railroad'.[45] King also told of how he prepared to launch Macro by cultivating relationships not just in Hollywood but in the political and financial realms too.[46] For King, these aspects of his work epitomised how he has sought to 'effectuate real change ... [by] advocating in one way to really evolve in a different way'.[47] Despite conceiving of his work as akin to 'the underground railroad',

King's shepherding of clients between media resembles widely used talent intermediary strategies. Such strategies are regularly used by talent intermediaries to manage their clients' career choices and encourage them to take on higher paid work sometimes at the expense of the clients' own ideas about their artistic integrity.[48] As an example of his advocacy, King cites Tim Story, whom he shepherded from the mid-budget independent film *Barbershop* to the blockbuster franchise *Fantastic Four* (2005). At the time of making *Fantastic Four*, Story stated:

> A few people called me about the Black thing and said: 'This is major. You're a Black director on *Fantastic Four*.' But all I was thinking was: 'I just don't want to screw up.' But then people were like, 'If you screw this up, we all got a problem,' and I said, 'Oh, man, I got that on me now?'[49]

On one hand, Story's comment shows the burden placed on Black people to speak for, and work towards benefiting, the Black community.[50] On the other hand, Story's comment indicates how King's Black clients did not necessarily see their career movement as a socially progressive act.

In her study of indie-auteurs' migrations to blockbuster filmmaking, Claire Molloy argues that these neoliberal entrepreneurs do not shed their radical politics but are 'from the start more closely aligned with the commercial end of indie filmmaking'.[51] How, and in what way, does race complicate this narrative? Does King's work demonstrate that well-established talent intermediary strategies can be used flexibility to advocate for diverse voices? Is King's work evidence of brand building initiatives being used to strengthen the positions of Black figures within the studio system?[52] Or, must Story's migration between media be understood as merely another manifestation of the Hollywood studios enlisting an indie-auteur brand to differentiate and promote a mainstream blockbuster? Moreover, is King's retrospective framing of his agenting work simply another example of performative rhetoric masking decades of equality inaction?[53] If so, is King another example of a Black figure working in Hollywood who has come to understand his work within 'the stipulated parameters of a neoliberal structure'?[54] These questions are difficult to answer definitively because, as Eithne Quinn argues, race is both a barrier and an opportunity. As Quinn explains:

> Race is an opportunity because Conglomerate Hollywood, though its growth since the 1980s seems overwhelming, is not all-absorbing or monolithically efficient – its racist assumptions present some opportunities for minority cultural producers. Indeed, when such corporate fault-lines are combined with the rich performative and subcultural resources of Black America in an increasingly synergistic, celebrity-fronted industry environment, the opportunities presented can be substantial.[55]

With all of this in mind, the next two sections explore in greater detail King's work with indie-auteurs. The first section analyses King's collaboration with Tyler Perry at William Morris during the early phases of Perry's career in Hollywood. The second explores King's collaboration with Ryan Coogler and Shaka King in the making of *Judas and the Black Messiah* at Macro. Doing so, the chapter considers how race is mobilised in promotion in ways that not only serves neoliberal market impulses by monetising diversity, but also sometimes sheds light on the barriers that Black practitioners face, enhances their positions in the wider industry, and may rearrange or reinforce images of Black professional legitimacy and respectability.

'I got this package with a cover memo from William Morris': innovative deal-making, 'authentic' Black production and Tyler Perry as indie-auteur

A writer, director, producer and actor, Tyler Perry is a highly entrepreneurial indie-auteur who has cultivated a reputation as a Hollywood outsider asserting industrial, economic and creative independence to produce purportedly authentic manifestations of his creative vision.[56] Unlike most of the other figures examined in this book, however, critics and scholars have called Perry's indie-auteur legitimacy into question because, they argue, his works include problematic or harmful representations and show Perry to be deficient as a visual storyteller. According to many scholars, Perry's work often includes derogatory depictions of Black women, problematic sexual politics and homophobic representations, a vilification of wealthy Black people, and minstrelsy modes-of-performance.[57] Perry's plays, which toured the African American or chitin-circuit, are frequently contrasted against so-called legitimate theatre,[58] while his films are often compared negatively to television's most denigrated genres, including the soap opera, reality television and chat shows.[59] These distinctions rest partly on Perry's claims to cater to a popular mainstream Black audience and rejection of pretension, prestige and critics' judgements.[60]

In these terms, Perry's works are effectively framed as 'negative' Black texts, which, as Racquel J. Gates explains, are often defined problematically by their distance from 'normative, White hegemonic standards of quality'.[61] Hence, critics' negative comparisons between Perry's filmmaking and certain modes of television clearly mark an important point of departure with indie-auteurs such as Steven Soderbergh, Cary Fukunaga and David Fincher, whose work is often perceived positively as being cinematic and unlike most television. Perry's denigration in these terms helps to explain why he has been so severely ignored from studies of American independent and indie film, despite Paul N. Reinsch calling him one of the 'most important independent American filmmakers of the past several decades'.[62]

Perry's indie reputation lies at the centre of what makes him such a controversial figure. As Reinsch points out, Perry is often treated by scholars as a problem that needs solving.[63] Contrasting Perry's features to the politically and socially critical films of the Los Angeles School of Independent Filmmakers and those of its legacy, Novotny Lawrence argues that Perry's films 'fall back upon Black stereotypes' and uphold 'the Hollywood status quo rather than challenging it'.[64] Leah Aldridge argues that Perry has adhered to 'neoliberalism's market logic and Hollywood's dismissive attitude toward Black representation'.[65] Aldridge argues that Perry has turned his 'Black body into a commodified image of Blackness' associated with non-threatening uplift messages that ultimately serve to 'curb resistance'.[66] Reinsch, however, argues that although a case can be made about the problematic representations of Perry's works, his adherence to Classical Hollywood modes of convention is a potentially radical act that transforms Hollywood aesthetics into a cinema of Black voices and faces.[67] Quinn, meanwhile, argues that by establishing an independent business model, Perry's productions, of which many were made at his own studio in Atlanta, have provided jobs for Black people in a poor region.[68] While acknowledging Perry's 'lamentable' efforts to resist his employees' attempts to unionise and pay them fair wages, Quinn argues that Perry 'has not enriched the major film companies', nor, she asserts, 'have his Black female-centered melodramas served to legitimate corporate interests'.[69] In these critiques, Perry is attributed significant agency as an entrepreneurial indie-auteur but is scrutinised in terms of whether he has used that agency for the good of other Black people both culturally and economically. Foregrounding Perry's William Morris representation, however, can help to provide a more complex picture. Specifically, it can: avoid simple binaries positioning the indie-auteur against a Hollywood core composed of the major studios; prevent tying him straightforwardly to a perceived Black audience; resist overstating Perry's autonomy and giving him too much credit; and challenges notions that he, rather than the industry, bears the responsibility for circulating the so-called negative Black images in his works.

Before becoming one of King's clients at William Morris and making his first feature film, *Diary of a Mad Black Woman*, in 2005, Perry had already secured a significant fortune estimated to have been between $50 million and $100 million from the sale of tickets of his plays, associated merchandise and home videos.[70] As well as mostly touring the African American theatre circuit, Perry's plays starred himself playing multiple roles including a Black gun-toting matriarch named Madea and appealed especially to churchgoing Black women. For Samantha N. Sheppard, Madea epitomises how Perry has built his brand partly by moulding himself into a 'marketable persona and product'.[71] Moreover, Perry exerted significant energy cultivating audience loyalty by interacting with his audience, and sharing stories about his life and career, both during his shows and online through his website.[72] Doing so encouraged repeat ticket-sales and enabled him to sell merchandise and home videos both at the live venues and online.

Despite having secured significant success in theatre, Perry was reportedly unknown in Hollywood until he signed with King and William Morris in 2003.[73] Asked how William Morris set about gaining Hollywood's attention, Perry explained that King told him, 'we've got to get you in here. We've got to get you to do this ... we want you to book a show here in town'.[74] Although Perry subsequently booked a show at the Wilshire Ebell Theatre, doing so brought disappointing results as the Hollywood executives sent their assistants in their place.[75] Consequently, Perry and King decided to make the 'biggest statement' they could by having Perry put on a play at the larger and more glamorous Kodak Theatre on Hollywood Boulevard.[76] Doing so was successful, Perry stated, as 'all of those executives came out and enjoyed the show'.[77]

Perry's collaboration with William Morris provides an important reminder of the relative control that talent intermediaries exert over their clients' careers. Contrary to Perry's repeated claims that he is motivated exclusively by an attempt to cater to his underserved Black working-class and female audience,[78] Perry's performances at the Ebell and Kodak theatres are examples of his efforts to secure attention from Hollywood studio executives. Perry's decision to attribute this strategy of gaining Hollywood's attention to William Morris and King represents typical rhetorical manoeuvring designed to deflect any attention away from the possibility that the indie-auteur may pursue commercial gain over artistic and, in this case perhaps, racial integrity. That is, Perry attributes his migration to Hollywood to the agency rather than to his own personal career ambitions.

The strategy of screening his play at the Kodak Theatre was successful with Perry and King subsequently entering negotiations with the Hollywood studios and networks to make a film adaptation of *Diary* and a television series, respectively.[79] Yet deals with Fox Searchlight and CBS collapsed after both the studio and network requested changes to the projects. 'The problem at CBS and at Searchlight', Perry declared, 'was that I kept being told that I needed other writers to make my projects work in Hollywood'.[80] After Fox Searchlight also began reportedly instructing Perry on who to cast, he explains that he 'handed the money back' with the intention of financing the film himself before releasing it on DVD as he had done his plays.[81] This narrative positions Perry as a Hollywood outsider willing to walk away from potentially lucrative deals if his creative control and integrity are threatened. Perry's straight-to-DVD plan was shelved, though, after he and King were contacted by Lionsgate, the largest independent studio, which offered Perry creative control, let him retain the rights, and gave him 50 per cent of the profits minus distribution and marketing costs in exchange for Perry putting up half the production finance.[82] Recalling this whole process, the then-president of production at Lionsgate, Steve Pasternak, stated:

> It isn't like we were tracking Tyler's activities. He did so much from a grass-roots level ... that he completely slipped under the radar of the film industry. I got this package with a cover memo from William Morris saying something like Tyler has done 57 gazillion dollars in sales, something outrageous for someone I'd never heard of.[83]

Consequently, Pasternak explains:

> I brought this with me to our management conference, and I asked everyone if they'd heard of him [Perry]. I thought at least the home entertainment people would have heard of him. Then I started to ask African American people that I know, or employees here, and they all knew who he was. I thought, 'We're not in on this secret'.[84]

Pasternak's comment is an example of racial prejudice in Hollywood. Suggesting that the management team and home entertainment people were White, Pasternak inadvertently highlights the fact that White privilege ran through Lionsgate's entire organisation. This adheres to broader findings that Hollywood is racialised as people of colour are usually employed as greeters, receptionists and assistants, while senior teams remain White.[85] Claiming to have 'asked everyone' while initially omitting the African Americans that he knew demonstrates how the opinions of Black people are treated as secondary and inferior. Pasternak's distinction between 'everyone' and his African American employees and acquaintances recalls Richard Dyer's finding that, when race is applied only to non-White peoples, it allows White people to 'function as a human norm' and 'claim to speak for the commonality of humanity'.[86] Moreover, Pasternak's phrasing, 'We're not in on this secret', wrongly implies something was being deliberately hidden rather than wilfully ignored. Pasternak's reliance on Black colleagues and friends for knowledge about Black culture, much like William Morris executives' interactions with King, demonstrates how major Hollywood institutions often lack the formal processes and systems necessary for tracking Black cultural trends. This ignorance is highly problematic because it is at once symptomatic of and perpetuates a marginalisation of Black culture and talent. Hence, drawing from a narrow pool of Black personnel for insight risks bolstering equally narrow conceptions of Black culture. The potential for a purposeful engagement with these issues is ultimately stymied, however, as Pasternak turns Hollywood's neglect of Black culture into a narrative about the discovery of a single indie-auteur. Perry's construction as an indie-auteur differentiates Lionsgate from the Hollywood studios and positions the company as more risk-taking.

In this context of racial prejudice, Perry and King reportedly collaborated to secure a savvy deal that maintained the indie-auteur's creative control and economic independence. According to Ndounou, Perry's business operations represent 'a viable, sustainable business model, especially for Black independent film'.[87] Citing Perry's collaboration with Lionsgate, Ndounou argues that Perry has managed to evade Hollywood's 'nearly impenetrable matrix of domination'.[88] Perry's efforts at retaining control over his script and project can be understood in these terms as being about more than merely fulfilling his creative vision. Rather, maintaining control enabled Perry to reduce the cost of production to minimise his financial risk while maximising his potential reward in the form of profit participation, and let Perry enhance his brand by ensuring that no very well-known star could outshine him (Figure 6.1).

Notions of Perry as a potentially archetypal independent filmmaker, however, are contentious given the extent to which Lionsgate's deal with him hinged on King's ability to leverage Perry's track record of substantial commercial success. Lionsgate's exposure to risk was minimal because Perry's prior commercial success highlighted the substantial audience that already existed for his works while Perry's contribution to the production finance decreased the company's upfront costs. Perry's ability to provide half of *Diary*'s production budget in exchange for retaining control reveals that Perry charted a route which is difficult for most independent filmmakers to follow. Moreover, taking Perry's collaboration with Lionsgate to be indicative of his independence and potential subversion of the Hollywood status quo is problematic, owing to how closely it adheres to the studio and indie-auteur's own promotional rhetoric. Boasting that his movie production budgets are significantly less than the Hollywood average, meanwhile, Perry stated: 'I look at others and see where they spent $30 or $40 million and wonder, "Where did the money go?" Into people's pockets, I guess'.[89]

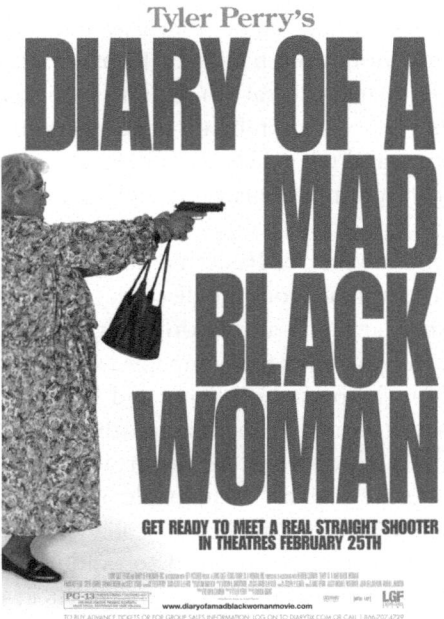

Figure 6.1 A poster for Tyler Perry's *Diary of a Mad Black Woman* featuring Perry starring as Madea. (Source: Photofest)

Perry's comment is reprehensible as he reduces costs to improve his share of profits and does so by reducing the pay of his employees.[90] Furthermore, by highlighting Perry's track record of commercial success, King conveyed impressions about the writer–director's significant entrepreneurial spirit. This entrepreneurial spirit is immensely appealing to Hollywood studios and talent agencies seeking to increase their bottom line, especially where it indicates an ability to open untapped markets.[91] In these ways, King and Perry's strategy is arguably symptomatic of a post-civil rights turn where Black producers and filmmakers have sought to appeal to Hollywood's capitalist impulses to secure jobs and financial independence.[92] In doing so, however, they may reinforce neoliberalism's privileging of individualism in ways that are often to the detriment of collective political action.[93]

King's experiences at William Morris around the same time highlights the challenges that marginalisation can have for individual Black employees. In an interview with *New York Times Magazine* that was published after he established Macro, King says that the week before *Diary* was due to be released in theatres, the film was not on the William Morris motion picture meeting agenda, as was protocol.[94] According to King, this represented one manifestation of how his ideas during the early phase of his career as an agent were frequently belittled.[95] The *Times Magazine* described King as being 'vindicated', however, after *Diary* became the highest-grossing film at the domestic box-office the following weekend before King and Perry 'learned to use being underestimated to their advantage'.[96] This narrative frames King's and Perry's experiences in ways that ultimately appear designed to highlight their entrepreneurial savvy.

King and Perry reportedly used 'being underestimated to their advantage' during negotiations over the production of Perry's debut series, *House of Payne*, with the syndication company Debmar-Mercury, which Lionsgate later acquired.[97] Specifically, King and William Morris's co-head of television, Mark Itkin, struck a 'unique' and 'pioneering' arrangement that industry commentators labelled the '10/90 deal'.[98] The 10/90 deal involved screening ten episodes of a series on a given channel or channels before securing an order for another ninety episodes if the show proved successful. In the case of *House of Payne*, this reportedly involved offering several channels the first ten episodes free of charge in exchange for a greater marketing push.[99] The strategy was designed to give *House of Payne* an opportunity to find an audience and guarantee the hundred episodes required for syndication while later giving them enough episodes to repackage the show as a DVD collection, thereby building on Perry's track record of generating substantial sales through home video.[100]

Debmar-Mercury press releases described this syndication model as having been 'inspired by the independent film platform distribution' model; a practice of releasing a feature on few screens in select territories before gauging audience appetite, building buzz and expanding wider.[101] This reference to independent film served to bolster impressions of Debmar-Mercury's syndication model as innovative and Perry as a Hollywood outsider who was circumventing Hollywood gatekeepers to reach his underserved Black audience. Recalling how he had walked away from the opportunity to make a sitcom with CBS, Perry asserted that a traditional network distribution order would have been a deal breaker because he wanted more of a commitment than the major networks typically offer.[102] Perry declared that he wanted 'to be a part of a system where an artist can create the art he thinks his audience wants' and, elsewhere, 'I know my audience, and I know what they want to see'.[103] Debmar-Mercury co-president Ira Bernstein also stated that Perry wanted to distribute *House of Payne* without Hollywood and network interference because the only way that he could guarantee that his 'unique and clearly defined brand' would be faithfully adapted to television was to 'get it on the air for his audience to see'.[104] Elsewhere, Bernstein added that Perry had repeatedly blown away the industry's established models and that *House of Payne*'s syndication was 'true to the independent spirit' of the project.[105] Summarising Debmar-Mercury's approach to the 10/90 model some years later, Bernstein stated that it began with Perry's insistence on creating a show that 'creatively he 100 per cent controlled'.[106] Bernstein continued, 'We said, we're basically a business of 50-year-old white guys judging and most times we're wrong. So how can we get an African-American sitcom on the air without all of us – including us – judging it?'[107]

Each of these comments made the 10/90 model appear to be a more democratic process where the underserved Black audience, rather than network executives, would determine *House of Payne*'s future. Such notions were contentious, however, as they elided the fact that the decision to commission ten episodes was itself an act of judgement. Contrary to its executives' efforts to portray Debmar-Mercury as risk-taking, the company's decision to make *House of Payne* was undoubtedly predicated once again on Perry's prior commercial success and the company's efforts to capture a potentially lucrative audience that had been increasingly neglected by major networks.[108] Hence Neal Sabin, vice president of the Weigel Broadcasting Co., the parent company to WCUI-TV Chicago which secured early rights to air *House of Payne*, stated, 'I like the ethnic skew, and I like Tyler Perry's track record'.[109]

House of Payne's approximately $500,000 per episode budget was roughly half of the network average for sitcoms.[110] This reduced not only Perry and Debmar-Mercury's costs for production but also the channels' subsequent costs of acquisition. Writing in *Forbes*, Merrill Barr hypothesised that efforts to launch later shows such as *Anger Management* (FX, 2012–14) and *Partners* (FX, 2014) using the 10/90 model failed because of their higher per episode budgets.[111] Itkin also argues that *House of Payne* succeeded because it reached a mass audience on TBS, whereas *Anger Management* and *Partners* targeted niche audiences on the prestige channel FX.[112] Consequently, *House of Payne* confirms Herman Gray's finding that the few Black shows on television are usually low cost and low risk.[113] While Perry's brand name helped to successfully launch *House of Payne*, the rhetoric of innovation surrounding its syndication model, and notions about fulfilling the indie-auteur's authentic vision, risk detracting attention away from a broader systemic problem of inequality. Moreover, the rhetoric of authorial independence and distribution innovation recalls the same rhetoric used to promote indie-auteur programmes such as *True Detective* and *The Knick* in the next decade. Yet while high-end shows such as *Twin Peaks* and *Band of Brothers* (HBO, 2001) were sometimes treated as antecedents to the 2010s cycle of indie-auteur–directed television,[114]

House of Payne never featured in the conversation. This omission is indicative of how low-budget Black productions targeting a Black audience are often denied the status of being a legitimate piece of art and are therefore omitted from histories of mainstream cultural production.[115]

Rhetoric about Perry catering directly to his audience is problematic because it is the same rhetoric that he uses to deflect criticism of the representations within his work. As several scholars have pointed out, Perry invokes his perception about what his audience wants and claims that his representations are based on authentic Black experiences as a shield against legitimate criticism.[116] In turn, Artel Great argues that Perry's productions can be understood according to a 'politics of thirst' whereby members of an underserved community are drawn to any emergent voice, even if, he says, that voice goes against their own interests.[117] Clearly, the construction of Perry as an authentic instinctual artist matters in these terms because it serves to bolster his association with his perceived core Black audience. Perry as indie-auteur legitimates his works as authentically of the Black community and obfuscates questions of his commercial motives and associations with Hollywood. This represents another example of rhetorical manoeuvring where the indie-auteur's operations are effectively framed in neoliberal terms as catering simply to the demands of the market. By bringing into focus King's and William Morris's roles in the management of Perry's career and pursuit of exposure within Hollywood, therefore, I challenge Perry's insistence that his representations are culturally acceptable simply because he works in service of a core Black audience.

According to King and Itkin, the syndication deal was 'another building block to extending the Tyler Perry brand in all media'.[118] King and Itkin's comment demonstrates how saturation of all media through the expansion of Perry's brand was their main strategy from very early in his Hollywood career. Since *Diary*, Perry has gone on to release feature films and television series, as well as often plays and other works such as books, at an astonishing rate. While pointing out that Perry's prolificacy may signal that he does not really write all of the works to which he attaches his name as lead or sole creator, however, Aymar Jean Christian and Khadijah Costley White argue that the expansion of his brand, and his positioning as Hollywood outsider and authentic Black voice, renders other Black voices 'unviable and unnecessary'.[119] This view is shared by some Black filmmakers such as Mario Van Peebles who stated:

> It's not that we shouldn't have our Tyler Perrys ... But we don't have our *A Beautiful Mind* [Howard, 2001] or *Lost in Translation* [Coppola, 2003]. The lack of variety gets to be reductive. ... Are there still cinematic minstrel shows? Absolutely.[120]

In the same article, however, King contended that Perry's success would open opportunities for other filmmakers by demonstrating to the studios that there was an unsated market demand for comedic vehicles with African American characters.[121]

King's rhetoric was indicative of how talent intermediaries attempt to not only build their individual clients' brands but also create an impression of demand in the marketplace to enhance the marketability and employability of other similar clients. In seeking to dispel accusations of harm to Black culture, King ignored the possibility that his and William Morris's strategy may have narrowed the parameters of Black storytelling by saturating the market with Perry's brand. This potential narrowing of parameters is reflected in the experience of producer D'Angela Steed when, upon pitching a TV drama, cable network executives reportedly asked her, 'What's the Tyler Perry version?'[122] Moreover, in a Hollywood industry providing few opportunities for Black talent in the belief that the market only has capacity for one Black figure, King's strategy arguably contributed to the growth of Perry's brand while leaving most other Black artists behind. Van Peebles's distinction between Perry and indie features such as *A Beautiful Mind* and *Lost in Translation*, however, acts as a reminder of Perry's frequent exclusion from legitimate culture. The issue for some of Perry's critics, therefore, was not so much that Perry was narrowing the parameters of Black film but that his negative images deviated from White normative standards of quality and some Black critics and filmmakers' efforts to secure acceptance within the White middle-class culture that Perry himself had shunned.

Perry's exclusion from legitimate culture has also led to him being significantly overlooked in studies of independent and indie film. While Perry's works are low cost and frequently disparaged, this section has shown that he is constructed as an indie-auteur with promotional, extratextual and critical discourse frequently invoking notions of his creative autonomy and economic independence. Recognising Perry's construction as an indie-auteur is important in adding greater complexity and colour to histories of independent and indie production as well as for, paradoxically, solving the 'Tyler Perry problem' that overstates his autonomy and positions him in narrow terms against a Hollywood core dominated by the major studios.

'Representing artists is a natural extension of that vision': *Judas and the Black Messiah*, Macro and coalition-building as promotion

This section analyses Macro and Charles King's collaboration with indie-auteurs Ryan Coogler and Shaka King in the production of *Judas and the Black Messiah*. A feature-length film released in 2021, *Judas* portrays Fred Hampton (Daniel Kaluuya), a deputy chairman of the Black Panther Party, in the days leading up to his assassination by the FBI following a betrayal by informant and Panther infiltrator William O'Neal (LaKeith Stanfield). *Judas* was co-produced by BRON Studios, Participant, Macro and Proximity Media. Proximity is owned by King and Macro's client, Coogler, who took a producing credit on *Judas* alongside King. *Judas* was also co-financed by Warner Bros., which acquired worldwide distribution rights. The film was directed by Shaka King, whose previous directing credits included one feature film, some short films and several television episodes. Shaka King also co-wrote the screenplay with his regular writing partner Will Berson, doing so by developing earlier drafts by brothers Kenneth and Keith Lucas. Significantly, *Judas* was released after the murder of George Floyd by police officer Derek Chauvin and during the Covid-19 pandemic when lockdown restrictions forced many cinemas to close. George Floyd's murder made the film highly topical in ways that increased dialogue around racial inequality and police brutality.[123] Lockdown restrictions prompted Warner Bros. to release *Judas* on its streaming service, HBO Max, on the same day as in cinemas.

Judas demonstrates how talent intermediaries and their collaborators may build an ethos of community activism into a film's promotion. While promoting *Judas*, Charles King, Shaka King and Ryan Coogler regularly implicitly and sometimes explicitly drew parallels between *Judas*'s depiction of Hampton's struggle and the experiences of Black filmmakers in Hollywood. On one hand, such parallels might be understood as signalling *Judas*'s continued social relevance in ways that were arguably designed to bolster support behind social equality activism. Charles King, for example, stated:

> I personally would hope that [what] people would take is understanding the incredible work and the voice that Chairman Fred had at 21 to uplift his community ... And that this also could be a moment in time, just like when Chairman Fred Hampton was bringing a coalition together, that the same thing is possible, and that with that coalition, real change for our communities here in this country and globally can happen.[124]

Such parallels may be understood in these terms as a form of social critique of the dominant neoliberal order and culture as represented through Hollywood.[125] On the other hand, such parallels may be understood as providing promotional and commercial functions, which potentially blunt social equality activism. Specifically, this chapter considers three interrelated promotional functions. First, parallels between *Judas*'s depiction of Hampton's struggle and the experiences of Black filmmakers in Hollywood promote *Judas* by generating interest in its narrative. Second, such parallels enhance the brands of King and his collaborators by positioning them as Hollywood outsiders struggling against the odds to create exceptional work. Third, emphasis on social barriers, social activism and coalition-building bolsters Macro's corporate mission and talent management business. It bolsters Macro's brand, generates investment in its productions by increasing a sense of their worth, and encourages more talent to join its management divisions by reiterating the necessity of a cohesive Black and minority filmmaking community. As King stated upon founding M88:

> Our work at MACRO is about lifting the culture and amplifying the voices and authentic narratives of Black people and people of color ... Representing artists is a natural extension of that vision and enhances our ability to find opportunities to collaborate with all of our various business verticals.[126]

Prior to the production of *Judas*, there were multiple points of interaction between Charles King, Shaka King and Ryan Coogler. First, Charles King has represented Coogler since the indie-auteur graduated from the University of Southern California and set out to make his debut feature, *Fruitvale Station* (2013). King helped Coogler to secure the finance to produce *Fruitvale* and has managed his career thereafter as Coogler proceeded to direct *Creed* (2015), a quasi-reboot of *Rocky* and the Disney-Marvel blockbuster *Black Panther* (2018). After King established Macro in 2015, Coogler came to occupy a highly privileged position as the only client that King continued to represent directly.[127] Asked after founding Macro which clients had played the most important role in his career, King described Perry as the client who inspired his entrepreneurialism and Coogler as the client who encouraged him to become more engaged in social activism.[128] Recalling having signed Coogler, King stated that the filmmaker had 'a mission and a purpose behind elevating culture and impacting communities that was far beyond what he was going to do as a filmmaker. And I really learned a lot about community activism frankly'.[129] In these terms, King's continuing representation of Coogler reinforces Macro's socially conscious brand and marks a point of departure with his more obviously corporate and commercial WME work. Moreover, whereas Perry was associated with negative images of Black people, King associates Coogler positively with Macro's mission of Black social and cultural uplift.

A second point of interaction, this time between King, King and Coogler, occurred in 2014 when the three figures collaborated with others including Ava DuVernay on a campaign called #BlackOutBlackFriday. Initiated by Coogler and DuVernay, the campaign encouraged consumers to boycott retailers on Black Friday to stop the unjust targeting of people of colour by law enforcement and the criminal justice system.[130] Described by Coogler as intending to make Black Friday 'a day of activism over consumerism', the campaign comprised various activities, including the release of a collection of short videos and a reading of Spike Lee's *Do The Right Thing* (1989) at New York's Lincoln Center.[131] One of the videos, which was directed by Shaka King, features a series of clips of police brutality set against Andy Williams's festive song, 'It's the Most Wonderful Time of the Year'.[132] The video's extreme juxtaposition of image and sound represents an example of 'shock effect' being used by Black artists to prompt social consciousness and critique. According to Herman Gray, the status quo can be disrupted in creative expression through the use of 'a tactical shock effect, something that disturbs and destabilizes the order of things, jarring us to see and imagine differently'.[133] During his participation in the Producers Guild panel on equality and diversity, Charles King smiles knowingly as he admits that he probably would not have worked on the campaign during his first year as an agent and felt empowered to participate in the campaign because he was leaving WME to establish Macro.[134] King's admission confirms how agents, and especially junior agents of colour, feel restricted in driving change within the Hollywood system. King's admission also serves to further differentiate between his more obviously commercial and corporate WME agenting work and Macro. While King depicts his own increasing empowerment, however, he also elides the fact that campaigns and short films tend to offer greater opportunities for experimentation, including tactical shock effects, than does mainstream film and television distributed by the Hollywood studios. While the #BlackOutBlackFriday campaign may reinforce Charles King's, Shaka King's and Ryan Coogler's reputations for social activism, therefore, one must be wary of accepting too readily the transference of this social activism and the successful deployment of similar shock tactics in feature filmmaking such as in the case of *Judas*.

The third area of interaction came in the form of a reportedly chance encounter between Shaka King and Coogler at Sundance in 2013. The narrative of how King and Coogler met was repeatedly communicated in the extratextual and critical discourse surrounding *Judas*'s release and must be understood as having been retrospectively configured. With their debut features, *Fruitvale* and *Newlyweeds* (2013), having made their world premieres at the festival, King and Coogler reportedly met 'among a sea of white faces' in Park City after a snowstorm grounded their flights home.[135] After reportedly arranging to meet for dinner that evening, Coogler and King exchanged stories about their very different experiences at the festival. *Fruitvale* received significant praise and went on to win Sundance's Grand Jury Prize and the Audience Award before being acquired by The Weinstein Company for just over $2 million.[136] With *Fruitvale* depicting the real-life events leading up to the manslaughter of Oscar Grant by police officers, Harvey Weinstein said that he was honoured to be able to share the film's 'earth-shattering story … with audiences everywhere'.[137] *Deadline*, meanwhile, described *Fruitvale* as having the potential to build on its festival success to become an unexpected hit akin to *Precious* (Daniels, 2009) and *Beasts of the Southern Wild* (Zeitlin, 2012).[138]

In contrast, *Newlyweeds* received no awards nor substantial bids from distributors. After the festival, King sold *Newlyweeds* to Phase 4 Films, a small Canadian distributor, for only $25,000.[139] In the promotional discourse surrounding *Judas*, King repeatedly described feedback that he allegedly received from a sales agent who refused to represent *Newlyweeds* at Sundance.[140] The sales agent, King explains, 'said he couldn't sell the film because there weren't any famous Black people in it'.[141] After retorting that Sundance is known for providing a platform for new actors and that many films screening at the festival feature unknown White actors, King says that the sales agent told him, 'Yeah, but they're white'.[142] Accordingly, King reflects:

> I knew that [*Newlyweeds*] didn't sell not because it didn't deserve to sell but because I wasn't entering a meritocracy. I was dealing with the same racist, systemic racism that, you know, had made my dad's life difficult, my mother's life difficult, my grandmother's life difficult, my grandfather's life difficult. You know, I understood that it wasn't me, so I wasn't like, 'ah man, I'm trash,' you know. But I was like, 'this sucks'.[143]

After this experience, King says that he made a short film, *Mulignans* (2015), from which he expected no remuneration but which restored in him 'the natural desire to create'.[144] Thus, King says that he has subsequently made a conscious effort to only undertake work that brings him fulfilment.[145] Elsewhere, King states that Black artists must be comfortable 'creating in the dark' because they may never secure backing in an industry where the executive levels remain White male dominated.[146]

This narrative of Coogler's and King's experience at Sundance invokes a context which positioned them as indie-auteurs and promoted *Judas* as an exceptional work that was made against the odds. Locating their relationship in the independent film realm recalls how promotional and extra-textual discourse invoked the Coens and Raimi's off-Hollywood living arrangements and friendship to position *Hudsucker* as an authentic indie film. Unlike the Coens and Raimi, however, the narrative of Coogler's and King's Sundance experience demonstrates clearly how their indie-auteur reputations were tied directly to their race. As one *Variety* interviewer put it, King is 'considered to be an "outsider" from Hollywood, both as a new filmmaker and as an artist of color'.[147]

On one hand, this narrative helps to highlight the barriers that Black filmmakers face in getting their films financed and distributed. King's description of *Newlyweeds*' rejection by a sales agent, for instance, is symptomatic of industry executives' and intermediaries' tendencies to perceive most films with predominantly Black casts as lacking marketability and box-office pizazz.[148] Meanwhile, *Deadline*'s comparison of *Fruitvale Station* to *Precious* and *Beasts of the Southern Wild* is indicative of an industry discourse that too often resorts to labelling any film with a predominantly Black cast, regardless of differences in narrative and aesthetic conventions, as belonging to a 'Black genre'. Such comparisons are not only reductive but extremely limiting as they contribute to industry perceptions that the market only has capacity for one significant 'Black film' to be distributed at a time.[149]

On the other hand, making race an inherent aspect of King's outsider indie-auteur brand risks undermining efforts at raising awareness of discrimination in the industry in general. After Sundance, for instance, King signed with William Morris and developed a television pilot for FX that was not picked up.[150] King also credits *Mulignans* with helping him to get his first professional unionised job directing several episodes of the TBS series *People of Earth* (2016–17).[151] Following his work on *People of Earth*, King has directed episodes of *High Maintenance* (HBO, 2016–20) and *Shrill* (Hulu, 2019–21). King's professional activity in the television realm thus implies that he is not quite the Hollywood industry 'outsider' that was described. In the promotion of *Judas*, however, King sought to differentiate between his television and film directing work:

> it is important that I differentiate how much energy and passion I give to, you know, a directing-for-hire job versus a film that, you know, I'm writing and directing. Just because, if you give all of yourself to a TV job and they take it and they just, you know, marginalise you, it really can feel hurtful, and I've experienced that to some degree, and so I know better, I know just to give a certain amount, and I know that

my 80 per cent is like a good amount, you know, 'cus basically I'm just not dreaming about it [the television project] ... but when you make a movie, you know how it is ... I'll do anything, I'll go through a wall, whatever, the answer's 'yes'.[152]

After asserting that television is also a writer's medium, unlike film where the director has authority, King stated that 'There's also something fun and a great education about committing to help[ing] someone else see what they want made, even if it isn't what you want made ... even satisfying studio notes'.[153]

Although King appears to be confessing to exerting less effort for employers in his television work, his comment represents rhetorical manoeuvring designed to ultimately enhance his reputation and obscure the realities of his network employment. Making even taking notes appear fulfilling serves to build and sustain his reputation as an authentic artist. In turn, King's comments reinforce simplistic distinctions and hierarchies positioning film over television and the indie-auteur above the director-for-hire. In positioning himself as an authentic artist, King seeks to cultivate authorship discourses and promote *Judas* as worthy of acclaim. King plays to elite conceptions of quality production in a way that Gray argues risks limiting experimentation and constraining Black expression.[154] In addition, King's distinctions between types of media and labour, which is underpinned by branding and talent management strategies, is antithetical to the creation of broad coalitions. King has publicly declared that he will never make commercial spots because, he says, they are a form of propaganda and he does not want to use his 'power as a visual storyteller' to do harm.[155] Recalling Dee Rees's work with Macro on *Mudbound* and filming of Walmart and Samsung commercials, King's comment demonstrates that no consensus exists between Macro's clients and collaborators about the relationship between media work and activism. Moreover, King's comments about the different types of media work confuse issues of quality and prestige with politics. Thus, King's dubious claims about his artistic authenticity and independence risk making old-fashioned conceptions of authorial practice the end-goal and detracting attention from broader industrial and social inequalities. Any conflation of Blackness and outsider status is highly problematic as, in King's case, conflating the two risks making him appear to be a 'sellout' when his links to Hollywood are realised and tightened.[156]

Shaka King's troubling experience with *Newlyweeds* provides a parallel in promotional discourse to the narrative of the difficulties that he, Charles King and Ryan Coogler experienced in making *Judas*. As I have mentioned, these narratives are also invoked to create parallels between

Judas's depiction of Fred Hampton's struggle for social equality and the Black filmmakers' experiences in Hollywood. On teaming up with Coogler and Charles King, for instance, Shaka King stated, 'If you're trying to kick down heavy doors, you need bodies to go up against that door. And I needed, like, big dudes'.[157] On securing Coogler as a producer of the film, King continued, 'So I got a big dude who I trust, whose politics I know are like mine'.[158] In the same interview, Charles King asserted that raising finance for Macro to become a film financier was the hardest thing he has ever done.[159] 'If the first Black partner in the history of Hollywood, who represented some of the biggest names in our industry, launches a company and still had challenges raising capital', King stated, 'that should tell you how challenging it is [gaining] access to capital for people who look like the three of us'.[160] While Charles King overstates his historical significance as he was the first Black partner in William Morris and not in Hollywood in general, Shaka King's and Charles King's comments clearly invoke an impression of these Black men, or 'dudes', as breaking down racial barriers.

Shaka King explains that racial barriers were encountered when, upon attempting to sell *Judas* to studios, he and his co-producers repeatedly received offers below the amount that they believed the film to be worth.[161] In one negotiation, King says that a studio executive made an insufficient offer after inputting data into an algorithm and determining that the movie would 'bomb'.[162] King says that he reminded the executive that the same algorithm had wrongly predicted that *BlacKkKlansman* (Lee, 2018) would fail at the box-office one year earlier.[163] Stating that the reason why they were 'lowballed' was because of 'mistruths' in Hollywood that films with Black casts perform poorly internationally, King says that it proves that 'even the math in Hollywood is racist'.[164] King's comments are supported by Ndounou's findings that distributors' assumptions that Black-cast films do not sell well abroad reduces opportunities for Black talent and limits the budgets for the few Black-cast films that are greenlit.[165] As a result, *Judas*'s marketing provided King and his colleagues with an opportunity to critique Hollywood's colour-coded dynamics and raise awareness about the continued barriers that Black talent face in Hollywood.

With *Judas* acquired by Warner Bros., however, it is paradoxical that King has found space to make such comments in the promotion of a studio co-financed and distributed film. King's ability to do so confirms Quinn's argument that Hollywood's 'corporate fault-lines' provide opportunities for minority talent mobilising the rich performative and subcultural resources of Black America within the celebrity-fronted industry environment.[166] Problematically, though, King's comment shows once again how authorship discourses circulated in Hollywood's celebrity-fronted environment are all too often masculinised. King's comment about big dudes breaking down doors recalls Joni Sighvatsson's description of Propaganda's director clients as flexing their creative muscles. Although framed in much more progressive terms, King's comment arguably represents a variation of the highly prevalent and problematic conceptualisation of the male indie-auteur as cultural innovator and maverick. Although promotional and extratextual discourse framed *Judas*'s production in terms of overcoming racial barriers, therefore, discussion of gender inequalities is conspicuously absent.

Having anticipated that Hollywood studios would be reluctant to greenlight a Fred Hampton biopic, King explained that he, along with Kenneth and Keith Lucas, made the strategic decision to couch the story in a thriller genre framework.[167] Comparing *Judas*'s focus on O'Neal's betrayal of Hampton to the police corruption narrative in *The Departed* (Scorsese, 2006), King described his film's genre framework as a 'Trojan horse' designed to give it mainstream and studio appeal.[168] Likewise, Charles King described *Judas* as an 'elevated thriller' and, pointing to its mainstream qualities, differentiated it from small independent art-house films.[169] In an article titled 'How "Judas and the Black Messiah" Reflects Charles D. King's MacroVision', King asserted that Macro's commitment to co-finance the film put them 'in a position to be partners'.[170] King went on to state, 'so this movie is not purely driven by the studio. That also helped us support Shaka's vision and how he cast the movie and to keep it as authentic as possible'.[171] Charles King also reveals how Shaka King had explained that although he had a background in the independent realm, he wanted *Judas* to be a commercial film that would be distributed and seen by audiences worldwide.[172]

Shaka King's and Charles King's comments indicate how *Judas* is symptomatic of indie modes of production where major studios became increasingly involved in the sector. In this context, Shaka King and his collaborators presented their decision to adopt a thriller genre framework as a strategy for exploiting Hollywood's corporate faultlines to create a film about racial and social equality. In turn, Charles King implied that Macro provided the conditions that enabled Shaka King to retain his autonomy and authentic vision despite working with a major studio. Yet Shaka King and his collaborators' adherence to a genre framework can also be understood as a form of acquiescence to studio pressures where the potential for radical social critique was compromised. It is certainly the case that efforts to make *Judas* a more commercial film by adopting a genre framework suited Shaka King's and Charles King's career and business objectives. It facilitated the writer-director's ascendency from the lower-budget independent realm to the Hollywood mainstream and the Macro CEO's efforts to grow his company and establish a partnership with Warner.

These dynamics are manifested clearly in *Judas*'s paratextual materials. For Shaka King, the film's political message and thriller genre narrative cohere around the opposing relationship and ideological positions of *Judas*'s two protagonists, Hampton and O'Neal. Indeed, King described the film as being about 'the capitalist in William O'Neal and the socialist in Fred Hampton ... and the coward in William O'Neal and the revolutionary in Fred Hampton'.[173] Thus, Warner's first poster has a large image of Hampton set against a marching crowd with a placard reading 'ALL POWER TO THE PEOPLE' in the top-right corner. Hampton and the marching crowd are coloured all in red, signalling Hampton's position as both leading the people and belonging to the people. The red colouring invokes a wave of revolution, as well as murder associated with the thriller genre. The use of red colouring to simultaneously invoke murder linked to the thriller genre is potentially problematic as it risks associating revolution with bloodshed over social change.

In contrast, a smaller image of O'Neal stands alone beneath Hampton with a subtle menacing grin. The film's title clearly evokes the theme of betrayal. The tagline below the trailer, 'You can kill a revolutionary but you can't kill the revolution', also written in bold white font, signals the film's balancing of a thriller murder narrative and Hampton biopic. The second poster, an image of Hampton standing proud and O'Neal appearing menacingly behind him entirely coloured in red, even more clearly positions the latter as a judas and foregrounds the narrative of betrayal (Figure 6.2). The second poster also features large bold text proclaiming *Judas* to be 'One of the best films of the year' with the crests of prestigious film festivals and organisations below it describing the film's award successes and nominations. It also describes *Judas* as being 'From producers Ryan Coogler & Charles D. King and Director Shaka King', thereby demonstrating how acclaim and the attribution of authorship are closely linked.

Although the posters convey Hampton as a revolutionary and O'Neal as a coward, they fail to adequately convey O'Neal as a capitalist and Hampton as a socialist. This is significant because the absence of motivation creates an impression of Black on Black crime and removes much sense of the social issues driving Hampton and the Black Panthers' push for change. The first of Warner Bros.'s trailers suffers from these issues too. This trailer achieves a significant energy through the fast pace of its editing which is cut to the tempo of the drumbeats and electronic horns

204 THE TALENT MANAGEMENT OF INDIE AUTHORSHIP

Figure 6.2 *Judas and the Black Messiah* poster. (Source: Photofest)

of its score. A significant proportion of the trailer also features Hampton loudly addressing his audience with chants such as 'I am a revolutionary', which repeats numerous times at the beginning and end, 'You can murder a freedom fighter but you can't murder freedom', and 'I'm gonna die for the people 'cause I live for the people'. In the middle, there are clips of O'Neal on the run, an explosion, a shootout and O'Neal throwing his gun. Collectively, these properties convey *Judas* as an accessible and cool mainstream thriller that aligns King, King and Coogler with indie-auteur cool.

As with the posters, however, there is no sense of the social injustices driving Hampton and the Panther's activism, nor of the capitalist social conditions and greed motivating O'Neal. Although the trailer features Hampton declaring that the Panthers are forming a 'rainbow coalition of oppressed brothers and sisters of every colour' and O'Neal protesting that they 'ain't no terrorists', there is little that adequately identifies the Panthers and Hampton as the victims of FBI persecution. Decontextualised, the explosion and shootout can be interpreted as acts of Panther efforts to sow hatred and terror, as FBI agent Roy Mitchell (Jesse Plemons) claims. Warner Bros.'s second trailer corrects these issues somewhat. It humanises Hampton through an emphasis on his relationship with Deborah Johnson (Dominique Fishback) and places more focus on the Panthers' social activism, which is said to include educating, nurturing, feeding and lobbying. The trailer also more clearly signals the FBI's detestable tactics by including clips of bureau director, Edgar J. Hoover (Martin Sheen), asserting that his officers must prevent the rise of the Black Messiah by neutralising Hampton 'through any means necessary'. Thus, the second trailer arguably strikes the kind of balance between conveying *Judas*'s thriller genre properties and its social message that Shaka King strived for, but it also effectively confirms the shortcomings of *Judas*'s other paratextual materials. Overall, the thriller genre conventions are promoted, and any substantial sense of *Judas*'s social critique is suppressed. As a result, *Judas*'s potential to disrupt the status quo with shock tactics is arguably compromised by its producers' adherence to prestige politics and mainstream genre conventions.

Conclusion

Following worldwide lockdowns that forced many cinemas to close in response to the Covid-19 pandemic, WarnerMedia took the decision to release its feature films for 2021, including *Judas*, in cinemas on the same day that they were released on its newly launched streaming service, HBO Max. The decision was an attempt to mitigate against losses in revenues from theatrical distribution while promoting HBO Max, which lagged behind Netflix, Amazon Instant Video and Disney+ for number of subscribers. As Macro was a co-financier and co-producer of *Judas*, the film's release on HBO Max severely limited the revenues that King's company could earn through profit participation.[174] Charles King recalled being disappointed in the way that Warner's day-and-date release strategy was communicated. 'Unfortunately', King says, 'we read [about it] in the trades, just like everyone else in our entire town'.[175] As well as empathising with HBO Max's market position, King stated that he was initially concerned about Macro's potential returns and ability to repay their investors.[176] King also described Warner's decision as potentially compromising Macro's stated mission of sharing *Judas*'s story about Hampton and his legacy with a wide audience.[177] Shaka King, meanwhile, responded to Warner's decision by claiming that it could harm Macro and the broader minority independent filmmaking community. Shaka King asserted, 'Really look at the role that MACRO plays in shepherding movies like this … If that company was not meaningfully compensated, the effect could be fairly disastrous to our filmmaking community'.[178]

Warner's decision to release *Judas* on HBO Max and in cinemas on the same day, therefore, represented another hurdle in an industry where the working conditions of Black talent and producers is already more precarious than those of their White counterparts.[179] Warner's decision to opt for a day-and-date release strategy also provides an important reminder of the precariousness of small and medium-sized enterprises such as Macro in a Hollywood industry where the major studios reduce their risk by signing unequal production and distribution partnerships. While Charles King claims that Macro is 'absolutely going to make the world better',[180] its dependency on much larger media organisations for co-production and distribution represents a threat to its future success. Thus, Warner's decision provides an important reminder that Black ownership of distribution infrastructure remains needed to drive more substantial change. As Charles King himself states, 'We know the value of our culture. And now we need to be part of the value chain of ownership'.[181]

While Tyler Perry has managed to secure a minority stake in the Paramount-owned BET Media Group, including its networks and streaming platform, and is reportedly in ongoing negotiations over completing a full takeover,[182] Macro has not yet entered into distribution and has more recently struck a first-look deal for the distribution of its feature films with Amazon.[183] In the meantime, Macro draws attention to the barriers it and Black talent face and, in doing so, seeks to strengthen their positions by bolstering their brands. Hence, Shaka King and Charles King used Warner's decision to release *Judas* on HBO Max to draw attention to an industrial context where Black filmmakers are marginalised and struggle for opportunities and exposure. As this chapter has argued, articulations about this context serve Macro and its clients' interests by bolstering their brand value, generating investment in their productions by increasing a sense of their worth, and encouraging more talent to join Macro's management divisions by reiterating the necessity of a cohesive Black and minority filmmaking community. Aligning an indie-auteur's outsider status with their race and racial unity with corporate missions can, however, be problematic. Black creators' adherence to old-fashioned notions of authorship risks reinforcing industrial and cultural hierarchies and constraining expression in ways that are potentially detrimental to collective progressive social activism. Macro's purported mission also risks creating an impression that above-the-line African Americans and other people of colour that do not become clients of a management company or agency that builds its brand around championing minorities are perceived as not supporting the community and its causes. As Macro adheres to mainstream conventions as it seeks to grow its sphere of influence, expand its revenue streams, and partner with major studios and distributors such as Warner and Amazon, it risks limiting opportunities for experimentation in expression for those figures working outside it. While King and Macro may make positive contributions to the industry and culture by advocating for Black talent and stories, therefore, they continue to work within, and sometimes reinforce, neoliberal capitalist structures and dynamics.

Notes

1. There are a number of socioeconomic factors behind such inequality. These factors include: Black people's lack of access to the socioeconomic capital more often enjoyed by White counterparts; problems with top intermediary companies' recruitment strategies where they too often rely on networking as a means of recruitment and recruit mainly from elite schools such as Stanford and Princeton while overlooking historically Black colleges; low levels of retention of Black agents stemming in part from their feelings of isolation; and, of course, more general industry prejudice (Buckley (2019); see also https://www.diverserepresentation.com).
2. Buckley (2019).
3. Ibid.
4. Mann (2008) p. 84.
5. Ndounou (2014) pp. 31–4.
6. Ibid. p. 31.
7. Ibid. p. 33.
8. Mack (2012) p. 52.
9. Ibid. p. 52.
10. Donnelly (2021).
11. On Black civil rights lawyers, see Mack (2012) p. 4.
12. Jarvey (2015).
13. Ndounou (2014); see also Gillespie (2016) p. 41.
14. Kennedy (2009) p. 3.

15. Hall (1993) p. 108.
16. Jarvey (2015); Littleton (2015b).
17. Littleton (2015b).
18. Jarvey (2015).
19. Low (2020).
20. https://web.archive.org/web/20220327091625/https://www.stayuncmmn.com.
21. Anon (2021).
22. Ndounou (2014) pp. 1–4; Havens (2013) p. 1.
23. See also Lotz (2014) p. 29.
24. https://www.staymacro.com/directory, under Charles D. King; Callahan-Bever (2017).
25. https://www.staymacro.com/directory, under Charles D. King.
26. Anon (2021); Kelly (2021).
27. Callahan-Bever (2017).
28. Ibid.
29. Ibid.
30. Ibid.
31. Ibid.
32. Ibid.
33. del Barco (2021).
34. Callahan-Bever (2017).
35. See Anon (2017b).
36. Squires (2014) p. 25.
37. Racquel J. Gates (2018, p. 45) notes that in the 1980s and 1990s 'the term "urban" became the preferred way to refer to music by African American artists because it signified blackness in a vague sense but avoided an explicit mention of race'. This, Gates says, was meant to allow the record companies to position the artists to crossover to appeal to White as well as Black audiences.
38. Roussel (2017) p. 84.
39. Gray (2016); Martin (2014); Himberg (2013); Gray (2005); Fuller (2010).
40. Ndounou (2014) p. 201; Harris and Tassie (2012) p. 322.
41. Ndounou (2014) p. 231; Harris and Tassie (2012) p. 322.
42. Ndounou (2014) p. 221.
43. Ibid. p. 221.
44. Tzioumakis (2017a) p. 88.
45. Anon (2015b).
46. Ibid.
47. Ibid.
48. Roussel (2017) p. 176.
49. Coates (2005).
50. Kobena (1994) pp. 234–5.
51. Molloy (2017) p. 373.
52. Ndounou (2014) p. 242.

53. Nwonka (2019); Nygaard and Lagerwey (2020) p. 55.
54. Nwonka (2019).
55. Quinn (2013).
56. Berg (2020); King (2020).
57. Sheppard (2016); Shaw (2016); Christian and White (2016); Lawrence (2013); Cartier (2014).
58. Shaw (2016) pp. 40–1.
59. Reinsch (2016) pp. 211–13.
60. Shaw (2016) pp. 46–7; Russworm (2016) pp. xiii–xxv.
61. Gates (2018) p. 17.
62. Reinsch (2016) p. 202.
63. Ibid. p. 200.
64. Lawrence (2013) p. 222.
65. Aldridge (2016) p. 228.
66. Ibid. p. 228.
67. Reinsch (2016) p. 216.
68. Ibid. p. 206.
69. Quinn (2013) pp. 206, 208.
70. Hughes (2004); Moore (2005).
71. Sheppard (2016) p. 3.
72. Blank (2003); see also Aldridge (2016) p. 226.
73. Johnson (2005).
74. Anon (2006a).
75. Ibid.
76. Ibid.
77. Ibid.
78. Sheppard (2016) p. 10; Christian and White (2016) pp. 149–50.
79. Johnson (2005).
80. Ibid.
81. Olsen (2005); Kaltenbach (2005).
82. Olsen (2005); Berg (2020).
83. Olsen (2005).
84. Ibid.
85. Caldwell (2013).
86. Dyer (2017) pp. 1–2.
87. Ndounou (2014) p. 84.
88. Ndounou (2014) p. 84; see also Quinn (2013).
89. Turner (2006).
90. Christian, and White (2016) pp. 146–7; Quinn (2013).
91. See also Christian and White (2016) p. 147.
92. Quinn (2013).
93. Ibid.
94. Baker (2017).
95. William Morris's undervaluing of the unestablished Black filmmaker's pro-

jects does not appear to be unique to Charles King and Tyler Perry. Indie-auteur Shaka King, who is discussed in the next section, has said that being left off William Morris's meeting agendas encouraged him to move to rival agency UTA (Blackhouse Foundation (2021)).

96. Baker (2017).
97. Ibid.
98. Anon (2018b); Barr (2017).
99. Kloer (2006); Barnes (2006).
100. Barnes (2006); Coyle (2007).
101. Anon (2006b); Anon (2006e).
102. Gray (2007).
103. McCauley (2006); Munoz (2007).
104. Ho (2006).
105. McCauley (2006); Anon (2006d).
106. Grego (2014).
107. Ibid.
108. See also Great (2016).
109. Barnes (2006).
110. Ibid.
111. Barr (2017).
112. Rose (2015b).
113. Gray (2005) p. 83.
114. Thompson (2015).
115. See also Gillespie (2016) pp. 75–6.
116. Sheppard (2016) p. 10; Christian, and White (2016) pp. 141–50.
117. Great (2016) p. 175.
118. Anon (2006c).
119. Christian, and White (2016) pp. 153–4.
120. Braxton (2008); see also Ava DuVernay in Molloy (2017) p. 369.
121. Braxton (2008).
122. Ibid.
123. Cobb (2021); Davis (2021).
124. N'Duka (2021).
125. See Ortner (2013) p. 29.
126. Sun (2021).
127. Nichols (2020).
128. Callahan-Bever (2017).
129. Ibid.
130. Macaulay (2014).
131. Ibid.
132. See Workneh (2014).
133. Gray (2005) p. 115.
134. Anon (2015b).
135. Ugwu (2021); Keegan (2021).

136. Fleming (2013).
137. Ibid.
138. Ibid.
139. Ugwu (2021).
140. Ugwu (2021); Cobb (2021); Davis (2021); Blackhouse Foundation (2021).
141. Ugwu (2021); Cobb (2021).
142. Ugwu (2021); Cobb (2021).
143. Blackhouse Foundation (2021).
144. Ibid.
145. Ibid.
146. Davis (2021).
147. Ibid.
148. Bielby and Bielby (2002); Ndounou (2014) pp. 174–5.
149. Ndounou (2014) p. 6.
150. Davis (2020).
151. Blackhouse Foundation (2021).
152. Ibid.
153. Ibid.
154. Gray (2005) pp. 192–3; see also: Gates (2018) pp. 8, 12.
155. Cobb (2021).
156. Since *Judas*, Shaka King has struck a first-look television deal with Disney's FX Productions (Petski (2021)).
157. Keegan (2021).
158. Ibid.
159. Ibid.
160. Ibid.
161. Cobb (2021).
162. Ibid.
163. Ibid.
164. Ibid.
165. Ndounou (2014) p. 57.
166. Quinn (2013).
167. Cobb (2021); Keegan (2021); Barboza (2021).
168. Barboza (2021).
169. Littleton (2021).
170. Ibid.
171. Ibid.
172. Ibid.
173. Ramos (2020).
174. Keegan (2021).
175. Davis (2020); see also Siegel (2021b).
176. Keegan (2021).
177. Ibid.
178. Ibid.

179. Warner (2016) p. 173.
180. Kelly (2021).
181. Ibid.
182. White (2023).
183. Jackson (2022).

Conclusion

The Migration of Indie-Auteurism and New Directions

Despite being made to appear cool and innovative, indie-auteurism often marks a continuation of old-fashioned industrial practices and strategies. From the indie films of the Coens and Soderbergh to the high-end commercials and series directed by Jonze, Rees, Fukunaga and Batmanglij, indie-auteurism has commonly been used to market projects and products aimed at White, young, male, middle-class and educated audiences with high levels of disposable income.

Indie-auteurism is not a consequence of creative freedom but is instead the result of talent management strategies enacted often in response to changing industrial factors, including fluctuations in investment, perceptions about consumer demand, and the adoption of new technologies. So, while indie-auteurs have usually been understood as autonomous filmmakers who succeed in making their best work in the realm of indie cinema, indie-auteurism is more productively understood as a discursive construct that is managed and mobilised by talent intermediaries to package and promote not only specialty films but also a range of other products and services. Indeed, indie-auteurism has substantial utility as producers, talent agents and talent managers use it to help those figures branded as indie-auteurs to secure jobs and finance for their so-called passion projects, sometimes doing so during unfavourable periods when investment in specialty content is withdrawn. Talent intermediaries' tendencies to portray indie-auteurs as innovators and pioneers not only boosts an individual's brand but opens doors to other employers or distributors to help other similar figures secure jobs or finance for their projects too. Talent intermediaries have significant incentives for facilitating the dissemination of indie-auteurism in this way as it increases the fees that they can collect from selling more projects and securing employment for more clients. It also enables them to bolster their own reputations as figures capable of discovering and nurturing talent, portray themselves as market leaders and increase their companies' valuations and secure investment.

Yet producers and talent managers help to promote their clients and their projects by depicting them as indie-auteurs whose cinematic creative visions make them superior to so-called directors-for-hire whose working conditions are often much more precarious. Doing so, they sustain and reinforce cinematization discourses that denigrate the creators and audiences of mass media by making most television and short-form production appear to be worthy of appreciation only when they adhere to the modes and standards associated with cinema. Indie-auteurism's value is thus underpinned by intertwined cultural and professional legitimation processes as industry perceptions about who the target audience is informs talent intermediaries', employers' and distributors' decision-making about the qualities and people needed to make and market screen productions. As a result, indie-auteurs tend to reflect their perceived audience as well as the intermediaries responsible for constructing indie-auteurism as a branded discourse. White and male talent intermediaries, financiers and distributors overwhelmingly favour young, White, male figures when selecting who to construct as indie-auteurs and which projects to greenlight. Simultaneously, the White masculinised discourse of the maverick or innovative indie-auteur remains pervasive as strategies for managing indie-auteurism contribute to delegitimating and devaluing the work of men of colour, White women, and women of colour. While talent intermediaries promote themselves as discovering unique talent and critics frame indie-auteurism as a form of unique vision, therefore, the management and mobilisation of indie-auteurism has contributed to the increased precariousness that women and people of colour face as it has played a role in sustaining the lack of diversity that has plagued the screen media industries for too long.

Signs emerged since the late 2010s, however, that women and people of colour have begun to be constructed as indie-auteurs more often than they had been before. This upturn has occurred as abuses against women and people of colour in Hollywood and broader society led to the #MeToo and #BlackLivesMatter movements, increased social consciousness about labour inequalities, and prompted slight improvements in their employment across the film and television industries.[1] After Emerson Collective acquired Anonymous Content, Anonymous hired more women in senior management roles, took on more Black and especially female clients, and diversified its productions with work such as *Carne y Arena*, *Eyes on the Prize: Hallowed Ground* and *Random Acts of Flyness*. Emerson's significant investment in Macro also facilitated Charles D. King and his co-executives' mission to amplify the voices of people of colour and provide a platform for more authentic storytelling as King and Macro used indie-auteurism to secure work for Black figures such as Ryan Coogler, Dee Rees, Boots Riley and Shaka King. More broadly, figures such as Ava DuVernay, Barry Jenkins and Issa Rae, who have sometimes been branded as indie-auteurs, have gained significant visibility, and struck lucrative production and distribution deals too. These examples show that indie-auteurism in fact can be used flexibly to enhance the brands and career opportunities of more talent constituencies.

Having begun by exploring the Coens' careers as indie-auteurs across three periods of indie film as outlined by Yannis Tzioumakis, the book has expanded the histories of specialty production by tracing how indie-auteurism is managed to package and market projects in other media and within wider contexts. Tracing the management and migration of indie-auteurs across media is, however, an open-ended process and several avenues remain for further exploration. More work could be done, for instance, around the management of indie-auteurs in the production of non-profit campaigns, documentary, video games and virtual reality. Will interactive media forms become a kind of new frontier for indie-auteurs or will video games and virtual reality continue to be regarded as peripheral in the overall organisation of their careers and production activities? How might indie-auteurs experiment with interactive media forms and what will the consequences be for indie culture and perceptions of autonomously authored modes of production?

The work and migration of indie-auteurs not only between employers and sectors but also across international contexts could also be explored, with talent agencies and management firms' international operations presenting one potential area to do so. As American subscription streaming services become increasingly global and seek to attract international audiences by commissioning and distributing projects made in different territories, Hollywood and international talent intermediary and production firms are adapting by expanding, consolidating and signing partnerships. Since 2017, for instance, Anonymous has: partnered with two UK talent agencies, Casarotto Ramsay and United Agents, to launch a London-based production company named Chapter One; partnered with Oslo-based production and management firm Einar Films, which is co-owned by its client Morten Tyldum, to establish Anonymous Content Nordic to produce 'premium content for the international and Nordic markets'; partnered with CAA and RT Features to launch RT Television with the remit of producing premium series in the Portuguese language; and partnered with European studio Federation Entertainment to create 'premium film and television content ... for local French and global audiences'.[2] Whether or not the management of indie-auteurs remains as central to Anonymous's business in this new climate as it was in the company's early years remains to be seen. Yet understanding how indie-auteurism is constructed outside the United States, how it is imported or exported, and what modifications occur as it crosses between international borders, could help to further sever perceptions that indie-auteurs are the success stories of an American independent cinema and could, instead, offer insight into the broader market and industry logics and strategies responsible for indie-auteurism's construction.

While the movement of indie-auteurs to new arenas may continue to draw the most attention from critics as it contributes to narratives of innovation, the relationship between indie-auteurs and class prior to the indie-auteurs' emergence also needs exploring further. Whether or not talent intermediaries involved in constructing indie-auteurs are more likely to select candidates from the upper classes and middle classes than from the working classes could tell us more about the media industries' roles in maintaining social and cultural hierarchies. The lives of above-the-line talent before they find fame are difficult to explore using secondary sources because they either go completely ignored or are retrospectively reported on and reconfigured as narratives of their journeys to success. Such narratives are often built around notions that the passion and talent of an individual led them to succeed against all other odds, which are notions that obscure systemic barriers and risk creating potentially misleading impressions that more people building successful careers in the media industries are coming from underprivileged backgrounds. Such narratives play neatly into the neoliberal notions espoused by major media industry distributors and financiers that free-market principles allow the best talent to rise to the top. Of course, many of the challenges faced and opportunities found in the management of indie-auteurism have broader resonance and the lessons learned can be applied to other above-the-line talent too.[3] The study of media management from a cultural industries vantage is relatively new, while much more work needs to consider the roles that talent intermediaries play in facilitating media industry recruitment processes, building stardom and selling products and brands in the contemporary era.

Whether or not talent intermediaries' claims about serving as 'agents of change' are effective and sustained in the long term also remains to be seen.[4] I am sceptical because talent intermediary practices adhere to much broader industry logics and while company executives often make announcements about new and pioneering directions and executives position themselves as great leaders, their strategies tend to be marked much more by continuity than change. If #MeToo and #BlackLivesMatter prompted greater consciousness of social inequalities and presented new market opportunities for distributors, talent intermediaries and their clients to exploit, then there is also a great risk that the slight gains in employment that have been made by people of colour and women over the last few years will disappear if and when those movements lose momentum. Yet even when women and people of colour are involved behind and in front of the screen, distributors' and brands' continued investment in so-called quality forms of production that tap into initiatives targeting mostly White middle-class audiences run the risk of denigrating women and people of colour that deviate from masculinised and White middle-class norms and are associated with more low-brow and less respected forms such as reality television, the soap opera or gangsta rap.

Emerson and Anonymous's claims about being a force for social change also masked the fact that Emerson's acquisition increased industry consolidation as it brought about co-ownership between Anonymous and Apple. Several commentators have linked industry consolidation to the death of mid-budget feature film production as a space for indie-auteurs,[5] while media industry consolidation and commercialism have often been understood as oppositional or detrimental to the creative freedom of talent.[6] Yet this book has argued that indie-auteurism has gained greater value and prominence as indie-auteurs are promoted as struggling artists making innovative work in the face of corporate pressures to differentiate their work, including those projects made for the media conglomerates, within the wider mediascape. Thus, indie-auteurism is not an endorsement of industrial economic independence or a critique of consolidation and free-market neoliberal economics. Instead, its connotations of innovation and originality mask consolidation and industry inequalities and preserve unequal industry relations between the media conglomerates and independent producers and talent, and these inequalities are felt more sharply across racial and gendered lines.

Going forward, we may ask how the careers and brands of indie-auteurs will be managed across media once Hollywood's industry relations stabilise following its period of flux created by the emergence and adoption of new digital and online technologies. Will high-profile indie-auteurs continue to migrate between film and television as regularly as they began to do in the mid-2010s and, if so, will indie culture become increasingly difficult to sustain or will invested individuals and institutions engage even more in acts of rhetorical manoeuvring that maintain cultural labels designed to preserve their leverage? If indie-auteurs increasingly sign overarching deals with single streaming services or platforms, will their migrations between media forms and genres continue to be perceived among the most important markers of their autonomy? If so, how will talent intermediaries and their clients work to sustain their leverage in an increasingly consolidated industry, and what opportunities will newer talent lacking the brand names of more established indie-auteurs receive?

Finally, while this book contributes to an expanded history of indie and specialty production, this is not necessarily a new or alternative history. Rather, the management and migration of indie-auteurism across screen media in an era of convergence draws from and reinforces established hierarchies privileging art over commerce, so-called cinematic production over traditional genres and more mass forms of entertainment, the indie-auteur over directors-for-hire, the ideal producer and 'great leader' over middle-management conformists and sycophants, and the White male maverick over people of colour and women. Whatever new directions indie-auteurism takes, therefore, we must remain mindful of the strategies and systems involved in its construction and of its various, often problematic and contentious, connotations, functions and repercussions.

Notes

1. Hunt and Ramón (2022) p. 3; Ramón, Tran and Hunt (2022).
2. Leffler (2023); see also Wiseman (2019a, 2019b).
3. Johnson, Kompare and Santo (2014) p. 11.
4. Anon (2016a).
5. Pomerantz (2012); Bailey (2014).
6. Banks (1996); Hesmondhalgh (2013); King (2016).

References

Akass, K. (2015) 'The Show that Refused to Die: The Rise and Fall of AMC's *The Killing*', *Continuum*, 29.5: 743–54.
Aldridge, L. (2016) 'To Brand and Rebrand: Questioning the Futurity of Tyler Perry', in T.M. Russworm, S.N. Sheppard and K.M. Bowdre (eds), *From Madea to Media Mogul: Theorizing Tyler Perry*, Jackson: University of Mississippi Press, pp. 225–32.
Alexander, H. (2015) 'Why *Beasts of No Nation* Fails to Tell the Whole Story About Child Soldiers', *Telegraph.co.uk*, 16 October, https://www.telegraph.co.uk/news/worldnews/africaandindianocean/ghana/11932578/Why-Beasts-of-No-Nation-fails-to-tell-the-whole-story-about-child-soldiers.html
Ali, L. (1997) 'The Kids Are All Right with a New Generation', *Los Angeles Times*, 11 May, https://www.latimes.com/archives/la-xpm-1997-05-11-ca-57594-story.html
American Film Institute (2019) 'Zal Batmanglij on Conceiving *The OA* Season 2 as an "Eight-Hour Movie"', *YouTube*, 2 April, https://www.youtube.com/watch?v=pf63YnyRZC4
Andreeva, N. (2019) 'Sam Esmail Inks Massive New Overall Deal with Universal Content Productions', *Deadline*, 8 February, https://deadline.com/2019/02/sam-esmail-overall-deal-universal-content-productions-mr-robot-homecoming-1202552446/
Andrew, G. (2003) 'Intolerable Cruelty', *Time Out*, 22 October, p. 69.
Andrew, G. (2008) 'Old Hands', *Time Out*, 2 January, pp. 55–6.
Andrews, D. (2013) *Theorizing Art Cinemas: Foreign, Cult, Avant-Garde, and Beyond*, Austin: University of Texas Press.
Andrews, H. (2014) *Television and British Cinema: Convergence and Divergence Since 1990*, Basingstoke: Palgrave Macmillan.
Anon (1995) 'Business', *Sight and Sound*, 1 April p. 4.
Anon (2006a) 'A Conversation with Tyler Perry', *The Charlie Rose Show*, 18 April, https://charlierose.com/videos/16542
Anon (2006b) 'Debmar-Mercury Partners with Actor/Writer/Director Tyler Perry to Distribute First Run Sitcom "House of Payne"', *Business Wire*, 2 March, p. 1
Anon (2006c) 'Debmar-Mercury Announces Historic Distribution Deals with TBS, FOX Station Group for First-Run Syndicated Sitcom "Tyler Perry's House of Payne"', *Business Wire*, 23 August, p. 1.

Anon (2006d) 'Debmar-Mercury Announces Stations to Air Tyler Perry's Original Comedy Series "House of Payne"', *Business Wire*, 27 April, p. 1.
Anon (2006e) 'Tyler Perry's *House of Payne* Off to Strong Start', *The Futon Critic*, 23 May, http://www.thefutoncritic.com/news/2006/05/23/tyler-perrys-house-of-payne-off-to-strong-start-21412/20060523debmar01/
Anon (2007) '*No Country for Old Men:* Ethan Coen, Joel Coen and Scott Rudin', *Daily Variety*, 18 December.
Anon (2014) 'Time Warner Inc. at Morgan Stanley Technology, Media & Telecom Conference', *Fair Disclosure Wire*, 5 March, https://www.proquest.com/globalnews/docview/1509066125/83E4438B04EC4567PQ/3
Anon (2015a) 'Sell of the Century', *Canberra Times*, 17 September, p. 19.
Anon (2015b) 'The Changemakers: Tactics for Equality and Diversity in Film & Television', Producers Guild of America, *YouTube*, 11 December, https://www.youtube.com/watch?v=tjhyCck_-jY
Anon (2015c) 'Violence in Israel; Picasso's Sculpture at MOMA; "Beasts of No Nation" in "The Charlie Rose Show"', *Transcripts*, 16 October.
Anon (2015d) 'What Leonardo DiCaprio Endured While Filming "The Revenant"', *Denver Post*, 31 December, https://www.denverpost.com/2015/12/31/what-leonardo-dicaprio-endured-while-filming-the-revenant/
Anon (2016a) 'Anonymous Content Receives Substantial Investment from Emerson Collective, Positioning Firm for Significant Growth', *PR Newswire*, 30 September, https://www.prnewswire.com/news-releases/anonymous-content-receives-substantial-investment-from-emerson-collective-positioning-firm-for-significant-growth-300337093.html
Anon (2016b) '*The Revenant* Best Director Iñárritu Golden Globes 2016', Patri, *YouTube*, 11 January, https://www.youtube.com/watch?v=gYH1NBtdkJo
Anon (2017a) 'Amazon Studios Head Roy Price Quits After Sexual Harassment Claims', *The Guardian*, 17 October, https://www.theguardian.com/technology/2017/oct/17/amazon-studios-roy-price-quite-sexual-harassment-claims
Anon (2017b) 'New Research Suggests that Effort at Work is Correlated with Race', *The Economist*, 4 February, https://www.economist.com/united-states/2017/02/04/new-research-suggests-that-effort-at-work-is-correlated-with-race
Anon (2018a) 'Harvey Weinstein Scandal: Who Has Accused Him of What?', *BBC News*, 25 May, https://web.archive.org/web/20180726025206/https://www.bbc.co.uk/news/entertainment-arts-41580010
Anon (2018b) 'Ira Bernstein', *Broadcasting & Cable*, 29 October, p. 12
Anon (2020) 'Antoine Fuqua: The Film that Lit My Fuse', Deadline Hollywood, *YouTube*, 30 June, https://www.youtube.com/watch?v=Mtiz9pKND9w
Anon (2021) 'Life as Entrepreneurs: Charles D. King & Stacey Walker King', *American Black Film Festival*, https://app.abffplay.com/video/268319/life-as-entrepreneurs
Anon (n.d.) 'Walmart: The Receipt', *Working Not Working*, https://workingnotworking.com/projects/120566-walmart-the-receipt

Ansen, D. (1985) 'Mixing Blood and Chuckles', *Newsweek*, 21 January, p. 74.
Ansen, D. (1994) 'A Blast of Hollywood Bile', *Newsweek*, 14 March, p. 72.
Atkins, O. (2017) 'Saatchi & Saatchi Unveils Oscars Walmart Challenge', *Shots*, 23 February, https://www.shots.net/news/view/92436-saatchi-saatchi-unveils-oscars-walmart-challenge
Attanasio, P. (1985a) 'Brothers in Film Noir; The Complicated Joys of Making Blood Simple', *New York Times*, 3 February, p. D1.
Attanasio, P. (1985b) 'Circle Sets Film Deal', *Washington Post*, 10 May, https://www.washingtonpost.com/archive/lifestyle/1985/05/10/circle-sets-film-deal/d9139baf-d724-4215-af58-38f345641dcc/
Aurthur, K. (2019) 'There Will Be No Wrap-Up Movie for "The OA"', *Variety*, 28 August, https://variety.com/2019/tv/news/oa-movie-netflix-brit-marling-1203317355/
Ayers, M. (2014) 'Steven Soderbergh on Why He Really Quit Movies', *Esquire*, 7 July, http://www.esquire.com/entertainment/movies/interviews/a29344/steven-soderbergh-interview/
Badley, L., C. Perkins and M. Schreiber (eds) (2016a) *Indie Reframed: Women's Filmmaking and Contemporary American Independent Cinema*, Edinburgh: Edinburgh University Press.
Badley, L., C. Perkins and M. Schreiber (2016b) 'Introduction', in L. Badley, C. Perkins and M. Schreiber (eds), *Indie Reframed: Women's Filmmaking and Contemporary American Independent Cinema*, Edinburgh: Edinburgh University Press, pp. 1–22.
Bailey, J. (2014) 'How the Death of Mid-Budget Cinema Left a Generation of Iconic Filmmakers MIA', *Flavorwire*, 9 December, https://flavorwire.com/492985/how-the-death-of-mid-budget-cinema-left-a-generation-of-iconic-filmmakers-mia
Baker, C. (2017) 'Driver's Seat', *New York Times Magazine*, 8 October, pp. 58–61, 64, 66.
Balio, T. (2013) *Hollywood in the New Millennium*, London: Palgrave Macmillan.
Banks, J. (1996) *Monopoly Television: MTV's Quest to Control the Music*, Boulder, CO: Westview Press.
Barboza, C. (2021) 'Panther Power', *Los Angeles Times*, 21 January, p. S12.
Barnes, B. (2006) 'Film Star Uses a Magic Word to Launch New Sitcom: Free', *Wall Street Journal*, 2 March, p. B1.
Baron, C. (2016) 'Not Just Indie: A Look At Films by Dee Rees, Ava DuVernay and Kasi Lemmons', in L. Badley, C. Perkins and M. Schreiber (eds), *Indie Reframed: Women's Filmmaking and Contemporary American Independent Cinema*, Edinburgh: Edinburgh University Press, pp. 204–20.
Barr, M. (2017) 'Was TV's 10/90 Model 10 Years Too Early?', *Forbes*, 6 June, https://www.forbes.com/sites/merrillbarr/2017/06/06/was-tvs-10-90-model-10-years-too-early/
Bart, P. (2013) 'Talent Agents Have Lost Their Leverage in a Buyer's Market', *Variety*, 8 May, http://variety.com/2013/film/news/talent-agents-have-lost-their-leverage-in-a-buyers-market-1200472365/

Bauder, D. (2015) 'USA Network Changing Look, Goes Grittier in Bid for Buzz', *Chicago Tribune*, 14 April, p. 7.

Baysinger, T. (2015) 'Networks Fiddle While New Series Burn', *Broadcasting & Cable*, 145.23: 6–7.

Beer, J. (2017) 'Walmart's Oscar Ads Were a Great Idea that Ultimately Flopped', *Fast Company*, 27 February, https://www.fastcompany.com/3068527/walmarts-oscar-ads-were-a-great-idea-that-ultimately-flopped

Belloni, M. (2016) 'Laurene Powell Jobs Goes Hollywood, Buys Minority Stake in "Spotlight" Producer Anonymous Content', *Hollywood Reporter*, 30 September, http://www.hollywoodreporter.com/news/laurene-powell-jobs-takes-minority-934139

Belloni, M. (2021) '"Sexual Misconduct" Claims: The Battle at Anonymous Content', *Puck*, 7 November, https://puck.news/anonymous-content-vs-fired-manager-multiple-instances-of-sexual-misconduct/

Berg, M. (2020) 'From "Poor as Hell" to Billionaire: How Tyler Perry Changed Show Business Forever', *Forbes*, 1 September, https://www.forbes.com/sites/maddieberg/2020/09/01/from-poor-as-hell-to-billionaire-how-tyler-perry-changed-show-business-forever/?sh=f8cdc5a34b51

Bergan, R. (2001) *The Coen Brothers*, London: Phoenix.

Bernstein, M. (2008) 'The Producer as Auteur (2006)', in B.K. Grant (ed.), *Auteurs and Authorship: A Film Reader*, Oxford: Blackwell, pp. 180–9.

Bettinson, G. (2015) 'Screen Acting and the New Hollywood: An Interview with Ethan Hawke (Part 1)', *Cinéaste*, 40.2: 4–11.

Bielby, D.D. and W.T. Bielby (2002) 'Hollywood Dreams, Harsh Realities: Writing for Film and Television', *Contexts*, 1.4: 21–7.

Billen, A. (1994) 'The Billen Interview: Andrew Billen Finds the Coen Brothers as Strange as Their Films', *The Observer*, 4 September, p. 10.

Birnbaum, D. (2016) 'The </real> mr. robot', *Variety*, 29 March, 331.9: 33–7.

Birnbaum, D. (2017) 'Actors on Actors', *Variety*, 6 June, pp. 51–71.

Blackhouse Foundation (2021) 'A Conversation with Shaka King', *Facebook*, 2 February, https://ms-my.facebook.com/blackhousefoundation/videos/a-conversation-with-shaka-king/902971313807307/?__so__=permalink&__rv__=related_videos

Blake, M. (2014) 'Winter Television Preview: *True Detective*: A Most Unusual Case', *Los Angeles Times*, 5 January, p. 5.

Blank, C. (2003) 'A Little Improv, Audience Interaction Keep Play Fresh', *Commercial Appeal*, 17 January, p. E1.

Booth, P. (2003) 'O Brothers, What Happened?', *St. Petersburg Times*, 9 October, p. W12.

Boston University (2010) 'BU in LA – An Evening with Joel Silver', *YouTube*, 29 June, https://www.youtube.com/watch?v=C2oiZRT4-So

Bourdieu, P. (1993) *The Field of Cultural Production: Essays on Art and Literature*, ed. R. Johnson, Oxford: Polity.

Bouw, B. (2001) 'Oh, the Car Is in There Somewhere: BMW Commissions Five A-List Directors for Film Series Featuring Bimmers', *National Post*, 26 April, p. 29.
Bowden, J. (2017) 'Amazon Cuts Ties with Weinstein Company After Assault Allegations', *The Hill*, 14 October, http://thehill.com/blogs/in-the-know/355443-amazon-cuts-ties-with-weinstein-company-after-assault-allegations
BoxOfficeMojo (n.d.a) '*No Country for Old Men* (2007)', https://www.boxofficemojo.com/title/tt0477348/?ref_=bo_se_r_1
BoxOfficeMojo (n.d.b) '*The Hudsucker Proxy* (1994)', https://www.boxofficemojo.com/title/tt0110074/?ref_=bo_se_r_1
BoxOfficeMojo (n.d.c) '*The Revenant* (2015)', https://www.boxofficemojo.com/title/tt1663202/?ref_=bo_se_r_1
Brady, T. (2016) 'Survival of the Fittest: Ain't No Mountain Tough Enough for Alejandro Gonzalez Iñárritu', *Irish Times*, 1 January, https://www.irishtimes.com/culture/film/alejandro-gonzalez-i-arritu-survival-of-the-fittest-on-set-and-in-hollywood-1.2476117
Braxton, G. (2008) 'Is "Madea" Effect Helping or Hurting? Filmmakers Meet Resistance if They Don't Follow Formula', *Chicago Tribune*, 6 April, p. 14
Brennan, J. (1992) 'Propaganda Switching On "Lights" Project with Bonet', *Variety*, 8 September, p. 4.
Bridges, D. (1993) 'PolyGram Filmed Entertainment Signs Film Distribution Agreement with MGM', *Business Wire*, 1 November, p. 1.
Brodie, J. (1994) 'Rookie Helmers Dish H'wood', *Variety*, 27 January, https://variety.com/1994/film/markets-festivals/rookie-helmers-dish-h-wood-117851/
Brodie, J. (1996) 'It's Been a Long Haul but Propaganda Works', *Variety*, 11 November, pp. 13, 79.
Brody, R. (2013) 'Steven Soderbergh Dissects Hollywood', *New Yorker*, 30 April, http://www.newyorker.com/culture/richard-brody/steven-soderbergh-dissects-hollywood
Brown, G. (1994) 'Mr Good Deeds Goes to Town', *The Times*, 1 September, https://www.proquest.com/docview/318180116/3A7B875D89554E82PQ/1
Brownstein, B. (2015) 'There's a War Coming; Netflix Is in the Feature-Film Business, and Theatre Chains Are Not Pleased', *Montreal Gazette*, 11 November, p. B7.
Bruzzi, S. (2013) *Men's Cinema: Masculinity and* Mise en Scène *in Hollywood*, Edinburgh: Edinburgh University Press.
Bruzzi, S. (2017) '"They Believe Every Fuckin' Word Because You're Super Cool": Masculine Cool '90s Style in *Reservoir Dogs*', in G. King (ed.), *A Companion to American Indie Film*, Chichester: Wiley, pp. 389–406.
Buckland, W. (ed.) (2014) *Hollywood Puzzle Films*, Abingdon: Routledge.
Buckley, C. (2015) 'Idris Elba's Toughest Role Yet: Going Brutal with Grace for "Beasts of No Nation"', *New York Times*, 8 September, https://www.nytimes.

com/2015/09/13/movies/idris-elbas-toughest-role-yet-going-brutal-with-grace-for-beasts-of-no-nation.html

Buckley, C. (2019) 'The Uphill Battles of Black Talent Agents in Hollywood', *New York Times*, 13 February, https://www.nytimes.com/2019/02/13/movies/black-talent-agents-hollywood.html

Burnside, A. (2015) 'Making It Big on Small Screen: Changing Scots Producer of *True Detective* on TV's Resurgence', *Daily Record*, 30 September, p. 28.

Busch, A.M. (1994) 'Candy's Last Film Held Up Amid Dispute', *Chicago Sun-Times*, 24 December, p. 22.

Cadwalladr, C. (2016) '*The Revenant* Is Meaningless Pain Porn', *The Observer*, 17 January, https://www.theguardian.com/commentisfree/2016/jan/17/revenant-leonardo-dicaprio-violent-meaningless-glorification-pain

Caldwell, J.T. (1995) *Televisuality: Style, Crisis, and Authority in American Television*, New Brunswick, NJ: Rutgers University Press.

Caldwell, J.T. (2008) *Production Culture: Industrial Reflexivity and Critical Practice in Film and Television*, London: Duke University Press.

Caldwell, J.T. (2013) 'Para-Industry: Researching Hollywood's Blackwaters', *Cinema Journal*, 52.3: 157–65.

Callahan-Bever, N. (2017) 'How Charles D. King Won Oscars and Made Millions with Multicultural Movies', *Complex: Blueprint*, 11 September, https://www.complex.com/pop-culture/2017/09/blueprint-with-charles-d-king

Carroll, R. and S. Levin (2017) '"Pack of Hyenas": How Harvey Weinstein's Power Fuelled a Culture of Enablers', *The Guardian*, 13 October, https://www.theguardian.com/film/2017/oct/13/harvey-weinstein-allegations-hollywood-enablers

Cartier, N. (2014) 'Black Women On-Screen as Future Texts: A New Look at Black Pop Culture Representations', *Cinema Journal*, 53.4: 150–7.

Chagollan, S. (1994) 'Propaganda on a Character Hunt: Duo Sheds Vid Tag with Pix', *Variety*, 7 July, p. 23

Chanko, K.M. (1990) 'Ben Barenholtz', *Films in Review*, 41.8/9: 416–17.

Chmielewski, D.C. (2018) 'NYT Report Details Harvey Weinstein Enablers; CAA Issues Apology "To Any Person the Agency Let Down"', *Deadline*, 5 December, http://deadline.com/2017/12/caa-apologizes-to-anyone-let-down-1202220778/

Chrisafis, A. (2023) 'Toxic Masculinity Fuels Dangerous Driving Like Drink, French Advert Says', *The Guardian*, 8 February, https://www.theguardian.com/world/2023/feb/08/toxic-masculinity-fuels-dangerous-driving-like-drink-french-advert-says

Christian, A.J. and K.C. White (2016) 'One Man Hollywood: The Decline of Black Creative Production in Post-Network Television', in T.M. Russworm, S.N. Sheppard and K.M. Bowdre (eds), *From Madea to Media Mogul: Theorizing Tyler Perry*, Jackson: University of Mississippi Press, pp. 138–58.

Christopher, J. (2003) 'Wolf Meets Fox', *The Times*, 23 October, p. 2.

Cieply, M. (2007) 'A Producer and a Studio Stay Close Despite Split', *New York Times*, 8 May, p. A1.
Clark, J. (1994) 'Strange Bedfellows', *Première*, 7.8: 61–4.
Clark, J. (1998) 'Irreverence, Umbrage & Him; Michael Moore Finds (Again) the Battle Isn't Over When He Puts a Finished Documentary in the Canister', *Los Angeles Times*, 11 April, https://www.latimes.com/archives/la-xpm-1998-apr-11-ca-38104-story.html
Clarke, P. (2021) '"True Detective" Director Cary Fukunaga Says It Was "Disheartening" Working with Writer Nic Pizzolato', *NME*, 24 September, https://www.nme.com/news/tv/true-detective-director-cary-fukunaga-says-it-was-disheartening-working-with-nic-pizzolato-it-didnt-feel-like-the-partnership-was-fair-3054565
Cling, C. (1995) 'Universal Pictures Cuts', *Las Vegas Review*, 10 April, p. E9.
Coates, T. (2005) 'The Color of Money', *New York Times*, 10 July, p. 21.
Cobb, J. (2021) 'Shaka King Grapples with Hollywood and History', *New Yorker*, 25 February, https://www.newyorker.com/culture/the-new-yorker-interview/shaka-king-grapples-with-hollywood-and-history
Coen, J. and E. Coen (dirs) (2011) 'An Exclusive Introduction', Blu-Ray bonus feature, *The Big Lebowski*, London: Universal Pictures.
Collin, R. (2015) 'Idris Elba Meets His Waterloo – in Africa', *The Telegraph*, 3 October, p. 16.
Columpar, C. (2016) 'The Feminist Politics of Collaboration in Lena Dunham's *Tiny Furniture*', in L. Badley, C. Perkins and M. Schreiber (eds), *Indie Reframed: Women's Filmmaking and Contemporary American Independent Cinema*, Edinburgh: Edinburgh University Press, pp. 276–87.
Corrigan, T. (1998) 'Auteurs and the New Hollywood', in J. Lewis (ed.), *The New American Cinema*, London: Duke University Press, pp. 38–63.
Covert, C. (2015) 'No Country for Young Men: Idris Elba Mesmerizes in *Beasts of No Nation*, as Does His Young Co-star', *Star Tribune*, 16 October, p. E8.
Cowan, N. (1993) 'Cloud of Mediocrity Casts Shadow on Sundance Fest', *Toronto Star*, 5 February, p. C3.
Coyle, J. (2007) 'Filmmaker Creates "Real" Characters', *Associated Press*, 2 March, p. W06.
Coyle, J. (2013) 'Netflix Shuffles the Deck with "House of Cards"', *The Ledger*, 27 January, https://eu.theledger.com/story/news/2013/01/27/netflix-shuffles-deck-with-house/8109098007/
Coyle, J. (2015) 'Elba, Fukunaga Subscribe for Netflix's "Beasts of No Nation"', *Charleston Gazette*, 13 October.
Coyle, J. (2017) 'Streaming Giants Play Hero and Villain in Oscar Season', *Yahoo!news*, 19 January, https://sg.news.yahoo.com/streaming-giants-play-hero-villain-205923207.html
Cullum, P. (2002) 'The Misfits: Four Killer Producers on the Cutting Edge of Independent Film', *L.A. Weekly*, 15 November, pp. 34–5.

Curtin, M. and K. Sanson (2016) 'Precarious Creativity: Global Media, Local Labor', in M. Curtin and K. Sanson (eds), *Precarious Creativity: Global Media, Local Labor*, Oakland: University of California Press, pp. 1–18.

D'Alessandro, A. (2023) 'Anonymous Content & Former Producer Manager Keith Redmon Settle', *Deadline*, 23 March, https://deadline.com/2023/03/anonymous-content-keith-redmon-settlement-1235308402/

Daniels, R. (2023) 'It's Not Just the Oscars that Fail Black Women. It's the Entire Awards Ecosystem', *Los Angeles Times*, 25 January, https://www.latimes.com/entertainment-arts/awards/story/2023-01-25/oscars-nominations-2023-academy-awards-season-black-women-commentary

Dargis, M. (2015) '"The Revenant" Welcomes You to Paradise. Now Prepare to Fall', *New York Times*, 24 December, https://www.nytimes.com/2015/12/25/movies/review-the-revenant-welcome-to-paradise-now-prepare-to-fall.html

Davis, C. (2020) '"Judas and the Black Messiah": Inside the Long Struggle to Bring Fred Hampton's Story to the Screen', *Variety*, 23 December, https://variety.com/2020/film/features/judas-and-the-black-messiah-shaka-king-1234871984/

Davis, C. (2021) 'Shaka King and George C. Wolfe on Casting Actors and Being Black in Hollywood', *Variety*, 25 February, https://variety.com/2021/film/awards/shaka-king-judas-and-the-black-messiah-george-c-wolfe-ma-raineys-black-bottom-1234914334/

Davis, K. (2007) 'Devastating for the World's Poor: Climate Change Threatens the Development Gains Already Achieved', *UN Chronicle*, https://www.un.org/en/chronicle/article/devastating-worlds-poor-climate-change-threatens-development-gains-already-achieved

Dawes, A. (1988) 'Propaganda, Polygram Ink Pic Pact', *Variety*, 9 September, pp. 1, 22.

del Barco, M. (2021) '"This Is About Lifting Culture," Says History-Making Producer Charles D. King', *npr*, 7 April, https://www.npr.org/2021/04/07/981655025/this-is-about-lifting-culture-says-history-making-producer-charles-d-king

DeSalvo, K. (2001) 'BMW Weaves Through the Web with Five Filmmakers', *Shoot*, 42.19: 1.

Dolan, D. (1999) 'Music Video Scores Without Any Glitz: Spike Jonze's Alter Ego Almost Fooled MuchMusic', *National Post*, 12 March, p. B5.

Dollar, S. (1995) 'Pop Music Preview', *Atlanta Constitution*, 31 March, p. 4.

Dominus, S. (2017) 'Refusing Weinstein's Hush Money, Rose McGowan Calls Out Hollywood', *New York Times*, 28 October, https://www.nytimes.com/2017/10/28/us/rose-mcgowan-harvey-weinstein.html

Donnelly, M. (2021) 'Tiauna Jackson Becomes First Black Woman Elected to Association of Talent Agents Board', *Variety*, 15 December, https://variety.com/2021/film/news/tiauna-jackson-association-talent-agents-board-1235134308/

Drake, P. (2008) 'Distribution and Marketing in Contemporary Hollywood', in P. McDonald and J. Wasko (eds), *The Contemporary Hollywood Film Industry*, Oxford: Blackwell, pp. 63–82.

Drake, P. (2013) 'Reputational Capital, Creative Conflict and Hollywood Independence: The case of Hal Ashby', in G. King, C. Molloy and Y. Tzioumakis (eds), *American Independent Cinema: Indie, Indiewood and Beyond*, New York: Routledge, pp. 140–52.

Dry, J. (2018) 'Dee Rees Directed this Oscars Commercial About a Black Girl with Sci-Fi Dreams and Two Mothers – Watch', *IndieWire*, 5 March, https://www.indiewire.com/2018/03/dee-rees-oscars-commercial-walmart-1201936217/

Dunning, J. (1985) 'Where to Get Off the Beaten Track', *New York Times*, 18 January, p. C1.

Dupler, S. (1989) 'L.A. Company Branches Out from Clip Base: Propaganda Nurtures New Talent', *Billboard*, 25 February, p. 43.

Dyer, R. (2017) *White: Twentieth Anniversary Edition*, Abingdon: Routledge.

Egner, J. (2015) 'Cary Fukunaga Isn't Trying to Educate You With "Beasts of No Nation,"' *New York Times*, 21 October, https://www.nytimes.com/2015/10/25/movies/cary-joji-fukunaga-on-the-perils-of-making-beasts-of-no-nation.html

Eller, C. and A. Dawtrey (1991) 'Polygram Buying Two Prod'n Firms', *Variety*, 25 September, pp. 1–2.

Elsaesser, T. (2013) 'Film Festival Networks, The New Topographies of Cinema in Europe', in D. Iordanova (ed.), *The Film Festival Reader*, St Andrews: University of St Andrews, pp. 82–107.

Emmerson Collective (2016) http://www.emersoncollective.com, accessed 6 November 2016.

Eyerly, A. (2015) 'Summer Television Preview', *Los Angeles Times*, 31 May, p. E7.

Fabrikant, G. (1992) 'Polygram to Buy 51 per cent Stake in Interscope's Film Division', *New York Times*, 11 August, https://www.nytimes.com/1992/08/11/business/polygram-to-buy-51-stake-in-interscope-s-film-division.html

Fairclough, N. (1995) *Media Discourse*, London: Bloomsbury.

Farrow, R. (2017) 'Harvey Weinstein's Army of Spies', *The New Yorker*, 6 November, https://www.newyorker.com/news/news-desk/harvey-weinsteins-army-of-spies

Felando, C. (2015) *Discovering Short Films: The History and Style of Live-Action Fiction Shorts*, New York: Palgrave Macmillan.

Fellowes, J. (2003) 'Leap of Faith', *Mail on Sunday*, 28 September, p. 32.

Filho, W.L, N.R. Matandirotya, J.M. Lütz, E.A. Alemu, F.Q. Brearley, A.A. Baidoo, A. Kateka, G.M. Ogendi, G.B. Adane, N. Emiru and R.A. Mbih (2021) 'Impacts of Climate Change to African Indigenous Communities and Examples of Adaptation Responses', *Nature Communications*, 12: art 6224, https://doi.org/10.1038/s41467-021-26540-0

Film Independent (2016) 'How "Mr. Robot" Creator Hacked the TV Model', *YouTube*, 23 October, https://www.youtube.com/watch?v=8cHKOPy-nWY

Fine, M. (1993) 'Will His "Bacon" Sizzle?', *Los Angeles Times*, 28 November, https://www.latimes.com/archives/la-xpm-1993-11-28-ca-61762-story.html

Fine, M. (2010) 'Antoine Fuqua Declares Independence', *Hollywood & Fine*, 4 March, https://web.archive.org/web/20141029220734/http://hollywood andfine.com/antoine-fuqua-declares-independence/

Fleming, M. Jr (2013) 'Sundance: The Weinstein Company Acquires "Fruitvale"', *Deadline*, 21 January, https://deadline.com/2013/01/fruitvale-sundance-film-festival-dea-weinstein-409114/

Fleming, M. Jr (2014) 'Alejandro G. Iñárritu And "Birdman" Scribes on Hollywood's Superhero Fixation: "Poison, Cultural Genocide" – Q&A', *Deadline*, 15 October, http://deadline.com/2014/10/birdman-director-aleja ndro-gonzalez-inarritu-writers-interview-852206/

Fleming, M. Jr (2016) 'Anonymous Content Finds Its New Strategic Partner: Laurene Powell Jobs' Emerson Collective', *IndieWire*, 30 September, http:// deadline.com/2016/09/anonymous-content-laurene-powell-jobs-emerson-collective-steve-jobs-1201828945/

Ford, J. (2018) 'Feminist Cinematic Television: Authorship, Aesthetics and Gender in Pamela Adlon's *Better Things*', *fusion journal*, 14: 16–29.

Ford, J. (2019) 'Women's Indie Television: The Intimate Feminism of Women-centric Dramedies', *Feminist Media Studies*, 19.7: 928–43.

Forristal, L. (2022) 'Netflix's Ad-Supported Plan Is Finally Here', *TechCrunch*, 3 November, https://techcrunch.com/2022/11/03/netflixs-ad-supported-plan-is-finally-here/

Fuller, J. (2010) 'Branding Blackness on US Cable Television', *Media, Culture & Society*, 32.2: 285–305.

Gallagher, M. (2013) *Another Steven Soderbergh Experience: Authorship and Contemporary Hollywood*, Austin: University of Texas Press.

Galloway, S. (2016) 'Oscars: Arnon Milchan's Big "The Revenant" Bet Paying Off', *Hollywood Reporter*, 14 January, http://www.hollywoodreporter.com/ news/oscars-arnon-milchans-big-revenant-856011

Galuppo, M. (2016) 'Why in the World Do TV Shows Go to Sundance?', *Hollywood Reporter*, 20 January, http://www.hollywoodreporter.com/news/ tv-at-sundance-stephen-king-857038

Garrahan, M. (2013) 'Lunch with the FT: David Fincher', *FT.com*, 1 February, https://www.ft.com/content/4161915e-1194-11e4-b356-00144feabdc0

Gates, R.J. (2018) *Double Negative: The Black Image and Popular Culture*, Durham, NC: Duke University Press.

Gaylin, A.S. (2001) 'Drive On', *Shoot*, 42.49: 30.

Gee, C. (2015) 'Idris Elba's *Beasts of No Nation* to be Boycotted by US cinemas', *Telegraph.co.uk*, 4 March, https://www.telegraph.co.uk/culture/film/film-news/11449158/Idris-Elbas-Beasts-of-No-Nation-to-be-boycotted-by-US-cinemas.html

Geier, T. (1999) 'Golin Putting Out Propaganda Pics as Citizen of USA', *Hollywood Reporter*, 3 November, pp. 6, 8.
Genette, G. (1982) *Palimpsestes: La Littérature au Second Degré*, Paris: Editions du Seuil.
Georgakas, D., B. Saltz and M. Moore (1998) 'Michael and Us: An Interview with Michael Moore', *Cinéaste*, 23.3: 4–7.
Gillespie, M.B. (2016) *Film Blackness: American Cinema and the Idea of Black Film*, London: Duke University Press.
Goldberg, L. (2020) 'Steven Soderbergh Inks Sweeping TV, Film Deal with WarnerMedia', *Hollywood Reporter*, 15 January, https://www.hollywoodreporter.com/live-feed/steven-soderbergh-inks-sweeping-tv-film-deal-warnermedia-1269831
Goldman, A. (2015) 'Director Alejandro González Iñárritu on Leonardo DiCaprio, "Birdman" and the Importance of a Proper Lunch', *Wall Street Journal*, 30 November, https://www.wsj.com/articles/director-alejandro-gonzalez-inarritu-on-leonardo-dicaprio-birdman-and-the-importance-of-a-proper-lunch-1448894869
Goldrich, R. (2000) 'Jonze Re-Ups for 3 Years at Satellite', *Shoot*, 41.7: 1, 12, 18.
Goldsmith, J. (2015) 'They Make the Deals that Make the Whole Town Sing', *Broadcasting & Cable*, 145.28: 8–11.
Goldstein, G. (2014) 'No Country for Gold Men?', *Variety*, 17 December, pp. 11–12, 14.
Goldstein, P. (2004) 'He's the Real Deal for Artists', *Los Angeles Times*, 30 March, p. E1.
Gomery, D. (1983) 'Television, Hollywood, and the Development of Movies Made-for-Television', in E.A. Kaplan (ed.), *Regarding Television: Critical Approaches – An Anthology*, Los Angeles: University Publications of America, pp. 120–7.
Goozner, M. (1998) 'Working-Class Hero Filmmaker Michael Moore Keeps on Needling Corporate America', *Chicago Tribune*, 12 April, p. 10.
Graham, J. and A. Gandini (2017) 'Introduction: Collaborative Production in the Creative Industries', in J. Graham and A. Gandini (eds), *Collaborative Production in the Creative Industries*, London: University of Westminster Press, pp. 1–14.
Graham, R. (1995) 'Don't Try This at Home', *Boston Globe*, 31 March, p. 63.
Graham, R. (1998) 'Delroy Lindo Getting His Due', *Boston Globe*, 5 July, p. N7.
Grainge, P. (2008) *Brand Hollywood: Selling Entertainment in a Global Media Age*, Abingdon: Routledge.
Graser, M. (2002) 'BMW Adds to Its Film Series: The Hire Still Attracting Big Talent for Car Shorts', *National Post*, 6 August, p. AL3.
Gray, E. (2007) 'Making "Payne" Pay: Tyler Perry Redefines the Sitcom Model', *Philadelphia Daily News*, 8 May, p. 53.
Gray, H. (1995) 'Black Masculinity and Visual Culture', *Callaloo*, 18.2: 401–5.

Gray, H. (2005) *Cultural Moves: African Americans and the Politics of Representation*, Los Angeles: University of California Press.

Gray, H. (2016) 'Precarious Diversity: Representation and Demography', in M. Curtin and K. Sanson (eds), *Precarious Creativity: Global Media, Local Labor*, Oakland: University of California Press, pp. 241–53.

Gray, H. and M. Iverson-Davis (2023) 'Feeling What I'm Seeing, Seeing What I'm Feeling', in A. Great and E. Guerrero (eds), *Black Cinema & Visual Culture: Art and Politics in the 21st Century*, New York: Routledge, pp. 17–35.

Gray, J. (2010) *Shows Sold Separately: Promos, Spoilers and Other Media Paratexts*, New York: New York University Press.

Gray, J. and D. Johnson (2021) *Television Goes to the Movies*, New York: Routledge.

Great, A. (2016) 'Bring the Payne: The Erasure of the Black Sitcom and the Emergence of *Tyler Perry's House of Payne*', in T.M. Russworm, S.N. Sheppard and K.M. Bowdre (eds), *From Madea to Media Mogul: Theorizing Tyler Perry*, Jackson: University of Mississippi Press, pp. 159–79.

Greenberg, J. (2015) 'Theater Owners Are Furious About Netflix's New Movie', *Wired*, 16 November, https://www.wired.com/2015/10/theater-owners-are-furious-about-netflixs-new-movie/

Greenberg, K. (2002) 'Super Reggie Winner: Crouching Brand, Hidden Bimmer', *Brandweek*, 18 March, 43.11: R4.

Greenwald, A. (2014) 'Indie TV: When Auteurs of the Art House Make the Move to Your Living Room', *Grantland*, 22 October, http://grantland.com/hollywood-prospectus/indie-tv-when-auteurs-of-the-art-house-make-the-move-to-your-living-room/

Grego, M. (2014) 'Blue Skies Over Debmar-Mercury', *Broadcasting & Cable*, 144.7: 28–9.

Gritten, D. (1999) 'Ethan and Joel Coen: Brothers in Film', *Creative Screenwriting*, 6.1: 55–9.

Groves, D. (1989) 'Working Title, Propaganda, Polygram Form Manifesto Sale Org', *Variety*, 14 July, p. 3.

Hadas, L. (2020) *Authorship as Promotional Discourse in the Screen Industries: Selling Genius*, Abingdon: Routledge.

Hale, M. (2015) '"The Knick" Season 2 Premiere Recap: Tied Up in Knots', *New York Times*, 17 October, https://www.nytimes.com/2015/10/18/arts/television/the-knick-season-2-premiere-recap.html

Hale, M. (2016) 'Steven Soderbergh on Rebooting "The Girlfriend Experience" for TV', *New York Times*, 1 April, https://www.nytimes.com/2016/04/03/arts/television/starz-the-girlfriend-experience.html

Hall, C. (1991) 'Jim & Ted's Excellent Adventure', *Washington Post*, 1 September, p. G1.

Hall, S. (1993) 'What Is This "Black" in Black Popular Culture?', *Social Justice*, 20.1/2: 104–14.

Hamedy, S. (2015) 'A Debut Guaranteed to Give Studio Goosebumps', *Los Angeles Times*, 19 October, p. E4.

Hanas, J. (2001) 'The Rise and Fall of Propaganda', *Advertising Age*, 1 December, http://adage.com/article/beat-sheet/rise-fall-propaganda/92280/

Harris, C.A. and K.E. Tassie (2012) 'The Cinematic Incarnation of Frazier's Black Bourgeoisie: Tyler Perry's Black Middle-Class', *Journal of African American Studies*, 16.2: 321–44.

Harris, D. (1999) 'Propaganda Vet Golin Back with a New Company', *Hollywood Reporter*, 2 August, pp. 3, 158.

Harris, S. (2019) '"Treated as a Criminal": Walmart Receipt and Bag Checks Anger Customers', *CBC News*, 12 November, https://www.cbc.ca/news/business/walmart-receipt-check-costco-1.5355527

Harvey, C. (2014) '*True Detective*, Sky Atlantic, Review: A Work of Depth and Cinematic Flair', Telegraph.co.uk, 22 February, https://www.telegraph.co.uk/culture/tvandradio/tv-and-radio-reviews/10654871/True-Detective-Sky-Atlantic-review-a-work-of-depth-and-cinematic-flair.html

Harvey, D. (2005) *A Brief History of Neoliberalism*, New York: Oxford University Press.

Harwell, D. (2015) 'Netflix Plan: Big-Screen Premieres on Small Screens', *Washington Post*, 15 October, https://www.washingtonpost.com/business/economy/netflix-plan-bring-big-screen-premiers-to-subscribers-small-screens/2015/10/14/cf197154-71d0-11e5-8248-98e0f5a2e830_story.html

Hatfield, S. (2003) 'The Go-to Guy', *Ad Age*, 1 March, https://adage.com/article/special-report-sports/guy/91599

Havens, T. (2013) *Black Television Travels: African American Media Around the Globe*, New York: New York University Press.

Havens, T. (2014) 'Towards a Structuration Theory of Media Intermediaries', in D Johnson, D. Kompare and A. Santo (eds), *Making Media Work: Cultures of Management in the Entertainment Industries*, New York: New York University Press, pp. 39–62.

Havens, T. and R. Stoldt (2023) 'Netflix: Streaming Channel Brands as Global Meaning Systems', in D. Johnson (ed.), *From Networks to Netflix: A Guide to Changing Channels*, 2nd edn, New York: Routledge, pp. 201–12.

Hayes, D. (2018) 'Dee Rees on Her "Otherworldly" Walmart Ad, Reuniting the "Mudbound" Band, and Why Netflix Is Indie Film's Best Hope', *Deadline*, 27 February, https://deadline.com/2018/02/dee-rees-on-mudbound-netflix-oscar-walmart-short-filmmaking-1202303280/

Helmore, E. (2014) 'Hollywood Directors Switch to TV as New Golden Age Beckons', *The Observer*, 16 March, p. 22.

Hesmondhalgh, D. (2013) *The Cultural Industries*, 3rd edn, London: Sage.

Heuman, J. (2013) '"Independence," Industrial Authorship, and Professional Entrepreneurship: Representing and Reorganizing Television Writing in the FCC Media Ownership Reviews', *Cinema Journal*, 52.3: 120–44.

Hiltbrand, H. (2014) 'Haunted Cops, a Scary Killer', *Philadelphia Inquirer*, 12 January, p. H1

Himberg, J. (2013) 'Multicasting: Lesbian Programming and the Changing Landscape of Cable TV', *Television & New Media*, 15.4: 289–304.

Hinson, H. (1985) 'Bloodlines', *Film Comment*, 21.2: 14–19.

Ho, R. (2006) 'Perry's Sitcom gets Atlanta Tryout', *Atlanta Journal*, 21 June, p. E1.

Hoberman, J. (1985) 'The Glitz, the Drab, and the Baffling', *Village Voice*, 22 January, p. 53.

Holdsworth, N. (2014) 'Anonymous Content Exec Michael Sugar Talks New Media, International Storytelling (Q&A)', *Hollywood Reporter*, 6 July, http://www.hollywoodreporter.com/news/anonymous-content-exec-michael-sugar-716840

Hollywood Reporter (2014) 'Emma Thomas, Marc Platt, John Lesher and More Producers on THR's Roundtables: Oscars 2015', *YouTube*, 19 December, https://www.youtube.com/watch?v=tD3hA2k5k0w

Holpuch, A. (2017) 'Harvey Weinstein Appears to Confess in Audio Released by the New Yorker', *The Guardian*, 10 October, https://www.theguardian.com/film/2017/oct/10/audio-released-by-new-yorker-appears-to-have-confession-by-harvey-weinstein

Holpuch, A. and J. Lartey (2018) 'Harvey Weinstein Appears in Court Charged with Rape and Other Sexual Offences', *The Guardian*, 25 May, https://amp.theguardian.com/film/2018/may/25/harvey-weinstein-surrenders-over-sexual-misconduct-charges

Holt, J. (2011) *Empires of Entertainment: Media Industries and the Politics of Deregulation, 1980–1996*, London: Rutgers University Press.

Hornaday, A. (2017) *Twitter*, 27 February, https://twitter.com/walmart/status/836034434977628160

Howe, D. (1994) '"Hudsucker Proxy": A Great Leap into the Void', *Washington Post*, 25 March, https://www.washingtonpost.com/archive/lifestyle/1994/03/25/hudsucker-proxy-a-great-leap-into-the-void/54a9f470-2c6f-49c0-92db-630c6f033ed1/

Howell, P. (2007) 'Best Western', *Toronto Star*, 9 November, p. E1.

Hughes, Z. (2004) 'How Tyler Perry Rose from Homelessness to a $5 Million Mansion', *Ebony*, 1 January, pp. 86–8, 90, 92.

Hunt, D. and A.C. Ramón (2022) *Hollywood Diversity Report 2022: A New, Post-Pandemic Normal? Part 1: Film*, Los Angeles: UCLA, https://socialsciences.ucla.edu/wp-content/uploads/2022/03/UCLA-Hollywood-Diversity-Report-2022-Film-3-24-2022.pdf

Hunt, D., A.C. Ramón, M. Tran, S. Amberia and D. Roychoudhury (2018) *Hollywood Diversity Report 2018: Five Years of Progress and Missed Opportunities*, Los Angeles: Ralph J. Bunche Center for African American Studies at UCLA, https://socialsciences.ucla.edu/wp-content/uploads/2018/02/UCLA-Hollywood-Diversity-Report-2018-2-27-18.pdf

Idato, M. (2014) 'Thriller on a Slow Boil', *The Age*, 9 January, p. 7.
Insdorf, A. (1984) 'New York's Film Festival Ready to Launch', *New York Times*, 23 September, https://www.nytimes.com/1984/09/23/movies/new-york-s-film-festival-ready-to-launch.html
Jackson, A. (2022) 'Amazon Studios, Macro Film Studios Ink Multiyear First Look Deal', *Variety*, 14 September, https://variety.com/2022/film/news/amazon-studios-macro-film-studios-first-look-deal-1235371913/
James, C. (2015) '"Beasts of No Nation" Hits Cinemas and Netflix', *Wall Street Journal*, 8 October, https://www.wsj.com/articles/beasts-of-no-nation-hits-cinemas-and-netflix-1444325085
Jancovich, M. and J. Lyons (2003) 'Introduction', in M. Jancovich and J. Lyons (eds), *Quality Popular Television: Cult TV, the Industry and Fans*, London: British Film Institute, pp. 1–8.
Jaramillo, D.L. (2013) 'Rescuing Television from "the Cinematic": The Perils of Dismissing Television Style', in S. Peacock and J. Jacobs (eds), *Television Aesthetics and Style*, London: Bloomsbury, pp. 65–75.
Jarvey, N. (2015) 'Agent Charles King Exits WME to Launch Multicultural Media Firm (Exclusive)', *Hollywood Reporter*, 5 January, https://www.hollywoodreporter.com/news/general-news/agent-charles-king-exits-wme-761010/
Jenkins, H. (2006) *Convergence Culture: Where Old and New Media Collide*, New York: New York University Press.
Jenner, M. (2016) 'Is This TVIV? On Netflix, TVIII and Binge-Watching', *New Media & Society*, 18.2: 257–73.
Jenner, M. (2018) *Netflix and the Re-invention of Television*, Cham: Palgrave Macmillan.
Johnson, C. (2012) *Branding Television*, Abingdon: Routledge.
Johnson, D. (2012) 'Cinematic Destiny: Marvel Studios and the Trade Stories of Industrial Convergence', *Cinema Journal*, 52.1: 1–24.
Johnson, D. (ed.) (2018) *From Networks to Netflix: A Guide to Changing Channels*, New York: Routledge.
Johnson, D. and J. Gray (2013) 'Introduction: The Problem of Media Authorship', in J. Gray and D. Johnson (eds), *A Companion to Media Authorship*, Chichester: Wiley, pp. 1–19.
Johnson, D., D. Kompare and A. Santo (2014) 'Introduction: Discourses, Dispositions, Tactics: Reconceiving Management in Critical Media Industry Studies', in D. Johnson, D. Kompare and A. Santo (eds), *Making Media Work: Cultures of Management in the Entertainment Industries*, New York: New York University Press, pp. 1–21.
Johnson, R. (2005) 'While Hollywood Studios Win Awards, Lions Gate, the Independent, Makes Money', *New York Times*, 7 March, p. C1.
Johnston, S. (1991) 'Interview: Double Fink', *The Independent*, 22 May, p. 18.
Johnston, S. (1993) 'Cannes Diary: Cause for Effect', *The Independent*, 21 May, p. 19.

Jones, C. (2017) 'Every Receipt Tells a Story: Walmart Pays Homage to Its Customers with First Oscars Ad Blitz', *USA TODAY*, 24 February, p. B1.

Jonze, S. (1994) 'Sighvatsson of Propaganda Films, Which Seized on the Music-Video Revolution and Encouraged a Generation of Gifted Young Filmmakers', *Interview Magazine*, 1 October, pp. 102, 104.

Jurgensen, J. (2016a) '"The Girlfriend Experience" Keeps Drama Compact', *Wall Street Journal*, 30 March, https://www.wsj.com/articles/the-girlfriend-experience-keeps-drama-compact-1459357093

Jurgensen, J. (2016b) 'Steve Golin: Hollywood's Anonymous Power Player', *Wall Street Journal*, 11 February, https://www.wsj.com/articles/steve-golin-hollywoods-anonymous-power-player-1455216887

Kaltenbach, C. (2005) 'Strong Black Women at Heart of Tyler Perry Films', *Baltimore Sun*, 13 March, p. 7F.

Kane, V. (2018) 'Leave It to Dee Rees to Turn a Walmart Commercial into One of the Year's Best Movies', *The Mary Sue*, 5 March, https://www.themarysue.com/dee-rees-the-box-walmart-commercial/

Kaplan, E.A. (2016) *Rocking Around the Clock: Music Television, Postmodernism, and Consumer Culture*, New York: Routledge.

Kay, J. (2014) 'Anonymous Content: Dramatic Leanings', *Screen Daily*, 19 June, https://www.screendaily.com/features/anonymous-content-dramatic-leanings/5073097.article

Keegan, R. (2021) 'Despite History-Making Noms, "Judas and the Black Messiah's" All-Black Producing Team Find Oscar Success to Be "Bittersweet"', *Hollywood Reporter*, 31 March, https://www.hollywoodreporter.com/movies/movie-news/judas-and-the-black-messiahs-all-black-team-on-bittersweet-feeling-of-making-oscar-history-4158240/

Kelly, J. (2021) 'Portrait: How this Black Mogul Is Disrupting the Movie Business', *Bloomberg*, 29 June, https://www.bloomberg.com/news/videos/2021-06-29/how-this-black-mogul-is-disrupting-the-movie-business-video

Kemp, E. (2022) 'Ethan Coen to Solo Direct Lesbian Road Trip Comedy', *NME*, 9 August, https://www.nme.com/news/film/ethan-coen-lesbian-road-trip-comedy-3286438

Kemper, T. (2010) *Hidden Talent: The Emergence of Hollywood Agents*, Los Angeles: University of California Press.

Kennedy, R. (2009) *Sellout: The Politics of Racial Betrayal*, New York: Vintage Books.

Keogh, J. (1993) 'Moore Goes the Way of All Hollywood Flesh', *Telegram & Gazette*, 4 March, p. 4.

Kerrigan, F. (2017) 'Marketing American Indie in the Shadow of Hollywood', in G. King (ed.), *A Companion to American Indie Film*, Chichester: Wiley, pp. 181–206.

Kilday, G. (2015a) 'Cannes: Impact of Netflix, Opportunities for Women in Focus at Panel', *Hollywood Reporter*, 16 May, http://www.hollywoodreporter.com/news/cannes-2015-impact-netflix-opportunities-796156

Kilday, G. (2015b) 'Netflix's $12M Oscars Gamble: How to Keep "Beasts of

No Nation" Alive', *Hollywood Reporter*, 5 November, http://www.hollywoodreporter.com/news/netflixs-12m-oscars-gamble-how-836265

King, A.S. (2020) 'Tyler Perry Is Ready to Defend Himself', *Level*, 15 January, https://level.medium.com/tyler-perry-is-ready-to-defend-himself-70b89f69129e

King, G. (2005) *American Independent Cinema*, London: I.B. Tauris.

King, G. (2009) *Indiewood, USA: Where Hollywood Meets Independent Cinema*, London: I.B. Tauris.

King, G. (2013a) *Indie 2.0: Change and Continuity in Contemporary American Indie Film*, London: I.B. Tauris.

King, G. (2013b) 'Thriving or in Permanent Crisis: Discourses on the State of Indie Cinema', in G. King, C. Molloy and Y. Tzioumakis (eds), *American Independent Cinema: Indie, Indiewood and Beyond*, New York: Routledge, pp. 41–52.

King, G. (2016) *Quality Hollywood: Markers of Distinction in Contemporary Studio Film*, London: I.B. Tauris.

King, G. (2017) 'Indie as Organic: Tracing Discursive Roots', in G. King (ed.) *A Companion to American Indie Film*, Chichester: Wiley, pp. 58–79.

King, L.C. (2014) *The Coen Brothers Encyclopedia*, London: Rowman & Littlefield.

Klemesrud, J. (1985) 'The Brothers Coen Bow in with "Blood Simple,"' *New York Times*, 20 January, https://www.nytimes.com/1985/01/20/arts/film-the-brothers-coen-bow-in-with-blood-simple.html

Klinger, B. (2010) 'Becoming Cult: *The Big Lebowski*, Replay Culture and Male Fans', *Screen*, 51.1: 1–20.

Kloer, P. (2006) 'From Madea to Mogul: Tyler Perry's Film Studio Adds to Whirl of Success', *Atlanta Journal*, 13 September, p. E1.

Kobena, M. (1994) *Welcome to the Jungle: New Positions in Black Cultural Studies*, New York: Routledge.

Krämer, P. (2013) 'The Limits of Autonomy: Stanley Kubrick, Hollywood and Independent Filmmaking, 1950–53', in G. King, C. Molloy and Y. Tzioumakis (eds), *American Independent Cinema: Indie, Indiewood and Beyond*, New York: Routledge, pp. 153–64.

Kronick, I. (1997) 'Daft Punk's Tale of Humble Hound Might Redefine Music Video', *The Gazette*, 20 March, p. 6.

Labuza, P. (2021) 'Op-Ed: How the Streaming Wars Are Changing What You Watch', *Los Angeles Times*, 18 July, https://www.latimes.com/opinion/story/2021-07-18/netflix-amazon-hulu-streaming-competition-hollywood-content

Lacey, L. (2003) 'Flirting with Cruelty', *Globe and Mail*, 10 October p. R1.

Lane, A. (2007) 'Hunting Grounds: "No Country for Old Men" and "Lions for Lambs,"' *New Yorker*, 12 November, https://www.newyorker.com/magazine/2007/11/12/hunting-grounds

Lane, C. (2016) 'Susan Seidelman's Contemporary Films: The Feminist Art of Self-Reinvention in a Changing Technological Landscape', in L. Badley,

C. Perkins and M. Schreiber (eds), *Indie Reframed: Women's Filmmaking and Contemporary American Independent Cinema*, Edinburgh: Edinburgh University Press, pp. 70–86.

Lang, B. (2015) 'Sundance Spending Could See Digital Lift', *Variety*, 20 January, p. 13.

Lang, B. (2022) 'Keith Redmon Sues Anonymous Content Over Ouster, Denies Sexual Misconduct Claims (Exclusive)', *Variety*, 23 March, https://variety.com/2022/film/news/keith-redmon-sues-anonymous-content-sexual-misconduct-claims-1235212466/

Lang, B. and R. Setoodeh (2016) 'Sundance: How Netflix and Amazon Are Dramatically Shaking Up the Market', *Variety*, 26 January, https://variety.com/2016/film/festivals/amazon-netflix-sundance-film-festival-1201688254/

Lawrence, N. (2013) 'Faux Real? *C.S.A. The Confederate States of America* as the Response to *The Birth of a Nation*', in G. King, C. Molloy and Y. Tzioumakis (eds), *American Independent Cinema: Indie, Indiewood and Beyond*, New York: Routledge, pp. 210–23.

Lee, A. (2015) '"Revenant" Producers, Alejandro G. Iñárritu Defend Budget, Sequential Shoot', *Hollywood Reporter*, 24 October, http://www.hollywoodreporter.com/news/revenant-producers-alejandro-g-inarritu-834442

Lee, B. (2015) 'Director Cary Fukunaga: "I Thought Nothing Could Be as Hard as *True Detective*, but *Beasts of No Nation* Eclipsed It"', *The Guardian*, 16 October, https://www.theguardian.com/film/2015/oct/15/cary-fukunaga-beasts-no-nation-netflix-interview

Leffler, R. (2023) 'French Talent Agent Rosalie Cimino to Lead Anonymous/Federation', *Screen Daily*, 19 January, https://www.screendaily.com/news/french-talent-agent-rosalie-cimino-to-lead-anonymous/federation/5178305.article

Leon, D. (1987) 'Blowing up Bunnies and Other Fun Moments', *Associated Press*, 4 May.

Leopard, D. (2009) 'Selling Out, Buying In: Brakhage, Warhol, and BAVC', in J. Staiger and S. Hake (eds), *Convergence Media History*, New York: Routledge, pp. 151–60.

Lepore, J. (2014) 'The Disruption Machine: What the Gospel of Innovation Gets Wrong', *New Yorker*, 23 June, http://www.newyorker.com/magazine/2014/06/23/the-disruption-machine

Levine, J. (2000) *The Coen Brothers: The Story of Two American Filmmakers*, Toronto: ECW Press.

Levy, E. (2018) 'Julia Roberts: A Big Name on the Small Screen', *FT.com*, 19 October, https://www.ft.com/content/d13dbec2-ce07-11e8-8d0b-a6539b949662

Likert, R. (1967) *The Human Organization: Its Management and Value*, New York: McGraw-Hill.

Linnet, R. (1999) 'Creative Focus: Future Shock', *AdWeek*, 18 October, http://www.adweek.com/news/advertising/creative-focus-future-shock-46726

Lipper, H. (1993) 'Another Fairy Tale from the Brothers Coen', *St. Petersburg Times*, 14 March, https://www.tampabay.com/archive/1993/03/14/another-fiery-tale-from-the-brothers-coen/

Littleton, C. (2015a) 'Anonymous Content Thrives on TV Boom, "Spotlight" and "The Revenant" Awards Heat', *Variety*, 16 December, http://variety.com/2015/biz/news/anonymous-content-true-detective-mr-robot-1201661360/

Littleton, C. (2015b) 'Charles King Leaves WME to Launch Content Company Macro', *Variety*, 5 January, https://variety.com/2015/biz/news/charles-king-leaves-wme-to-launch-content-company-macro-1201392716/

Littleton, C. (2016) 'Showrunner Q&A: Sam Esmail and David Levien on Antiheroes, Casting, and Shooting in New York', *Variety*, 6 June, https://variety.com/2016/tv/news/mr-robot-sam-esmail-billions-david-levien-1201789845/

Littleton, C. (2021) 'How "Judas and the Black Messiah" Reflects Charles D. King's Macro Vision', *Variety*, 10 February, https://variety.com/2021/film/news/charles-king-judas-and-the-black-messiah-macro-1234905096/

Lotz, A.D. (2007) *The Television Will Be Revolutionized*, New York: New York University Press.

Lotz, A.D. (2014) 'Building Theories of Creative Media Industry Managers: Challenges, Perspectives, and Future Directions', in D. Johnson, D. Kompare and A. Santo (eds), *Making Media Work: Cultures of Management in the Entertainment Industries*, New York: New York University Press, pp. 25–38.

Lotz, A.D., R. Lobato and J. Thomas (2018) 'Internet-Distributed Television Research: A Provocation', *Media Industries Journal*, 5.2, https://doi.org/10.3998/mij.15031809.0005.203

Low, E. (2020) 'WME Partner Phillip Sun, Macro's Charles D. King Launch M88 Representation Firm, With Michael B. Jordan as Sun's First Client', *Variety*, 24 August, https://variety.com/2020/tv/news/wme-phillip-sun-m88-management-firm-macros-charles-d-king-1234746988/

Lowry, B. (2015) 'TV Review: *Mr. Robot*', *Variety*, 23 June, https://variety.com/2015/tv/reviews/mr-robot-review-usa-network-1201523347/

Luers, E. (2015) 'IFP Announces Two New Award Categories For Annual IFP Gotham Independent Film Awards', *ifp.org*, 17 September, https://web.archive.org/web/20150926002646/http://www.ifp.org/press/ifp-announces-two-new-award-categories-for-annual-ifp-gotham-independent-film-awards/#.WJMOJIOLSUk

Lury, C. (2004) *Brands: The Logos of the Global Economy*, Abingdon: Routledge.

Lyons, J. (2016) '"A Woman with an Endgame": Megan Ellison, Annapurna Pictures and American Independent Film Production', in L. Badley, C. Perkins and M. Schreiber (eds), *Indie Reframed: Women's Filmmaking and*

Contemporary American Independent Cinema, Edinburgh: Edinburgh University Press, pp. 54–69.

Lyons, J. and Y. Tzioumakis (eds) (2023) *Indie TV: Industry, Aesthetics and Medium Specificity*, New York: Routledge.

Macaulay, S. (2014) 'Filmmakers Launch #BlackoutBlackFriday Day of Activism, Events and Retail Boycott', *Filmmaker Magazine*, 28 November, https://filmmakermagazine.com/88466-filmmakers-launch-blackoutblack-friday-day-of-activism-events-and-retail-boycott-plus/#.YXAe-RrMKUk

Macdonald, G. (2001) 'Driven to Sell', *Globe and Mail*, 28 April, p. R1.

MacDowell, J. (2013) 'Quirky: Buzzword or Sensibility?', in G. King, C. Molloy and Y. Tzioumakis (eds), *American Independent Cinema: Indie, Indiewood and Beyond*, New York: Routledge, pp. 53–64.

Mack, K.W. (2012) *Representing the Race: The Creation of the Civil Rights Lawyer*, Cambridge, MA: Harvard University Press.

Mahar, K.W. (2006) *Women Filmmakers in Early Hollywood*, Baltimore, MD: Johns Hopkins University Press.

Mallore, D. (2002) 'Screen Test', *AdWeek*, 43.46: 20.

Malone, M. (2016) 'As Royal Gives Way to Robot, USA Eyes New Skies', *Broadcasting & Cable*, 146.25: 18.

Mann, D. (2008) *Hollywood Independents: The Postwar Talent Takeover*, Minneapolis: University of Minnesota Press.

Marin, R. (1994) 'MTV's Ruling Vidiot Savant', *Newsweek*, 27 November, http://www.newsweek.com/mtvs-ruling-vidiot-savant-186470

Markowitz, D. (2015) 'TV Review: What Happened with "True Detective"?', *University Wire*, 21 August, https://www.proquest.com/globalnews/docview/1705910971/E24E8242D024603PQ/3

Martin, A.L. Jr (2014) 'Scripting Black Gayness: Television Authorship in Black-Cast Sitcoms', *Television and New Media*, 16.7: 648–63.

Maslin, J. (1997) 'King Lear (Just Call Him Larry) In Iowa: [Review]', *New York Times*, 19 September, p. 12.

McCabe, J. (2013) 'HBO Aesthetics, Quality Television and *Boardwalk Empire*', in S. Peacock and J. Jacobs (eds), *Television Aesthetics and Style*, London: Bloomsbury, pp. 185–97.

McCauley, M.C. (2006) 'With Plays, Movies, TV Show, Perry Tells It Like It Is', *Knight Ridder*, 12 June, p. 1.

McClintock, P. (2015) 'Netflix Movies: Producers Weigh Hidden Downsides', *Hollywood Reporter*, 19 March, http://www.hollywoodreporter.com/news/netflix-movies-producers-weigh-hidden-782403

McClintock, P. (2016a) 'Box Office: "Star Wars" Beats "The Revenant" in U.S., Storms China with Record $53M Debut', *Hollywood Reporter*, 10 January, http://www.hollywoodreporter.com/news/box-office-star-wars-beats-853756

McClintock, P. (2016b) '"The Revenant" Producer on the Bear Scene that Took on "Myths of Its Own"', *Hollywood Reporter*, 19 February, http://

www.hollywoodreporter.com/news/revenant-bear-attack-producer-scene-864106
McClintock, P. and T. Siegel (2016) 'Focus Features Shake-Up: What's Behind Peter Schlessel's Abrupt Exit', *Hollywood Reporter*, 9 February, https://www.hollywoodreporter.com/news/focus-features-shake-up-whats-862969
McCracken, C. (2016) 'Rethinking Television Indies: The Impact of American Playhouse', *Screen*, 57.2: 218–34.
McDonald, P. (2008) 'The Star System: The Production of Hollywood Stardom in the Post-Studio Era', in P. McDonald and J. Wasko (eds), *The Contemporary Hollywood Film Industry*, Oxford: Blackwell, pp. 167–81.
McDonald, P. (2017) 'Flexible Stardom: Contemporary American Film and the Independent Mobility of Star Brands', in G. King (ed.), *A Companion to American Indie Film*, Chichester: Wiley, pp. 493–520.
McHugh, K.A. (2016) 'Miranda July and the New Twenty-First-Century Indie', in L. Badley, C. Perkins and M. Schreiber (eds), *Indie Reframed: Women's Filmmaking and Contemporary American Independent Cinema*, Edinburgh: Edinburgh University Press, pp. 239–55.
McKenna, A.T. (2012) 'Independent Production and Industrial Tactics in Britain: Michael Klinger and *Baby Love*', *Historical Journal of Film, Radio and Television*, 32.4: 611–31.
McMurria, J. (2007) 'A Taste of Class: Pay-TV and the Communication of Television in Postwar America', in S. Banet-Weisner, C. Chris and A. Freitas (eds), *Cable Visions: Television Beyond Broadcasting*, New York: New York University Press, pp. 44–65.
Merritt, G. (2000) *Celluloid Mavericks: A History of American Independent Film*, New York: Thunder's Mouth Press.
Miller, J. (2015) 'Leonardo DiCaprio Explains Why He Ate Actual Raw Bison Liver for *The Revenant*', *Vanity Fair*, 17 December, https://www.vanityfair.com/hollywood/2015/12/leonardo-dicaprio-the-revenant-raw-bison-liver
Miller, L.S. (2015) 'In the Age of Auteur Television, What Does It Mean to Be a Director?', *Indiewire*, 2 March, http://www.indiewire.com/2015/03/in-the-age-of-auteur-television-what-does-it-mean-to-be-a-director-64584/
Miller, T. (2016) 'Cybertarian Flexibility – When Prosumers Join the Cognitariat, All That Scholarship Melts into Air', in M. Curtin and K. Sanson (eds), *Precarious Creativity: Global Media, Local Labor*, Oakland: University of California Press, pp. 19–32.
Milvy, E. (2001) 'BMW at Intersection of Art and Commerce', *Los Angeles Times*, 4 April, https://www.latimes.com/archives/la-xpm-2001-may-04-ca-59071-story.html
Mitchell, E. (2003) 'A Lawyer's Good Teeth Help in Court and Love', *New York Times*, 10 October, https://www.nytimes.com/2003/10/10/movies/film-review-a-lawyer-s-good-teeth-help-in-court-and-love.html
Mittell, J. (2015) *Complex TV: The Poetics of Contemporary Television Storytelling*, New York: New York University Press.

Molloy, C. (2010) *Memento*, Edinburgh: Edinburgh University Press.

Molloy, C. (2013) 'Christopher Nolan and Indie Sensibilities', *Revue Française d'Études Américaines*, 2: 40–51.

Molloy, C. (2017) 'Indie Cinema and the Neoliberal Commodification of Creative Labor: Rethinking the Indie Sensibility of Christopher Nolan', in G. King (ed.), *A Companion to American Indie Film*, Chichester: Wiley, pp. 368–88.

Moniuszko, S.M. and C. Kelly (2018) 'Harvey Weinstein scandal: A Complete List of the 87 Accusers', *USA Today*, 1 June, https://eu.usatoday.com/story/life/people/2017/10/27/weinstein-scandal-complete-list-accusers/804663001/

Monk, K. (1994) 'Selling Cars on the Information Superhighway', *Vancouver Sun*, 2 April, p. D2.

Moore, R. (2005) 'Tyler Perry Has Hit it Big for a Man Who Goes Unnoticed', *Orlando Sentinel*, 25 February, p. 18.

Moorhouse J. (2020) *Unconditional Love: A Memoir of Filmmaking and Motherhood*, Melbourne: Text Publishing.

Mowe, R. (2014) 'The Sweet Smell of Success', *Eye for Eye*, 10 July, http://www.eyeforfilm.co.uk/feature/2014-07-10-interview-with-michael-sugar-about-anoymmous-content-feature-story-by-richard-mowe

Munoz, L. (2007) 'Tyler Perry Makes His Own Rules In Hollywood', *Los Angeles Times*, 11 May, p. D10.

Murray, S. (2005) 'Brand Loyalties: Rethinking Content Within Global Corporate Media', *Media, Culture & Society*, 27.3: 415–35.

Natale, R. (1995) 'Moore Better News: War on the Horizon', *Los Angeles Times*, 19 February, https://www.latimes.com/archives/la-xpm-1995-02-19-ca-33673-story.html

Nathan, I. (2008) 'The Complete Coens', *Empire*, January, p. 173.

Ndounou, M.W. (2014) *Shaping the Future of African American Film: Color-Coded Economics and the Story Behind the Numbers*, New Brunswick, NJ: Rutgers University Press.

N'Duka, A. (2021) '"Judas And The Black Messiah" Team on Why "There's a Fred Hampton in Everyone" – Deadline Virtual House', *Deadline*, 4 March, https://deadline.com/video/judas-and-the-black-messiah-team-on-why-theres-a-fred-hampton-in-everyone-deadline-virtual-house/

Newman, M.Z. (2009) 'Indie Culture: In Pursuit of the Authentic Autonomous Alternative', *Cinema Journal*, 48.3: 16–34.

Newman, M.Z. (2011) *Indie: An American Film Culture*, New York: Columbia University Press.

Newman, M.Z. and E. Levine (2012) *Legitimating Television: Media Convergence and Cultural Status*, Abingdon: Routledge.

Ng, P. (2014) 'Cinemax Gives Steven Soderbergh's "The Knick" Early Season 2 Renewal', *Hollywood Reporter*, 10 July, http://www.hollywoodreporter.com/live-feed/cinemaxs-knick-renewed-season-2-717845

Nichols, M. (2020) 'Macro Taps Jerome Martin, Natalia Williams to Expand Management Arm (Exclusive)', *Variety*, 29 June, https://variety.com/2020/

tv/news/jerome-martin-natalia-williams-macro-management-charles-king-1234719892/

Nordyke, K. (2018) 'Matthew Weiner on Sexual Misconduct Allegation: "I Don't Remember Saying That"', *Hollywood Reporter*, 30 September, https://www.hollywoodreporter.com/tv/tv-news/matthew-weiner-denies-sexual-misconduct-allegation-1148105/

North, A. (2018) '#MeToo at the 2018 Oscars: The Good, the Bad, and the In Between', *Vox*, 5 May, https://www.vox.com/2018/3/5/17079702/2018-oscars-me-too-times-up-frances-mcdormand-jimmy-kimmel

Nugent, J. (2021) '*No Time To Die* Review', *Empire*, 29 September, https://www.empireonline.com/movies/reviews/no-time-to-die/

Nwonka, C.J. (2019) 'The New Babel: The Language and Practice of Institutionalised Diversity in the UK Film Industry', *Journal of British Cinema and Television*, 17.1: 24–46.

Nygaard, T. and J. Lagerwey (2020) *Horrible White People: Gender, Genre, and Television's Precarious Whiteness*, New York: New York University Press.

O'Carroll, L. (2017) 'Harvey Weinstein: English Actor Says Alleged Sexual Assault Ruined Film Career', *The Guardian*, 13 October, https://www.theguardian.com/uk-news/2017/oct/12/harvey-weinstein-alleged-assault-sophie-dix-english-actor-ruined-career

O'Connell, S. (2015) 'Why Leonardo DiCaprio Made Himself Vomit While Shooting *The Revenant*', *Cinemablend*, 28 September, https://www.cinemablend.com/new/Why-Leonardo-DiCaprio-Made-Himself-Vomit-Shooting-Revenant-85047.html

O'Falt, C. (2016) 'It's Complicated: How Netflix and Amazon Add a Big Wrinkle to Sundance Deal-Making', *IndieWire*, 21 January, http://www.indiewire.com/article/its-complicated-how-netflix-and-amazon-add-a-big-wrinkle-to-sundance-deal-making-20160121

O'Steen, K. (1994) 'Propaganda, Partners Seek to Fill Indie Niche', *Variety*, 4 April, p. 14.

O'Sullivan, M. (2003) 'Cruel? Yes. Intolerable? No', *Washington Post*, 10 October, https://web.archive.org/web/20150822125109/http://www.washingtonpost.com/wp-dyn/content/article/2003/10/10/AR2005033116239.html

Olsen, M. (2000) 'Discovery: Mike Mills', *Film Comment*, 36.3: 16–17.

Olsen, M. (2005) 'Pages from Perry's "Diary"', *Los Angeles Times*, 24 February, https://www.latimes.com/archives/la-xpm-2005-feb-24-wk-movies24-story.html

Omar, Y. (2020) 'Why Did the Oscars Fail to Nominate Any Female Directors Again?', *Harpers Bazaar*, 14 January, https://www.harpersbazaar.com/uk/culture/entertainment/a30505280/oscars-female-directors/

Onstad, K. (2017) 'Brit Marling's Impossible Dream', *Vulture*, 23 January, https://www.vulture.com/2017/01/brit-marling-the-oa.html

Ortner, S.B. (2013) *Not Hollywood: Independent Film at the Twilight of the American Dream*, London: Duke University Press.

Ortner, S.B. (2017) 'The Making of the Indie Scene: The Cultural Production of a Field of Cultural Production', in G. King (ed.) *A Companion to American Indie Film*, Chichester: Wiley, pp. 42–57.

Otterson, J. (2019) 'Alfonso Cuarón Sets TV Overall Deal at Apple', *Variety*, 10 October, https://variety.com/2019/tv/news/alfonso-cuaron-sets-tv-overall-deal-at-apple-1203366172/

Pallotta, F. (2016) '"Mr. Robot" Creator Says Freedom of Cable TV Helped Show Succeed', *CNN Wire Service*, 16 March, https://money.cnn.com/2016/03/16/media/mr-robot-sam-esmail-south-by-southwest/index.html

Palm Pictures (2003) *The Work of Director Spike Jonze: A Collection of Music Videos, Short Films, Documentaries, and Rarities* [DVD], produced by Vincent Landay and Richard Brown.

Palmer, R.B. (2004) *Joel and Ethan Coen*, Chicago: University of Illinois Press.

Patterson, J. (2007) '"We've Killed a Lot of Animals"', *The Guardian*, 21 December, https://www.theguardian.com/film/2007/dec/21/coenbrothers

Pearson, E. (2017) 'Structuring Indie and *Beasts of the Southern Wild*: The Role of Review Journalism', in G. King (ed.) *A Companion to American Indie Film*, Chichester: Wiley, pp. 155–80.

Pearson, R. (2011) 'Cult Television as Digital Television's Cutting Edge', in J. Bennett and N. Strange (eds), *Television as Digital Media*, London: Duke University Press, pp. 105–31.

Pendreigh, B. (1994) 'Coen for the Big One', *The Scotsman*, 10 August.

Peplow, G. (2023) 'The Anatomy of an Oscar Winner', *Sky News*, https://news.sky.com/story/oscars-2023-diversity-v-data-what-analysis-of-94-years-of-winners-tells-us-about-the-academy-awards-11635455

Perkins, C. (2016) 'My Effortless Brilliance: Women's Mumblecore', in L. Badley, C. Perkins and M. Schreiber (eds), *Indie Reframed: Women's Filmmaking and Contemporary American Independent Cinema*, Edinburgh: Edinburgh University Press, pp. 138–53.

Perren, A. (2012) *Indie, Inc.: Miramax and the Transformation of Hollywood in the 1990s*, Austin: University of Texas.

Perren, A. (2023) 'Same Word, Different Medium: The Evolution of Indie TV Since the 2000s', in J. Lyons and Y. Tzioumakis (eds), *Indie TV: Industry, Aesthetics and Medium Specificity*, New York: Routledge, pp. 59–77.

Persall, S. (1995) 'John Candy's Real Last Movie', *St. Petersburg Times*, 3 February, https://www.tampabay.com/archive/1995/02/03/john-candy-s-real-last-movie/

Petruska, K. (2023) 'Amazon Prime Video: Scale, Complexity, and Television as Widget', in D. Johnson (ed.), *From Networks to Netflix: A Guide to Changing Channels*, 2nd edn, New York: Routledge, pp. 235–46.

Petski, D. (2021) '"Judas And The Black Messiah" Writer-Director Shaka King Inks First-Look Deal with FX Productions, *Deadline*, 1 October, https://deadline.com/2021/10/judas-and-the-black-messiah-shaka-king-first-look-deal-fx-productions-1234848120/#comments

Pevere, G. (2003) 'Coens Dodge the Romance in No-Holds-Barred Comedy', *Toronto Star*, 10 October, p. F02.

Pierce, S. (2016) 'Sundance Preview: Oscar-Winner Soderbergh Finds Happiness in TV', *Salt Lake Tribune*, 19 January, https://archive.sltrib.com/article.php?id=3415295&itype=CMSID

Pierson, J. (1996) *Spike, Mike, Slackers & Dykes: A Guided Tour Across a Decade of American Independent Cinema*, London: Faber.

Pomerantz, D. (2012) 'Disney's Success and The Death of Mid-Budget Movies', *Forbes*, 28 August, https://www.forbes.com/sites/dorothypomerantz/2012/08/28/disneys-success-and-the-death-of-mid-budget-movies/#eaeeeec4bd8a

Portman, J. (1997) 'Obstacles Impede "Serious" Movies', *Ottawa Citizen*, 18 September, p. D11.

Powers, A. (1999) 'Rock Music Videos as an Art Form with a Festival of Its Very Own', *New York Times*, 14 May, https://www.nytimes.com/1999/05/14/movies/rock-music-videos-as-an-art-form-with-a-festival-of-its-very-own.html

Powers, J. (2015) 'One Direction', *Vogue*, 1 November, https://archive.vogue.com/article/2015/11/one-direction

Powers, P. (2007) 'The Philosophical Foundations of Foucaultian Discourse Analysis', *Critical Approaches to Discourse Analysis Across Disciplines*, 1.2: 18–34.

Pulleine, T. (1985) 'Brothers in Gore', *The Guardian*, 31 January, p. 23.

Quinn, E. (2013) 'Black Talent and Conglomerate Hollywood: Will Smith, Tyler Perry, and the Continuing Significance of Race', *International Journal of Media and Culture* 11.3: 196–210.

Ramón, A.C., M. Tran and D. Hunt (2022) *Hollywood Diversity Report 2022: A New, Post-Pandemic Normal? Part 2: Television*, Los Angeles: UCLA, https://socialsciences.ucla.edu/wp-content/uploads/2023/11/UCLA-Hollywood-Diversity-Report-2023-Television-11-9-2023.pdf

Ramos, D.R. (2020) '"Judas And The Black Messiah" Trailer: Director Shaka King Puts Shine on Timeless Story of Black Revolutionary Chairman Fred Hampton', *Deadline*, 6 August, https://deadline.com/video/judas-and-the-black-messiah-trailer-shaka-king-chairman-fred-hampton-ryan-coogler-charles-d-king-macro/#comments

Randee, D. (2015) 'On Television; Long Reach of "Mr. Robot"', *Los Angeles Times*, 24 November, p. S56.

Rao, S. (2022) 'David O. Russell is Latest Face of Hollywood's Workplace Abuse Problem', *Washington Post*, 7 October, https://www.washingtonpost.com/arts-entertainment/2022/10/07/david-o-russell-movie-allegations/

Rea, S. (1994) 'Hudsucker Proxy: The Spawn of an Unlikely Hollywood Marriage', *The Philadelphia Inquirer*, 27 March, p. G02.

Redmond, A. (2015) *Constructing the Coens: From* Blood Simple *to* Inside Llewyn Davis, Lanham, MD: Rowman & Littlefield.

Reinsch, P.N. (2016) 'The Case for Calling George Lucas the "White Tyler

Perry'", in T.M. Russworm, S.N. Sheppard and K.M. Bowdre (eds), *From Madea to Media Mogul: Theorizing Tyler Perry*, Jackson: University of Mississippi Press, pp. 200–24.

Repass, S. (2002) 'Reviews: "Being John Malkovich"', *Film Quarterly*, 56.1: 29–36.

Richards, R.W. (2021) *Cinematic TV: Serial Drama Goes to the Movies*, Oxford: Oxford University Press.

Richardson, J. (1990a) 'Producers: Propaganda Films', *Premiere*, 1 June, p. 60.

Richardson, J. (1990b) 'The Joel & Ethan Story', *Premiere*, 1 October, pp. 94–101.

Rife, K. (2017) 'An Incomplete, Depressingly Long List of Celebrities' Sexual Assault and Harassment Stories [Updated]', *AV Club*, 22 November, https://www.avclub.com/an-incomplete-depressingly-long-list-of-celebrities-se-1819628519

Rizzo, C. (2014) 'Series Thrive with a Single Director Instead of a Group', *Variety*, 18 June, https://variety.com/2014/tv/awards/going-with-a-solo-helmer-instead-of-a-group-1201221666/

Rohter, L. (1990) 'For Producers, Their Way Is the Right Way', *Los Angeles Times*, 15 October, p. 13.

Romney, J. (2016) 'Alejandro Gonzalez Iñárritu: "When You See *The Revenant* You Will Say 'Wow'"', *The Observer*, 8 January, https://www.theguardian.com/film/2016/jan/03/alejandro-gonzalez-inarritu-interview-the-revenant

Rose, L. (2015a) 'Netflix's Ted Sarandos on "Beasts of No Nation" Allure: "It Was Not a Focus-Grouped Film"', *Hollywood Reporter*, 21 December, http://www.hollywoodreporter.com/news/netflixs-ted-sarandos-beasts-no-849506

Rose, L. (2015b) 'TV Agent Mark Itkin on Why He's Retiring, How Reality TV Can Recover and a Lost Oprah-Lee Daniels Show', *Hollywood Reporter*, 17 December, https://www.hollywoodreporter.com/news/general-news/tv-agent-mark-itkin-why-848511/

Rosenberg, A. (2015) '"Beasts of No Nation" Is a Powerful Story About the End of Childhood', *Washington Post*, 16 October, https://www.washingtonpost.com/news/act-four/wp/2015/10/16/beasts-of-no-nation-is-a-powerful-story-about-the-end-of-childhood/

Rottenberg, J. (2016) 'To Stream or Not to Stream: Filmmakers Are Seeking Ways to Cross the Digital Divide', *Los Angeles Times*, 22 May, https://www.latimes.com/entertainment/movies/la-ca-mn--blur-decision-20160511-snap-story.html

Roundtree, C. (2022) '"He Needs to Be Stopped": Sources Say Cary Fukunaga "Abused His Power" To Pursue Young Women on Set', *Rolling Stone*, 31 May, https://www.rollingstone.com/tv-movies/tv-movie-features/cary-fukunaga-no-time-to-die-1359656/

Roussel, V. (2016) 'Talent Agenting in the Age of the Conglomerates', in M. Curtin and K. Sanson (eds), *Precarious Creativity: Global Media, Local Labor*, Oakland: University of California Press, pp. 74–87.

Roussel, V. (2017) *Representing Talent: Hollywood Agents and the Making of Movies*, Chicago: Chicago University Press.

Russworm, T.M. (2016) 'Media Studies Has Ninety-Nine Problems … But Tyler Perry Ain't One of Them?', in T.M. Russworm, S.N. Sheppard and K.M. Bowdre (eds), *From Madea to Media Mogul: Theorizing Tyler Perry*, Jackson: University of Mississippi Press, pp. xiii–xxxiv.

Ryan, C. and A. Greenwald (2017) 'Ep. 106: The Year in TV with "Mr. Robot" Creator Sam Esmail', *The Watch*, formerly available at: https://soundcloud.com/the-watch-podcast/ep-106-the-year-in-tv-with-mr-robot-creator-sam-esmail

Ryan, P. (1994) 'Independents' Day', *Irish Times*, 17 September, p. 3.

Sacks, E. (2015a) 'Hollywood Look Out – Here Comes Netflix', *New York Daily News*, 9 June, https://www.pressreader.com/usa/new-york-daily-news/20150609/281573764314496

Sacks, E. (2015b) 'This "Beast" Has Brains: Taut Tale Shifts Film Landscape', *New York Daily News*, 11 October, p. 18.

SAG-AFTRA Foundation (2017) 'The Business: Zal Batmanglij & Brit Marling on Collaboration and The OA', *YouTube*, 15 March, https://www.youtube.com/watch?v=0ta0brryNCw

Sandberg, B. (2019) 'TV's New Math: What if $100M Netflix Deals Actually Shortchange Creators?', *Hollywood Reporter*, 25 April, https://www.hollywoodreporter.com/news/general-news/tvs-new-math-what-100m-netflix-deals-actually-shortchange-creators-1203846/

Santo, A. (2008) 'Para-television and Discourses of Distinction: The Culture of Production at HBO', in M. Leverette, B.L. Ott and C.L. Buckley (eds), *It's Not TV: Watching HBO in the Post-Television Era*, New York: Routledge, pp. 19–45.

Sarris, A. (2008) 'Notes on the Auteur Theory in 1962 (1962)', in B.K. Grant (ed.), *Auteurs and Authorship: A Film Reader*, Oxford: Blackwell, pp. 35–45.

Schatz, T. (2009) 'The Genius of the System', in L. Braudy and M. Cohen (eds), *Film Theory and Criticism: Introductory Readings*, 7th edn, Oxford: Oxford University Press, pp. 523–8.

Schatz, T. (2017) 'Going Mainstream: The Indie Film Movement in 1999', in G. King (ed.) *A Companion to American Indie Film*, Chichester: Wiley, pp. 257–78.

Schilling, M.K. (2013) 'Steven Soderbergh on Quitting Hollywood, Getting the Best Out of J. Lo, and His Love of Girls', *Vulture*, 27 January, http://www.vulture.com/2013/01/steven-soderbergh-in-conversation.html

Schreiber, M. (2013) '"I'm Absolutely the Right Person for this Job": Allison Anders and Mary Harron on Lifetime Television', in L. Badley, C. Perkins and M. Schreiber (eds), *Indie Reframed: Women's Filmmaking and Contemporary American Independent Cinema*, Edinburgh: Edinburgh University Press, pp. 87–103.

Scott, A.O. (2017) 'Review: "Wonder Woman" Is a Blockbuster that Lets

Itself Have Fun', *New York Times*, 31 May, https://www.nytimes.com/2017/05/31/movies/wonder-woman-review-gal-gadot.html

Scott, J. (1984) 'Festival of Festivals', *Globe and Mail*, 7 September, p. E3.

Seidenberg, R. (1985) 'Out of NYU into Independence', *New York Times*, 27 January, https://www.nytimes.com/1985/01/27/arts/out-of-nyu-into-independence.html

Seitz, M.Z. (2015) 'The Binge Director: Steven Soderbergh Can Make a Whole Season of *The Knick* Almost as Fast as You Can Watch It', *Vulture*, 5 October, https://www.vulture.com/2015/10/on-set-steven-soderbergh-the-knick.html

Seitz, M.Z. (2016) '*The Girlfriend Experience* Is One of the Best Shows of the Year', *Vulture*, 8 April, http://www.vulture.com/2016/04/girlfriend-experience-is-one-of-the-best-shows-of-the-year.html

Sellors, C.P. (2010) *Film Authorship: Auteurs and Other Myths*, New York: Wallflower Press.

Sepinwall, A. (2021) 'Steven Soderbergh on the Gore, the Grind, and the Glory of Making "The Knick"', *Rolling Stone*, 25 February, https://www.rollingstone.com/tv-movies/tv-movie-features/steven-soderbergh-interview-knick-hbo-max-1131019/

Setoodeh, R. (2015a) 'Cary Fukunaga Offers New Details on Why "It" Remake Fell Apart', *Variety*, 2 September, https://variety.com/2015/film/news/cary-fukunaga-it-exit-1201584416/

Setoodeh, R. (2015b) 'Unleashing The Beast', *Variety*, 1 September, pp. 28–33.

Sexton, J. (2022) '"Everything About Being Indie Is All Tied to Not Being Black": Indie Music, Race, and Identity in *Medicine for Melancholy* and *Pariah*', *Music, Sound, and the Moving Image*, 16.2: 129–52.

Sexton, M. and D. Lees (2021) *Seeing It on Television: Televisuality in the Contemporary US 'High-End' Series*, London: Bloomsbury Academic.

Sharf, Z. (2021) 'Cary Fukunaga: Working on "True Detective" Became "Disheartening" as Nic Pizzolatto Got More Power', *IndieWire*, 22 September, https://www.indiewire.com/features/general/cary-fukunaga-criticizes-true-detective-creator-nic-pizzolatto-1234666628/

Shaw, D. (2013) *The Three Amigos: The transnational filmmaking of Guillermo del Toro, Alejandro González Iñárritu and Alfonso Cuarón*, Manchester: Manchester University Press.

Shaw, R.Z. (2016) 'From the Margins to Center Stage: Tyler Perry's Popular African American Theatre', in T.M. Russworm, S.N. Sheppard and K.M. Bowdre (eds), *From Madea to Media Mogul: Theorizing Tyler Perry*, Jackson: University of Mississippi Press, pp. 30–51.

Shepherd, D. (1985) 'Texas Strangers', *San Diego Reader*, 25 April, pp. 26–7.

Shepherd, J. (2016) 'HBO Reveals Why *True Detective* Season 2 Sucked', *The Independent*, 6 January, https://www.independent.co.uk/arts-entertainment/tv/news/hbo-reveals-why-true-detective-season-2-sucked-a6798516.html

Sheppard, S.N. (2016) '"Tyler Perry Presents …": The Cultural Projects,

Partnerships, and Politics of Perry's Media Platforms', in T.M. Russworm, S.N. Sheppard and K.M. Bowdre (eds), *From Madea to Media Mogul: Theorizing Tyler Perry*, Jackson: University of Mississippi Press, pp. 3–29.

Shope, K. (2006) 'The Final Cut: How SAG's Failed Negotiations with Talent Agents Left the Contractual Rights of Rank-and-File Actors on the Cutting Room Floor', *Journal of the National Association of Administrative Law*, 26.1: art 3, http://digitalcommons.pepperdine.edu/naalj/vol26/iss1/3

Siegel, T. (2021a) '"Everyone Just Knows He's an Absolute Monster": Scott Rudin's Ex-Staffers Speak Out on Abusive Behavior', *Hollywood Reporter*, 7 April, https://www.hollywoodreporter.com/features/everyone-just-knows-hes-an-absolute-monster-scott-rudins-ex-staffers-speak-out-on-abusive-behavior

Siegel, T. (2021b) 'Producer Roundtable: Andy Samberg, Dede Gardner, Charles D. King and More on the Streaming Rise Amid COVID and Their Awards Contenders', *Hollywood Reporter*, 22 January, https://www.hollywoodreporter.com/movies/movie-news/producer-roundtable-andy-samberg-ashley-levinson-charles-king-and-more-on-the-streaming-rise-amid-covid-and-their-awards-contenders-4118121/

Silberg, J. (2001) 'Short Takes: BMW Hits the Infobahn', *American Cinematographer*, 82.7: 85–8.

Sim, G. (2016) 'Individual Disruptors and Economic Gamechangers: Netflix, New Media, and Neoliberalism', in K. McDonald and D. Smith-Rowsey (eds), *The Netflix Effect: Technology and Entertainment in the 21st Century*, London: Bloomsbury, pp. 185–201.

Sinwell, S.E.S. (2020) *Indie Cinema Online*, New Brunswick, NJ: Rutgers University Press.

Sinwell, S.E.S. (2023) '(Re-)Branding Sundance: Entering the Indie TV Market', in J. Lyons and Y. Tzioumakis (eds), *Indie TV: Industry, Aesthetics and Medium Specificity*, New York: Routledge, pp. 81–97.

Smith, N.M. (2013) 'Interview Steven Soderbergh, Part 1: "Side Effects," "Behind the Candelabra" and His Friendship With David Fincher', *IndieWire*, 5 February, http://www.indiewire.com/2013/02/interview-steven-soderbergh-part-1-side-effects-behind-the-candelabra-and-his-friendship-with-david-fincher-41382/

Smith, P.J (2021) 'Behind the Money: Alejandro González Iñárritu as career director', *Studies in Spanish and Latin American Cinemas*, 18.1, pp. 9–18.

Spangler, T. (2015) 'Amazon Studios to Produce Movies for Theatrical, Digital Release in 2015', *Variety*, 19 January, http://variety.com/2015/digital/news/amazon-studios-to-produce-movies-for-theatrical-digital-release-in-2015-1201408688/

Sperb, J. (2013) *Blossoms and Blood: Postmodern Media Culture and the Films of Paul Thomas Anderson*, Austin: University of Texas Press.

Spicer, A., A.T. McKenna and C. Meir (2014) 'Introduction', in A. Spicer, A.T. McKenna and C. Meir (eds), *Beyond the Bottom Line: The*

Producer in Film and Television Studies, New York: Bloomsbury Academic, pp. 1–23.

Squires, C.R. (2014) *The Post-Racial Mystique: Media & Race in the Twenty-First Century*, New York: New York University Press.

Steinberg, B. (2018) 'Walmart Will Return to Oscars Ads, Enlisting Female Directors', *Variety*, 22 January, https://variety.com/2018/tv/news/walmart-female-directors-oscars-advertising-1202671774/

Stern, M. (2014) '"True Detective" Director Cary Fukunaga's Journey from Pro Snowboarder to Hollywood's Most Wanted', *Daily Beast*, 26 February, https://www.thedailybeast.com/true-detective-director-cary-fukunagas-journey-from-pro-snowboarder-to-hollywoods-most-wanted

Sternbergh, A. (2014) 'The Age of the Streaming TV Auteur', *Vulture*, 21 September, https://www.vulture.com/2014/09/age-of-the-auteur-on-streaming-tv.html

Stewart, A. (2013) 'Revamped Focus Features Led by Peter Schlessel Relocating to LA', *Variety*, 2 October, http://variety.com/2013/film/news/breaking-focus-features-ceo-james-schamus-out-peter-schlessel-to-take-over-1200688551/

Stolley, K., F. Kerrigan and C. Yalkin (2022) 'Branded Entertainment: A Critical Review', in P. McDonald (ed.), *The Routledge Companion to Media Industries*, New York: Routledge, pp. 372–81.

Stone, N. (2016) 'Golden Globes: Alejandro G. Iñárritu Wins Best Director', *Hollywood Reporter*, 10 January, http://www.hollywoodreporter.com/news/alejandro-g-inarritu-wins-golden-853890

Strauss, B. (2015a) 'Acclaimed Child Soldier Novel "Beasts of No Nation" Comes to Theaters, Netflix', *Los Angeles Daily News*, 16 October, https://www.dailynews.com/2015/10/16/acclaimed-child-soldier-novel-beasts-of-no-nation-comes-to-theaters-netflix/

Strauss, B. (2015b) 'There's More to 2015's Fall Movie Releases than "Star Wars" – but Does It Matter?', *Telegram*, 11 September, https://www.presstelegram.com/2015/09/11/theres-more-to-2015s-fall-movie-releases-than-star-wars-but-does-it-matter/

Strauss, N. (1995) 'Critic's Notebook: Hit Bands You See But Don't Listen To', *New York Times*, 1 April, https://www.nytimes.com/1995/04/01/arts/critic-s-notebook-hit-bands-you-see-but-don-t-listen-to.html

Straw, W. (2001) 'Scenes and Sensibilities', *Public*, 22/23, https://public.journals.yorku.ca/index.php/public/article/view/30335

Stubbs, A. (2020) 'Packaging *House of Cards* and *The Knick*: How Talent Intermediaries Manage the Indie-Auteur Brand to Sell Premium Television', *Critical Studies in Television*, 15.2: 129–47.

Sun, R. (2021) 'M88's Mission to Create New, Diverse Roadmap for Hollywood Management', *Hollywood Reporter*, 26 August, https://www.hollywoodreporter.com/business/business-news/m88s-mission-diverse-roadmap-hollywood-management-1235002216/

Swisher, K. (2018) 'Can Laurene Powell Jobs Save Storytelling?', *New York Times*, 27 November, https://www.nytimes.com/2018/11/27/opinion/laurene-powell-jobs-emerson-pop-up.html

Swisher, K. (2019) 'Full Transcript: "Mr. Robot" Creator Sam Esmail on Recode Decode', *Vox*, 19 November, https://www.vox.com/2016/11/19/13654544/full-transcript-mr-robot-sam-esmail-hacking

Takaki, M. (2002) 'Dirs. Scott, Woo, Carnahan Answer "The Hire" Calling', *Shoot*, 16 August, https://shootonline.com/news/share/28580

Taubin, A. (2001) 'Driven to Perfection', *Village Voice*, 26 June, https://www.villagevoice.com/driven-to-perfection/

Thompson, A. (2006) 'Risky Business', *Hollywood Reporter*, 12 May.

Thompson, A. (2007) 'The Ol' "Country" Switcheroo', *Variety*, 19 April, p. 4.

Thompson, A. (2008) 'Slow Burn Keeps "Old Men" Simmering', *Variety*, 4 February, pp. 14; 24.

Thompson, A. (2015) 'How Steven Soderbergh Made "The Knick" Must-See TV, and More', *IndieWire*, 31 May, https://www.indiewire.com/2015/05/how-steven-soderbergh-made-the-knick-must-see-tv-and-more-187380/

Truffaut, F. (2008) 'A Certain Tendency in French Cinema (1954)', in B.K. Grant (ed.), *Auteurs and Authorship: A Film Reader*, Oxford: Blackwell, pp. 9–18.

Tryon, C. (2013) *On-Demand Culture: Digital Delivery and the Future of Movies*, London: Rutgers University Press.

Tryon, C. (2015) 'TV Got Better: Netflix's Original Programming Strategies and Binge Viewing', *Media Industries Journal*, 2.2, http://www.mediaindustriesjournal.org/index.php/mij/article/view/126/180

Turner, M. (2006) 'Mad for Madea; Popular Character Isn't Only Thing Keeping Prolific Tyler Perry Busy', *Chicago Tribune*, 24 February, p. 56.

Turow, J. (1992) *Media Systems in Society: Understanding Industries, Strategies, and Power*, New York: Longman.

Twohey, M., J. Kantor, S. Dominus, J. Rutenberg and S. Eder (2017) 'Weinstein's Complicity Machine', *New York Times*, 5 December, https://www.nytimes.com/interactive/2017/12/05/us/harvey-weinstein-complicity.html

Tzioumakis, Y. (2006) *American Independent Cinema: An Introduction*, Edinburgh: Edinburgh University Press.

Tzioumakis, Y. (2011) 'Academic Discourses and American Independent Cinema: In Search of A Field of Studies, Part 2 – The 1990s to Date', *New Review of Film and Television Studies*, 9.3: 311–40.

Tzioumakis, Y. (2012) *Hollywood's Indies: Classics Divisions, Specialty Labels and American Independent Cinema*, Edinburgh: Edinburgh University Press.

Tzioumakis, Y. (2013) '"Independent", "Indie" and "Indiewood": Towards a Periodization of Contemporary (Post-1980) American Independent Cinema', in G. King, C. Molloy and Y. Tzioumakis (eds), *American Independent Cinema: Indie, Indiewood and Beyond*, New York: Routledge, pp. 28–40.

Tzioumakis, Y. (2017a) *American Independent Cinema: An Introduction*, 2nd edn, Edinburgh: Edinburgh University Press.

Tzioumakis, Y. (2017b) 'From Independent to Indie: The Independent Feature Project and the Complex Relationship Between American Independent Cinema and Hollywood in the 1980s', in G. King (ed.), *A Companion to American Indie Film*, Chichester: Wiley, pp. 233–56.

Ugwu, R. (2021) 'Shaka King Goes to Hollywood', *New York Times*, 12 February, https://www.nytimes.com/2021/02/12/movies/shaka-king-judas-black-messiah.html

Uhlin, G. (2020) 'David Fincher's Righteous Workflow: Design and the Transmedial Director', in C. Vernallis, H. Rogers and L. Perrott (eds), *Transmedia Directors: Artistry, Industry, and New Audiovisual Aesthetics*, New York: Bloomsbury Academic, pp. 136–49.

Van Gelder, L. (1989) 'At The Movies', *New York Times*, 10 February, https://www.nytimes.com/1989/02/10/movies/at-the-movies.html

Vernallis, C. (2013) *Unruly Media: YouTube, Music Video, and the New Digital Cinema*, New York: Oxford University Press.

Vernallis C., H. Rogers and L. Perrott (eds) (2020) *Transmedia Directors: Artistry, Industry, and New Audiovisual Aesthetics*, New York: Bloomsbury Academic.

Vice, J. (2007) 'Coens Return to *Fargo* Form', *Desert Morning News*, 21 December, https://www.proquest.com/docview/351565143/667F5FFEF9C420CPQ/6

Villarreal, Y. (2014) 'USA Network to Embrace Darkness', *Los Angeles Times*, 11 November, p. B1.

Walker, D. (2013) 'Nic Pizzolatto, New Orleans-Born Novelist, Discusses HBO's Upcoming "True Detective"', *The Times-Picayune*, 8 July, http://www.nola.com/tv/index.ssf/2013/07/nic_pizzolatto_new_orleans-bor.html

Warner, K.J. (2016) 'Strategies for Success? Navigating Hollywood's "Postracial" Labor Practices', in M. Curtin and K. Sanson (eds), *Precarious Creativity: Global Media, Local Labor*, Oakland: University of California Press, pp. 172–85.

Wartofsky, A. (1999) 'Shooting for the Hip: Video May Have Killed the Radio Star, but Spike Jonze Is a Cultural Force to be Reckoned with in the Music Video Business', *Ottawa Citizen*, 11 November, p. C5.

Wasko, J. (2005) *How Hollywood Works*, London: Sage.

Watercutter, A. (2015) '*Beasts of No Nation*'s Director Has Big Ideas for Netflix', *Wired*, 16 October, https://www.wired.com/2015/10/beasts-no-nation-fukunaga-netflix/

Weintraub, S. (2010) 'Exclusive: David Fincher Talks "Social Network," "Zodiac," His Filmmaking Process, and More', *Collider*, 30 December, http://collider.com/david-fincher-interview-social-network-girl-with-dragon-tattoo/

Weisbard, E. (1997) 'Join the Club', *Village Voice*, 4 March, p. 55.

Westrup, L. (2016) 'The Long and the Short of Music Video', *The Projector*, 16.2: 19–35.

Wexman, V.W. (2020) *Hollywood's Artists: The Directors Guild of America and the Construction of Authorship*, New York: Columbia University Press.

White, A. (2023) 'Tyler Perry Says He Is "Beyond Interested" in Majority Stake in BET', *Hollywood Reporter*, 5 April, https://www.hollywoodreporter.com/tv/tv-news/tyler-perry-bet-sale-majority-stake-1235367947/

White, P. (2016) 'Killer Feminism', in L. Badley, C. Perkins and M. Schreiber (eds), *Indie Reframed: Women's Filmmaking and Contemporary American Independent Cinema*, Edinburgh: Edinburgh University Press, pp. 36–53.

Willens, M. (1998) 'From Miller Lite to the Making Of Movies Lite?' *New York Times*, 6 September, p. 7.

Williams, K. (2003) *Why I [Still] Want My MTV: Music Video and Aesthetic Communication*, Cresskill, NJ: Hampton Press.

Williamson, M. (2016) *Celebrity: Capitalism and the Making of Fame*, Cambridge: Polity.

Wiseman, A. (2019a) '"Ad Astra" & "Call Me By Your Name" Outfit RT Features Launches TV Venture With Anonymous Content & CAA', *Deadline*, 15 October, https://deadline.com/2019/10/ad-astra-call-me-by-your-name-outfit-rt-features-launches-tv-venture-with-anonymous-content-caa-1202760229/

Wiseman, A. (2019b) 'Anonymous Content & "The Imitation Game" Director Morten Tyldum Launch Anonymous Content Nordic', *Deadline*, 28 May, https://deadline.com/2019/05/anonymous-content-morten-tyldum-launch-nordic-1202622822/#comments

Wollaston, S. (2014) 'G2: The Weekend's TV: Is it McConaughey? Is it Harrelson? Or is Louisiana the Star of *True Detective*?', *The Guardian*, 24 February, p. 21.

Workneh, L. (2014) '#BlackoutBlackFriday: A National Call to Boycott Black Friday for Ferguson and Beyond', *HuffPost*, 28 November, https://www.huffingtonpost.co.uk/entry/blackout-black-friday_n_6237108

Zelenski, D. (2003) 'Talent Agents, Personal Managers, and Their Conflicts in the New Hollywood', *Southern California Law Review*, 76.4: 979–1002.

Zhong, F. (2016) 'Amy Seimetz on the Powder Keg That is "The Girlfriend Experience"', *W Magazine*, 14 April, http://www.wmagazine.com/story/amy-seimetz-the-girlfriend-experience-riley-keough-monica-lewinsky

Index

Note: n denotes a note.

13 Reasons Why, 73, 133
21st Century Fox, 148; *see also* Twentieth Century Fox
500 Days of Summer, 153
8½, 96, 116n

A&M Films, 64
ABC, 31, 107, 110, 122
above-the-line talent, 3, 6, 36, 98, 134, 207, 216
Academy Awards, 75, 89, 107–13, 159, 161, 170–1
action movies, 34, 38, 73, 81, 158–60
adaptation, 42–4, 47, 49–50, 77, 82, 140, 156, 187, 191–2
Addis-Wechsler & Associates, 14–15
Adlon, P., 140
adventure movies, 150
Adventures of Ozzie and Harriet, The, 31
advertising, 6, 25, 47, 72, 80, 83, 88–9, 97–100, 106–9, 114, 131
agency, 5, 11, 176, 186
agents, 3–6, 8, 10, 12, 14, 16, 18, 20n, 34–6, 48, 57, 67, 99, 115n, 123, 167, 176–85, 187, 190–1, 197, 201, 207n, 213, 215–16
Aldridge, L., 186
Alfred Hitchcock Presents, 124
Amazing Spider-Man, The, 152–3, 156
Amazon, 2, 7, 15, 108–10
Amazon Instant Video, 7, 52, 108, 122, 128–9, 149, 205–7
Amazon Studios, 1–3, 7, 15, 136
'Ambush', 102

AMC, 122
American Film Institute, 61, 74
Amiel, J. and Begler, M., 74, 120, 125
Amores Perros, 103, 105, 155
Anderson, P.T., 48
Anderson, W., 54n, 90
Andrew, G., 47
Andrews, D., 87n
Andrews, H., 50
Anger Management, 192
Anonymous Content, 9, 15, 17–18, 57–60, 71–84, 87n, 88–9, 97–108, 110–11, 114, 118–43, 145n, 147n, 148–56, 158, 161, 163–4, 168–70, 178, 214–15, 215, 217
anonymous figures, 8–11, 59
Ansen, D., 28–9, 41
Ant-Man, 153–4
Apatow, J., 140
Apple, 75, 77, 217
Apple TV+, 52, 77, 149, 171
Araki, G., 73, 121
Arnold, A., 121, 126
art, 5, 9, 12, 18, 25–6, 35, 52, 60, 62, 67, 76, 87n, 89, 97, 104, 125, 136, 151, 155, 157–8, 161, 166–7, 169, 191, 193, 202, 218
art cinemas, 87n, 104, 202
art-house cinemas, 2, 7, 24, 160
Association of Independent Commercial Producers, The, 72
AT&T, 144n
attorneys, 14, 28, 42, 76, 165, 177
audiences, 2–3, 7, 10–12, 20n, 22–6, 29, 31, 36, 38, 40–2, 47–8, 50–2, 55n,

59, 62, 69–70, 73, 75–6, 80, 89, 94, 96–7, 100–1, 103, 105–6, 108–9, 111–14, 119, 122, 124, 128, 131–2, 138, 141–3, 148–51, 156, 158, 160–2, 165–6, 170–2, 172n, 179, 183, 185–7, 189, 191–4, 198, 202, 204, 206, 208n, 213–17
authenticity, 2, 7, 24–5, 27, 36–8, 41–3, 47, 49, 55n, 62, 68, 71, 74–5, 81, 90–2, 112, 124–5, 136, 142, 149, 151–2, 154, 156–8, 160, 162, 167–8, 176–8, 180, 183, 185, 192–3, 196, 198–200, 202, 214–15
autonomy, 1–2, 5–9, 16, 23, 26, 28, 34–5, 42, 62–4, 66, 72, 81, 92, 97–8, 107–8, 110, 118–19, 125–9, 166–7, 172, 178–9, 186, 188, 192, 194, 202, 213, 215, 218
awards, 23–4, 33, 37, 72, 74–5, 90, 103, 109, 134, 158–9, 161, 166, 170–1, 198, 203
Axios, 77

Badley, L., Perkins, C. and Schreiber, M., 138
Balio, T, 148
Band Apart .35mm, A, 98
Band of Brothers, 192–3
Banks, J., 61–2
Barbershop, 18, 177, 182, 184
Barenholtz, B., 22, 24, 27, 29, 31
Baron, C., 13, 112
Barr, M., 192
Barton Fink, 23, 33–5, 41
Batmanglij, Z., 18, 120–1, 125, 127–8, 131–2, 139, 213
Battsek, D., 48
Bazawule, B., 177, 180
Beach Bum, The, 73, 155
Beastie Boys, 93, 96
Beasts of No Nation, 18, 134–5, 149–50, 163–71
Beasts of the Southern Wild, 198–9
Beautiful Mind, A, 193–4
Beer, J., 109
Being John Malkovich, 57, 90, 93

benefactor, 2, 7, 100, 127, 164–5
Berkus, J., 34–5
Bernstein, I., 191–2
BET Media Group, 206
Bevan, T., 42, 65
Bezos, J., 15, 109
Big Lebowski, The, 42, 47, 55n
Big Little Lies, 121, 126
Big Miracle, 73–4
'Big Train', 93
Bildsten, B., 98–9, 101–2
Birdman or (The Unexpected Virtue of Ignorance), 155–6, 158, 160, 162
Birth of a Nation, 170
Black cultural production, 18–19, 76, 78–81, 89, 101, 110–14, 176–207, 207n, 208n, 209n, 214–15
Black List, The, 135
Black Panther Party, 195, 204
#BlackLivesMatter, 214, 216
#BlackOutBlackFriday, 197
blockbusters, 149, 151, 153–7, 160, 169, 184, 196
Blood Simple, 22–9, 32, 34, 37, 41, 43, 51, 54n
'blue skies' programming, 130–1, 135
BMW, 72, 97–105, 107, 109, 112, 114
Booth, P., 47
Bourdieu, P., 9–10
Box, The, 17, 89, 107, 110–14
box-office, 26, 41, 47, 55n, 66, 82, 158, 160, 163, 166, 170, 191, 199, 201
brand, 2–4, 6–9, 13, 17–18, 24, 26, 28–9, 35–7, 48, 50, 52, 55n, 58–60, 62–3, 70, 72, 74–5, 80, 83–4, 88, 90–1, 99–102, 108–9, 111, 119, 121–6, 128, 130–3, 135–8, 140, 142–3, 146n, 151, 153–4, 156, 158, 160, 162–3, 166–8, 170, 172, 179–80, 184, 187, 189, 191–4, 196, 199–200, 206–7, 213–18
branded content, 17, 58, 72, 79, 88, 97–107, 123, 180
broadcast television, 7, 11, 31, 69, 92, 101, 107, 110, 113, 128, 132, 144n, 185

Brolin, J., 50
Brown, D., 70
Brown, G., 41
Brown, R., 91, 120, 125
Bruzzi, S., 102, 161
'Buddy Holly', 96–7
Burton, T., 98–9

cable television, 7, 61, 118, 121–2, 127–8, 131, 134, 146n, 148, 167, 172n, 194
Cadawalladr, C., 161
Cadillac, 113
Cagaanan, D., 91–2
Caldwell, J., 9, 16, 46
'California', 93, 97
Cambern, D., 82
Campion, J., 78, 82
Candy, J., 69
Cannes Film Festival, 23, 27, 33–7, 98
Cannon, 24
capitalism, 40, 71, 132, 162, 167, 190, 203, 205, 207
'Car Song', 93
Carne y Arena, 76, 214
Carter, D., 98
Casablanca, 96, 115n
CBS, 187–8, 191
chat shows, 185
Chauvin, D., 195
'Chosen', 102
Christian, A.J., and White, K.C., 193
Christopher, J., 47
Cinema 1, 24–5
cinematization, 11, 18, 49, 73, 88–114, 118–43, 154–5, 168, 185, 214, 218
Circle Films, 22–34, 46
Citizen Kane, 96, 115
Civil Rights Movement, 76, 190
class, 3, 7, 11–12, 41, 68–70, 89, 96–7, 100–1, 105–6, 108–9, 112–14, 122, 128, 187, 194, 213, 216–17
Clooney, G., 42, 44–6
Coen brothers, 17, 22–53, 54n, 55n, 57, 96, 124, 199, 213, 215
collaboration, 17–18, 22–3, 28, 33–5, 37, 42, 47, 49–50, 52, 57, 97, 111, 113, 119, 140, 185, 187, 189, 195
comedy, 25, 30–1, 33, 40, 52, 69, 70, 73, 81, 105–6; *see also* romantic comedy
Comet, 135, 137
commerce, 9, 35, 52, 60, 62, 67, 72, 89, 114, 136, 158, 218
commercial spots, 4, 17, 58–9, 62, 64, 68, 72, 74, 78–80, 88–91, 98–100, 103, 107–14, 128, 131, 200, 211
communism, 59
convergence, 1, 4–8, 11–13, 17, 19, 22, 26, 36, 38, 42, 46, 48, 53, 55n, 57–9, 61–8, 71–2, 75, 77, 84, 90–1, 115, 119, 122, 127, 129, 132, 137–8, 144n, 149, 152, 171, 184, 191, 206, 217–18
control, 6, 16, 22, 27–8, 43–4, 61, 67, 71, 74–5, 79, 83, 100, 110, 112, 124, 128, 134, 150, 153–4, 171, 176, 187–9, 192
Coogler, R., 18, 177, 180, 185, 195–205, 215
Corrigan, T., 4
corruption, 35, 40, 50, 68, 140, 160, 178, 202
Covid-19 pandemic, 195, 205
Cowan, N., 36
Creative Artists Agency (CAA), 14, 215
credits for screen media, 24, 32, 38, 41, 43–7, 50, 70, 82–3, 95–6, 102, 119, 124, 133–5, 140, 162, 164, 177, 182, 186, 195
critics, 10–11, 20n, 23, 28, 34, 36–8, 41–2, 47–8, 62, 90–1, 95, 97, 109, 111, 119, 125, 132, 134–5, 142, 156, 160–1, 163, 170–1, 185, 194, 214, 216
Cruise, T., 78, 123
Cuarón, A., 77–8, 121, 123
Cullum, P., 9, 12, 16
cultural hierarchies, 3, 11, 13, 18, 25–6, 31, 34, 52, 97, 101, 114, 119, 126, 141, 160, 200, 207, 216, 218

'Da Funk', 93, 97
Dahl, J., 66, 123
Dargis, M., 160–1
dark tone, 22, 29, 33, 40, 51, 67, 103, 105–6, 130, 135
Deadline, 156, 198–9
deal-making, 3, 5–6, 8, 26–8, 48, 61, 64–5, 68–70, 72–3, 75–7, 79, 87n, 90, 107, 116, 121, 127, 136–7, 140, 158–9, 165, 168, 172n, 173n, 177, 182, 185, 187–93, 206, 211n, 215, 217
de la Mora, G.R., 103
Debmar-Mercury, 191–2
Diary of a Mad Black Woman, 18, 177, 186–91, 193
DiCaprio, L., 75, 157–9, 161–2, 169–70
Dick, N., 60, 68, 71
Dickinson, 73, 77
digital, 4–5, 76, 99, 171, 179, 217
directors-for-hire, 119, 124, 126–7, 129, 133, 135, 139, 143, 199–200, 214, 218
Directors Label DVD series, 91, 93
Disclaimer, 77, 121
discourse, 1, 3, 6, 8–12, 16–17, 23–5, 27–9, 34–8, 40–2, 47–8, 50–2, 55n, 58–60, 74–5, 84, 89–91, 97, 99, 101, 104, 110–11, 118, 120–1, 124, 132, 134–5, 137, 141–2, 150, 154, 156, 158–66, 168–71, 175n, 180–1, 185, 194, 197–200, 202, 213
Disney, 1, 16, 48, 152, 171, 196, 211n
Disney+, 171, 205
disruption, 112, 150, 164–8, 171–2, 180–3, 197, 205
distinction, 3, 25, 35, 43, 49–51, 62, 84, 89, 114, 127, 132, 136, 143, 160, 185, 188, 194, 200
distribution, 2–5, 12–13, 23–8, 35–6, 41, 48–9, 52, 60–1, 66, 69–70, 77, 115n, 127, 129, 132, 143, 149–50, 152, 158, 160, 163–8, 170–1, 188, 191–2, 195, 198, 201, 205–7, 213–17

diversification, 4–5, 74, 133, 181, 214
diversity, 8, 13, 76–7, 84, 98, 101–3, 108–9, 112, 114, 166, 175n, 179–80, 183–5, 197, 214
documentary, 4, 68, 76, 92–3, 215
Don't Worry, He Won't Get Far on Foot, 73, 155
Drake, P., 6, 173n
drama films, 149, 151
'Drop', 94–5
Dry, J., 111
Dunham, L., 140
Dunning, J., 24
DuVernay, A., 112, 121, 197, 215
Dyer, R., 188

Elba, I., 163–4, 169, 180
Elsaesser, T., 25–6, 55n
Emerson Collective, 75–9, 147n, 178, 214, 217
emotion, 47, 51, 57, 76, 82–3, 138, 141, 161, 169
entrepreneurialism, 23, 65, 75, 129, 140, 181–2, 184–6, 190–1, 196
Eraserhead, 24, 29
Esmail, S., 18, 77, 120, 125–6, 128, 133, 135–8
Esmail Corp., 136–7
Eternal Sunshine of the Spotless Mind, 57, 72–3, 105
Evans, K., 108
exclusivity, 25, 41, 50, 61, 168
exploitation film, 2, 25–6
'Express Yourself', 115n
Eyes on the Prize: Hallowed Ground, 76

Fairclough, N., 10
Fallen Angels (Showtime, 1993–6), 78, 123
Fallon, 83, 97–102, 108
family films, 73
Fantastic Four, 184
Fargo (Coen, 1996), 42, 47, 51
Fatlip, 94
FCC, 129
Feinberg, K., 76

Fellner, E., 42
Fellowes, J., 47
femininity, 11, 14, 48, 51–2, 89, 114, 119, 138, 142–3, 161, 187, 214
field of cultural production, 7, 121, 128, 134
film festivals, 2, 7, 14, 23–5, 33, 35–8, 55n, 74, 99, 203
FilmDistrict, 1
financial crash of 2008, 148
financier, 3, 107, 152, 155, 162, 168, 201, 205, 214, 216
Fincher, D., 17, 60–2, 71, 77, 83, 89–90, 93, 96–8, 101, 105–6, 115n, 120, 166–8, 185
Finney, A., 31–2
Fitzgerld, J.B., 176
Floyd, G., 195
Focus Features, 1–2, 48, 52, 72, 134, 148, 163, 165
'Follow, The', 102, 104–6, 112
Ford, J., 138
Foster, J., 79, 147n
Fox Searchlight, 48, 128, 158, 163, 165, 170–1, 187–8
franchise, 132, 137, 148, 151–6, 158, 172, 184
Frankenheimer, J., 98, 101
freelance, 6, 43, 135, 168
Fruitvale Station, 196, 198–9
Fukunaga, C., 15, 18, 73–4, 79, 120–1, 125–7, 133–5, 139, 149, 152, 154, 163–70, 175n, 185, 213
Fundamentals of Caring, The, 2, 149
Fuqua, A., 17, 77, 81, 107–9
FX, 122, 192, 199

Gallagher, M., 6, 43
Gambit, 44
Game, The, 90, 105
gangster genre, 32–3
Gates, R.J., 113, 185, 208n
gender, 13, 16, 59, 77–84, 89, 100–1, 105, 107, 110, 114, 138–43, 150, 155, 160, 162, 172, 202, 217; *see also* femininity; masculinity

genre, 1, 6, 9, 11, 29, 31, 33, 35, 44, 46, 63, 69, 73–4, 127, 140–1, 146n, 155, 172, 185, 199, 202–5, 217–18
play with genre, 22, 29, 31, 33, 39–41, 46, 90, 95–6, 112
Gerima, H., 183
Gillespie, M., 112
Gimlet Media, 77
Girlfriend Experience, The, 119, 121, 138–43, 144n
Global South, 101
Glynn, K., 70
Goldberg, E., 107–8
Golden Globes, 74–5, 161
Golin, S., 9, 17, 57–8, 60–2, 64–5, 67–72, 74–6, 79, 81–4, 87n, 90, 97, 99–101, 120, 122–4, 149–52, 154–5, 158, 161
Gondry, M., 17, 57, 91
Good Machine, 1–2
Gordon, K., 15
Gotham Awards, 74
Gramercy Pictures, 66, 70
Granik, D., 73, 79
Graves, P., 70
Gray, H., 112–13, 192, 197, 200
Gray, H. and Iverson-Davis, M., 76
Gray, J., 10
Gray, J. and Johnson, D., 6
Grazer, B., 23, 42–7, 49, 53n
Great, A., 193
'great leaders', 12, 181–2, 216, 218
Greenberg, K., 99
guerrilla filmmaking, 102–4
Guggenheim Partners, 75, 123

Hackett, I., 15
Hadas, L., 136–7
Hall, S., 178–9
Hamilton, C., 135–6
Hampton, F., 195–6, 201–6
Hanas, J., 71
Hanks, T., 78, 123
Harrelson, W., 125–7
Harris, C.A and Tassie, K.E., 183
Harvey, D., 77

INDEX

Havens, T., 143n
HBO, 76, 122, 127–8, 130, 132, 134, 146n, 166
HBO Max, 76, 137, 146n, 195, 205–6
Heaven's Gate, 157–8
Heinberg, A., 154
Hesmondhalgh, D., 64–5
Heuman, J., 129, 143
hip-hop gangsta films, 182–3
Hire (The), 17, 72, 83, 88, 97–108, 110, 112, 114, 160, 162
Hitchcock, A., 29, 124
Hoberman, J., 24–6
Hollywood, 2, 4, 6–7, 9, 14–16, 18, 20n, 22–30, 33–8, 40–2, 44, 46–8, 50–1, 54n, 60, 66–70, 72, 74, 80–4, 87, 90, 96, 98–100, 108–10, 118, 126, 135, 139, 149–50, 152–3, 155–8, 160, 162–5, 173n, 176–7, 179–91, 193–203, 206, 214–17
  'Hollywood's plantation scheme', 176, 178, 180
Hollywood Reporter, The, 137, 170
Home Before Dark, 73, 77
Homecoming, 77, 120, 125–6, 133, 136
home video, 5, 148, 187–8, 191
Hood, G., 18, 73, 152
Hope, T., 1–2, 7–8
Hornaday, A., 109
horror, 1, 9, 23
House of Cards, 120, 122, 165, 167–8
House of Payne, 18, 177, 191–3
Howe, D., 41
Howell, P., 51
Hudsucker Proxy, The, 23, 34–42, 47, 50, 54n, 55n, 199

I Am the Night, 79, 126
'If I Only Had a Brain', 92–3
'I'll Be Your Shelter', 115n
Imagine Entertainment, 43–6
imperialism, 68, 81, 162
Iñárritu, A.G., 17–18, 73, 75–6, 79, 98, 101, 103–5, 112, 149, 155–64, 170

Inception, 105, 150
independent company, 8, 17, 24, 26, 61, 64–6, 72, 84, 148, 158, 186, 188
indie film, 1–13, 17, 19, 19n, 22–52, 55, 57n, 61, 64–71, 74–7, 81, 84, 87n, 89–90, 93, 103, 120–4, 128, 134, 136–9, 141, 148–54, 160, 164, 166–7, 170–1, 172n, 177, 183–4, 186, 189, 191, 194, 198–9, 202–3, 206, 213, 215–16
indie television, 2, 4–6, 79, 89, 114, 118–43, 143–4n, 151, 177, 191–4
indiewood, 22, 48–9, 52, 149, 152, 173n
innovation, 2, 7–9, 12, 18, 23–4, 28–9, 33, 47–8, 58, 63, 65–7, 69, 72–3, 81, 88–9, 95, 97–102, 105, 107–9, 114, 118–20, 122–3, 127–8, 130–2, 135–7, 139–40, 143, 153, 158, 161, 164, 167, 169, 185, 191–3, 202, 213–14, 216–17
Insdorf, A., 24
interactive productions, 72, 215
Interscope Communications, 64, 68
Intolerable Cruelty, 23, 42–8, 51
investment, 7, 18, 23, 28, 34–5, 58, 61–2, 64–5, 67–8, 71–2, 75–7, 79, 123, 129–30, 149–51, 155, 161, 163, 178, 196, 206, 211, 213–14, 217
irony, 41, 138
Itkin, M., 191–3
'It's Oh So Quiet', 96

Jackson, J., 61, 115n
Jackson, M., 81
Jackson, S.L., 73, 77, 126
Jackson, T., 177
Jaramillo, D., 126
Jenkins, B., 121, 139, 215
Jenkins, P., 18, 79, 121, 139, 152–4
Jenner, M., 166, 171, 172n
Johnson, C., 9
Johnson, D., 205
Johnson, D., Kompare, K. and Santo, A., 11
Johnston, S., 35

Jonze, S., 17, 63, 81, 88–97, 106, 112, 115n, 213
Judas and the Black Messiah, 18, 177, 185, 195–206, 211n

Kalifornia, 66, 70, 90
Kane, V., 111
Karlovy Vary International Film Festival, 73, 151
Kaufman, A., 166–7
Kaufman, C., 57
Keaton, M., 76, 155
Kemper, T., 13
Kennedy, R., 178
Kerrigan, F., 28
Kerrigan, L., 119, 121, 139–41
Kidman, N., 67, 126
Kill Me Again, 66, 81
King, C.D., 18, 176–207, 209n, 214–15
King, G., 5, 23, 25, 27, 36, 150, 152, 173n
King, S., 18, 177, 195–206, 210n, 211n, 215
Knick, The, 18, 73–4, 120–1, 123, 125, 127–8, 130, 132–3, 139, 145n, 192
Kodak Theatre, 187
Korine, H., 73, 155
Krämer, P., 6
Kring, M., 108
Kuhn, M., 65–7

L.A. Weekly, 9, 12
labour, 4, 6, 8–9, 11, 129, 137, 143, 163, 200, 214
Labuza, P., 171
Lacey, L., 47
Ladykillers, 42, 51
Landmark Theatres, 165, 170
Lane, A., 51
Lane, C., 102
Last Days of Ptolemy Grey, The, 77, 126
Laundromat, The, 73, 76, 155
Lawrence, N., 186
Lee, A., 79, 98, 100–2
Lee, S., 22, 28, 121
legitimation, 2, 7, 11, 37, 63, 88–9, 95, 97, 101, 107, 112–14, 121–2, 125, 127, 138, 141–3, 144n, 154, 160–1, 166, 169, 172, 179, 185–6, 192–4, 214, 217; see also cinematization
Leopard, D., 5
Lesher, D., 48, 50
'Let's Wait Awhile', 115n
Levine, J., 43
Levy, A., 66
liberals, 69, 76, 160
Libra Films, 24
Lichter, L., 165
Linklater, R., 22, 107
Lionsgate, 188–9, 191
Lipper, H., 34
Lombardo, M., 128, 134
López, I., 147, 177
Los Angeles School of Independent Filmmakers, 186
Los Angeles Times, 57, 97
Lost in Translation, 193–4
Lotz, A., 20n, 27
Lotz, A., Lobato, R. and Thomas, J., 145n
Louis C.K., 140
Lynch, D., 24, 29, 66, 121–3, 144n

M88, 180, 196
McCarthy, C., 48–51
McCarthy, M., 107, 110
McCarthy, T., 73, 155
McClintock, P., 160
McConaughey, M., 67, 125–6
Macdonald, G., 101
McDonald, P., 75
MacDowell, J., 55n
McDowell, J., 100
McGowan, R., 14–15
McHugh, K., 81, 162
Mack, K.W., 177
Mackay, A.M., 63, 80–1
McKenna, A.T., 164
Macro, 18, 77, 176–85, 190, 195–207, 214
macro- and micro-industrial, 10–11
Mad Men, 15, 168
made-for-television movie, 78, 168

INDEX

Madison Avenue, 99
Madonna, 61, 98, 102, 106, 115n
mainstream, 2, 5, 7, 22–6, 28–9, 31, 33–4, 36, 38, 40–2, 44, 46–8, 52, 54n, 55n, 63, 67–70, 73–4, 84, 88–9, 96–7, 109, 114, 119, 131–2, 138, 143, 146n, 156, 158, 160, 162, 166, 172, 172n, 178, 181–3, 185, 192–3, 197–8, 202–7, 214, 218
Make it Yours, 113
Manchester by the Sea, 2, 149
Maniac, 18, 73, 120, 125, 133
Manifesto Film Sales, 65
Mann, D., 6, 20n, 176
marketing, 2–5, 9–11, 13, 16, 23, 28–9, 31, 35–7, 40, 43–50, 52, 63, 70, 84, 88–9, 100, 102, 107–8, 121, 129, 131, 136, 142, 152, 156, 158, 163, 168, 170, 180, 184, 188, 191, 194, 198–9, 201, 209n
markets, 4, 7, 13, 18, 25–6, 35, 41, 65, 84, 99, 138, 179, 183, 190, 194, 215–16
Marling, B., 18, 120–1, 125, 127–8, 131–2
Marvel, 151–3, 156, 196
Mascis, J., 93
masculinity, 11–12, 50–2, 81–3, 89, 102, 105–7, 112, 114, 139, 141–2, 150, 157, 160–3, 169–70, 178, 187, 202, 213–14, 217
maverick, 8, 12–13, 16, 18, 20n, 71, 81–4, 139, 150, 154–5, 162–3, 168–9, 172, 178, 191, 193, 196, 199, 202, 214, 218
MC 900 ft. Jesus, 91–3
Messick, J., 14–15
#MeToo, 15, 80, 110, 114, 214, 216–17
Metropolis, 96, 115
Meyers, N., 107, 110
MGM/UA, 69–71
Miller's Crossing, 22, 31–3, 41, 51
Milvy, E., 99
minstrel shows, 185, 193
Miramax, 1, 14–16, 48–50, 52, 128, 148
Missing in Action 2, 24

Mitchell, E., 47
Mittell, J., 141
Molloy, C., 8, 23, 54n, 102, 105, 184
Monk, K., 38
Moore, M., 17, 59, 67–71
Moorhouse, J., 17, 78, 82–3
Mr. Robot, 18, 73–4, 119–20, 125–6, 130–3, 135–7
MTV, 61–3, 80–1, 91, 97
Mudbound, 110–11, 177, 200
Mulignans, 198–9
multiculturalism, 179, 183
music video, 4, 17, 58, 60–4, 68, 71–4, 77, 80–1, 84, 88–97, 99, 112, 114, 123
Music Video Producers Association, 72

Nance, T., 76, 79
Nathan, I., 51
National Association of Theatre Owners (NATO), 165–7
NBCUniversal, 1–2, 119, 131, 136–7; *see also* Universal
Ndounou, M.W., 176, 183, 189, 201
neoliberalism, 4, 8, 52, 77, 101–3, 107, 109, 129, 132, 137, 167, 181–2, 184–6, 190, 193, 195–6, 207, 216–17
Netflix, 3, 52, 119–20, 122, 127–9, 131–2, 134, 149–50, 163–72, 172n, 205
Never Stop Arriving, 113
new media, 72, 99
New Regency, 148–9, 157–8, 161
New York Film Festival, 23–4, 32
New York Times, 14, 16, 62, 76, 97, 154, 190
Newlyweeds, 198–200
Newman, M., 25–6, 36, 55n, 96
Newman, M. and Levine, E., 11, 89, 119, 138, 144n
Newsweek, 28–9, 97
niche, 3, 7, 11, 22, 24–6, 34, 38, 41–2, 50, 52, 68, 70, 89, 105–6, 111, 122, 148–9, 158, 160, 172n, 183, 192, 213

Nike, 62, 72
No Country for Old Men (Coen and Coen, 2007), 23, 42, 48–52
No Time to Die, 152, 154
noir film, 23, 28
Nolan, C., 105–6
non-profit campaigns, 4, 197, 215
Nugent, J., 154
Nygaard, T. and Lagerwey, J., 12, 20n, 87n

O'Neal, W., 195, 202–5
O'Sullivan, M., 47
OA, The, 18, 120, 125, 131–3, 164
'Oh Father', 115n
Olmstead, D., 79, 87n
online technologies, 2, 4–5, 101, 149, 217
originality, 2–3, 7, 28–9, 63, 81, 93, 95, 118, 130, 134, 149, 163, 165, 217
Ortner, S., 7–8, 76, 103
Ottawa Citizen, 82, 97
Owen, C., 98–100, 125
Ozy Media, 77

packaging, 3–5, 11, 18, 42, 48, 55n, 118–21, 123, 125–7, 138–9, 144–5n, 162, 180, 185, 188, 213, 215
Palmer, R.B., 55n
Pantera, 80
Paramount, 1, 48, 206
Paramount Vantage, 1, 48–50, 148
paratexts, 10, 28–33, 38–40, 43–7, 50–1, 54n, 91, 98, 101, 130–1, 134, 141–2, 158–60, 166, 169–70, 190, 203–5
Pariah, 111, 113
Participant Media, 164, 195
Partners, 192
passion projects, 150–1, 153, 156–8, 164, 166, 168–9, 199, 213
Pasternak, S., 188–9
patriarchy, 81, 140, 169
pay-TV, 118, 121, 127–9, 132, 167
Peacock, 136

'Peak TV', 118, 123
Pearson, E., 48
Pedas brothers, 22, 24, 27, 31
Perren, A., 132, 137, 171–2
Perry, T., 18, 177, 185–94, 196–7, 206, 209–10n
Petruska, K., 7, 171
Pevere, G., 47
Pharcyde, The, 94
philanthropic, 75, 77
Philips Electronics, 55n, 61, 66, 71, 89
Pizzolatto, N., 120, 133–6
police brutality, 195, 197–8
politics, 8, 40, 59, 64, 68–71, 76, 93, 102, 114, 122, 138, 144n, 154, 162, 176–7, 183, 186, 190, 196–7, 200, 205, 207
PolyGram Filmed Entertainment, 34, 55n, 65–71
PolyGram, 61–71, 84, 89–90
Portrait of a Lady, 78, 82
'Powder Keg', 102–5, 112
Powell Jobs, L., 75–7, 87
Powers, J., 169
Powers, P., 10
'Praise You', 94–5, 97
precarious employment, 8, 13, 129, 158, 206, 214
Precious, 198–9
prestige, 16, 31, 75, 108, 134, 137, 171, 185, 192, 200, 205
Price, R., 1, 7, 15
procedural shows, 128, 136
producers, 1–3, 8–9, 11–18, 22–6, 34–6, 38, 40–4, 46–7, 49–50, 52, 53n, 57–60, 62–3, 67–72, 79, 82–3, 89, 91, 102, 106, 110, 120–1, 123–4, 126, 129, 133, 135–8, 140–1, 146n, 149, 151, 155, 157–8, 161, 164–70, 176–7, 184–5, 190, 194, 201, 203, 205–6, 213–14, 217–18; *see also* showrunners
Producers Guild, 183, 197
Propaganda Films, 17–18, 57–72, 74, 77–84, 88–97, 99, 114–15, 118, 120, 122–3, 178, 200, 202

Proximity Media, 195
Public Broadcasting Service, 122
public relations, 10, 59, 87n, 114, 123
publicist, 6, 14
puzzle films, 104–5

quality production, 2, 9–10, 24, 33–4, 43, 51, 57–8, 60, 69–71, 73–4, 87n, 89, 97, 125–7, 132–7, 150–5, 160–1, 164, 166–7, 169, 172, 172n, 177–8, 200, 217
Quinn, E., 184, 186, 201
quirky, 22, 30–4, 39, 47, 54n, 90, 97, 122

race, 11–13, 18, 59, 77–83, 101, 113, 169, 175–207, 207n, 208n, 214, 217–18
Raimi, S., 34, 47, 199
Raising Arizona, 22, 27, 30–2, 34–5, 46, 50
Random Acts of Flyness, 76, 214
rap, 81, 217
reality television, 185, 217
Receipt (The), 89, 107–11, 114
record labels, 61–3, 80–1, 92, 97
Red Rock West, 66, 81
Redmon, K., 15, 58, 79, 87n, 161
Rees, D., 17, 79–80, 89, 107, 110–13, 177, 200, 213, 215
Reinsch, P.N., 186
Reservoir Dogs, 16, 66
retail, 7, 25, 89, 107, 110, 197
Revenant, The, 15, 18, 73, 75, 120, 149, 155–64, 168, 170–1
rhetorical manoeuvring, 8–10, 26, 38, 49, 63, 65, 67, 75, 92, 99–100, 108, 110, 132, 136, 151, 154, 158, 187, 193, 200, 217
Riley, B., 177, 215
Ritchie, G., 17, 98, 101, 105–6
Robbins, T., 35, 40–1
Roberts, Julia, 125–7
Roberts, Juliana, 63
Romanek, M., 71–2, 91
Romanoffs, The, 15

romantic comedy, 42, 45–8, 51, 73
Roussel, V., 5–6, 12–13, 123–5, 152–3
Rudin, S., 15–16, 23, 42, 48–52, 57
Russell, D.O., 15, 37, 76

'Sabotage', 96–7
Sabin, N., 192
sales agent, 65, 198–9
Samsung, 113, 200
Sarandos, T., 164–6, 168
Satellite Films, 89–92, 95
satire, 47, 68, 155, 162
Schamus, J., 1–2, 8
Schlessel, P., 1
Schreiber, M., 51
Scott, A.O., 154
SCP Private Equity Partners, 71, 90
SCTV Network, 69
Seagram, 46, 55n, 61, 71–2
Seeking a Friend for the End of the World, 73, 79
Seimetz, A., 119, 121, 138–43
Sellors, P., 150
Sena, D., 60–2, 66, 90, 96–7, 115n
Sex, Lies, and Videotape, 16, 128
Sexton, M. and Lees, D., 144–5n
sexual abuse, 14–17, 79, 110, 141
sexuality, 111–12
'Shady Lane', 93
Shepherd, D., 24
Sheppard, S.N., 187
'shock effect', 197, 205
Shoot, 97–8
short film, 17, 88–9, 98–9, 101–2, 107–8, 110, 114, 135, 195, 197–8
showrunners, 118, 122, 133, 136
Sighvatsson, S., 60–2, 64–5, 68–9, 71, 81–2, 90, 92, 122, 202
Silver, J., 23, 34–42, 47, 53n, 55n, 57
Sim, G., 166, 168
Sin Nombre, 126, 134, 163, 175n
Sinwell, S., 149
Skarsgård, S., 98, 102
Slater, C., 126, 133
Smith, P.J., 155
soap opera, 119, 138, 143, 185, 217

social hierarchies, 11, 16, 18, 25, 52, 59, 75, 77–84, 97, 101, 107, 110, 114, 119, 123, 138–43, 155, 160, 172, 182, 195–7, 200–2, 207, 216–18
Soderbergh, S., 16, 18, 22, 55n, 73, 76, 119–21, 123–30, 132, 137–42, 144–5n, 155, 166–7, 185, 213
Sony, 16, 152
South by Southwest Festival, 38, 74, 133
specialty production, 1–6, 9, 11–13, 18–19, 19n, 20n, 38, 48, 50, 52–3, 58, 60, 68, 73–4, 81, 134, 148–72, 172n, 213, 215, 218; *see also* indie film; indie television
Spotlight, 59, 73–5, 120, 155
Squires, C.R., 182
'Star', 102, 105–6
stardom, 4, 8, 16, 44, 46, 108, 118, 152, 155, 164, 202, 216
Starz, 122, 141
Steed, D., 194
Sternbergh, A., 128
Stolley, K, Kerrigan, K and Yalkin, C., 99
Stone, E., 73, 125, 156
Story, T., 18, 177, 184
Strauss, B., 160
streaming, 2, 7, 52, 118, 122, 127–9, 131–2, 134, 136–7, 145n, 159–50, 163–8, 171–2, 195, 202, 205, 215, 217
subversive, 9, 47, 57, 70
Sugar, M., 58, 120, 123, 125–6, 130, 139, 151–4, 164–5, 168, 170
Sundance Film Festival, 2, 5, 14, 36–7, 69, 75, 128, 170, 197–9
'Sure Shot', 93
Sweet, J., 98
Swisher, K., 76
syndication, 168, 191–3

talent managers, 3–6, 8–12, 17–18, 20n, 57–84, 87, 89–90, 93, 97, 99, 101–2, 104, 114, 115n, 120–1, 123, 127, 129, 133, 135, 139, 143, 145, 149, 151–5, 164, 177–85, 196, 200, 206–7, 213–16
talent migration, 6, 53, 114, 118, 121, 123, 125, 127, 143, 166, 184, 187, 215, 217–18
Tarantino, Q., 16, 98
taste, 12, 16, 22, 48, 58, 67, 70, 121–2, 126–7, 150–1, 157, 160, 162
Tauber, J., 66
TBS, 192, 199
television drama, 11–12, 15, 18, 73–4, 79, 89, 101, 118–43, 146n, 148–51, 154–5, 163, 214–15
test-screenings, 36, 38, 70
There Will be Blood, 48, 52
Thor: The Dark World, 153–4
Thousand Acres, A, 78, 82
thriller genre, 29, 48, 51, 73, 140–1, 144n, 202–5
'Time Online', 37–8
Time Warner, 37–8, 144n
Timex, 98
Too Old to Die Young, 121, 144n
Toronto Film Festival, 23, 53n
trade press, 1, 10, 49, 52, 61, 148
True Detective, 18, 73–4, 119–21, 125–7, 132–5, 139, 148, 151, 154, 163–4, 166, 168, 192
True Detective: Night Country, 147n
Tsotsi, 153
Twentieth Century Fox, 26–8, 30–1, 33, 148–9, 152, 158–60, 163, 171
Twin Peaks, 118, 122, 144n, 192–3
Twin Peaks: The Return, 121–2
Tyldum, M., 77, 215
Tzioumakis, Y., 5, 10–11, 17, 22, 26, 48, 52–3, 151, 163, 173n, 215

Underground Railroad, The, 121, 144n
'Undone (The Sweater Song)', 93
United Talent Agency (UTA), 34, 176, 210n
Universal, 1–2, 19n, 43–4, 46, 52, 55n, 61, 66, 71–2; *see also* NBCUniversal
Universal Cable Productions, 136–7, 146n

urban culture, 181–3, 208n
USA Films, 71–2
USA Networks, 71, 128, 130–1, 133, 136

Vallée, J., 121, 126
value chain, 12, 206
Van Peebles, M., 193–4
Van Sant, G., 73, 121, 155
Variety, 1–2, 37, 49, 64, 74, 120–1, 123, 137, 199
Vernallis, C., 91
Vernallis, C., Rogers, H., and Perrott, L., 6
Vice, J., 51
video games, 38, 68, 143n, 215
violence on-screen, 29, 48–51, 83, 103, 105, 144n, 161
virtual reality, 4, 76, 136, 215
Vonder Meulen, K., 99–100

Wachtel, J., 137
Walker, A.K., 98, 102
Walmart, 17, 89, 107–14, 200
Warner, K., 79
Warner Bros., 1, 34, 37, 68, 152, 154, 195, 201, 203
Warner Independent, 1, 48, 148
WarnerMedia, 119, 137, 140, 144n, 146n, 205–7
Washington, D., 81
Washington Post, 109, 166
'Weapon of Choice', 93

Webb, M., 18, 152
Weigel Broadcasting Co., 192
Weiner, M., 15
Weinstein Company, The, 14, 198
Weinstein, H., 14–17, 48, 110, 198
western movies, 51, 150
Wexman, V.W., 82–3, 140
What Do You Care About? #VoteYourFuture, 76
When They See Us, 121, 144n
Whitaker, F., 98, 104
Whiteness, 12–13, 77–84, 87n, 91, 95, 97, 112–14, 162, 168, 207n, 175n, 176–8, 181–6, 188, 192, 194, 198, 206, 207n, 208n, 213–14, 217–18
William Morris/WME, 18, 67, 177, 179–83, 185–91, 193–4, 196–7, 199, 201, 209–10n
Williams, K., 80
Wired, 166–7
Wonder Woman, 152, 154
Wong, K., 17, 79, 98, 101, 104–5, 112
Working Title, 34, 42, 52, 55n, 64–6
World Cinema, 80, 96, 162
Writers Guild, 74, 129

X-Men Origins: Wolverine, 152–3

youth culture, 62, 73, 181–3, 213

Zeta-Jones, C., 42, 44–6
Zelenski, D., 115n
Zhong, F., 142

EU Authorised Representative:
Easy Access System Europe Mustamäe tee 50, 10621 Tallinn, Estonia
gpsr.requests@easproject.com

Printed and bound by CPI Group (UK) Ltd, Croydon, CR0 4YY
02/03/2026
02063702-0002